Praise for Tim Lawrence's *Love Saves the Day: A History of American Dance Music Culture, 1970–1979*

"One of the sharpest books on dance music to date, striking a balance between you-are-there club descriptions, socioeconomic analysis, and musical critique." —Tricia Romano, *The Village Voice*

"*Love Saves the Day* not only gets dance-music history right—it refocuses that history to include those unjustly excluded from it." —Ethan Brown, *New York*

"This is as close to a definitive account of disco as we're likely to get, and as entertaining as a great night out." —Richard Smith, *Gay Times*

"A densely detailed and heartfelt account of the era." —Bruce Tantum, *Time Out New York*

"Essential reading for anyone who wants to know the who, what and where of disco's earliest years and why a musical style came to symbolize an entire decade." —John-Manuel Andriote, *Lambda Book Report*

"[An] exhaustive journey through the pulsating dance floors of '70s New York." —Mike Gwertzman, *New York Post*

"Should become a fixture in the libraries of serious students of American pop." —Philip Christman, *PASTE*

"A fully comprehensive . . . analysis of dance culture. . . . Tim Lawrence has done his homework, and his dynamic delivery possesses a delightful, intimate style." —Roberta Cutolo, *Straight No Chaser*

"Lawrence has documented the scene with a fan's affection and a scholar's thoroughness. . . . His interview subjects, veteran DJs and clubgoers all, best convey in their own words what it was like to be on the dance floor at the Loft, the Gallery or the Paradise Garage when the crowd—drenched in sweat, screaming and whistling, arms in the air—gave itself up to rapture."
—Tom Beer, *Newsday*

"The definitive book on dance music in the 1970s."—Lisa Neff, *Chicago Free Press*

"*Love Saves the Day* works as an eye-opening history of a movement that found a nation taking time out to dance."—Andy Battaglia, *Onion*

"Lawrence's astounding research and wide focus make this the music's definitive chronicle so far."—Michaelangelo Matos, *Seattle Weekly*

"Lawrence has accomplished the seemingly impossible feat of cuing up every famed and arcane component of disco's ethos and executing a narrative possessed by a seamless grace that's comparable to the work of the legendary DJs who are duly chronicled."—Frank Halperin, *Philadelphia City Paper*

"This book is more than a historical document; indeed, it houses more anecdotes . . . and reminiscences than a million different lifestyle magazines, with the added bonus that these aren't about over-hyped 'celebrities'; they're about people who were 'faces' in a time and place that is directly responsible for the hedonism and the heartbreak that comprises modern clubbing."—Manu Ekanayake, Trustthedj.com

"An extraordinarily rich work that ought to transform the ways we write the history of popular music."—Mitchell Morris, *Journal of Popular Music Studies*

"This brilliant study of the birth of disco and the spawning of a million different subgenres . . . is crucial reading for anyone who thinks they know their club culture. Because until you've read this, you might as well know nothing, nada, zilch."—Susan Corrigan, *i-D Magazine*

"Will surely stand as the definitive history of dance music's early years."
—Joe Madden, *Jockey Slut*

Hold On to Your Dreams

Hold On to Your Dreams

Arthur Russell and the
Downtown Music Scene,
1973–1992

Tim Lawrence

Duke University Press Durham and London 2009

© 2009 Duke University Press
All rights reserved

Printed in the United States of America
on acid-free paper ♾

Designed by Jennifer Hill
Typeset in Arno Pro and Univers
by Tseng Information Systems, Inc.

Library of Congress
Cataloging-in-Publication Data
appear on the last printed page
of this book.

Alan Abrams Kathy Acker Mustafa Ahmed JoAnne Akalaitis Rik Albani Ali Akbar College of Music Laurie Anderson Another Side Bob Ashley Bob Babbitt Afrika Bambaataa Barefoot Boy Wilbur Bascomb Battery Sound David Behrman John Bernd Bessie Schönberg Theater Billboard Bill's Friends Bob Blank Lola Blank Blank Tapes Studios Blue Green Bohannon Bond's Bonzo Goes to Washington Joyce Bowden Bright and Early Ernie Brooks Jim Burton David Byrne John Cage Cornelius Cardew Casual Gods CBGB's CETA Orchestra Jesse Chamberlain Rhys Chatham Mel Cheren Don Christensen Columbia Records Cooper-Hewitt Museum Frankie Crocker Merce Cunningham Steve D'Acquisto Dance Music Report Danceteria Doug DeFranco Vince Delgado Dinosaur Dinosaur L Les Disques du Crépuscule Arnold Dreyblatt Bob Dylan Julius Eastman Experimental Intermedia Foundation Face Fast Food Band Barry Feldman Felix Sammy Figueroa Flying Hearts Henry Flynt Riccardo Fogli Jim Fouratt Franklin Street Arts Center Chris Frantz Mark Freedman Johnny Fu Gallery Kyle Gann Walter Gibbons Jon Gibson Allen Ginsberg Philip Glass Peter Gordon Kent Goshorn Robert Green Steven Hall John Hammond Jerry Harrison Steven Harvey Yogi Horton Butch Ingram Jimmy Ingram John Ingram Timmy Ingram William Ingram Institute of Contemporary Art Scott Johnson Tom Johnson Kailas Shugendo Kennedy Center François Kevorkian Kevin Killian Kitchen Knitting Factory Jill Kroesen Joan La Barbara La MaMa Richard Landry Elodie Lauten Mary Jane Leach Tom Lee Larry Levan Mark Levinson George Lewis Eric Liljestrand Lincoln Center Annea Lockwood Loft Logorhythm Lola Glen Lomaro Loose Joints Love of Life Orchestra Lower Manhattan Ocean Club Gary Lucas Mabou Mines Jackson Mac Low David Mancuso Manhattan School of Music Kurtis Mantronik William Allaudin Mathieu Max's Kansas City Leon McElroy Melody Maker Denise Mercedes Mercer Arts Center Modern Lovers Charlotte Moorman John Moran Bill Morgan Mudd Club Donald Murk Sydney Murray Rome Neal Necessaries Paul Nelson New Musical Express New York Rocker New York Times Phill Niblock Ninth Circle Yuko Nonomura Normal Music Band Peter Orlovsky Le Orme Other End Frank Owen Toni Pagliuca Andy Paley Robert Palmer Palo Paradise Garage Jon Pareles Wendy Perron Poetry Project at St. Mark's Poet's Building Record World Steve Reich R.E.M. Simon Reynolds Jonathan Richman Terry Riley Rock Lounge John Rockwell Michael Rosenblatt Bob Rosenthal Rough Trade **Arthur Russell** Bill Ruyle Frederic Rzewski Sailboats Larry Saltzman Alison Salzinger Roger Sanchez San Francisco Conservatory of Music John Scherman Carlota Schoolman Allan Schwartzberg 1750 Arch Street Jon Sholle Nicky Siano Jimmy Simpson Mark Sinclair Singing Tractors Sire Sleeping Bag Sobossek's Will Socolov SoHo Weekly News Robert Stearns Seymour Stein David Stubbs Studio 54 Ned Sublette Sundragon Studios Talking Heads Elias Tanenbaum Steven Taylor Television Todd Terry Tier 3 Ed Tomney Stan Tonkel David Toop Geoff Travis "Blue" Gene Tyranny Upside Records Myriam Valle David Van Tieghem Walker Arts Center Warner Bros. Jennifer Warnes Ajari Warwick Washington Square Church WBLS West End Jerry Wexler Tina Weymouth Jeff Whittier Robert Wilson Kirk Winslow Christian Wolff Stephanie Woodard Melvina Woods World Music Hall WUSB Stony Brook Ellen Ziegler Robert Ziegler Peter Zummo

Contents

Illustrations

"Arthur wrote classical music, avant-garde dance music, rock and roll, R&B, and sometimes country, too," Steve D'Acquisto declared in between spoonfuls of soup as he gave me the lowdown on Arthur Russell during a late-lunch interview in May 1998. "How can I explain it? He was like Picasso. He was a fantastic artist." A pioneering DJ who had worked as a coproducer with Russell, D'Acquisto delivered his overview with the fervid surety of an evangelist. "Arthur was one of the great songwriters of the twentieth century. I put him up there with Rogers and Hart, with Cole Porter. He had a whole new way of talking, a whole new way of saying things." At that point D'Acquisto started to sing "Tell You (Today)," a song he recorded with Russell in the early 1980s.

> Walking down the street
> I knew it was my chance
> My chance today
> New shoes on my feet
> I thought that they could dance
> Dance away
> It makes me come alive
> I remember the look of sadness on your face
> But that was before
> I want to tell you today.

"It's like you've broken up with somebody, but you still love them," he enthused. "If I told you the words to some of his other records, you would flip out." Transported by a rush of memories, D'Acquisto proceeded to sing "Let's Go Swimming," "Janine," and "List of Boys." It was a while before he realized his soup had gone cold.

Occupied with researching the history of U.S. dance culture, I had agreed to set aside an afternoon to talk about Russell, because I needed to find out more about two of his twelve-inch singles, "Go Bang! #5" and "Is It All Over My Face?"—and Russell wasn't around to tell me about them. But D'Acquisto ended up spending more time talking about Russell's songs than his remixes, and by the end of the interview, I had noted down a series of names whose proximity seemed to violate some kind of musical taboo. Unable to explain how Russell had come to work with David Byrne, Allen Ginsberg, Philip Glass, and John Hammond, as well as Walter Gibbons, François Kevorkian, Larry Levan, and Will Socolov, D'Acquisto challenged me to write a biography about his low-profile friend, whom he had met at David Mancuso's Loft, the influential private party that would frame my account of New York dance. I replied by noting that I already had my hands full with the dance book. Privately I wondered if it would be possible to write a book about such a manifestly diffuse figure.

When D'Acquisto died from a brain tumor four years later, it seemed as though the opportunity to find out more about Russell's scattered existence had passed on as well, and the sensation of having experienced a double loss stayed with me until I traveled to the EMP Pop Music conference in 2003, where I had a chance conversation with the Cuban music specialist Ned Sublette. "'Is it all over my face? / You caught me love dancing,'" Sublette crooned the moment I told him about my forthcoming dance book. "'Is it all over my face? / I'm in love dancin'.'" A downtown composer, musician, and record-label owner, Sublette had been friends with Russell and wanted to talk. He also offered to put me in touch with the composer-musicians Peter Gordon and Peter Zummo, who had worked closely with Russell over a number of years. Imagining future interviewees, I wondered if they would sing to me as well.

As a route into Russell's history presented itself, I began to float the idea of a biography, only to hear questions about its marketability raised. They dampened my hopes but not my intrigue, so when Gordon visited London in June 2003, I took him up on his offer to "talk Arthur," and by the time I boarded a flight the following February to attend Mancuso's party for the Loft's thirty-fourth anniversary, Russell's shadowy silhouette had been transformed. Responding to the simultaneous release of two posthumous compilations of Russell's work, David Toop and the *Wire* ran a cover feature about the composer-musician in January 2004, and as Mancuso's guests rolled into his East Village gathering, I met Steve Knutson, who was hoping to give the Loft host a vinyl copy of *Calling out of Context*—one of the albums that had prompted Toop to write his piece. "Arthur Russell is my favorite artist," Knutson told me a couple of days later as I photocopied a pile of archival documents he was holding on behalf of Tom Lee, Russell's long-term lover. "His music is pure spirit." I went on to spend long afternoons talking with Lee and Zummo, and a couple of weeks later the *New York Times* and the *New Yorker* ran prominent features about Russell. Something strange was unfolding, while the potential for a biography had become much clearer.

Beyond a clutch of occasional reviews, the archives revealed that Frank Owen, Toop, and Zummo had published interview-led features about Russell in *Melody Maker*, the *Face*, and the *SoHo Weekly News*. Subsequently, Gary Lucas, Sublette, and Toop penned articles to coincide with Russell's passing and the posthumous release of *Another Thought*, a collection of Russell's voice-cello recordings released in 1994.[1] Informed by this material, I began to approach anyone who was willing to talk, and quickly generated a list of contacts that, beginning with Alan Abrams and ending with Zummo, resembled a phantom address book of Russell's acquaintances. The task of pinning down milestone dates became easier after Chuck and Emily Russell (Russell's parents) and Muriel Fujii (an ex-girlfriend) sent me copies of the letters Russell had written to them (which I quote throughout the book). By the time Tom Lee invited me to rummage through an old box of flyers and letters, I was confident that the details of his life could be mapped out in credible detail. But one key question remained unanswered: were these the specifics of a life that would matter only to a band of dedicated listeners, or was there a reason to think they might amount to something more?

As my research deepened, I began to realize that it wasn't just Russell who cut an oblique figure; so, somewhat strangely, did the city in which he made his music. Between 1970 and 1985 disco, punk, new wave, no wave, hip-hop, and electro forged their distinctive sounds, the eclectic compositional movement of "new music" fashioned a compositional alternative to serialism, and free jazz continued to accelerate away from bebop, hard bop, and modal jazz. Yet while these sounds had been historicized as self-contained movements, no meta-account had been written to explain why this extraordinary rush of sonic innovation had originated in the lofts, clubs, bars, and community halls that stretched across lower Manhattan (save for hip-hop, which germinated in the boroughs). Indeed with the exception of *Between Montmartre and the Mudd Club*, in which Bernard Gendron explores the exchange that took place between new music, new wave, and no wave, little had been written on how these downtown sounds didn't exist as a series of discrete scenes but instead began to meet and blend until downtown resembled a mashed-up jukebox of illegitimate fusions. Revealing the way downtown New York came to function as a space of explorative flows, Russell's blurry movements between pop, rock, folk, dance, hip-hop, and orchestral music did indeed resonate more widely still. In addition to describing the life of a musician, his biography could also help articulate the contours of a dynamic network: downtown New York during the 1970s and 1980s.

This shift in scope resolved a related problem. Setting out, I had wondered how I would negotiate the apparent requirement that every biography must elevate the life of its subject to the point where it plays into a rather insidious form of individualism. Artists and composers might relish this kind of exalted write-up, because recognition can be emotionally and financially rewarding, and so might record companies, because individuals are easier to sell than amorphous collectives, but a less partial interpretation of the world requires a different approach. As Manuel DeLanda notes in *A New Philosophy of Society*, while individuals are not the passive products of a grand macrostructure, nor is the macrostructure a "mere aggregate"; it comprises not a sum of individuals but the way in which those individuals *interact* with each other.[2] This idea of interaction (or what happens when two elements come into contact and develop a reciprocal exchange) was pivotal for Russell, who moved from Oskaloosa to Iowa City to San Francisco to New York because each new location offered him a greater opportunity to form relationships and explore sound. He didn't settle in downtown New York because the statistics looked good—it's likely more composers and musicians were living uptown during the early 1970s—but because downtown was a better place to exchange ideas, struggle over structure, fool around, and get good sound. Russell's biography, it follows, needed to emphasize not only his individuality but also his collaborative outlook and rootedness in a dynamic network.

In case an explicit disclaimer is necessary, *Hold On to Your Dreams* isn't intended as a history of that network. As a result the jazz loft scene is referenced only in passing, because although Russell grew up with jazz and introduced jazz aesthetics into many of his recordings, he didn't frequent venues such as Studio Rivbea and Ali's Alley, and he didn't become involved in the improvisation scene that developed out of the Knitting Factory in the 1980s. Similarly the no-wave scene charted by Simon Reynolds in *Rip It Up and Start Again* and Marc Masters in *No Wave* is referenced only briefly, because Russell didn't make music with its key protagonists, including the influential downtown figure Glen Branca. One of Branca's peers, the new-wave/no-wave composer Rhys Chatham, has a significant role because of his friendship with Russell and his heavyweight, institutional presence at the Kitchen Center for Video and Music. The unquestionably influential Kitchen is also a little more prominent than it might have been in a nonbiographical account of downtown because Russell curated its music program for the 1974–1975 season.

Along with the topography of Russell's choices, the testimonies of Russell's family, friends, and collaborators have heavily shaped this book. Whether it's clearer or foggier, hindsight is always a description of a past event rather than the event itself, and the memories and insights of interviewees can only be refracted through the present. I quote them because their recollections and opinions are either important or interesting, and although that's not the same thing as saying they're indisputably correct, their value becomes clearer when considered alongside the voices that are absent. Often cryptic and cagey when interviewed, Russell might have obstructed the writing of this biography if he was still around, but his passing has made it difficult to capture his voice, never mind check his movements and motives. Lovers, friends, mentors, and collaborators such as Louis Aquilone, John Bernd, Julius Eastman, Walter Gibbons, Allen Ginsberg, John Hammond, Larry Levan, Yuko Nonomura, and Kirk Winslow have also passed away, as has the more contentious figure of Ajari Warwick. I regret having interviewed Steve D'Acquisto about Russell on just the one occasion and that I was unable to locate the studio owner and engineer Mark Freedman, a significant figure in Russell's life.

Drawing on all available sources, I've attempted to combine the burrowing mentality of the archaeologist with the presentational outlook of the museum curator and the emotional sensibility of a diarist. I have tried to evoke the delicate, calibrated, and immersive mode of Russell's day-to-day music-making existence without letting minutiae suffocate his story, so while significant recording sessions and performances receive detailed descriptions, the kind of micro-detail that can be found in his notebooks is only included when it doesn't threaten to wreck any semblance of flow and structure. Whenever I wondered about whom to include or exclude, I asked myself the question: would Russell have wanted this friend to appear in a photo album of his life? Having shaped this book around his favorite people and places, I also have attempted to infuse this crucial biographical information with an equally important level of contextual analysis. The hope is for this analysis to illustrate the importance of a figure who was soft-spoken.

The chapters that follow are divided into seven chronologically ordered and overlapping blocks of time: Formations (1951–1973), Explorations (1973–1975), Alternatives (1975–1977), Intensities (1977–1980), Variations (1980–1984), Reverberations (1984–1987), and Tangents (1987–1992). The chronological framework allows the biography to carry out its first basic task, which is to outline the story of Russell's life, because this work hasn't been carried out beyond article-length detail. Far from forcing his story into an ill-fitting straitjacket, the chronology helps draw attention to the way in which, when faced with an array of choices, Russell's modus operandi was one of inquisitive digression. Instead of "progressing" from one style of music to another, or even one group of musicians to another, Russell followed an illogical logic, pursuing a bemusing number of sounds. Like a vine, he only moved up or down if that movement helped him move sideways, and his striking simultaneity—his wanting to do everything at once—didn't so much stop time as open up other ways of experiencing it.

In the mid-1980s Russell worked on a song titled "Get Around to It," but before I follow his advice, I should note a few points about the "it" that's about to begin. Regarding the mode of biographical address, Russell is called Russell in the preface, introduction, and epilogue, but in the narrative description of his life he becomes Charley, Jigmé, and then Arthur, because he wanted to connect emotionally and wasn't keen on formalities. Of course music provided Russell with his primary mode of connection, and although this cannot be replicated or displaced, some background information hopefully will enrich future listening. For readers who want to find out more, all of Russell's published recordings are listed in a discography at the end of the book, and the bibliography contains a list of websites of relevant record labels, musicians, and articles. Unless otherwise referenced, all quotations are taken from interviews that I conducted between 1998 and 2008.

Regarding the title of the book, I decided to opt for the unashamedly uplifting "Hold On to Your Dreams," the name of a song Russell wrote in the early 1980s for the producer and remixer François Kevorkian. Hatched while he was living in San Francisco, Russell's dream was simple: he wanted to write music as it came to him, move between and even bring together different sonic-social worlds, and earn enough money to pay the rent as he went about his work. Financial difficulties and record company fallouts disrupted this ambition repeatedly, and from the mid-1980s onwards ill health threatened to end it once and for all. But Russell only gave up pursuing the perfect studio mix (as well as an integrated downtown music culture) when sickness finally overtook his body. Full of improbable transitions and vivid flashes, Russell's life also took on the form of a dream, and while it's impossible to capture that dream in its entirety as it fades from consciousness, the shards that survive continue to enthrall.

Acknowledgments

My name appears on the spine of this book, but my primary task has been to coordinate, transcribe, and organize the memories of Arthur Russell's friends, family, and collaborators. Many writers describe their profession as a lonely one, but the experience of working on this book has been collective and sociable, and when I sing Russell's line "I wanna see all my friends at once," as I often do, I think of many of the people I have been lucky enough to meet while researching his biography.

I was admitted into Russell's inner circle because his intimates were open, generous, and trusting, as well as willing to take a gamble and confide in an author who had only one book to his name—a book about *disco*. Everyone who contributed to this book also made the most difficult acknowledgment of all: that however precious their memories might be, Russell was and remains beyond the proprietorship of any single person, and that this book would contain only part of "their Arthur." Russell could be fearless and contentious, especially if his activity seemed likely to lead to something interesting or even inspire personal growth, and because of this, it proved to be impossible to navigate an entirely smooth passage through the research and writing process. I remain grateful to those who might have been confronted with more information than they wanted to know at certain points, and hope I've learned a few things from the time bombs Russell left ticking after he died.

I remain indebted to the following interviewees, many of whom spoke with me several times while contributing to an archive of more than six hundred emails: Alan Abrams, Mustafa Ahmed, Bob Blank, Lola Blank, Joyce Bowden, Ernie Brooks, Rhys Chatham, Mel Cheren, Don Christensen, Steve D'Acquisto, David DePino, Arnold Dreyblatt, Barry Feldman, Jim Fouratt, Muriel Fujii, Colin Gate, Bernard Gendron, Jon Gibson, Philip Glass, Peter Gordon, Kent Goshorn, Steven Hall, Steven Harvey, David Hill, François Kevorkian, Kevin Killian, Steve Knutson, Jim Kohn, Jill Kroesen, Joan La Barbara, Elodie Lauten, Sister LaVette, Mary Jane Leach, Tom Lee, Robbie Leslie, George Lewis, Eric Liljestrand, Gary Lucas, David Mancuso, William Allaudin Mathieu, John Moran, Bill Morgan, Donald Murk, Sydney Murray, Rome Neal, Phill Niblock, Thomas R. O'Donnell, Toni Pagliuca, Gladys Pizarro, Bob Rosenthal, George Ruckert, Chuck Russell, Emily Russell, Julie Russell, Kate Russell Henry, Bill Ruyle, Larry Saltzman, Alison Salzinger, Roger Sanchez, John Scherman, Carlota Schoolman, Nicky Siano, Jim Smith, Will Socolov, Robert Stearns, Ned Sublette, Elias Tanenbaum, Anne Tardos, Todd Terry, Geoff Travis, "Blue" Gene Tyranny, David Van Tieghem, Leon Van Weelden, Paul Waldman, Daniel Wang, Jennifer Warnes, Jeff Whittier, Christian Wolff, Ellen Ziegler, Robert Ziegler, and Peter Zummo. These individuals supplied the memories and insights that underpin this biography. Without them it would have amounted to a moribund fusion of press cuttings, reworked secondary sources, and personalized interpretations of recordings. With them, I hope it's something more.

Because it was so difficult to get hold of Russell's music when I started my research, and because so much of his music remains unreleased, I turned to his collaborators and collectors, who supplied me with rare recordings. Ernie Brooks dug out a selection of Flying Hearts tapes and also made copies of the two Necessaries albums he worked on with Russell. Steven Hall sent me "C-Thru," a track he recorded with Russell and Walter Gibbons. Working with Tom Lee, Steve Knutson passed on recordings of Russell's interview on WUSB Stony Brook and his performance at 1750 Arch Street; a rare copy of *Tower of Meaning*; a bootleg of the Walter Gibbons mix of "Go Bang! #5"; and a selection of Bright and Early, Flying Hearts, Loose Joints, and solo efforts. Gary Lucas put together a compilation that included a recording of Russell's rap session with Mark Sinclair. Nick the Record assembled a selection of Russell's dance tracks, including the seven-inch version of "Pop Your Funk." Sandro Perri provided me with his own Polmo Polpo remix of "Kiss Me Again." Alex PeWin gave me another bootleg version of the Walter Gibbons remix of "Go Bang! #5." Larry Saltzman copied more Flying Hearts material, including the group's demo session with John Hammond. Matt Wolf forwarded Russell's performance of "Eli" at the Kitchen. I also received valuable discographical assistance from Ernie Brooks, Steven Hall, Tom Lee, Chris Menist, Niki Mir, Nick the Record, Will Socolov, Lee White, and, above all, Steve Knutson, who has become the unrivalled authority on Russell's unreleased tapes.

I've also benefited from generous assistance during my documentary research. Rachael Dorsey-McGowen, Richard Guerin, Ben Hyman, Matthew Lyons, and Edith Whitsitt helped me access material from the Kitchen's archives. Muriel Fujii was bold enough to send me the love letters she exchanged with Russell. Bernard Gendron shared information he had collected on early rock gigs that took place in the Mercer Arts Center as well as on Rhys Chatham's work with Morton Subotnick. Steven Hall made copies of the impassioned faxes he swapped with Russell while he was living in Hong Kong. David Hill handed over material gathered in his own research on Russell, including Point Music's inventory of Russell's tape archive, which was completed on 7 December 1992. Steve Knutson fuelled the idea of writing a biography when he invited me to rummage through the archives he was holding in his office at Audika. Tom Lee welcomed me into the apartment he co-inhabited with Russell and took my breath away as he opened up the boxes of letters and notebooks he had refused to discard, and which we leafed through together across long afternoons. Chuck and Emily Russell sent copies of the precious letters written by their son, as well as pamphlets about their hometown. Robert Stearns made a photocopy of the delicate *Kitchen Yearbook* he compiled for the 1974–1975 season and also sent details from the even more fragile 1975–1976 edition. David Toop shared the handwritten notes he made during his interview with Russell for the *Face* magazine. Kurt B. Reighley forwarded a transcript of his interviews with Laurie Anderson and Steve D'Acquisto. Additional support in tracking down books and articles was provided by the library staff at the University of East London (especially Hugh Bowman) and the British Library.

Collecting the artwork that appears in this book required much work, partly because Russell was notoriously camera-shy, and partly because photography was an expensive hobby in the 1970s and most of Russell's friends were poor. A significant portion of the material came from the private collections of Tom Lee and Chuck and Emily Russell, as well as the archive held by Audika. In addition I would like to thank Mustafa Ahmed, Bob Blank, Maria Blondeel, Teri Bloom, David Borden, Joyce Bowden, Patricia Brennecke, Ernie Brooks, Pat Clare, Paula Court, Steve D'Acquisto, R. Dulman, Frances Eastman, Johnny Fu, Muriel Fujii, Jon Gibson, Allen Ginsberg, Michael Gomes, Peter Gordon, Peter Hale, Steven Hall, Andy Harris, David Hill, Patricia Kelly, François Kevorkian, Mary Jane Leach, Leonedis Designs, Gary Lucas, William Allaudin Mathieu, Mike Meagher, Sydney Murray, Phill Niblock, Yuko Nonomura, Wendy Perron, Robert Poll, Marsha Resnick, Richard Rogers, Marion Rosendahl, John Rosenfelder, Bob Rosenthal, Jo Sherman, Nicky Siano, Teri Slotkin, Robert Stearns, Ned Sublette, Joanna Voit, Carrie Waldman, Paul Waldman, Edith Whitsitt, Matt Wolf, Ellen Ziegler, and Peter Zummo, all of whom provided valuable help. I have attempted to contact Jo Bonney and Robert Longo, Richard Landry, Daniel Sussman, and Henry Wang without luck, but I remain grateful for their photographs and artwork, which enrich this book.

Although it will involve repeating a number of names, extra-special thanks must go to Tom Lee, the unswerving and unsung friend, lover, and devotee, who has been courteous, gentle, and generous in answering all manner of inquiries; Chuck and Emily Russell, whose dedication to their son across the decades remains striking; Joyce Bowden, Ernie Brooks, Peter Gordon, Steven Hall, Elodie Lauten, and Peter Zummo, who continue to wrestle with the complicated legacy of their friend; Steve Knutson, whose work at Audika has done so much to raise Russell's profile, and who has been generous with information and resources; Steve D'Acquisto for letting his enthusiasm get the better of him and me when we started to talk about Russell; Arnold Dreyblatt, Donald Murk, Ned Sublette, and Jeff Whittier for their willingness to share rich insights; Robert Stearns for digging deep in order to help me get the Kitchen story straight; and finally to Philip Glass, whose enthusiasm and support for a younger and less successful composer-musician has barely dimmed across a period of some twenty-five years.

I would also like to thank Enrica Balestra, Andrew Blake, Bernie Gendron, Maggie Humm, and Helen Lane for reading earlier drafts of this book with such care; Danny Wang for initiating a conversation with one of this book's most important interviewees; Drew Daniel for coming up with the theme for EMP's 2006 gathering, which helped a great deal; Stuart Baker, Mel Cheren, Barry Feldman, David Hill, Gary Lucas, Will Socolov, Seymour Stein, Geoff Travis, and, especially, Philip Glass and Steve Knutson, for releasing Arthur Russell's music, which can't have ever been straightforward, but which lies at the heart of everything that follows; Stuart Aitken, Daniela Cascella, Sasha Frere-Jones, Jess Harvell, Tom Lee, Gary Lucas, Chris Menist, Thomas R. O'Donnell, Ben Ratliff, Kurt B. Reighley, Walter Rovere, Ned Sublette, Peter Zummo, and, in particular, David Toop for publishing articles that have already made the case for Russell's music; Matt Wolf for the excellent *Wild Combination: A Portrait of Arthur Russell* as well as the check-ins; Donald Murk for flattering me with the thought that I'm a "good match"; Will Straw for supporting my application to the British Academy; Aaron Lecklider for inviting me to contribute an article about Russell to the *Journal of Popular Music Studies*; Michael LeVan for overseeing the publication of my ambitious piece about Arthur Russell and rhizomatic musicianship in *Liminalities*; and Ryan Dohoney for the Julius Eastman clarifications.

More generally, I would like to thank Sarah Baker, Jeremy Gilbert, Maggie Humm, Mica Nava, Anat Pick, Ashwani Sharma, and Debbie Shaw in the Centre for Cultural Studies Research collective for the conversations about culture and politics; Enrica Balestra, Daphne Brooks, Garnette Cadogan, Maurizio Clemente, Jeremy Gilbert, Steve Goodman, Judith Halberstam, Yum Hara Cawkwell, Jason King, Charlie Kronengold, Josh Kun, David Mancuso, Fred Maus, Colleen Murphy, Carlos Palombini, Stefan Prescott, Alexandra Vázquez, Danny Wang, and Tim Watson for the conversations about music and politics; Eric Weisbard, Ann Powers, and the organizers and attendees at the EMP Pop Music conference in Seattle, who generate the most urgent conversations about popular music; my students in the music culture program at the University of East London for keeping me on my toes; Maurizio Clemente and Francesca Sulis (with Giovanni Ranieri and Luca Benini) for the Italian support; Tess and Greg, Helen and David, Rita and Nonna, and Giorgio and Elsa for the good food and feisty conversations; and Jeremy Gilbert and Colleen Murphy plus the rest of the Lucky Cloud Sound System collective—Ilaria Bucchieri, Lili Capelle, Guillaume Chottin, Simon Coppock, Cyril Cornet, Claude Dousset, Estelle du Boulay, Adrian Fillary, Emma Halpin, Simon Halpin, Darren Henson, James Hoggarth, Jo Kemp, Cedric Lassonde, Fabien Lassonde, Jo Littler, Iain Mackie, David Mancuso, Pauline Moisy, Darren Morgan, Pete Morris, Alex Pe Win, Alejandro Quesada, Sharon Reid, Janette Rosing, David Starsky, Tan Ur-Rehman, Elin Vister, Shannon Woo, and John Zachau—for the Journey through the Light parties, which couldn't be more rewarding.

I have once again been fortunate enough to work with the staff at Duke University Press, who published my first book, *Love Saves the Day: A History of American Dance Music Culture, 1970–1979*. Molly Balikov has been rigorous and flexible in overseeing the production process, and Courtney Berger, Katie Courtland, Jennifer Hill, Michael McCullough, and Laura Sell have been as professional, responsive, and friendly as any writer could wish. Jan Williams, not of Duke but a good fit here, has created an index that is elegant and insightful. Extra special thanks must be reserved for my editor, Ken Wissoker, with whom I have shared some memorable evenings, and whose taste in music and food is never less than excellent. Boundless in his enthusiasm and global in his outlook, Ken has been good enough to allow me to run with ideas that have appeared improbable, and has also revealed a knack for making key suggestions at decisive moments. Above all, he has established Duke as a publishing house that nurtures dissenting voices with care and integrity, as well as urgency and wonder, even when these voices aren't easily marketed. Could there be a better home for a biography of Arthur Russell?

Writing a book about someone who has passed away has reminded me continually of my parents, who died when I was young, but who continue to inform so much of what I do; I wish they were around. During the final weeks of writing, my mother's cousin Helen Franks, who must have been the first member of my family to publish a book, succumbed to a terrible illness; her vivacious mind and warm hospitality are missed. This book is dedicated to my wife, Enrica, who means everything to me and who helps me make sense of the world, and also to my two young daughters, Carlotta and Ilaria, who are such wonderful little and not-so-little human beings, and who carry such joy and hope. I'm lucky and thankful.

Introduction

Arthur Russell hailed from the Midwest, yet felt at home in downtown New York. Outwardly normal to those who observed his checkered shirt and acne-scarred face, he trod the mazelike streets that ran from the battered tenements of the East Village to the abandoned piers on the West Side Highway for hours at a time, and on a daily basis. The labyrinthine infrastructure and contrasting neighborhoods of lower Manhattan suited his purpose: equipped with a portable tape recorder or, when it became available, a Sony Walkman, Russell would play Abba alongside Mongolian throat music, or Bohannon back-to-back with Terry Riley, or Peggy Seeger followed by Grandmaster Flash—selections that were drawn from the global spectrum of sound and summoned the disjunctive backdrop of the city. Stopping only to offer his headphones to a friend, or to note an idea on one of the score sheets he stuffed into his bulging pockets, or to watch the sunset over the Hudson, Russell was a musical nomad who had downtown imprinted onto his sneakers.

New York, a hub for sonic invention, hosted a spell of particularly manic productivity during the 1970s and 1980s, and Russell, who lived in the city from 1973 to 1992, became one of its most audacious musicians. Striving for a level of sonic mobility that matched his winding walks and unpredictable tape selections, Russell wrote and recorded folk, pop, new-wave, dance, and orchestral music while composing songs for the cello, all in a rush of scene-hopping simultaneity that carried him through many of downtown's most vital spaces. Disco at the Loft, the Gallery, and the Paradise Garage; new music at the Kitchen Center for Video and Music (better known simply as "the Kitchen") and the Experimental Intermedia Foundation; country at Sobossek's and the Lower Manhattan Ocean Club; new wave and experimental pop at CBGB's and Danceteria; hip-hop and electro at the Roxy; poetry at St. Mark's; salsa on the streets of the East Village—skipping between these sounds and scenes with the nonchalant ease of a kid playing hopscotch, Russell embodied the creative mayhem of an era in which parties shimmered with energy and gigs brimmed with intent. A roamer at heart, Russell's performances and recordings made him uniquely qualified to navigate the baroque complexity of the downtown music scene during this period.

It would have been forgivable if Russell's music sounded like the work of an amateur idealist, such was the scope of his migrant hike, but in fact his contributions were consistently notable. As an orchestral musician he worked as the music director at the Kitchen, the groundbreaking venue for experimental composition, and recorded pieces for the pioneering composer Philip Glass and the avant-garde theatre director Robert Wilson. In the pop/rock sphere Russell put together demos for Columbia Records' legendary A&R executive, John Hammond, who believed Russell had the potential to become the next Bob Dylan, and he also played with the Necessaries, a new-wave band signed to Sire Records. Exploring the outer reaches of dance, he recorded a series of twelve-inch singles that blazed a trail between disco and house, working with pioneering engineers, producers, and remixers such as Bob Blank, Walter Gibbons, François Kevorkian, and Larry Levan. As he deepened his work, he cultivated a critically acclaimed voice-cello aesthetic that drew on orchestral music, dub, folk, and dance. Along the way he cofounded Sleeping Bag Records, one of the most influential independent labels for hip-hop and club music in the 1980s.

Russell recognized that the new-music compositional movement, minimalist rock, and disco/dance shared an interest in stripped-down instrumentation, trancelike repetition, and affective intensity, and so he worked between genres; while many of his contemporaries found his vision unconvincing, history has demonstrated he was simply ahead of his time. As a composer, Russell helped pioneer the eventually prolific dialogue between orchestral music and pop/rock, and he reached out to black dance with more energy than any of his downtown peers. His use of classical Indian, Western orchestral, and jazz techniques helped establish the future coordinates of mutant disco, or disco-not-disco. And although some deemed his introduction of a skittish syncopation into his twelve-inch repertoire to be undanceable, the sound went on to be popularized by broken beat and then dubstep years down the line. Anticipating the emergence of indie music, Russell also developed a strand of folk-oriented pop that was emotionally honest and delicately vulnerable. By the time indie had established this style as its own, he was busy introducing a black funk and hip-hop sensibility into his electronic pop—a combination that remains a leap too far for most guitar bands to this day.

Despite his itinerant sensibility, Russell has been recognized largely for just one set of recordings, his dance productions, which charted an aesthetic escape from the commercial cul-de-sac of late disco. Featuring David Byrne's highly-strung rhythm guitar, the twelve-inch single "Kiss Me Again" contained enough dissonance for it to become Sire's first foray into the disco arena. Remixed by Larry Levan, "Is It All Over My Face?" supplanted the polished aesthetic of late seventies disco with the bumpier atmosphere of the downtown dance floor. The equally pivotal "Go Bang! #5" featured a combination of orchestral and R&B musicians as well as the studio trickery of François Kevorkian. Even "Let's Go Swimming" and "School Bell/Treehouse," which failed to impress DJs when they were released, have resonated with gathering force over time. Russell's twelve-inch dance singles outsold his nondance releases by some distance, and this trend continued for several years after he died, during which time they appeared with gathering frequency on compilations that explored the less commercial recordings of the disco era as well as its mutant aftermath. Yet they also reverberated beyond dance, for Russell was set on taking the marginalized aesthetics of disco and even hip-hop into the heart of downtown.

Quirky, fragile, and pensive, Russell's songs didn't have anything like the same kind of impact as his dance productions, in part because so few of them were released, but a series of posthumous albums have highlighted this side of his craft. "I don't think there's any other songwriting where the music and the lyrics are of the same order," says the bass player and songwriter Ernie Brooks, who worked with Russell across the better part of two decades. "Musically Bob Dylan was not nearly as advanced as Arthur. John Lennon comes close. There are songs and there are songs, but Arthur's songs are the ones I always want to listen to." Unsure of his looks as well as his voice, Russell was always on the lookout for a vocalist who could deliver his compositions to a wider audience, yet most of the candidates ended up deferring back to Russell, whose agile technique enabled him to sail across his hieroglyphic lines. Invention came easily to him, and in May 2004 the *Wire* included Russell among its list of sixty writers who have contributed to the reinvention of the song form.[1]

The ability to move without inhibition—to record and listen without prejudice—was pivotal to Russell. When asked how his voice-cello album *World of Echo* (1986) related to earlier dance releases, he replied, "I think, ultimately, you'll be able to make dance records without using any drums at all," forgetting to mention that choreographers were already working with his acoustic songs.[2] As if to demonstrate the mutability of sound, Russell enjoyed rolling the same set of lyrics over a range of instrumental backdrops, and he ended up moving with such freedom it became impossible to associate him with a single style. This set him apart from other radically open-minded downtowners, such as Rhys Chatham, Philip Glass, Peter Gordon, and Peter Zummo, who worked across art music, pop, rock, and jazz, yet were ultimately rooted in the compositional scene, as well as from Laurie Anderson and David Byrne, whose eclecticism could be located in experimental pop. No navigation system could pinpoint the whereabouts of Russell. "He was way ahead of other people in understanding that the walls between concert music and popular music and avant-garde music were illusory, that they need not exist," comments Glass, who participated in the exploration of rock while remaining rooted in orchestral music. "He lived in a world in which those walls weren't there."

It's tempting to believe that each time Russell picked up a musical instrument or entered a recording studio, he paused to wonder what would happen if he tried to do things differently. Russell devolved the responsibilities of the conductor to his musicians during rehearsals for an orchestral performance; he shepherded a bunch of percussion-happy dancers into Blank Tapes Studios in order to capture their energy on vinyl; he opened windows to let the "musicianship of the street" feed into his mixes; he encouraged gospel-trained vocalists to unlearn what they had been taught in order to become more expressive; and when he spotted an old school friend playing a broken guitar, he whisked him into the studio because, as Donald Murk (a companion from that moment) notes, he believed that "everybody has a voice." As Russell explored the limits of musicianship, accomplished collaborators gleaned ideas about how they could develop their practice. "Arthur played a 'classical/acoustic' instrument, yet embraced and experimented with every new electronic gadget he could afford or get his hands on," explains the percussionist Mustafa Ahmed. "Whenever he learned about a new drum machine or synthesizer, he would tell me about it. In spite of my initial opposition, he purchased electronic drum pads and gave them to me to use when I performed with him. That forced me to learn the new technology, and I eventually came to incorporate these new devices into other aspects of my music."

In the end Russell spread himself across too many scenes and worked with too many musicians to build up a major reputation in a single genre, yet his lack of commercial success cannot be attributed solely to the music industry's distrust of eclecticism. Russell's perfectionism was peppered with obstinacy—on one occasion he spent a whole day fine-tuning the sound of a kick drum while his co-musicians waited to begin—and collaborators became so accustomed to his protracted methods they learned to stop asking what they were working on, or when a certain piece might be finished. The Walkman contributed to Russell's indecisiveness inasmuch as it enabled him to switch between two versions of a demo recording again and again as he tried to decide which was superior. But although Russell found it easy to become embroiled in a cycle of introspection, his recordings rarely suffered from the attention to detail. Like that of an accomplished improviser, the ease of his sound masked the prodigious amount of work that went into its making.

There was something beautiful about Russell's reluctance to decide on a final mix for many of his works. Playing, recording, and mixing amounted to a process of possibility, with every route a choice almost too tempting to resist, and the step of deciding on a final version—when a song would become static and therefore experience a form of death—often too painful to take. Instead Russell preferred to see music as a process that could reproduce itself in infinite ways and, in so doing, hint at the complexity and innate possibility of the universe. When he wrote orchestral music, Russell was drawn to the "generative" or "open form" approach championed by Christian Wolff (one of his mentors) because it allowed the musicians to embark on an uncharted exploration of sound. Dance music appealed in part because the practice of remixing allowed songs to experience several lives. Opportunities to release multiple versions of the same song were otherwise scarce, yet Russell generated something like a thousand reel-to-reel tapes of unreleased recordings. Because much of that music was unfinished, it contained the promise of future life.

Nevertheless Russell's perfectionism and philosophical resistance to finishing shouldn't obscure the fact that his output was substantial before he died in 1992 of complications arising from AIDS. In addition to his twelve-inch singles, Russell released four albums of his own music and two albums with the Necessaries, even though he didn't release any of the music recorded during the last five years of his life—a period of deliberate procrastination that risks overshadowing the years in which he was notably more successful (in terms of delivering an end product). "In those days it was hard to get a record released, and Arthur released more records than any of us," notes Ned Sublette, a downtown collaborator. "That was part of his mystique. Despite everything, he was visibly in the process of creating a body of work on record." Russell also laid down enough electronic pop, folk-oriented rock, acoustic songs, and off-the-wall dance tracks to fill four posthumous albums of previously unreleased material—*Another Thought* (1994), *Calling out of Context* (2004), *Springfield* (2006), and *Love Is Overtaking Me* (2008)—while another posthumous release, *First Thought Best Thought* (2006), included previously unreleased compositional pieces. With more albums of fresh material promised, Russell is beginning to look prolific, especially for a so-called serial procrastinator.

Whether they nestled within or between the coordinates of genre, these recordings always sounded particular. "Russell's work is stranded between lands real and imagined: the street and the cornfield; the soft bohemian New York and the hard Studio 54 New York; the cheery bold strokes of pop and the liberating possibilities of abstract art," wrote Sasha Frere-Jones in the *New Yorker* in 2004. "Arthur Russell didn't dissolve these borders so much as wander past them, humming his own song."[3] Innocent yet sophisticated, light yet serious, smooth yet angular, Russell's sonic identity contained seemingly irreconcilable contradictions, something that the Loft host David Mancuso captures when he describes him as being "Dylan and Coltrane rolled into one." The guitarist Gary Lucas, who has worked with the "trailblazers" Captain Beefheart and Jeff Buckley, remains captivated by Russell, with whom he worked in the 1980s. "There was the Corn-Belt-transplanted-to-New-York sensibility, the gay sensibility, the Buddhist sensibility — everything was in the mix," he comments. "That's what the best artists do. They give you a striking sense of personality."

Given his dynamic musical personality, it is perhaps surprising that Russell was also a bashful, complicated musician whose career could double as a tutorial in the frustration of narrative — including the tropes of self-made success and self-inflicted tragedy that run through so many biographies of musicians. Subdividing into a series of unresolved tangents, Russell's life and work lacked a defining arc, and because his overwhelming concern was to get the music right, moments of commercial promise ended in argument or anticlimax. In the end Russell died a marginal figure because he wasn't sufficiently self-centered, competitive, or coherent to convince the marketing departments of New York's record companies to embrace his vision. But for those who judged him according to his ability to work collectively, creatively, and with contradiction, all without recourse to materialism and celebrity, his subjugated story suggested an alternative way of working in the world. "This was a musical revolt . . . and Arthur was part of it," Glass noted in a 1995 interview. "We all became accepted except Arthur . . . He was an underground musician to the end of his life."[4]

Russell remains a relatively marginal figure, even in accounts of the downtown era. Tom Johnson's eyewitness account of downtown's orchestral scene in the 1970s and early 1980s, *The Voice of New Music*, overlooks Russell, perhaps because the author (in the words of Sublette) "didn't have a clue what our generation was doing." Michael Musto was much more open to the innovative possibilities of popular culture, but his book *Downtown* celebrates the brash, the fashionable, and the extrovert, and Russell, who scored poorly on all of those counts, doesn't get a mention. Marvin Taylor's impressive edited collection from 2006, *The Downtown Book*, emphasizes the primitive anger, anxious nihilism, and postmodern confusion that ran through lower Manhattan between 1975 and 1984, and once again Russell doesn't quite fit, even though downtown is lauded for having become a home for outsiders. Bringing together the photographs of Paula Court with a series of short essays by downtown players, the Soul Jazz publication *New York Noise: Art and Music from the New York Underground, 1978–88* seemed certain to correct the historical record, but Russell was notoriously camera-shy and somehow slips away.[5] A self-declared admirer,

Simon Reynolds mentions Russell only briefly in his groundbreaking history of postpunk, *Rip It Up and Start Again*, because Russell didn't have a significant impact on postpunk consciousness.[6] Nor did Russell feature in Kyle Gann's collection of writings on the downtown experimental scene, *Music Downtown*, perhaps because, as Gann wrote in his obituary of Russell, "he simply vanished into his own music."[7]

The omission of Russell doesn't amount to a conspiracy, or even an act of negligence, because he didn't insist upon being heard or seen. "His importance has not been appreciated as broadly as it should because he left such a small paper trail," comments Bernard Gendron, author of *Between Montmartre and the Mudd Club*, who didn't include Russell alongside Laurie Anderson, Glenn Branca, Rhys Chatham, and Peter Gordon in his list of the key representatives of downtown's "borderline aesthetic" because Russell left so little evidence of his work.[8] As with many other histories of U.S. popular music, however, the foregrounding of downtown's more audible and visible performers has resulted in the masculine and the straight being privileged above the feminine and the queer, as well as the white above the black and the Latin. While there is no disputing the influence of individuals such as Glenn Branca, James Chance, Rhys Chatham, and Richard Hell, as well as groups such as Blondie, the New York Dolls, the Ramones, Sonic Youth, Suicide, the Swans, Talking Heads, and the Velvet Underground, the historical focus on rock and its exchange with the noisier end of compositional music has helped strengthen the reputations of players who were already prominent. Insofar as they are recognized, African Americans have managed to appear on the periphery when they are masculine (such as the breakdancers and DJs of hip-hop, and the intrepid performers of free jazz) or when they have augmented white players (such as the session musicians who performed on *Remain in Light*). Meanwhile women have appeared, in general, if they reproduced the masculine (e.g., Lydia Lunch, Patti Smith), embraced a boyish techno-coldness (e.g., Laurie Anderson), or played the blonde seductress (e.g., Debbie Harry). Even given these restraints, downtown's producers of pop, folk, and—above all—disco haven't featured at all.

Russell's story, which is also a story of his collaborations, counterbalances rather than displaces these versions of the downtown era. Russell lived in a neighborhood that was heavily Latin, went to clubs that were predominantly gay and black, hung out with women who were drawn to the ethereal, and wrote songs with guys who were interested in the sublime. As he went about his work, Russell recorded rock and orchestral music, and when these scenes appeared to be trapped in a demographic or aesthetic loop, he mixed things up. "Arthur was always the one to bring in people from different backgrounds—blacks, gays, people from Brooklyn and the Bronx," notes Zummo. "To him there was no question that these people could be drawn into the white downtown avant-garde scene. I would have never met Mustafa Ahmed if it hadn't been for Arthur." No other downtowner engaged with the visceral, creative, transcendental world of black gay aesthetics to the same degree as Russell, and the results could be heard in his performances and recordings. "Many New York artists around that time were using aggression and anxiety in their work," wrote Ben Ratliff in the *New York Times* in 2004. "Russell's work had no aggression in it whatsoever, but patience and kindness instead; this is one of the reasons it doesn't now feel stuck in its time."[9]

If downtown was violent, poor, dangerous, competitive, and macho— and it's worth questioning the extent to which the macho element might have overstated the toughness of the conditions—Russell tried to not let it get to him. He lived in the East Village because as well as being hazardous, it was rich in rhythm and community. He frequented the seedy dives where desolation and unease were de rigueur, but preferred to hang out in the celebratory venues of downtown dance. And while a number of downtowners expressed a combination of poetic aggression and anxious frustration, he chose to introduce fun, sensitivity, and humor into his music. Along with Tom Lee, his supportive partner, these factors might have helped Russell survive, for while most of his peers ended up leaving downtown for more moderate climes, he stuck it out until the end of his life. "Downtown was a discourse on the nullification of absolutes that needs the full cacophonous chorus to be heard," comments the popular-culture critic Carlo McCormick in *The Downtown Book*. Because his inquisitive ear, light feet, and generous spirit led him to work in so many scenes, Russell offers a rather lovely way to explore the musical elements of this chorus.[10]

1 **Formations** (1951–1973)

Charles Arthur Russell—or Chuck—was born in Oskaloosa, Iowa, to a Methodist father and a Quaker mother in 1922. Having graduated from high school, he attended Parks Air College until he was expelled for spending too much time in Missouri, where his Oskaloosan girlfriend, Emily Alsop, was studying liberal arts. During World War II Chuck joined the U.S. Navy, after which he was accepted into flight school and married Emily, who gave birth to their first daughter, Kate, in 1946. By then Chuck had enrolled at Iowa State University to study civil engineering, and as he supplemented his GI Bill income with a series of unglamorous jobs, Chuck switched programs before he gave up his studies in order to open an insurance agency in the fall of 1948. Chuck and Emily's second child, Julie, was born in 1949, and a couple of years later, on 21 May 1951, the arrival of their first son, Charles Arthur, marked the completion of the family. Although nobody remarked upon it at the time, it would later appear significant that he was born on the night of a full moon.

Like John Cage, Captain Beefheart, La Monte Young, Harry Partch, Steve Reich, Lou Reed, Tom Waits, Frank Zappa, and other maverick musicians and composers born in the United States, Charles Arthur ended up developing a bold aesthetic practice that appeared to bear no relation to his place of birth. Founded in 1835 by Captain Nathan Boone, who had been ordered to find some land and build a fort, Oskaloosa was situated in the heart of the Corn Belt, some sixty miles southeast of Des Moines, the state capital of Iowa. It matured into a small municipality of some ten thousand residents, which made it the third largest town in Iowa. In 1938 *Fortune* magazine ran a feature titled "Oskaloosa vs. the U.S.," having selected Oskaloosa as the subject because it was considered to be a perfectly typical town, and in 1950 the town was honored with a Freedom Foundation Award. Born the following year, Charles Arthur would later conclude that his idea of freedom could be best pursued elsewhere, and he ended up running away from home at the age of sixteen. Within a few years he was writing post-minimalist orchestral music, angular folk songs for the cello, and avant-garde disco—music that sounded strange to Chuck and Emily, never mind their Oskaloosan friends.

Yet although Oskaloosa was a conservative town situated in a conservative state, Charley (as he liked to be referred to) was also challenged with the task of escaping a conservative era. "With the help of the GI Bill, men were ushered into schools and professions that would boost their economic status," explains his sister Kate. "At the same time, the government, the corporations, and the media pushed for larger families, forcing women to give up their wartime jobs and settle for so-called woman's work. But it was also an era of hope." Having worked hard and seized his opportunities, Chuck flourished in his new insurance business, while Emily's parents, the owners of the largest department store in Oskaloosa, also profited from the postwar economic boom. Elsewhere in the United States, economics and culture moved according to a similar rhythm. "Although activists and liberals may have been disappointed at the slow pace of social reform after World War II, the attention of most Americans was so riveted on the astonishing new world of consumerism and prosperity that social issues—for the moment, at least—seemed relatively unimportant," writes the historian William Chafe. "Rarely has a society experienced such rapid or dramatic change as that which occurred in America after 1945."[1]

Prosperity didn't make the Russells synonymous with traditionalism, and they revealed themselves to be significantly less conservative than some of their friends at their country club when they adopted plans (put together by Chuck's architect brother) to build a redwood home in the style of Frank Lloyd Wright. But they could find no reason to challenge other widely accepted conventions, so Kate, Julie, and Charley would return from school to find Emily curled up in a chair, reading the latest selection from the Book-of-the-Month Club, and when Chuck returned from his office a little later, Emily would cook up a casserole while he put on a record. Stretching to the end of the flat Iowan horizon, the only clouds that lingered were "lucky ones" (as Charley would write later in his song "Lucky Cloud"). "Life was getting better, and my parents, along with almost everyone else, embraced the new lifestyle," adds Kate. "Who wouldn't after fifteen years of depression and war?"

Relocating to Iowa City and then to San Francisco before settling in New York City, Charley would move farther and farther away from the calm, protected enclave of Oskaloosa, and each departure would add weight to his maverick credentials. As Michael Broyles argues, the tradition of the maverick musician lies at the center of "possibly the strongest and most sacred myth of American society, that of rugged individualism," and the "inability or in some cases conscious unwillingness of the mavericks to compromise has been precisely why their voices have remained clear, or at least why they were not overwhelmed by the predominant European culture."[2] Charley certainly found it difficult to compromise, and he left the Midwest not in order to lead an equivalent lifestyle in another part of the country, but instead to find a different group of friends, a contrasting set of social expectations, and ultimately, a more vibrant music culture. "Oskaloosa is a nice-sized town, but it's certainly rural," comments Emily. "The opportunities in a community of this size for a boy like Charley were limited." Chuck adds that his son needed to leave Oskaloosa in order to pursue his dream. "Looking back, I don't think we would be talking about him today if he hadn't run away. If he had stayed at home, he might have become an insurance agent or something."

For all his rebellious tendencies, however, Charley never left the experience of his childhood in Oskaloosa entirely behind. As a kid, he loved to listen to Chuck tell stories about the wind and the high seas of the South Pacific, where he had served on a minesweeper, and Chuck's passion for music was another formative influence. Milling around the stereo, Charley would have heard Chuck select a range of classical composers, including Brahms, Bach, Beethoven, Chopin, Mozart, and Vivaldi, while on other occasions his father would opt for the songs of Frank Sinatra, Aretha Franklin, or Bessie Smith. More often than not, however, Chuck would pick out some jazz from his collection of three to four hundred LPs. Dave Brubeck, the Modern Jazz Quartet, and Ahmad Jamal featured regularly, as did Leonard Bernstein's *What Is Jazz?*. Instrumentalists who played with "real rhythm," such as Louis Armstrong, Benny Goodman, and Fats Waller, raised the temperature, as did the full-throttle Dixieland of Bob Crosby and his Bobcats, Tommy Dorsey, and Jimmy Rushing. When Chuck was in the mood for something calmer, he favored the more sophisticated playing and writing of Duke Ellington, Jimmy Giuffre, and Teddy Wilson, along with the musicals and film scores of André Previn. This music continued to run through Charley long after he thought he had left Oskaloosa behind.

Emily's musical influence might have been even more profound. Having played the bass viola in her younger years, she took up the cello around the time Charley started to go to school, and when she wasn't practicing in the family's music room, she would sit down with Charley and talk about classical music as it played on the stereo. More musical than his sisters, Charley took up the piano when he was in second grade, aged six, and soon started to play by ear. His first tutor, Cecil Penniston, one of a handful of African Americans who lived in Oskaloosa, focused on theory, after which Raymond Comstock, who led the high-school orchestra, concentrated on getting him to read music — specifically because this was something Charley believed he could avoid. In the fourth grade Charley thought about switching to the trombone, but chose the cello when he was told he could join the school orchestra straight away (rather than wait a semester) if he opted for a stringed instrument. That decision deepened Charley's musical bond with his mother, even if the two of them ended up fighting over access to the cello until Chuck bought his wife a $650 replacement. When he reached sixth grade, Chuck and Emily agreed to let him travel alone to Des Moines in order to take private classes at Drake University. Acknowledging Charley's progress and talent, the school asked him to compose music for its production of *The Emperor's New Clothes*, which was performed in the spring of 1966. After someone complimented Charley on the music he replied, "Just wait till I finish it."[3]

Charley's musical progress couldn't paper over his shortcomings, however, and as he grew older Chuck and Emily began to worry about his social skills. Unlike his father, who was an athletics enthusiast, Charley preferred dinosaurs, Erector Sets, astronomy, fish, puppet-making, and magic to sports, and he broke his arm attempting the high jump on one of the few occasions he tried to be more athletic. Charley's refusal to take sports

Four-year-old Charley takes a bath with Kate (left) and Julie (center), 1955. Photograph by Charles Arthur Russell Sr. Courtesy of Charles Arthur Russell Sr. and Emily Russell.

seriously became a major source of friction, especially with Emily and Kate, who feared it would mark him out as being irredeemably different from other boys, and some fierce battles ensued. "He was named exactly like my father, and it seemed like he had to be like my father," says Kate, who attempted to play the role of mediator when arguments broke out, but usually ended up backing her parents. Having made Charley run laps around the backyard pond when he went through a chubby-boy phase, Chuck took to admonishing him for being a "poor sport" when he reacted badly to things not going his way, and although the barb was delivered with ribbing humor, it always drove Charley crazy. "At that moment when he really needed us, I think we failed him to a certain degree," adds Kate.

As Charley's adolescent angst deepened, an aggressive rash of acne erupted over his face and back, and it's possible that the success of Kate (who was outgoing, creative, and flamboyant), Julie (who blossomed into a popular homecoming queen), and Chuck (who became mayor of Oska-loosa in January 1964) compounded his sense of being an outsider and maybe also a failure. Morose and timid, awkward and dreamy, self-absorbed

Charley during his astronomy phase, 1962. Photograph by Charles Arthur Russell Sr. Courtesy of Charles Arthur Russell Sr. and Emily Russell.

and self-conscious, Charley was an outwardly square kid, and although he was undoubtedly bright, his cleverness could be irritating. The owner of an unpleasant temper, Charley also required only the mildest provocation or mishap to go into a sulk or a rage, and he became something of a loner. "He was *abnormal* from the point of view of the all-American boy," says Chuck. "He was different, and I think kids made fun of him." At this juncture nobody could have imagined that he would only come into his own in downtown New York; even less that he would manage this with many of his personality traits intact.

Charley wasn't completely friendless, however, and it came as some relief to Chuck and Emily when he struck up a friendship with Kent Goshorn, who had been "kind of impressed" when he saw Charley react with laughter rather than tears after breaking his arm at the high jump. Although Goshorn was used to hanging out with what he calls "jock types," he shared Charley's interest in the arts as well as his frustration with life in Oskaloosa, and they started to get together for music-listening sessions when Chuck

Charley Russell, 1964. Photographer
unknown. Courtesy of Tom Lee.

and Emily went out on a Saturday night and the house was theirs to claim.
During these evenings Goshorn would regularly pick out "British invasion"
rock, while Charley would select a mix of classical music, folk, and jazz. "I
would go over to his house to trade records, and trying to be precocious, I
would bring out Bob Dylan or James Brown or something like that," Goshorn commented later. "Arthur would bring out Stravinsky and John Coltrane." At the same time, Charley also attempted to influence the taste of
his parents, who didn't appreciate rock and roll. "[Chuck and Emily] had a
stereo system and the speakers went into their bedroom," recalls Goshorn.
"Charley would play the Rolling Stones at very low volume when they were
sleeping to 're-programme them,' so he said."[4]

Entering into the countercultural spirit of the era, Charley and Goshorn also read poetry, smoked pot, and grew their hair long, and when
the high school authorities started to quash this modest wave of opposi-
tional culture in the fall of 1964, Charley refused to conform. "Come on,
Charley," Chuck and Emily would say. "You can't rock the boat too much."
But the rocking had only just begun, and during 1965, Chuck's second year
as mayor, Charley started to spend time with a group of older boys and

young men who bonded around a commitment to rock and roll, folk music, and the arts, as well as a willingness to experiment with marijuana and LSD. "To me it was a spiritual awakening," says Leon Van Weelden, one of Kate's former high-school sweethearts and an established member of the group. "Having grown up in a conservative, fundamentalist religious community and family, it was an opening for me to see life through a totally different lens."

Appearing in black jeans and a white shirt, and demonstrating a preference for music that the rest of the group found uninteresting or incomprehensible, Charley became an awkward presence. "Some people saw him as a kind of nuisance," recalls Van Weelden, who had been a dedicated sports enthusiast until he tried acid to the accompaniment of Eastern music and the *Book of Dao*. "He was a goofy little kid and we weren't sure whether he was cool enough to hang out with us, or trustworthy enough to keep his mouth shut, or stable enough not to get into trouble one way or another." Possessing the right combination of determination and intellectual flair, however, Charley was allowed to stick around, and in 1966, the group judged him to be ready to trip. "There were times when he would do marijuana or LSD for two or three days in a row and every weekend," adds Van Weelden. "He sometimes went to school while he was tripping. He was pretty indiscriminate and really didn't have any boundaries at that point. It was a blessing and a curse. It allowed him to explore without judgement. It helped form who he was."

Chuck's and Emily's tolerance reached its limit during this period. Although they didn't discover he was experimenting with LSD until later, the realization that he was reading Timothy Leary — one of the key philosophers of the psychedelic movement — left them deeply worried. When they realized he was smoking marijuana, a relatively unknown drug at the time, they booked a session with a psychologist. Charley's sophomore-year grades were disappointing rather than disastrous — he received a middling mixture of Bs and Cs, plus a D for P.E. — but Chuck and Emily believed he could do better and remained troubled by his disobedient, slothful, belligerent demeanor. Tempers spilled over eventually when Charley refused to cut his hair and swore in front of Emily, which prompted Chuck to "bounce him on the floor" (as Chuck puts it). The Russells were both furious and distraught that they had lost control of their wayward son, while Charley's overriding concern was to escape from Oskaloosa.

Iowa City

The Russell family had always traveled around. Languid summers were spent in Minnesota, where Emily's parents owned a cabin by one of the state's ten thousand lakes, and it was there that C. C., Emily's father, taught Charley how to drive a boat and fish. Cutting through Texas, the Russells also went on a road trip to Mexico and headed to the Gulf of Mexico before they made their way to Acapulco, where they came face to face with the Pacific Ocean. On a subsequent holiday they went to Chicago, where they visited museums and journeyed on the subway in order to witness the city's tenements and slums. Chuck and Emily had built their home in the Midwest, but they wore UN-tinted spectacles and wanted their children to see the world.

The vacations helped create a striking impression of the land that lay beyond Oskaloosa, as well as a working knowledge of how to get around, and when Goshorn traveled with his family to live in California, Charley was left with one less reason to remain in his hometown. In 1967 the Summer of Love broadcast the news that the best action was happening on the West Coast, and when Van Weelden moved to the liberal outpost of Iowa City, a realistic escape route began to materialize. Having already visited Iowa City, Charley declared a preference for continuing his high school education at University High, a progressive institution that was open to the children of professors at the University of Iowa. So toward the end of 1967, when he was sixteen years old, Charley ran away from home and went to camp on Van Weelden's sofa in Iowa City.

Responding to Chuck's and Emily's concern, a well-connected friend helped Charley enroll in University High, while Chuck and Emily agreed to give Van Weelden (who had conducted himself well during his relationship with Kate) a contribution toward his living expenses. "Letting Arthur [as Charley would soon call himself] go to Iowa City and live with Leon was really smart," says Kate. "Leon was on Arthur's wavelength and Arthur needed space. He needed to follow whatever dream he was dreaming. He ran away and we had to let go. It was a good thing." Chuck and Emily attempted to ease their anxiety by acquiring a thirty-foot, two-mast sailboat.

In the end, Charley didn't spend much time with Van Weelden. Once classes at University High were over for the day, he would head off with

Left: Charley (far right) with his sisters and cousins while on vacation at Gull Lake, Minnesota, 1956. Photograph by Charles Arthur Russell Sr. Courtesy of Charles Arthur Russell Sr. and Emily Russell. *Right*: Charley on a beach in Mexico in the summer of 1963, shortly after he broke his arm. Photograph by Charles Arthur Russell Sr. Courtesy of Charles Arthur Russell Sr. and Emily Russell.

The Russell family during a trip to Chicago in 1959. Photographer unknown. Courtesy of Charles Arthur Russell Sr. and Emily Russell.

friends, or make his way to a rented house where a rock and roll band from Oskaloosa had taken up residence. "Charley came and went pretty freely," remembers Van Weelden. "He'd come in late at night and then he'd go to school. It wasn't problematic. He was just unrestrained." When Van Weelden left for California, Charley stayed in Iowa City and moved in with a preacher, but he didn't settle down, and it appears that he spent a good number of nights out, often sleeping on the floor of a musician friend's house. Unsurprisingly, he continued to slip further behind in his studies.

San Francisco

Shacking up in an apartment of some "druggy friends" from Oskaloosa and Iowa City that was located between Haight-Ashbury and the old Fillmore District, Charley and Goshorn visited San Francisco during spring break of 1968 and returned to live there in the summer. "We didn't ask if we could stay," remembers Goshorn. "We just moved in and found a place on the couch." Indifferent to the wider countercultural movement, Charley avoided discussing the Vietnam War and also steered clear of the rock scene that had gelled around the Monterey Pop Festival of June 1967, perhaps because, as Goshorn maintains, it was easier for him to be "different and 'ahead' of everyone else" if he was into Cage rather than Hendrix. Goshorn also felt Charley became distant and elusive during this period, and as LSD became an inconsequential part of their lives and their Oskaloosan bond weakened, they drifted apart. Enough of a connection remained for them to stick together when they decided to move out of the apartment; their roommates were heavily into heroin, and after a while it became too much. Charley found the two of them a room in a nearby commune, and they started to sell psychedelic newspapers to earn some money. But their relationship continued to sour, and a month or two later Goshorn moved to a rural commune.

Left to his own devices, Charley appears to have drifted until he was arrested in early 1969. "The police explained to me that he was in a place where they investigated and found marijuana," recalls Chuck. "Since he was underage, they wouldn't release him until he turned eighteen." The police were familiar with this kind of situation—the number of minors living outside parental care in San Francisco had skyrocketed during the second half of the 1960s—and they proceeded to ask the Russells if they wanted Charley to be held in a detention home or sent back to Oskaloosa. "We consulted a friend who worked in law enforcement and he said, 'If you force him home, you may never see him again.' So I called back and said, 'Hold and release!'" Rather than stay in the detention center, or return to Oskaloosa, however, Charley joined Kailas Shugendo, a Buddhist commune, on 14 February 1969, and he was released to its custody.

Combining the teachings of the Tibetan Buddhist priest Lama Anagarika Govinda with the mountain asceticism practiced by the Shugenja followers of Japanese Shingon Buddhism, Dr N. G. Pemchekov Warwick founded Kailas Shugendo in the late 1960s. The name reflected his mongrel outlook: *Kailas* alludes to the revered Mount Kailas in Tibet, while *Shugendo* is the name given to the Shugenja's brand of mountain asceticism. Mountain walking became a regular activity, while fire ceremonies (during which mantras were recited and participants walked across burning coals) took place on a weekly and later daily basis. Fair-skinned, dark-haired, and in possession of a Buddha-like paunch, Warwick called himself Ajari, which is the Japanese translation of the Sanskrit term for "senior teacher."

The circumstances of Charley Russell's entry into Kailas Shugendo remain hazy. He had shown an interest in Buddhism back in Iowa, and the public adoption of the religion by the beat writers Richard Alpert, Gary Snyder, Jack Kerouac, and Allen Ginsberg, who were read by Charley, might have created a lasting impression. He didn't get involved in Buddhism during his first months in San Francisco, and Kailas Shugendo was also a nonproselytizing organization, but Ajari Warwick was a charismatic public figure who needed to build up his commune's numbers, and it's conceivable that Charley joined the organization a little more readily than might have otherwise been the case when the police asked him to identify an adult guardian as a condition of his release. At the very least, Charley joined Kailas Shugendo at a time when he was alone and vulnerable.

Because the commune lacked its own building, Charley stayed in a single room on Bush Street, and when Goshorn called on him that summer, they headed off to the Santa Cruz mountains for three days, during which time Goshorn hiked while Charley stayed put and played his cello (which he originally had left behind in Oskaloosa but had now recovered). After that Charley was taken into the Mill Valley home of Terry and Lorna Mills, who were both members of Kailas Shugendo, and when Terry and Lorna started to call Charley "Jigmé," the name stuck, maybe because Charley thought it would enable him to shed another layer of his Oskaloosan skin. Following Kailas Shugendo's purchase of its first house at 1551 Octavia Street in April 1970, Jigmé moved into the premises, and he remained a resident when the commune relocated to a tall wooden house on Pine Street, near Japantown, in July.

An intimate and devoted disciple of Warwick, Jigmé cut his long hair in order to be inaugurated as a "tonsured novice priest"; he took part in liturgical training and spiritual guidance; and he was given the responsibility of stocking the commune with food and drink. In addition, he participated in the organization's fire walking rituals, played cello at its fire ceremonies, and joined the Kailas Shugendo Mantric Sun Band, a country-Buddhist outfit led by Warwick. Settling into his new surroundings, he also became a drug-free, vegetarian teetotaler and enrolled at a local community college, where he would go on to earn the equivalent of a high-school diploma. "My life is definitely taking direction in the mountains," he wrote to Chuck and Emily in March 1970.

Loaded with duties, Jigmé barely had time to practice cello, yet the commune paid for him to start taking private lessons with Andor Toth, the youngest player in the San Francisco Symphony Chamber Orchestra, and in April Jigmé reported to Chuck and Emily that his playing was "coming along very nicely." "Each time I visit my teacher there is improvement, and with it in all of my life," he added. "Problems which I was confounded with a year ago no longer exist." Jigmé took to practicing in his closet, not because playing was forbidden, but because it was a quiet spot where he wouldn't be disturbed, and he also loved the acoustics of the confined space. As the sound swirled around and through his body, he lost the capacity to distinguish between himself and music, and playing became a form of meditation.

Chuck and Emily Russell visited Charley (as they continued to call him) in January 1971 and could barely conceal their delight at his transformation. Dr. Warwick's brand of West Coast Buddhism might have seemed strange to their Midwestern Christian sensibility, but as far as they were concerned, the Kailas Shugendo guru had weaned their son away from drugs and enabled him to return to school and the cello. Kate visited later in the spring and glimpsed the commune's magnetic appeal when she attended one of

Jigmé and Emily Russell at a farmer's market in San Francisco, 1971. Jigmé drove such a hard bargain over the cost of vegetables his parents were reminded of Emily's entrepreneurial father. Photograph by Charles Arthur Russell Sr. Courtesy of Charles Arthur Russell Sr. and Emily Russell.

the daily fire ceremonies. Sitting in yoga postures on tiered benches, some twenty-five congregants chanted as Jigmé played cello, and as the fire grew stronger, the chanting became louder. "I was almost transformed," she remembers. "I could have seen myself getting involved." Kate recalls being concerned about Dr. Warwick's level of control over his followers, which made her "shudder," yet she also recognized that the commune had given Jigmé a sense of perspective and an opportunity to "grow up."

A North Indian classical musician, Ali Akbar Khan established the Ali Akbar College of Music at the end of 1967, the annus mirabilis for Indian music in the West, during which the Beatles released *Sgt. Pepper's Lonely Hearts Club Band* (featuring George Harrison's sitar on "Within You Without You"); Ravi Shankar performed at the Monterey Pop Festival (sharing the bill with Jimi Hendrix, Janis Joplin, Otis Redding, and the Who); and Shankar and Yehudi Menuhin won a Grammy for their album *West Meets*

East (after which they performed at a UN human rights concert that was broadcast around the world).[5] Initially based in a rented room in Berkeley, the college relocated to Marin County when Khan decided the noise generated by the antiwar protests wasn't conducive to study, and a little later it moved again, this time to San Rafael.[6] As Khan's profile soared—his album *Shree Rag* was nominated for a Grammy in 1970—G. S. Sachdev, a *bansuri* (bamboo flute) musician, and a stream of teachers from India worked with musicians such as the Grateful Dead drummer Mickey Hart, the folk artist Jody Stecher, Great Society's lead guitarist Darby Slick, and the bass and saxophone player Peter Van Gelder. An unprecedented number of Western players wanted to absorb Eastern classical music, and Arthur Russell became part of this movement.

Lacking a formal structure, the college's program encouraged indefinite study, and Arthur (as Jigmé preferred to be called in this environment) gave himself up to the musical vortex, taking instrumental and vocal classes with Khan and Sachdev, as well as vocal classes with Sengupta Ghosh, another teacher in the college. Even though it lay outside the conventions of Indian classical music, Arthur held on to his cello, and in a chance meeting he was joined on the instrument by Mark Levinson, whose unparalleled audiophile amplifiers would eventually power the sound system at the Loft in New York City (and bring perfect clarity to Arthur's future dance recordings). Playing against the drone—a single note played over an extended period of time—Arthur practiced hard, and carried out a good deal of this work with Jeff Whittier, a flautist he met on Mount Shasta in August 1969.

A follower of Mother Mary Mae Maier, a spiritual leader who had traveled widely in India and Tibet before settling on the north Californian mountain, Whittier had been sitting with his teacher when a member of Kailas Shugendo approached to see if Mother Mary would be prepared to meet the group. The representative left a copy of *The Way of the White Clouds* by Lama Anagarika Govinda, Warwick's guru, and when Mother Mary caught sight of the picture of Govinda she said, "He's real. I want to meet with them."[7] Dressed in a Hawaiian shirt and sneakers, Whittier walked across the glacier at an altitude of eleven thousand feet to relay the news, and later that evening, when Kailas Shugendo returned from the top of the mountain to its campsite at Bunny Flat, Ajari lit a great fire and Mother Mary spoke for hours. "We spent the whole night up on the mountain, and Arthur and I talked," remembers Whittier, who was struck by his new friend's intelligence and grasp of Buddhist philosophy. "We discovered that we were both interested in Indian music right away." Arthur and Whittier stayed in touch, and following the death of Mother Mary in 1970, Whittier traveled to the Ali Akbar College of Music; he enrolled in the program in June 1971.

Forming a close friendship, Arthur and Whittier practiced the scales of unusual *ragas* and, echoing the structure of the *bhajan* (devotional song), in which poetic lines are repeated with subtle variations, they also developed riffs. Because Whittier played the flute, Sachdev's bow-flute class — on music for bowed instruments and the flute — provided them with practice material, and, teaming up with a tabla player, they worked on playing in rhythm cycles. As Arthur's practice deepened, he began to explore the particularities of the classical Indian idiom, including the existence of notes that appeared only as "accidentals" in Western music. It was as if Arthur had something in common with these notes: unclassifiable in the West, they were fully recognized, integrated, and liberated in the parallel framework of the East. But instead of exchanging one tradition for another, Arthur hoped to fuse the two together. "Arthur was very interested in the forms of Indian music," says Whittier. "It was giving him pause for thought. He was soaking it up."

Through Whittier, Arthur also became close with Ellen Ziegler, who enrolled in the College full-time after graduating from Antioch College, and Alan Abrams, who joined as a way of pursuing a non-sectarian spiritual practice, having studied meditation in India with the guru Nimkroli Baba, the author of *Be Here Now*. "We all lived in these group houses, drifted back and forth, and stayed up all night," recalls Ziegler, a vocalist who also played the flute and drums. "We were a bunch of enthusiastic, mind-altered Americans, and we all became obsessed." Ziegler says she would sit down with Arthur and create "little rivers of music" in which they tried to bring "all these diverse elements together." Abrams remembers taking part in practice sessions where students played or sang a single note until it drew everyone into its inescapable logic. "Arthur was also doing his other music on the side," adds Abrams. "We played acoustic guitar together a lot — folk music. He wasn't letting anyone dictate to him that he needed to make a choice."

In many respects the college embodied the experimental freedom of the countercultural movement; contrary to established educational practice, for example, female and male students shared dorms and shower rooms. Yet it was also a conservative institution ruled by a powerful patriarch in which, according to Whittier, a core group (including Ziegler) became the personal disciples of Khan while others (including Abrams, Whittier, and Arthur) were made to feel peripheral. Instrumental choice was often a determining factor—Khan played the sarod and tended to prefer those who did the same—and although Arthur would comment later that the cello was Khan's "favorite instrument," it appears to have predetermined his failure to enter the honored inner circle, which bothered him.[8] College politics didn't come between Arthur, Abrams, Whittier, and Ziegler, however, and as conversations about Buddhism segued into dusk-to-dawn, free-flowing jams, they took to meeting in Mill Valley, where Ziegler and Whittier rented a room, or in Abrams's vine-covered abode in San Geronimo Valley, or at the bottom of a tree in Bolinas where Abrams took occasional refuge, or Mount Shasta, where they would head at every opportunity, instruments strung over their shoulders, rucksacks strapped onto their backs.

Having enrolled as a part-time student in the San Francisco Conservatory of Music in the summer of 1970, around the time he joined the Ali Akbar College, Arthur also pursued a conservatory education in Western art music. His educational experience there was less frigid than it might have been had he enrolled some ten or fifteen years earlier, when serialist composers, such as Pierre Boulez, Karlheinz Stockhausen, and Milton Babbitt, dominated. Abandoning melody, harmony, progression, and resolution in favor of twelve-tone theory and complex atonality, the composers of serial music produced deliberately discordant works because the world remained riven with conflict, and they believed it was their responsibility to write pieces that revealed rather than papered over these fissures. "[New music] abandons the deception of harmony that has become unsustainable in the face of the catastrophe toward which reality is veering," argues Theodor Adorno, the celebrated theorist of serialism, in *Philosophy of New Music*. "It has taken all the darkness and guilt of the world on itself. All its happiness is the knowledge of unhappiness; all its beauty is in denial of the semblance of the beautiful."[9] The theories of the postwar serialists, who often held university positions that insulated them from the need to write music that attracted a wide listenership, were challenged by John Cage's exploration of audience engagement and indeterminacy, as well as La Monte Young's work in the realm of improvisation, simplicity, and sustained sounds. Young had started out as a serialist, and he made no clear-cut break with that approach, but the composer slowed down his rows of notes to such a degree he ended up producing a drone, and his work became the key influence for a new wave of composers who wanted to break with the establishment's homogeneous makeup, innate elitism, and preference for an aesthetic that was (to many) unlistenable: namely, Terry Riley, Steve Reich, and Philip Glass.

A disciple of Pandit Pran Nath, who had also formed an important relationship with Young, Riley generated modular musical structures that, in permitting musicians the freedom to decide how long they played a set phrase, made chance central to the performance of his music (which, true to the democratic outlook of the countercultural movement, became music that wasn't only "his"). Inspired by Riley, Reich used tape loops of recorded voices and instruments to create a phasing effect, in which two identical recordings, running at slightly different speeds, moved in and out of synch with each other. And drawing inspiration from Indian musical aesthetics as well as the intentionally repetitive and cyclical plays of Samuel Beckett, Glass composed in rhythmic cells that mutated almost imperceptibly. Tonal, rhythmically fixed, and slow burning, the music of these composers avoided (in the words of Keith Potter) the "fragmented discourses of serialism and indeterminacy" while bypassing the "reassuring continuities" of neoclassicism.[10] Glass would go on to become particularly explicit about the break with what he described as the "wasteland" of European serialism, which was dominated by "maniacs" who were "trying to make everyone write this crazy, creepy music."[11] The reaction against the aesthetic and institutional power of the serialists was judged by Robert T. Jones to have amounted to "an eruption of the times, an inevitability."[12]

This countermovement became an important reference point for Arthur, initially because West Coast musicians enjoyed a geographical connection to the work of three of its pioneers. Young had enrolled as a graduate student at the University of California, Berkeley, where he began to "discover reasons for moving beyond the twelve-tone system" and went on to compose pieces such as *Vision* and *Poem*, the latter having been inspired while Young sat on a wooden bench in a campus laundromat.[13] Riley had premiered *In C*—a modular composition that consisted of fifty-three short patterns of music, each of which was to be played by the musicians in the same order, but with each musician repeating each fragment as many times as she or he liked before moving onto the next — at the San Francisco Tape Center in November 1964.[14] After attending the premiere of *In C*, Reich recorded the voice of a black preacher who was giving a sermon in Union Square in San Francisco and copied the tape in order to loop the voices on *It's Gonna Rain*. Although these compositions generated less local attention than the turbulent strains of acid rock and the exotic notes of Indian classical music, they were rooted in San Francisco and pointed to a West Coast–style metamorphosis in orchestral music.

Instead of attempting to evoke a world riven with dissonance, Glass, Reich, Riley, and Young were interested in constructing a hypnotic, transcendent, pleasurable plateau of shifting sound, and the composer and writer Michael Nyman drew attention to their coalescing objectives when he coined the term "minimal music" to describe their work.[15] Drawing a parallel between the goals of these composers and Gilles Deleuze's concept of the decentralized work (which doesn't rely on teleological development and lies outside of history), the Belgian composer Wim Mertens would later highlight minimalism's use of "singular intensities" that are "ever changing and shifting" and have "no content" beyond themselves.[16] Mertens added that minimalist music shifted the listener's attention from the content of change to the process of change. "In repetitive music this change is a kind of new content, and in a way one gets the suggestion of an entirely free flow of energy," he explained. "The ecstatic state induced by this music, which could also be called *a state of innocence, an hypnotic state,* or *a religious state,* is created by an independent libido, freed of all the restrictions of reality."[17]

Ecstasy, innocence, hypnotic and religious states, the libido, freedom; these terms were commonplace for West Coast residents during the late 1960s and early 1970s, and it made sense that San Francisco's academic institutions would support the development of this aesthetic. The Center for Contemporary Music at Mills College, which had Darius Milhaud and Luciano Berio on its faculty, attracted Reich to its master's program. After Reich enrolled, the director Robert Ashley assembled a teaching team that included Nath, Riley, and "Blue" Gene Tyranny. Meanwhile, minimalism also received a sympathetic reception at the San Francisco Conservatory of Music, where Loren Rush and Robert Moran were, according to William Allaudin Mathieu, "very attuned to Terry," "up-to-the-minute," and "hip." "I heard a performance of *In C* by a conservatory ensemble and I wasn't very impressed by it," remembers Mathieu, who also worked at the conservatory. "But shortly thereafter I met Terry and became extremely engaged with his work, as well as a close friend of his, with many common bonds."

Arthur had been following Mathieu's work for a while and, having completed the conservatory's Fundamentals of Musicianship course over the summer, for which he received a "B," he enrolled to take a counterpoint class and Mathieu's keyboard harmony class in the fall. "In addition to being an excellent improvisationalist, he [Mathieu] is well versed in the classical repertoire, and has the ability to tell me how I will play the piano without hearing me play," Arthur wrote to Chuck and Emily in September 1970. "I had always made note of his writing in *Down Beat* because of its intelligence and always hoped to meet him. Now, at the outset of 'studying' with him, and all hero-worship aside, I find myself rather pleased to say the least." Arthur added: "When I auditioned for his class, he told me I could study with him privately, which will certainly cut more directly to the problems of harmony, piano playing, and composition than being in a class of fifteen people, all of them waiting for a piano."

Mathieu's background was impressive. He had studied theory and harmony with Easley Blackwood (a protégé of Nadia Boulanger, the influential French-born composer, conductor, and teacher) and worked as a composer and arranger for Stan Kenton and Duke Ellington (who recorded two of his arrangements) before becoming director of the Sufi Choir in San Francisco in 1969. He remembers seeing Arthur, who was "part of the same spiritual-artistic community," at these performances, and that prompted him to offer to teach the student privately for a reduced fee. "The Conservatory had legit teachers who knew how to play well," says Mathieu. "Many of them were excellent teachers of basic pedagogy and quite a few were extremely creative in their work. But I did find, to my dismay, that the subtlety and depth of European harmonic practice that I had studied were almost unknown on the West Coast. It was like the Rocky Mountains got in the way." According to Mathieu, the conservatory resembled a hippie city. "It was a free and easy place. An awful lot of us smoked dope. It was all the faculty could to do keep up the appearance of an accredited school."

Mathieu, or Allaudin as he began calling himself in 1971, a year after meeting his guru Pandit Pran Nath, became intrigued by his new student. "At our first meeting he spent a great deal of time explaining what he was

William Allaudin
Mathieu in 1975.
Photographer
unknown.
Courtesy of William
Allaudin Mathieu.

doing and why he was doing it and who he was. He was a hundred percent self-involved. Now he would be on meds." Allaudin adds that Arthur
displayed an extraordinary talent for writing avant-garde folk. Drawing
on Walt Whitman, Bob Dylan, William S. Burroughs, and perhaps even
Donovan, his lyrics, which didn't scan or rhyme, were elliptical and visionary. As for the accompanying music, it drew on the pentatonic simplicity of
the blues and country, but it was also composed, polyphonic, and harmoni-
cally adventurous, foregrounding strange chords and melodies that leapt
in unexpected directions. "It was a very strange mix of intellectual process
and pop influence," explains Allaudin. "It had mindful details, yet it also
had the sweep and scope of contemporary poetry. The lines were tuneful,
but not simple. There was a great deal of worked-out complexity—a my-
opic complexity."

Allaudin tried to teach Arthur what he "needed next" by examining his
compositions, which the student would play on guitar and then attempt to
notate, and pointing out Arthur's "own brilliance" to him. "Bill has a rare
skill and a well tuned mind," Arthur wrote to his parents in late September
1970, "and has taught me more in three sessions than most teachers have in
all my experience." The admiration was mutual. "Arthur was so deeply into
his perceptions of experience," notes Allaudin. "He really experienced what
he experienced, and he experienced it through an unusually limited filter,

because he was so self-involved. He was very eclectic and very lost, and I liked that, because that was the temperament of the times."

Fourteen years his senior, Allaudin became a mentor to his troubled, highly sensitive pupil. "He had conflicts and a particular anger that he had no idea how to cope with. He was a kid. But we had a surprisingly warm, even fond, person-to-person friendship. I kind of loved him." If the feeling was mutual, Arthur might not have recognized it. "Any attraction would have taken some allied form—adulation, loyalty, or something similar," reflects the tutor. "In any case, I was not aware of Arthur being attracted to anyone or anything, and it was all I could do to keep him on course tracking his own love for music, and his talent in it."

Back at the Kailas Shugendo commune, where Arthur continued to live, the charismatic Ajari Warwick was more interested in strengthening his own mystique and power than nurturing a democratic, spiritual community. He provided the lost with structure, and helped Jigmé (as Arthur was still known in the context of the commune) off of the street, but in exchange he required devotion and obedience. "Dr. Warwick had a public persona of great beneficence and Jupiterean generosity, but actually he had a very mean streak, and he liked to dominate people," says Allaudin, who had a superficially "bright and sunny" relationship with the Kailas Shugendo figurehead. "He was a male dominatrix—very tortured inside and very powerful outside. The people who lived on the commune were his slaves, and Arthur was totally caught up in the life of the rooming house. He told me stories of subjugation and humiliation that were sad and anger-making to me."

Though he cut an impressive figure when he established Kailas Shugendo, Warwick's credibility came under increasing scrutiny with the passing of time, and his overenthusiastic implementation of the practice of fire walking led some to suspect his sanity. Whereas Japanese Shingon leaders walked across fire once or twice a year and treated the ritual with extreme caution, Warwick carried out the practice on a weekly and eventually, it appears, daily basis. Spiritual teachers in the Bay believed that the overdose could have contributed to the guru's increasingly erratic behavior, which included him attacking members of the commune, with Jigmé hit on more than one occasion.

Yuko Nonomura, a Shingon priest, provided an alternative Buddhist outlook and, after a while, a spiritual escape route for Jigmé. Born in Japan, Nonomura was already a priest when he migrated to the United States with his parents in the 1930s, after which he and his family were incarcerated in a Japanese internment camp at Tula Lake during the Second World War. Following his release, Nonomura lived the outwardly normal life of an insurance agent, and his background remained a secret until Warwick discovered it and invited him to lecture at the commune. Nonomura was taken aback by what he saw there. He found it difficult to accept that Warwick was disseminating a number of closely guarded Shingon mantras with casual abandon, and he was particularly concerned by Warwick's elevation of the obscure tradition of fire walking (which Nonomura practiced only occasionally in Japan and gave up altogether when he moved to the United States) to the center of his organization's ritual.

Jigmé met Nonomura when the Shingon priest gave a lecture at Kailas Shugendo, and the two of them struck up a close relationship. Nonomura introduced the young Buddhist musician to *Kukai: Major Work*, a compilation of writings by the monk who established the Shingon sect, and that book, along with *The Way of the White Clouds* and *The Tibetan Book of the Dead*, could almost always be found in Jigmé's backpack. More importantly, Jigmé came to appreciate the way Nonomura was able to explain Shingon concepts without resorting to complicated philosophical constructions or assuming the role of the charismatic guru. "Yuko was someone who Arthur could look to for answers," says Jeff Whittier, who would accompany his friend on visits to Nonomura's house, where they would discuss Buddhism and drink sake. "He was the opposite of Ajari, who had initiated him [Arthur] in these practices, but wasn't inclined to explain them."

Back in the commune, tensions between Jigmé and Warwick began to mount. In June 1970 the guru leader made a pilgrimage to Japan that was beyond the financial means of Kailas Shugendo, and in the autumn Jigmé reported to his parents that resources were so stretched he was finding it difficult to ask the organization to pay for his music education. Jigmé still maintained he was benefiting from his association with the commune. "Slowly I believe that I am relieving you of the various emotional weights I put on you in younger years," he declared in a letter sent to his parents in the autumn, and the following January he wrote enthusiastically about the climbs he had made over the holidays, one of them at night in a raging, 90-mph wind. Yet Warwick was also becoming openly critical of Jigmé's immersion in music, which he believed was undermining his spiritual practice and commitment to Kailas Shugendo, and Kate remembers the Buddhist leader being visibly unhappy when she accompanied her brother on a trip to the Ali Akbar College of Music during her earlier visit to San Francisco. "Music was definitely a point of conflict," recalls Whittier, who received firsthand accounts of the relationship.

Sensing that Chuck and Emily were concerned about his well-being, Jigmé decided to ask Allaudin to write a semi-fictional letter on his behalf in order to provide reassurance, and Allaudin agreed in order to give his student "maximum autonomy" in his relationship with his parents. "When Charles first came to study music with me he seemed to be in a period of severe inner struggle," wrote Allaudin (under the name of William Mathieu of the San Francisco Conservatory) in June 1971. "I'm sure this condition didn't slip by unnoticed by you, his father. Since in your notes to me you've expressed your concern, and your kind willingness to help him out, I thought I'd share with you the good feeling I have begun to have about his musical progress, and about his general good health." Allaudin went on to deliver a frank assessment of "Charles." "He certainly finds difficult what others find easy. But there are certain things he does—like musical composition—in which he is gifted. He hears well and is creative to a high degree—and what I hope you see—toward a highest purpose. Don't let the strangeness of his practices put you off." Allaudin concluded with the most reassuring words of all. "He is in excellent hands in the case of Dr. Warwick, and strict ones in my case. Charles is a person about whom one could worry with ease. But his growth has been strong. So don't worry. He's OK."

Off the record, Allaudin also encouraged Jigmé to leave Kailas Shugendo. "I mistrusted Ajari Warwick enormously," he says. "He had tremendous power and had probably aggrandized his Buddhist studies in order to accrue power, or so it seemed to me at the time. You'd see this deadness in the eyes of the disciples, and after a while, that happened to Jigmé. I tried to get him out of there." Allaudin's advice hit home; Jigmé left the commune at the end of June and moved into a six-bedroom house that was perched on the crest of a hill in San Raphael. After that he went to spend time with his family and, during a holiday by the lakes in Minnesota, played cello against the backdrop of lapping water. The contrast with the claustrophobic

Arthur Russell playing the cello on a beach in Minnesota, c. September 1971. Photograph by Charles Arthur Russell Sr. Courtesy of Charles Arthur Russell Sr. and Emily Russell.

setting of the cupboard where he practiced in the Kailas Shugendo house couldn't have been greater.

On his return to San Francisco, Arthur discussed his decision to leave Kailas Shugendo with Alan Abrams, Jeff Whittier, and Ellen Ziegler. Attempting to work out if he was the one who was crazy rather than Warwick, he questioned if his beatings might have been deserved, of if they formed part of a grander spiritual lesson. As their conversations opened out, Arthur surprised his friends by toeing the line of conservative orthodoxy within Buddhist philosophy and ritual—something that seemed unlikely given his irreverent outlook and contrary nature. Yet Arthur also distanced himself from Kailas Shugendo, which he took to describing as "dogmatic," and moved instead into the gentle if somewhat detached orbit of Yuko Nonomura. "Although Yuko wasn't a celebrated teacher from the Zen Center or the Tibetan movement, he was every bit as evolved as these people, and came without their whole following and bunch of claptrap," recalls Abrams, who was also introduced to the priest by Arthur. "Yuko was very genuine and he was a very powerful influence on Arthur."

Drawn into the logic of Nonomura's wisdom, Arthur announced in a taped letter to his parents (recorded around the end of 1971 or the beginning of 1972) that he needed financial support to visit Mount Koya in Japan, where Nonomura had lived in a monastery, after which he hoped to travel to India. "I can buy flutes in India for 50 cents and sell them for ten dollars when I get back and the school would buy at least a hundred from me . . . that is, unless someone does it before I do when I get back," he explained, knowing that the stash of flutes brought to the college from India by G. S. Sachdev had run out recently. "That's almost a thousand dollars' worth right there, so I know it's possible to do it, plus what a great educational undertaking it would be." Arthur called his parents soon after and asked for two thousand dollars to pay for the trip as well as the instruments. "We said no, so the idea was erased," recalls Chuck. "Truthfully I think he wanted to take a vacation. But we did admire his spunk. Now I wish we had done it." The news that Arthur had left Kailas Shugendo might have influenced the decision to turn him down; was he about to revert to his ill-disciplined, pre–Kailas Shugendo ways? The fact remained that Warwick had forced him to choose between Kailas Shugendo and music, and he had made his choice.

Arthur's eccentricity could be disconcerting. Even the strange considered him strange, and in social situations he often came across as being shy and awkward. Yet he had a knack for approaching people, including influential people, and relating to them as if there was no good reason why they shouldn't be friends. So it was that during his time in San Francisco, a time in which he was on the lookout for inspirational mentor figures, he became friends with Allen Ginsberg.

Having moved to San Francisco in 1954, Ginsberg was catapulted to beat fame (with Jack Kerouac and William S. Burroughs) after he read parts of "Howl" at the Six Gallery the following year. City Lights Books published the poem in the collection *Howl and Other Poems* in 1956, and a year later law enforcement officials read one of its racier lines and initiated an obscenity trial, which cast Ginsberg into the international spotlight and concluded in his favor. As he cemented his reputation as an important poet with the completion of "Kaddish," a groundbreaking poem that meditated on the death of his troubled mother, Ginsberg became a leading figure in the countercultural movement. He defended the First Amendment; he criticized U.S. military involvement in Vietnam; he spent time with Timothy Leary and explored LSD; and he became a Buddhist. Having already recorded "Howl" onto vinyl, Ginsberg released an album titled *Allen Ginsberg Reads Kaddish: A Twentieth-century American Ecstatic Narrative Poem*, and in 1970 he delivered his third LP, *William Blake's Songs of Innocence and Experience*, which came out on the Verve record label.[18] A short while later Ginsberg met Arthur, who transformed his musical outlook.

A Buddhist acquaintance of Warwick, Ginsberg first saw Arthur playing cello with the Kailas Shugendo Mantric Sun Band in a park— "He was wearing a strange composite Buddhist uniform, semi-military, semi-Mongolian," Ginsberg recounted later—and they quickly discovered mutual interests in music, poetry, and Buddhism.[19] Openly and politically gay, as well as charming and persistent when in pursuit, Ginsberg was drawn to Arthur, who started to provide him with musical backing at his poetry readings. After a performance at Grace Cathedral, a center for peace activism and psychedelic shows, Ziegler joined them in Ginsberg's apartment, where they played and sang Ginsberg's Blake adaptations until the early hours. "Arthur was a fabulous improviser," says Ziegler, who remembers Arthur being both comfortable and happy that evening. "He had the skills of being classically trained, and the freedom of being Arthur." Working his tiny harmonium, a two-octave keyboard mounted on a *shruti* box (a small, hand-operated instrument that produces a drone), Ginsberg also liked to play *bhajans* to the accompaniment of Arthur. "It was all very informal," says Whittier, who participated in some of these sessions. "This was something Arthur was into musically."

Ginsberg paid Russell $255 to play cello on his next Blake album, which he recorded at the "inexpensive" Pacific High Studios in July and August of 1971. Playing alongside Ginsberg (vocals, harmonium, finger cymbals, Tibetan human-thigh-bone trumpet), Jon Meyer (flute), Jon Sholle (guitar), Alan Senauke (mandolin), and Peter Hornbeck (violin, viola), Arthur appeared on "A Cradle Song," "Infant Joy," "The Fly," "School Boy," "A Dream," and "Pacific High Studio Mantras," while on "Voice of the Bard" he performed solo with Ginsberg, who later explained that he was "interested in Arthur Russell's rich cello unison underlining."[20] Featuring an old Tibetan mantra, "Pacific High Studio Mantras" included a cameo appearance by Warwick and the Kailas Shugendo Mantric Sun Band; Ginsberg had already performed with the group in a concert that same July.[21] On the recording, the group chanted, "Om ah hum vajra guru padma siddhi hum," which translates as "body speech mind diamond teacher lotus power amen," or "tough teacher tender teaching." Hearing those lines must have given Russell, who had just left the commune, pause for thought.

If the past caught up with the present during Arthur's studio debut, the present began to resemble the future when Ginsberg took him to New York to record "A Dream" (featuring "lyrics" by William Blake) with Bob Dylan at the end of 1971. At the Record Plant, they were joined by Peter Orlovsky (vocals), Jon Sholle (guitar), Anne Waldman (vocals), David Amram (French horn, piano), Perry Robinson (clarinet), Happy Traum (guitar), and Maruga (drums, bells, toys), and when Dylan proved to be a reluctant session leader — Ginsberg says he "balked at the mantras," maybe thinking they were a "mind-trap" — Arthur stepped into the void.[22] "He did *a lot* on that session in terms of arranging and producing," notes Ernie Brooks, the bass player with the Modern Lovers, who would become good friends with Arthur a few years later. "Ginsberg had a lot of confidence in Arthur. He would always refer to Arthur as a musical genius." Staying with Ginsberg in his apartment at 408 East Tenth Street, Arthur saw a city that made San Francisco seem parochial, and finding himself in a studio with Dylan and others, he discovered he had no reason to be timid about his musical knowledge. Although he held a deep affection for Ginsberg, Arthur told his parents that performing with him for three nights in San Francisco on their return to the West Coast had been "time down the drain." Arthur's ambitions, it had become clear, extended beyond even the most appealing session work.

Back in the crucible of Allaudin's master class at the San Francisco Conservatory, Arthur continued to develop a form of composition that combined the principles of avant-garde art music with Buddhist mantra and philosophy (a project that was beyond Ginsberg, who was unable to grasp Arthur's more complex musical suggestions). Drawing on the chance practices established by John Cage and Christian Wolff, Arthur asked each musician to wear a set of headphones and sit back-to-back in two rows of chairs, after which he provided each with a script, which combined text and music, and a link into a long line of string. On feeling a tug on the string from another student, the recipient was required to select a section from the script—maybe a line from the *Diamond Sutra*, or a sequence of notes drawn from sheet music, or a raga—that related to the Indian or Western tone playing through the headphones at that particular moment, and as the collage of mantra, voice, and sound developed, Russell began to play cello. "An incredible harmony came out of this cacophony of sounds," remembers Alan Abrams. "Everyone was blown away. People tended to think that Arthur was trying to freak them out, but he was really sincere."

Arthur didn't venture into San Francisco's acid-rock scene, and showed no interest in the camp theatre music of the Cockettes, whose shows were described by Ginsberg as "transvestite-glitter-fairy satiric masques."[23] But he did explore a series of niche settings that confirmed his interest in reaching beyond the compositional avant-garde. Whittier recalls sharing "a secret thing for country" with Arthur, and adds that his friend would also visit the Center for World Music, which opened in San Francisco in 1963. When Miles Davis played in North Beach, Arthur sat in the audience, and during a Terry Riley concert held in an amphitheatre on Mount Tamalpais in Mill Valley he was struck by the composer's indebtedness to Indian classical music rather than his minimalist trajectory. In addition, Arthur took part in the jam-oriented sessions that were organized at the African Orthodox Saint John Coltrane Church, which had been established to preserve the spirit of Coltrane, who died in 1967, and he must have met Alice Coltrane in this setting because a later curriculum vitae records that he played on tour with the widowed musician. It's possible Arthur started to experiment with hooking up his cello to an amplifier during these performances; this was something he began in 1972.[24]

Accompanied by the Ali Akbar College musicians John Bergamo (vibraharp, percussion) and Vince Delgado (darbukka), as well as Brian Godden (guitar), Charles Amir Lewis (hands and mouth), and Karen Nelson (piano), Russell performed his own work in public for the first time on 16–17 March 1973 at 1750 Arch Street—an important venue for experimental music in Berkeley.[25] The concert, which was broadcast live on the listener-sponsored KPFA station, opened with an orchestral duet featuring piano and cello before it moved into a jazz set and culminated with a surreal sound clash that consisted of insane, random drum rolls, nonsensical overlapping voices, demented laughter, and bursts of discordant cello. In between the acts, an announcer read extracts from an essay about the spiritual qualities of Bugs Bunny, "the archetypal mystic," who was "devised to teach important esoteric lessons." Noting that Russell was a very young composer, the announcer remarked that the performance might have been "a little bit unskilled in a lot of ways, but there's a spark of something there. . . . If we watch Arthur Russell, I think in ten years from now we may see him in a very surprising position in the world of music."[26]

Arthur's potpourri of styles had been assembled in a somewhat blunt manner, and there was also no discernible market within the contemporary art-music scene for this kind of explicitly cross-genre performance. Yet the composer was already moving between a range of sharply contrasting sounds as if no form was superior to another, and as if this kind of adaptability was more logical than the alternative of grounding himself in a single generic field. When Arthur studied Indian classical music, it didn't occur to him to ditch Western art music, and his affection for Buddhist mantra didn't lead to a rejection of Southern folk. Why make a choice when no choice was required? The 1750 Arch Street concert was an early attempt to bring together several styles in a single piece of music, and an audience for this approach would emerge when the minimalist aesthetic of the late 1960s began to sound a little tired during the 1970s. The announcer, it would become clear, overestimated the time it would take Arthur to make a name for himself by eight-and-a-half years.

Arthur could have explained his striking openness to different musical styles as being an expression of his Buddhism, but according to Whittier, Arthur was more likely to focus on how an ordinary sound might be impregnated with spiritual energy. At the same time, Arthur developed a commitment to the Indian musical concept of *riaz*, or "practice," and he began to explore the implications of this rigorous approach during his time in San Francisco. "Arthur would talk about the process being as important as the goal," recalls Whittier. "I didn't entirely agree, because as a musician you are defined by how you play at any given time, and the product is the measure of the riaz. But Arthur would say that the process was more important than the end product." Easily confused with a tendency toward procrastination, practice became the most important element of Arthur's work—the space in which he could move most freely. Yet in a world that was defined in-

Muriel Fujii in her bedroom, a walk-in closet on Ashbury Street, San Francisco, in 1972. Photographer unknown. Courtesy of Muriel Fujii.

creasingly by commodification—or the marketing of end products—the approach would also undermine his chances of "making it," and by 1973 that was something he wanted quite badly.

Arthur, remembers Muriel Fujii, was always playing or composing music. "He just had a real need to write music and create music," she says. "It was something he did *constantly*." A Hawaiian-born, English-lit major at the University of San Francisco, Fujii met Arthur at a benefit concert to support the United Farm Workers that featured readings from Lawrence Ferlinghetti, Robert Bly, and Ginsberg (who Arthur accompanied on cello). Arthur approached Fujii at the end of the performance, and a little later he got her phone number from a friend. The next day Fujii returned home to find Arthur waiting on her doorstep, and not wanting to be rude, she invited him in. They talked until Fujii realized Arthur wasn't going to leave of his own accord, at which point she pretended she had to study for an exam the following day. An expert in persistence, Arthur volunteered to sleep on the couch while Fujii spent the night preparing for her imaginary test, and when she returned from school the next day he was still there. "At that point I just didn't know how I was going to get rid of him," she recalls.

In the end, Arthur finally announced he had to leave, and Fujii, who wanted to make sure his word was good, said she would accompany him to wherever he had to go. As they drove to San Raphael in Arthur's beaten-up VW Beetle, his cello angled across Fujii as its neck stuck out of the window, a Boccherini piece piped out of the radio, and when Arthur remarked that he could play the piece, she began to see him differently. On their arrival at his home, Arthur took Fujii to his room, which was crammed with an old stand-up piano, a guitar, a string bass, and a shruti box, and proceeded to play Bach on his cello. "I think that's when I fell in love with him," she recalls. "It took twenty-four hours, or something like that."

Arthur spent a lot of time talking about artists such as John Cage and Morton Subotnick, whose records he would borrow from the library, and was "almost scornful of pop culture," remembers Fujii. If he disliked a song he would describe it as being "Neil Diamond," she adds, and he also made it clear that if Fujii wanted to check out a rock act at the Fillmore she would have to go with a friend. Arthur preferred the kind of "rock" that could be found at Mount Tamalpais and Mount Shasta, where, settling under an oak tree that looked out onto the Californian landscape, he would play to Fujii as the day drifted toward dusk. On their way home, Arthur would sit in the passenger seat and compose music that combined avant-garde experimentalism with the incidental quality of everyday life, writing songs about the wind blowing in his hair, or the experience of passing through a town, or the sight of insects splattering onto the windshield of the car. The world was simple, strange, and beautiful, and Arthur captured this in his work.

Back at his San Rafael home, which was known as the Sufi house because all the other residents were Sufis, Arthur's dreaminess, devotion to music, and permanent lack of money could upset his housemates. As was typical of the time, the household costs were divided, and Arthur, whose only independent source of income came from freelance musical transcription and very occasional session work, would end up asking his parents to help him catch up on missed payments. He was less concerned about making good on his unfulfilled chores, however, and every now and again would be called to account at a house meeting, where he would often turn to Jonni Sue Bartel, one of the other residents and a tolerant ally. In contrast to Fujii, who was shy, Bartel radiated confidence and she ended up hitting it off so well with Arthur they had an affair. Fujii didn't mind because she was also involved with someone else.

Toward the beginning of 1973 Arthur left San Rafael and moved into another Sufi house in Novato, just north of San Rafael, in order to live nearer to Allaudin, who had started to tutor him out of his basement studio in San Anselmo, a suburb in Marin County. "Arthur's compositions increased in complexity, but he became less and less able to finish them," Allaudin recalls of these later lessons. "He was fascinated by the complexity, but he couldn't figure out a way to use it. He was fixated on the piece and didn't want to know what he was doing." Yet in other respects Arthur's vision was clearer than it had ever been, for in April 1973 he went camping with Whittier and Abrams on Mount Shasta, and when the late winter snow fell so hard their car became stuck for days, Arthur turned to his friends and declared, "I'm going to New York to make it in music!" Whittier teased Arthur that it sounded faintly un-Buddhist to be talking about his career in the presence of the timeless mountain, only for his friend to respond with a shrug.

The announcement came as a surprise. Arthur had a steady girlfriend, a number of close buddies, an exceptional music tutor, and plenty of ongoing performance projects in San Francisco, while Yuko Nonomura and the city's surrounding countryside met his spiritual needs. Yet a sense of stasis was also gnawing away at Arthur's sense of well-being. As entrepreneurs and artists cashed in on the countercultural movement, and as the acolytes of LSD realized that it was going to take more than a tab of acid to change the world, the political promise of the late 1960s began to fade. By 1973 the party appeared to be moving toward its conclusion, in part because, as Eric Hobsbawm has argued, the economic growth that underpinned sixties radicalism had come to an abrupt end.[27] "The culture couldn't sustain itself any longer," remembers Ellen Ziegler, who traveled to India with Ali Akbar Khan before moving to Seattle to retrain as a graphic designer in 1974. "Nobody had a job. People shared as best they could, but after a while they wanted to get a real life."

The beneficiary of an economic cycle in which families found themselves better off than ever before, Arthur, like so many of his baby-boomer peers, had rebelled against the conformism and materialism of the 1950s by experimenting with LSD in Oskaloosa and turning to Indian classical music, Buddhism, and Ginsberg in San Francisco. He was able to lead a

Arthur Russell walking on Mt. Tamalpais, which overlooks the Pacific Ocean, in April 1973. "It was the closest 'wilderness' to the Ali Akbar College of Music," says Ellen Ziegler. Photograph by and courtesy of Ellen Ziegler.

communal-creative-spiritual lifestyle for five years, not because the internal economy of the countercultural movement was robustly self-sufficient, which it wasn't, but because his parents were prepared to subsidize what they understood to be his rehabilitation. By the spring of 1973 that support had become a source of embarrassment, so Arthur started to look to the example of Ginsberg (who shuttled between the East and West Coasts as he melded creativity, spirituality, and professional success), and also to Allaudin (who had turned his expertise in Western and Eastern music into a career). Within a couple of months he resolved to try and "make it" as a musician by taking San Francisco's unique amalgam of Eastern and Western music to an unknowing yet potentially receptive audience in New York. "Arthur wanted to find a commercial outlet for his music," says Abrams. "He was trying to reconcile how he could make a living while doing what he wanted to do, and he wanted to combine this with a spiritual existence. He wanted it all."

Arthur hoped he would be able to continue his relationship with Fujii, who was planning to stay in the Bay Area, but after Fujii's Japanese American parents were introduced to Arthur during her college graduation ceremony, they presented her with an ultimatum: either she return to live with them in Hawaii or they would disown her forever. Fujii broke the news to her boyfriend during a journey to Mount Tamalpais. "Arthur said, 'Let's get married then,'" she remembers. "It wasn't at all romantic. It was very practical. He was driving and I told him what my father said, and he replied, 'Well, let's get married.'" The proposal took Fujii by surprise, and she was left with the impression that it might have taken Arthur by surprise too. Whittier says Arthur loved Fujii, but notes that he found her emotional signals difficult to read, and that he also "really liked Jonni Sue." While Arthur and Fujii enjoyed spending time with each other and exchanged exuberant love letters during holidays, Fujii also remembers seeing less of him during 1973.

Fujii kept her eyes firmly on the windshield and didn't reply to Arthur's proposal. If she had, she says, she would have said "no." "Arthur would have just stifled me," she explains. "He was so unlike me. He was really driven and knew what he wanted to do." Breaking the silence, Arthur suggested Fujii travel with him to New York, but she was already committed to vacationing with her parents, at the end of which she would return with them to Hawaii. Arthur and Fujii met one more time, but didn't talk about getting married, or breaking up. As a parting gift, Arthur handed Fujii two of his favorite items of clothing: his red wool sweater, which had a reindeer emblazoned across the chest, and his suede tan coat. After that, Fujii left San Francisco at the beginning of June, and Arthur, his cello attached to his back like the shell of a tortoise, traveled to New York.

2 Explorations (1973–1975)

New York was in a state of physical and economic decline at the beginning of the 1970s, and the malaise deepened as the decade progressed. Pollution hung in the air, rubbish collected on street corners, traffic congestion intensified, and a combustible racial tension hissed across ethnically divided neighborhoods. The white middle class judged the East Village (including Alphabet City, or Avenue A through Avenue D), Harlem, and Brooklyn too black and too Latin to be safe, while the Cast Iron District was deemed terrifying because it lacked any kind of demographics at all—it was without residents and light industry had relocated to calmer, more functional zones. Exacerbated by the manufacturing exodus, the incendiary problem of rising unemployment was also linked to the relaxation in 1965 of the pernicious quota laws that restricted the movement of non–Western Europeans into the United States, which contributed to the arrival of 435,000 immigrants from Latin America, Asia, and the Caribbean to the city during the 1960s.[1] Approximately one million white New Yorkers fled to the cordoned-off tranquility of the suburbs and beyond, but unemployment continued to skyrocket, with the city hemorrhaging 613,000 jobs between 1969 and 1977.[2] "The whole country hated New York," notes Bob Rosenthal, who worked for Allen Ginsberg and would become friendly with Arthur. "It just stood for ethnicity."

The backlash against the 1960s was less pronounced in

New York than in San Francisco, because New Yorkers had placed less faith in acid's emancipatory potential. As the author and downtown impresario Ron Kolm put it, "You couldn't drop acid and take the A Train."[3] But by the early 1970s the city had also declined so sharply that Johnny Carson took his *Tonight Show* out of New York and relocated it to California, from where he joked, "Some Martians landed in Central Park today . . . and were mugged."[4] Favorable statistics were hard to come by; as the number of governmental employees swelled, services were cut, and crime and rape figures spiraled while tax revenues plummeted. Responding to New York City's surge toward bankruptcy in 1975, President Gerald Ford refused to bail out its government, which prompted the *Daily News* to run the headline, "Ford to City: Drop Dead." Called to explain the president's position, Ford's spokesman compared New York to a drug-abusing child and commented, "You don't give her a hundred dollars a day to support her habit." In a seemingly choreographed response, the subway danced with graffiti, fire hydrants hissed out water, and sirens wailed out their disapproval. "New York in the 1960s and 1970s was a city with serious problems," comments Vincent Cannato, author of *The Ungovernable City*.[5]

Ford needed a scapegoat because other urban centers in the United States were also struggling to hold on to the economic gains of the postwar era. "It wasn't just New York, though New York was an advanced case," notes Ned Sublette, a composer-musician who would soon become friends with Arthur. "The country's cities were rebounding from white flight and loss of revenue, and inner cities were in terrible shape. The shaping experience of our parents' lives was the Great Depression. We thought we had escaped it because we grew up in an age of unprecedented prosperity, but we hit a wall in the first half of the seventies with the oil price shocks, the floating of the dollar, high unemployment, and inflation." As unemployment shot up to nine percent and inflation to eleven percent, the United States entered a period of "stagflation"—a combination of stagnation and inflation, which would continue until 1980. "That recession was one of the shaping historical events of our lifetime and had a direct impact on our lives," adds Sublette.

The deepening decay played itself out in different ways across New York. When viewed from the commercial grid of midtown, the residential zones of the Upper West Side and the Upper East Side, or the college-dominated territory of Morningside Heights, the decline looked like a disaster. Yet the very same process was experienced as a loosening up of space and aesthetic codes in the Cast Iron District, which was located in downtown New York. As the clunking machines of the onetime manufacturing base became a distant echo, artists grasped the potential of its high-ceilinged lofts and started to move into evacuated buildings. Having opened the Paula Cooper Gallery in 1968, Paula Cooper was the first dealer to realize the zone's potential as an art haven, and Ivan Karp, Max Hutchinson, Betty Cuningham, Leo Castelli, and others launched rival galleries soon afterwards. Rents remained low because few thought about living there, since there were no stores, no boutiques, and beyond Broadway, few pedestrians and cars, with only a single bar to serve the neighborhood's thirst. During this period industrial buildings could be bought for next to nothing because so many restrictions remained on their use. "You were always afraid of being found out," the art dealer Charles Cowles commented later. "Everybody had a fold-up bed and you had to hide the shower."[6]

Taking care to conceal telltale signs of habitation from the city's building inspectors, artists, musicians, and sculptors began to open up their flexible living spaces to neighborhood friends and the knowing public, and as the city relaxed its insistence that the neighborhood should be preserved exclusively for industrial use, alternative names for these reinvented areas began to circulate. In 1973 the Cast Iron District was renamed "SoHo," an abbreviation of "South of Houston Street," which marked the shift away from manufacturing, and a few years later residents in the Lower West Side adopted the name "TriBeCa," which was short for "Triangle below Canal Street." No matter how informal or temporary its status, any venue that opened in SoHo, TriBeCa, or NoHo (as the area north of Houston Street was renamed in the late 1980s) derived an inevitable cachet from the cutting-edge location. First-time visitors were known to become unsettled when they journeyed to the semi-deserted district to go to an exhibition or a concert, and their nervousness intensified when they made their way home after sunset. Back then the neighborhood's cobbled streets were pitch black at night.

If New York was washed up and dirty as far as the rest of the country was concerned, downtown was its abject Other, a decadent zone full of unusable buildings that had been all but obliterated from the city's consciousness. But toward the middle of the 1970s perceptions began to shift, at least within the city, and in May 1974 *New York* magazine ran a front-cover story that claimed SoHo's galleries, lofts, and performance venues made it "The Most Exciting Place to Live in the City."[7] Artists and musicians began to migrate to the area in even greater numbers following the passing of the Emergency Tenant Protection Act on 15 June 1974, which introduced a regulatory framework for the commercial lofts and legalized the previously shady practice of loft living. By specifying that residents had to be verifiable artists (or manufacturers), the act also encouraged creative practitioners to live in an area that spanned no more than twenty square blocks and came to resemble, in the words of one resident, an "artists' colony."[8] In this manner the conditions were established for the emergence of what would come to be known as the downtown scene. "Rarely has there been such a condensed and diverse group of artists in one place at one time, all sharing many of the same assumptions about how to make new art," notes Marvin J. Taylor, editor of *The Downtown Book*.[9]

As artists, choreographers, musicians, poets, sculptors, and video makers moved to downtown, they started to recognize each other on the walkways. Framed by an environment in which transgression and possibility were architecturally and socially embedded, conversations and collaborations began to occur. And as these interactions multiplied, downtown became a movement of boundary-breaking, interdisciplinary collaborations that defied definition yet featured a set of recurring aesthetic priorities. "The vernacular of Downtown was a disjunctive language of profound ambivalence, broken narratives, subversive signs, ironic inversions, proliferate amusements, criminal interventions, material surrogates, improvised impersonations, and immersive experientiality," comments the art critic Carlo McCormick. "It was the argot of the streets, suffused with the strategies of late-modernist art, inflected by the vestigial ethnicities of two centuries of immigration, cross-referenced across the regionalisms of geographic and generational subculture, and built from the detritus of history on the skids as a kind of cut-up of endless quotation marks."[10]

The origin of downtown's experimental music culture can be traced back to 1960, when Yoko Ono staged a concert series organized by La Monte Young and Richard Maxfield in her TriBeCa loft on Chambers Street. Evoking a cultural mindset as much as a geographical location, downtown music came to be understood in relation to the institutionalized music establishment of uptown, where the ethos of serialism was propagated from fortified campuses (i.e., Columbia University and the Manhattan School of Music), the prestigious Lincoln Center (where serial music would be programmed alongside more popular classical pieces), and a cluster of other venues (including Merkin Hall, the Ninety-second Street Y, and Carnegie Hall). Although some suggest that downtown amounted to a "deliberate rejection of Uptown elitism," others maintain that downtowners were "blissfully unaware" of what was happening uptown.[11] Downtown composers such as Philip Glass and Steve Reich, who had premiered works in Lincoln Center and Carnegie Hall, were certainly aware of the divide. "The [uptown] audience jeers, and the critics lose a lot of sleep trying to figure out how to prove objectively that the music is inept, without revealing stylistic biases," reported Tom Johnson in the *Village Voice*.[12] Versions of the battle between uptown and downtown unfolded across the United States—including San Francisco—but in New York it was at its most concentrated and compelling.

The conflict was social as well as aesthetic. While uptowners were for the most part middle-aged, sober academics who were uninterested in attracting a wider audience, downtowners tended to be younger bohemian types who had been moved by the radical populism of the 1960s and hoped (or even needed) to attract a paying public. "The uptown serialists posited that their music was created by experts for experts," notes Peter Gordon, who joined the downtown fray in the mid-1970s. "As Milton Babbitt stated in his famous essay, 'Who Cares if You Listen?' This was seen as a complex music, and the uninitiated listener was supposed to find it as difficult to understand as advanced physics. The composer's 'audience,' therefore, was a small group of fellow composers, academics, and aficionados." Downtowners went about their work in an entirely different manner. "What we posited was a populist philosophy: new music could be composed which addressed both the sensual needs of the listener as well as the intellect. The audience for this music was seen as being the members of the community—artists, writers, neighborhood people."

As they produced music that drew inspiration from their spectacular yet sparse surroundings, downtowners survived as best they could, taking on odd jobs in order to pay the rent. Even the relatively successful Glass drove a taxi and, along with the similarly successful Reich, formed a moving company in order to support his art. "We worked at whatever jobs we could— playing in bands or shows, plumbing, carpentry, proofreading, bartending, cutting tape, dancing," comments Gordon, who adds that the profusion of talent combined with the scarcity of cash encouraged musicians to develop "an extended net of favors," which led them to regularly rehearse for free (in preparation for performances that were paid for).[13] With public funding of the arts channeled overwhelmingly toward uptown's opera and orchestral venues, downtowners prioritized creativity and friendship above money and security, and Taylor notes they circulated their works among themselves with barely an eye on the wider market. "Artists worked in multiple media, and collaborated, criticized, supported, and valued each other's works in a way that was unprecedented," he writes.[14]

Rarely born in Manhattan, downtowners hailed from far and wide, including towns as remote as Oskaloosa, Iowa. Introduced to New York's oasis of dereliction for the first time when he stayed with Ginsberg on East Tenth Street at the end of 1971, Arthur would eventually consider downtown to be his home, and he ended up leaving infrequently because the neighborhood satisfied almost all of his needs. Yet Arthur also yo-yoed between downtown and midtown for several years, not because he was interested in midtown's department stores or discotheques, but because he wanted to strike a deal with one of the major record companies that were nestled there. Shuttling between downtown's initially discrete music scenes with as much energy and determination as anyone, Arthur refused to choose between orchestral music, new wave, and disco, and his performances and studio work reflected his eclectic agenda. The question was: could Arthur's spontaneous embodiment of downtown's musical network be commodified by the record companies that were located halfway up the volatile island of Manhattan?

Manhattan School of Music

Having applied to study at the Manhattan School of Music (MSM), Arthur traveled to New York to attend an interview in June 1973, and on arriving he camped in the West End Avenue apartment of Alan Cauldwell, an Oskaloosan exile who had hosted the music and drug-taking sessions that were so important to him when he was a teenager. Arthur's initial response to his new surroundings was one of doubt. Although Central Park was a short walk away, Arthur pined for the environment he had left behind, and when Muriel Fujii sent him a postcard of a rural scene, he replied, "Real trees!" before noting that the New York subway was "very dark" and "smell[ed] of urine." In another letter Arthur commented on the way everybody was walking around with big, blaring radios. "It feels like the end of the American civilization, but I don't want to make it seem any worse than it is," he commented. His analysis was echoed elsewhere. "New York City has become a metaphor for what looks like the last days of American civilization," the *New York Times* film critic Vincent Canby wrote the following November.[15]

Arthur was offered a place at MSM on 19 June, and by the end of the following day, he had spent four hours hanging out in John Cage's house, hand-delivered tapes of his music to the offices of Columbia and Vanguard, and listened to Pierre Boulez conduct the New York Philharmonic orchestra in Lincoln Center. Just as he had announced at Mount Shasta, he did indeed want to "make it," and he resolved to stay in the city when he received a rejection letter from Oberlin College in Ohio, where he had also applied to study. "He [Arthur] seems to have a talent in the area of vernacular music," ran the letter. "His compositions show cohesiveness and sensitivity to the style of current, commercial music. We are not as impressed by his endeavors in styles which we would characterize as 'serious' contemporary compositions." Making the most of the summer, Arthur traveled to Maine (to visit Kate and her newborn son, Beau), returned to Manhattan (to take an admission test for Columbia University, which formed part of his MSM academic requirement), and then headed out to the West Coast (to pick up his remaining possessions, see old friends, and attend an Ali Akbar Khan concert). Finally he made his way to Iowa to see his parents, and when Chuck asked him if he regretted his move, he replied, "No, New York is where it's happening. San Francisco is nicer, but New York is where it's happening." When Chuck asked him if he wanted to return home, he replied, "I don't think I would like the plains."

Renowned for its rigorous adherence to the academic, atonal strains that had dominated twentieth-century art music, the Manhattan School of Music was always going to be an unforgiving setting for a utopian dreamer. When the influential uptown serialist Charles Wuorinen took umbrage at one of Arthur's compositions—"City Park," a repetitive piece that fused music with writings of Ezra Pound and Gertrude Stein—Arthur explained that he was excited by the way its nonnarrative structure meant listeners could "plug out and then plug back in again without losing anything essential." Wuorinen replied, "That's the most unattractive thing I've ever heard."[16] Conflicts such as these persuaded Arthur to consider the possibility of transferring to study with Christian Wolff at Dartmouth College in Hanover, New Hampshire, soon after he enrolled at the Manhattan School of Music. "Christian's a really good composer, and a beautiful cat," he wrote to Fujii in October 1973. "He has a real appreciation for acoustic sounds and natural occurrence." Arthur traveled to Hanover—"which is not a short distance from New York," says Wolff—and the tutor remembers the two of them spending time together. "Arthur was having interesting problems with Charles Wuorinen," he confirms. "Wuorinen is this hyper-controlling, rationalized serial composer, so he was completely at the other pole of what I imagine Arthur was interested in doing and what I was doing. The idea of him studying with Wuorinen blew my mind. They were at loggerheads the whole time." Wolff figured that Arthur was an open-minded kind of guy and probably wanted to find out what, if anything, the MSM had to offer. "The uptown guys were big on discipline and rigor, so maybe Arthur thought he should look at it."

A class in linguistics at Columbia University offered Arthur a refuge, and he also pursued an interest in electronic music with Elias Tanenbaum, an eclectic and sympathetic composer. "Arthur never had the skills of the usual conservatory composer, nor was he interested in acquiring them," recalls Tanenbaum, whose tiny classroom doubled as an electronic-music studio, which contained a series of tape decks plus two state-of-the-art ARP synthesizers. "He was interested in going his own way, and I allowed him to do that."

It was in Tanenbaum's classroom that Arthur got to know David Van Tieghem, who had applied to the Manhattan School of Music in order to study with Paul Price, a pioneer of modern percussion, and James Preiss, who played percussion with Steve Reich. Like Arthur, Van Tieghem sported a beard and long hair that he sometimes wore in a ponytail, and as they stopped to chat in the corridor they discovered they agreed on a key matter: that the college wasn't a place where they hoped to forge an academic career in serious music, but instead functioned as an outlet where they could learn while they explored how else they might earn a livelihood as composer-musicians. Though he was outwardly nonchalant during their initial exchanges, Arthur became interesting to Van Tieghem when he gave him a tape that included a recording by Arthur of "Goodbye Old Paint" that mixed Americana, the cello, and tablas. Arthur's voice and cello blended beautifully and generated a sound that was neither folk nor pop, recalls Van Tieghem.[17]

Drawing on the kind of "generative" music that was running through the work of composers such as Alvin Lucier, Steve Reich, Terry Riley, Frederic Rzewski, and Christian Wolff, as well as the non-intentional composition methods of the poet Jackson Mac Low, Arthur's earliest performances in New York toyed with form and chance. In the autumn of 1973 he took part in the "Avant-Garde Festival," which was organized by the cellist and performance artist Charlotte Moorman, and presented a piece that required his musicians (including Van Tieghem) to memorize an individual melody as well as the melodies of the other players. Performing on a platform in Grand Central Station, the musicians walked around with pieces of wood and attempted to make stick-to-stick contact whenever they thought of another player's melody. Around the same time, Arthur developed an equally playful and esoteric piece on WKCR-FM, Columbia University's radio station, in which he and Van Tieghem played cello and drums while listening through headphones to two separate vinyl LPs of animal noises and sound effects that had been deliberately scratched—and adjusted their playing to the meter of the scratches. "The radio audience didn't hear the LPs," remembers the percussionist. "It was sort of annoying to listen to, but a fun idea."

Initially based at International House on West 125th Street and then at 500 Riverside Drive during his first weeks at the MSM, Arthur ended up spending a good portion of his first semester in Ginsberg's apartment, which was located in the dystopian wasteland of Tenth Street and Avenue C. "On Avenue B the heroin was the purest and the cheapest in the whole country," notes Bob Rosenthal, who was living on Twelfth Street when he met Ginsberg in 1974. "Gregory Corso would fly in from San Francisco just to score. It was worth it. So the whole of the East Village was scary." Ginsberg was mugged during his time on Tenth Street, remembers Rosenthal, but the poet refused to let that alienate him from the East Village, which he championed as a neighborhood of diversity and freedom. "I think it's real dangerous around here, but nothing ever happens to me," Arthur wrote to Fujii in July. "Down in Little Italy, where the Mafia lives, it's real clean and safe."

Carrying unresolved sexual tension in their relationship, Arthur and Ginsberg played a revolving game of teacher and student. Ginsberg, a voracious learner, sucked musical information from Arthur, such as how to play the twelve-bar blues and ragas, and in return he tutored Arthur in poetry writing, providing Arthur with self-belief and encouraging him to follow a spontaneous and creative life. During this period Ginsberg traveled regularly and often visited Boulder, Colorado, where he was preparing to launch the Jack Kerouac School of Disembodied Poetics at the Naropa Institute. In a postcard written while he was away in September 1973, the poet applauded Arthur's "precision in words" and the way he showed both "courage" and an "understanding of basic reality" to "rely on so delicate a fact and persevere with confidence in memories drawn from actual rather than idealized life." Arthur's work, he added, reached the "final loveliness and Buddha smallness of the Actual." Ginsberg concluded with warm words of reassurance. "Staying with the real . . . is a rare art you have."[18]

At a glance, Arthur didn't really fit into the East Village. With his handsome face eroded by acne and his rather conservative preference for checkered shirts, he looked like a nerd, and the fact that he was introverted and aloof contributed to his anonymity. Yet Arthur's awkwardness was also laced with a genuine, unaffected oddness that could become a source of fascination. On one occasion, he went to an Eastside loft party with Elodie Lauten and Denise Feliu, two members of the all-female rock band Flaming Youth who were also living in Ginsberg's apartment, and following the band's performance he started to write a letter to Fujii on a musical score sheet. After a while he was asked if he was writing an article about the party, and later another guest wondered if he was penning her biography. "Arthur was inspired by the performance and felt like writing a letter to his girlfriend, so it must have been a very emotional moment," says Lauten. "I don't think he was trying to be weird or rude. He was just being Arthur."

Ridiculed for being a misfit in his hometown, Arthur became an eccentric curiosity in parts of the East Village, yet he also found it difficult to settle in his new habitat, in part because he missed Fujii. In October 1973 he explored the idea of transferring to the University of Hawaii, an unlikely place for him to pursue his musical career but a good place for him to find Fujii, and although he abandoned the plan when he found out that his SAT scores didn't match the entrance requirements, he continued to talk of traveling to the island. In the end Fujii visited New York and remembers eating French fries in Arthur's favorite greasy diner, as well as traveling to Columbia University. Dressed in an olive-green military parka with a fur-trimmed hood, Arthur was "very upbeat" during the visit, and his good spirits continued to flow when he persuaded his girlfriend to share the steering wheel during a trip to Oskaloosa. As Fujii battled with the gear stick, Arthur composed music. At points it must have seemed as though the prior six months hadn't happened.

Oskaloosa surprised Fujii. "I was expecting everything to be provincial, but it wasn't at all," she says. Uncomfortable silences peppered the dinner table conversation, but Fujii and the Russells also warmed to each other, and she got to see another side of her boyfriend when they visited his grandmother. "Arthur didn't show a lot of emotion and was often glib about things, but with his grandmother he was like a grandson," she remembers. "He was affectionate." That wasn't quite enough for Fujii, however, and her next stop-off—in Boston, where her other boyfriend from San Francisco, Andy, was now living—confirmed her hunch that the relationship with Arthur was coming to an end for emotional as well as logistical reasons. "Andy was a loving, warm person, whereas Arthur was more intellectual," she notes. "Arthur wasn't self-centered, but he was very focused on what he wanted to do. He had this focus to him that Andy didn't have."

Back in New York, Arthur met the prominent flautist and saxophonist Jon Gibson, who had played in the premier performances of *In C* (Riley), *Music in the Shape of a Square* (Glass), and *Drumming* (Reich) before joining the Philip Glass Ensemble. Gibson, who was urbane, curious, and mellow, asked Arthur to play in a concert of his own "reduced" music at the Washington Square Church in March 1974, and was pleased enough with Arthur's effort, even if he "wasn't a stellar-ace, nail-it-on-the-first-read kind of guy." Then, in April, Wolff invited Arthur to play in a concert alongside Jackson Mac Low and Michael Cooper that was broadcast on WBAI-FM. "I think Arthur and I played a duet of one of my pieces, *For 1, 2, or 3 People*," recalls the composer. "In many respects it was a completely open piece. The ground rules were clear, but they were set up in a way that you were constantly confronted with surprises."

Wolff was pleased with Arthur's contribution. "He generally seemed kind of depressed, but not in a way that got other people down, and when he played it didn't seem to matter so much," the composer recalls. "His cello playing was not brilliant but it was very musical and lay somewhere between folk and popular music, although obviously with some classical training. It was very congenial to me because my own music and perform-

Left to right: Martha Siegal (cello), Arthur Russell (cello), Barbara Benary (violin), and Jon Gibson (soprano saxophone) in rehearsal for Gibson's concert at the Washington Square Church, New York City, 5 March 1974. Photograph by Richard Landry. Courtesy of Jon Gibson.

ing is like that. I have no virtuosic talent whatsoever." In a letter to Fujii, Arthur revealed he was happy enough with the way things went. "The gig was pretty good," he wrote. "Christian came down. Jackson Mac Low did some pieces . . ." As with Ginsberg and Dylan, Arthur wasn't overawed, because he had confidence in his musical ability. And he wouldn't have flinched when, a couple of months later, his final MSM transcript for 1973–1974 showed a below-average student, because he had long since concluded that the things he wanted to learn weren't being taught at the school.

The Kitchen

The WBAI-FM appearance turned out to be significant, not because of Arthur's deepening relationship with Wolff, but because Rhys Chatham approached the Oskaloosan exile at the end of the performance. "We *instantly* started arguing about music philosophy, although not in a heated way," remembers Chatham. "He had a very quiet, soft-spoken manner, yet was very rigorous and somewhat contrary. I was really challenged by his way of speaking. Arthur was a real trip."

Chatham's credentials were impressive. As a teenager, he had attended the renowned Third Street Music School Settlement, where he became interested in serial music, and after he graduated Morton Subotnick took him "under his wing" and let him use his studio at New York University. "It was considered a compromise to write music with even a veneer of accessibility, for accessibility was not a part of the theoretical platform," Chatham noted later. "It seemed one needed to be a specialist in modern music, or perhaps in love with someone who was, in order to fully appreciate the music which was being written around that time."[19] Having become a full-fledged member of the Composer's Workshop at NYU, which was headed by Subotnick, Chatham developed an interest in noise, and that was what he thought he was going to get when he went to see Terry Riley play at the Electric Circus. When Riley turned out to be a "long-haired guy playing circus music," Chatham tried to get a refund, but his request was turned down, and so he resolved to return to the concert and sulk. "It changed my life," he remembers. "That was the moment I became interested in tonality." Soon after Chatham started to write his own music of long duration, and then in the fall of 1971 he became the first music director at the Kitchen Center for Video and Music.

Founded by the video artists Steina and Woody Vasulka earlier that same year, the Kitchen was located in the Mercer Arts Center, a collection of rooms (including a former kitchen) devoted to the performing arts that occupied the second floor of the Broadway Central Hotel. (Hotel residents used the Broadway entrance, while habitués of the Mercer Arts Center entered via Mercer Street.) The Vasulkas met Chatham through the choreographer Daniel Nagrin and were excited when the young composer gave them a private demonstration of the new Buchla synthesizer—a modular, voltage-controlled machine that, in contrast to the Moog synthesizer, didn't have a standard keyboard. The Buchla in question had been presented to Subotnick by Don Buchla, who had worked alongside Subotnick at the San Francisco Tape Center. When Chatham noticed that Monday nights at the Kitchen were always "dark," he asked if he could stage a music series. The Vasulkas ushered him in.

Piecing together a program that was about 50 percent electronic, Chatham started off booking friends from the Composer's Workshop, including Maryanne Amacher, after which he turned to downtown composers such as Jon Gibson, Tom Johnson, Frederic Rzewski, and La Monte

Young. In between, he also performed the single-note drone piece *Two Gongs*, which explored, in the words of Johnson, who began to review the downtown compositional scene for the *Village Voice* at the end of 1971, the "strange microscopic world" of tone.[20] "Everyone who played was doing me a favor," says Chatham, who would open the doors and scatter pillows around the floor before each performance. "It was really a community spirit." Infectiously enthusiastic and intellectually engaged, Chatham established the music program as the heartbeat of a buzzing downtown experimental scene that also included occasional events at the Paula Cooper Gallery and the Leo Castelli Gallery, as well as more frequent concerts at 112 Greene Street, the Artist's Space, 98 Greene Street, 10 Beach Street, the Clocktower on Broadway, and the Elaine Summers Experimental Intermedia Foundation (which was commonly referred to as the Experimental Intermedia Foundation, or Experimental Intermedia). "The Kitchen was the center of that universe because of the sheer volume of activity," notes Robert Stearns, who worked at the Paula Cooper Gallery and was a regular at the Kitchen. "I have to credit Rhys with that."

Having given the Kitchen as much time and energy as they could muster, Chatham and the Vasulkas handed over their unpaid directorships to the downtown composer Jim Burton (who took on the music program) and the video artists Shridar Bapat and Dimitri Devyatkin (who took on the more developed video program) in the fall of 1972. The new directors lacked the chemistry of their predecessors, however, and an argument broke out when Burton asked if he could expand the music program into the weekend, only for Bapat and Devyatkin to offer him Tuesdays as a compromise. At that point Burton teamed up with Stearns, who was his roommate, and together they staged a rival music series in their SoHo loft that featured Chatham, Patti Smith, and others. The series continued until mid-December, when the director of the nonprofit agency that supported the Kitchen asked Burton and Stearns to take over the running of the venue, and added that he would withdraw his aid to the Kitchen if they refused. Having already established himself as a hardworking volunteer, Stearns was made director, while Burton resumed his work as music director.

Stearns and Burton took up their positions in January 1973 and enjoyed a month or two of tranquility before the landlord of the Mercer Arts Center threatened to double their rent. The turn of events proved to be fortuitous. Having decided to vacate, Stearns and Burton had already packed up

The interior of the Kitchen on Wooster Street. Courtesy of the Kitchen, New York City.

most of the Kitchen's equipment by the time the Broadway Central Hotel collapsed as a result of structural problems in August, and they reopened in a cut-rate space on the second floor of 59 Wooster Street and 484 Broome Street—both addresses for the same building—in the autumn.[21] "The 7,500 square-foot, second-floor space had previously served as the luxurious, if Bohemian, residence of the gallery owner Joseph LoGiudice," says Stearns. "A real kitchen, sleeping quarters, and storage area occupied an L-shaped space in the back of the building, and a large, bright, generously windowed south-facing space became the primary location for performances, with access from Wooster Street. The oak hardwood floors, stately columns, and clean white paint lent an air of legitimacy to the venue, whether or not it was deserved."

The Kitchen re-opened with a concert for John Cage's sixtieth birthday party in early December 1973—the rumbling from the trucks on Broome Street that were heading to the Holland Tunnel accompanied the instrumentation—and, as Burton's season drew to a close, the search for a new music director began in the early summer of 1974. Although the details are hazy, Stearns appears to have canvassed Chatham, who recommended the intense, provocative musician he had met at the Wolff concert back in April. Having bumped into Arthur at a number of other events, Chatham believed his friend's no-bullshit attitude, intellectual energy, and musical open-mindedness meant he was perfectly suited to take up what had become the most prestigious position on the downtown circuit. "Arthur was someone who was known on the scene," says Chatham. "The most important thing was the desire to do the job." Chatham wasn't concerned that Arthur was only twenty-three, because he had done the job himself when he was nineteen.

Arthur had played at the Kitchen—perhaps for the first time—toward the end of May 1974 when Christian Wolff (organ) invited him to play cello alongside David Behrman (viola), Garrett List (trombone), and Jon Gibson (soprano saxophone and flute) on *Exercises and Songs*.[22] "We sang political songs and played these pieces that consisted of a series of melodic fragments," recalls Wolff. "John Cage was there and he remarked that the music sounded like the classical music of some civilization that we hadn't discovered." Arthur would have relished the prospect of being able to organize similar concerts, yet he hesitated over the offer to become music director, not because he thought the Kitchen was too illustrious for him to handle, and not because he was worried about the pressure of administering the music program, but because he had yet to feel settled in New York. "I still don't know where I'll be next year," he wrote to Fujii in the middle of July, by which point he had applied to return to the San Francisco Conservatory, if only to keep his options open. "I don't like the idea of not seeing you for a year or more. I don't know what to do." Come August, Arthur was still riven with doubt. "If I go to the conservatory I could be near Yuko, Mt. Shasta, the Pacific Ocean, and you," he reasoned. "If I stay in New York I'll be closer to getting temporarily rich, hence I could come and see you."

In the end Arthur decided to stay in New York, because its music scene was much more developed than the one in San Francisco. His season at the Kitchen got underway on 12 October 1974 when Annea Lockwood, a New Zealand–born locally-based musician, performed *Humming: and Other Sensory Meditations*, a quirky piece that invited audience participation. Working alongside Carlota Schoolman, a young video artist who had been made the Kitchen's video director, Arthur's next concert featured the Louisiana-born Richard Landry, who combined tenor saxophone and video in a concert that mixed minimal orchestral music with Cajun sounds.[23] Then, at the end of November, Arthur appeared alongside thirty-seven other performers in a festive "Soup and Tart" event organized by the French Fluxus artist Jean Dupuy, in which the participants performed for two minutes each, while others dined on soup and apple tart. The lineup included JoAnne Akalaitis, Laurie Anderson, Jon Gibson, Philip Glass, DeeDee Halleck, Joan Jonas, Richard Landry, Gordon Matta-Clark, Charlemagne Palestine, Yvonne Rainer, Richard Serra, Nancy Topf, and Hannah Wilke—a virtual compendium of downtown invention.[24] When his slot arrived, Arthur sat on a chair and played "Eli," a dirgelike, voice-cello song about an unwanted dog.[25] "It was very poignant," remembers Schoolman, who adored the enigmatic poetry of Arthur's lyrics as well as his mix of melody and dissonance. "Arthur's playing was just sublime."

From December to February, Arthur programmed experimental composers such as Jim Burton, Cornelius Cardew, Alvin Curran, Garrett List, Ingram Marshall, Phill Niblock, and Richard Teitelbaum. "The parameters were highly defined," comments Chatham, who had become a member of La Monte Young's Theater of Eternal Music in 1973. "We were coming out of a post-Cagean, post–Phil and Steve kind of thing, so Arthur had to move tentatively." Many of the concerts featured composer-musicians who lived in the neighborhood and were used to turning to each other when they needed someone to provide them with instrumental support, or even a booking. "These were people who were already somewhat established Kitchenettes," adds Stearns. "They would have simply contacted Arthur and said, 'Hey, I want a gig!'" Arthur was also committed to the events he programmed, so when Cardew was criticized for "trying to make music for the masses," he defended the composer's attempt to make music for his students as well as to "get back to a state of mind he was in when he was sixteen years old."[26]

According to Kitchen insiders, Arthur was a relaxed and sometimes dreamy music director, but his demeanor became focused and quietly insistent when he booked Jonathan Richman and the Modern Lovers to perform in March 1975. The move was entirely counterintuitive, since the Kitchen had forged a reputation for being (as the New York Times described the Mercer Arts Center) "a kind of downtown Lincoln Center seen through the wrong end of a telescope."[27] Arthur wanted to initiate a conversation about aesthetics between art and rock musicians, however, and although the decision threatened to undermine the Kitchen's cutting-edge status, he booked Richman to play at the venue for four consecutive nights from 19 March to 22 March 1975. In order to emphasize his point, Arthur promoted the concert as a "rock and roll show." A band with commercial aspirations was being invited into the front room of the noncommercial and extremely esoteric avant-garde.

The Kitchen's art-rock conversation had almost got going when the venue was located in the Mercer Arts Center. The electronic-rock-jazz band Robert Mason and Stardrive played Friday nights between March and June of 1972, and a video rock presentation featuring the New York Dolls, Satan, and the Magic Tramps was screened toward the end of Mason's run, although these events occurred outside of the auspices of the music program. In addition, the New York Dolls held a four-month residency in the Oscar Wilde Room, which shared the same corridor as the Kitchen, from June to October 1972; and other bands, including Ruby and the Rednecks, Suicide, and Teenage Lust, also played in the Oscar Wilde Room. "We were aware the Dolls were performing at the Mercer Arts Center," recalls Stearns. "They were such a freak act you couldn't miss them. We thought we were doing weird stuff, but the Dolls made our clan look like eggheads from Columbia University." According to Stearns, a number of composers who were involved with the Kitchen were "guardedly hostile" toward their rock neighbors, and although he wonders if the bands helped create "a distinct atmosphere that influenced the whole environment of the Mercer Art Center," the players maintained their distance. When the Kitchen moved to Wooster Street it was widely accepted that its newfound autonomy—including its freedom from raucous rock—was desirable.

Whereas the psychedelic rock of the late sixties and the progressive rock of the early seventies appear to have been too self-consciously complex and bombastic to appeal to Arthur, a performance by the Modern Lovers at the Townhouse Theatre in New York toward the end of January 1974 captured his imagination. Delivering nonchalantly idiosyncratic lyrics in a plain-speaking style, the pre-punk Richman left a deep impression, as did the band's tall, rugged bass player, Ernie Brooks, whom Arthur approached at the end of the concert in order to exchange phone numbers. "There was something in the style of the Modern Lovers that he related to," recalls Brooks of his early conversations with Arthur. "Jonathan was abrasive and hard-edged, while Arthur was lyrical and flowing, more pop than rock.

But they both wrote with a directness that could be quotidian and almost banal, yet was also poetic." For Arthur, attending the Modern Lovers concert amounted to a revelatory confirmation of an idea raised by a linguistics class at Columbia University: he was more interested in vernacular communication than formal structure.[28]

Several months later, as he traveled to visit Kate in Maine, Arthur stopped off to see Brooks in Cambridge, Massachusetts, unaware that the Modern Lovers were about to split. He sat on the floor and played songs such as "I Forget and I Can't Tell" (also known as "The Ballad of the Lights") and "My Sister Knows the Saddest People." An English-lit graduate from Harvard who had worked on the college literary magazine, Brooks believed he had "some insight into lyrics" and recalls being swept away by what he heard. "They were beautiful songs, and Arthur sang them with this Iowan twang," he says. "They were quirky in terms of chords and words, and had a folky sound to them." Arthur told Brooks he wanted them to record music together, and when the Mercury A&R representative Paul Nelson offered Arthur some free studio time to produce a demo, he drove up to Boston to pick up Brooks and Jerry Harrison, the keyboard player for the Modern Lovers, who had studied with Brooks at Harvard. Completing the lineup, Andy Paley, the bandleader of the Sidewinders, who had opened for the Modern Lovers at the Townhouse, was invited to play drums. The players recorded four tracks—"Bobby," "Holding Hands with a Heartbreaker," "I Forget and I Can't Tell," and "I Guess This Must Be the Place"—only for Nelson to pass.[29] But Arthur and Brooks had found each other—and soon they would have the Kitchen's "Rock and Roll Show" to look forward to.

Arthur drummed up interest among his experimental peers on the opening night of the Richman series. "You can't leave now!" he told Schoolman, who was deeply suspicious of popular culture and had no intention of staying for the evening. "You realize who is playing here tonight? It's Jonathan Richman and the Modern Lovers! This is bubblegum music gone wacko!" His band having split up, Richman appeared in front of a packed venue in a revised acoustic formation alongside Ernie Brooks (guitar, vocals), "Hope Bacon" (guitar, vocals), Andy Paley (percussion, vocals, guitar), Jonathan Paley (guitar, vocals), Miranda Remington (violin, vocals), and Jody Thaxter (vocals, percussion). In the first half of the concert the group mixed Modern Lovers songs with old standards, while in the second half members of the audience—ecstatic Modern Lovers devotees plus a small

Arthur Russell writing music in Maine in the early 1970s. Photograph by Charles Arthur Russell Sr. Courtesy of Charles Arthur Russell Sr. and Emily Russell.

number of downtowners—were given the opportunity to put in requests. "When Jonathon [*sic*] sings, he literally cries," reported an enthused Peter Gordon, who had just moved to New York after studying at the Center for Contemporary Music at Mills College. "I want to believe the Modern Lovers are just plain folk, ordinary men and women singing the songs they love to people who love to hear them. A fan told me that Jonathon performs mostly in hospitals and nursing homes and the only reason he wants to be famous is so it will mean more to those people. Beautiful."[30] Stearns was also moved. "It was new for the Kitchen," he says. "I remember my ears feeling as though they were hearing something for the first time, even if it was sentimental. It was a grin instead of a grimace. It was enjoyable, fun, loud. Arthur was the first to draw on avant-garde pop culture. It was both nostalgic and cutting edge."

A broader exchange between rock and art music had already started to unfold. Drawing on Igor Stravinsky and Edgard Varèse, Frank Zappa and the Mothers of Invention explored the intersection between rock and art music, and Zappa also put on a concert with Zubin Mehta, the musical

Ernie Brooks (right) playing with the Modern Lovers at a free Sunday afternoon concert in Cambridge, Mass., c. 1970. Photograph by Richard Rogers. Courtesy of Ernie Brooks.

director of the Los Angeles Philharmonic orchestra, in 1970.[31] Released the same year, Soft Machine's "Out-Bloody-Rageous" referenced the work of Terry Riley, as did "Baba O'Riley," the opening track on the Who's 1971 album, *Who's Next*. After that, the citations and collaborations began to flow more freely. Mike Oldfield's 1973 album, *Tubular Bells*, drew on Steve Reich. John Cale and Angus Maclise (of the Primitives and the Velvet Underground) worked with La Monte Young, and brought his devices of drone and repetition into their music. Brian Eno declared Young to be "the daddy of us all" and looked to Philip Glass's 1970 composition *Music with Changing Parts* when he recorded his first album with Robert Fripp, *No Pussyfooting*.[32] Lou Reed introduced wind and string instruments into his pre-punk pop, and, according to Gordon, he acknowledged Young to have been the inspiration behind his 1975 album *Metal Machine Music*.

Composers had also begun to explore the popular terrain, and the Center for Contemporary Music at Mills College was a key location for this activity. The center's director, Robert Ashley, asserted the center's hybrid agenda by developing a series of mixed-media operas, and he also employed the pianist "Blue" Gene Tyranny (born Robert Nathan Sheff), who had played in the Prime Movers and contributed to the band's decision to hire Jim Osterberg (later known as Iggy Pop) to play drums. Terry Riley, who collaborated on *Church of Anthrax* with John Cale, made music that combined art and popular forms while based at Mills. And Peter Gordon premiered *Machomusic* for six saxophonists and electronics during his graduate studies in San Diego, after which he enrolled at Mills to continue his work. Elsewhere, Richard Landry, a player in the Philip Glass Ensemble, brought together tape-delay techniques with southern Louisiana Cajun and Zydeco music; the philosopher, musician, and anti-art activist Henry Flynt explored related ground with his country-style violin compositions; Tony Conrad played with Young as well as the German Krautrock group Faust; and Jim Burton teamed up with Rhys Chatham and Garrett List to deliver a Hank Williams–inspired country-and-western concert that featured an atonal horizontal slide guitar and vocals sung on helium (all performed in front of a mock Western saloon).

However, whereas these art-driven explorations were concerned with integrating rock gestures into a compositional framework, Richman's post–Modern Lovers lineup was rooted in rock, and their appearance at the Kitchen provoked some disquiet. "You didn't have to be close-minded to feel some resistance toward the Modern Lovers," reasons Ned Sublette. "The people who were playing at the Kitchen were sophisticated musicians who had put a great deal of thought and study into what they did. In contrast, the music of the Modern Lovers was very simple-minded, and Richman's lyrics were utterly—and proudly—infantile. When I arrived in New York I felt like I had escaped the places where the only music people could imagine was rock." Grounded in a commitment to experimentalism that was sometimes mistaken for cultural elitism—especially in rock circles—most downtown composers opposed rock not because it sounded like rock, but because it only sounded like rock. Why would any musician want to be governed by such a limiting set of aesthetic rules? "The concert was called the 'Rock and Roll Show,' and rock and roll was the bad guys, the commercial stuff, which was out of our territory," adds Stearns.

Then again, Arthur was more interested in forging connections than entrenching difference, and his invitation to Richman broke new ground because it implied that some forms of unadulterated rock didn't just have minimalist potential, but were actually minimalist already. Once that conclusion was reached, it became much harder to sustain the idea that institutions should be segregated by genre. Post-classical minimalists had plied their trade through progressive colleges and alternative performance spaces, while rockers (save for Zappa) stayed rooted in their recording studios and established concert venues. Indeed Bernard Gendron, author of *Between Montmartre and the Mudd Club: Popular Music and the Avant-Garde*, argues that "for all its eclecticism and testing of this or that musical boundary, the Kitchen, during its first five years, always remained firmly fixed in the classical musical avant-garde tradition, never breaching the walls separating it from other musical fields, such as jazz and rock," and in this respect the Kitchen was typical of the way downtown music culture was largely made up of discrete and segregated scenes.[33] In fact, Arthur, a contrarian cast amidst a band of troublemakers, had set about subverting the institutional framework of art music and rock halfway through the Kitchen's fourth year, and he might have been pleased when his cross-generic deed was covered by the *Village Voice*, which reviewed one of the concerts.[34] "Arthur was trying to bring other things into the Kitchen," confirms Brooks. "He liked fighting with the powers. He would have thought, 'Well, if they don't like pop or rock, I'm going to bring it into the Kitchen.'"

The trombonist and composer Garrett List, who met Arthur during Burton's tenure as music director at the Kitchen, was also interested in moving beyond the demarcated confines of compositional minimalism. "Arthur was very much influenced by the whole minimalist thing," says List, who had already played in Young's drone band for a couple of years (during which time he was given "something like four notes" to play). "It was hard not to be hit on the head by minimalism during that period, and Arthur's take on it was that Buddhism could lead to minimalism. But we didn't want to be minimalists, so we tried to find a way of dealing with it without jumping on the bandwagon. We wanted to go from minimalism into popular language, and it was very much in the air at the Kitchen to break down these barriers." Peter Gordon was another willful trespasser, and like Arthur and List, he made a point of highlighting the wider move toward a jazz-rock-compositional interaction that included the composer-performers Anthony Braxton, Karl Berger, Garrett List, Robert Sheff, Jon Gibson, Jill Kroesen, Arthur Russell, and Fred Rzewski, as well as himself. "Art and entertainment are not two separate worlds never to intermix," Gordon noted in his essay on the appearance of the Modern Lovers at the

Kitchen. "They are two coexisting fields, each performing in necessary social functions. It's time for the intellectual impetus of art—the exploring, questioning, positing of problems—to join forces with the broader bases of entertainment."[35]

Arthur was the first person to bring unadulterated rock (entertainment) into the downtown compositional scene (art), and the Richman series became a key moment in the evolution of the Kitchen. By the end of the run it had become clear that the small cluster of subway stops that lay between the Kitchen and Lincoln Center disguised an increasingly vast cultural divide, because a form of sonic democracy, in which sounds would be treated equally, was being ushered into the downtown scene. "Arthur and I shared this thing about wanting to deal with a language that was more open than minimalism or Cagean music or the uptown scene," adds List. "We were all talking about trying to find alternatives to this, and the fact Arthur programmed the Modern Lovers was more like saying, 'Let's really do this shit—let's not just talk about it.'" The doing had a direct impact on at least one member of the audience. "Rock was somehow less," remembers Chatham. "Back in the early seventies, people were still questioning rock's validity. Arthur's unique contribution was to introduce rock groups to the programming, which was considered heresy at the time, but proved to be prophetic in its vision. I was shocked. But it made me think, and I ended up joining in. What can I say?"

Hammond

Arthur had been engaging with popular forms and figures for some time. He wrote twisted folk songs, recorded with Allen Ginsberg, and hooked up his cello to an amplifier while he was studying at the San Francisco Conservatory and the Ali Akbar College. During his first trip to New York, he also met John Hammond, the highly influential Columbia A&R representative who could list Count Basie, George Benson, Benny Goodman, Billie Holiday, Bob Dylan, and Bruce Springsteen among his discoveries.[36] However Arthur and Hammond came into contact—and it's entirely possible Hammond would have accompanied Dylan into the studio for the Ginsberg recording session—Arthur is unlikely to have missed the opportunity to hand the Columbia talent scout a cassette (in effect, an electromagnetic calling card).

Hammond believed Arthur was special. Just like Dylan and Springsteen, the Oskaloosan emitted an aura of organic truth, while his Midwestern twang and unusual guitar progressions were sufficiently distinctive for him to be marketed as a unique talent. When the Columbia executive became aware that Paul Nelson was also pursuing Arthur, he asked the singer-songwriter to lay down a demo in August 1974. During that session Hammond introduced Arthur to his secretary as "the most advanced and talented of all the young artists," after which he added that he wanted to sign him. A few days later, just as Arthur was about to become the music director at the Kitchen, Hammond invited him back into the studios to mix the tapes. "He was very encouraging, and said that if Mercury didn't sign me he'd try to get Columbia to do it," Arthur wrote to Fujii. "He actually said that. But it's still really uncertain. Even though John Hammond is a big wig at Columbia, he still said 'try.'" Filled with the excited doubts of a kid going ice-skating for the first time, Arthur added he was "super-ambitious" and "pretty stupid" because he had nothing to "justify" his ambition. "I've got so much to do," he signed off. "All the music in the world."[37]

Having received the call to return to the Columbia studios in March 1975, just as he was preparing to stage the Jonathan Richman series at the Kitchen, Arthur asked Ernie Brooks (bass) and Andy Paley (drums) to join him for the session—a straightforward proposition thanks to the fact that Robert Stearns was already covering their travel expenses. Jon Gibson (alto saxophone, soprano saxophone, and clarinet) and Jon Sholle (guitar) were also invited, as were two newer acquaintances from the downtown experimental scene, Garrett List (trombone) and Peter Gordon (tenor saxophone and keyboards). All of them were impressed: to have anyone pay for a recording session was significant; for it to be Hammond was momentous. As they made their way into the studio, the presence of Stan Tonkel behind the mixing desk did nothing to diminish the sense of occasion. Tonkel had engineered many of Columbia's recordings with Miles Davis.

Rather than recording to multitrack tape in order to generate a clear separation of sounds, which was the favored approach during the 1970s, Hammond and Arthur (who played guitar and keyboards and sang) recorded directly to two-track stereo because they were concerned primarily with the "feel" of the session. The arrangements were also unusual, with Gibson, Gordon, and List asked to play lines that were more typical of strings than the idiomatic punches and stings normally written for horns.

"Arthur wanted us to back up his music and to let the instruments support the voice and words," recalls List. "The music was song-like and had something to do with folk. There was something unsophisticated about it. It was another sound that hadn't happened." The eclectic lineup revealed Arthur's interplanetary trajectory: Brooks and Paley were confirmed pop-rock performers, while Gibson and List were deep into avant-garde composition, but in the Columbia studio, under Arthur's direction, their paths merged, at least for one session. "Arthur didn't follow the standard rock quartet lineup," notes Gordon, who relished the upheaval.

Hammond, however, was displeased. Having planned a solo session with Arthur, he was disappointed when his latest handpicked protégé showed up with a bunch of other musicians who obscured their one-on-one rapport. "I think Hammond had hoped to do with Arthur what he had done with Bruce Springsteen and Bob Dylan at the beginning of their careers—go into the studio with the artist, solo, record about thirty songs, raw, and use that to start the process with the company," explains Gordon. "I recall Hammond being peeved at Arthur for bringing such a large group along."[38] According to List, the Columbia executive became irritable almost right away. "Hammond didn't really lock into it too much. You could tell he wasn't that excited about it. He was hoping he would uncover another Bob Dylan." Instead he uncovered a musician who believed the most compelling work came out of collaborative exchange. "Arthur was ambitious, but he was ambitious for other things," adds List. "Arthur would have probably liked to be a star, but he also had a larger vision of what music was for, and that was one of the reasons we were friends—because of these ideas we shared."

Introducing each song, Hammond became more and more vexed until he finally turned to the mike and said: "And the next song will be performed by Arthur Russell *and his symphony orchestra.*" At the end of the session Hammond hovered around List. "He kept asking me about my trombone playing and the different things I had been doing, and then he said, 'Where are you going now? Why don't you walk to my office with me?'" Having cold-shouldered Arthur, the A&R man found out everything he could about his new interest. "Well, this is my telephone number," Hammond told List. "It goes directly to my desk. You won't even speak to my secretary. You call me and let's go and have lunch some day." The trombonist only called a few years later when he needed to find a way to make some money, by which time Hammond's contact details had changed. Meanwhile, Arthur's story with the Columbia boss would twist and turn in other directions.[39]

Instrumentals

Jill Kroesen and Peter Gordon, who had studied with the mixed-media pioneer Robert Ashley at the Center for Contemporary Music at Mills College in San Francisco, joined Arthur in his art-meets-pop quest. "Bob Ashley was an extraordinary teacher," says Kroesen, who played keyboards and congas. "There was a Buchla and a Moog at Mills, and we also had an eight-track studio. It was very fertile ground. I was friends with Peter. He was even my boyfriend for about two weeks." Kroesen wrote her thesis on rock and the blues, around which she composed a song titled "Fay Shism Blues," and remembers it being a "big deal" that she was bringing popular sounds into art music. "But there was no resistance to what we were doing," she adds. "Because of Bob Ashley, we didn't think of ourselves as composers doing music, but as artists doing art, with music one of our components. We didn't think too much about combining art music and rock. We just sort of did it."

Kroesen met Arthur soon after she moved to New York in 1974, and when Carlota Schoolman invited her to perform *Dear Ashley in the Kitchen* in January 1975, she asked Arthur (along with Rhys Chatham) to accompany her. During the performance Kroesen sent questions via video and microphone to Ashley, who was sitting in the next room, and Ashley was also given free rein to meander about, as well as ask members of the audience he had spotted on his monitor to join him backstage. "The extremely open-ended format precluded any sense of 'performance' as such," reported Peter Frank in the *SoHo Weekly News*, downtown's local newspaper. "This irritated those spectators who came to see a capital *P* Performance and led to various analyses concerning the difference between East Coast Boring and West Coast Boring."[40] Kroesen would go on to collaborate with Arthur on many occasions. "He seemed very uncomfortable with himself," she recalls. "I always had a lot of affection for him."

Gordon also flung himself into the pop-art cauldron without pausing to reflect on their theoretical incompatibility. Born in New York City, he moved to Munich at the age of thirteen, and played in soul and R&B bands while studying at the American Army School. In his spare time he hung

out at rock clubs and listened to the Munich Opera perform Anton We-
bern and Arnold Schoenberg. "I also heard Ellington, Basie, Ray Charles,
James Brown," he says. "I once even had the opportunity to perform with
Chuck Berry. This was all in my musical vocabulary." Gordon continued
his high school education in Los Angeles, where he met Don Van Vliet /
Captain Beefheart in Canoga Park. He listened to the maverick bandleader
extemporize on the relationship between music and art, as well as shout at
his band when the recording of *Trout Mask Replica* didn't go as planned.
"I was influenced by Zappa, but it was Beefheart who got me interested
in vernacular music as art. I began to see the possibilities of a serious pop
music."

While attending the University of California, San Diego, Gordon met
Kathy Acker (who was also drawn to the idea of throwing together disparate syntaxes) and formed a pop band that morphed top–one hundred
chart songs into free-form improvisations. After that he went to Mills College, where he studied with Robert Ashley, Terry Riley, and "Blue" Gene
Tyranny, and spent hours mixing rock, electronic, and abstract recording
techniques in the college's studio. Convinced that contemporary art music
was inherently elitist, Gordon sought to create a popular form that was
"intelligent but musical in a larger sense," and ended up looking to minimalism without feeling that he was obliged to follow its pioneers. "The
hegemony of the 'big four'—Reich, Glass, Riley, Young—wasn't so clearly
laid out," he explains. "There were numerous currents of musical thought
going on." Hot on the heels of Kroesen, Gordon traveled to New York in
February 1975 and moved into a railroad apartment on East Fifth Street
with Acker (who shared the $150-per-month rent). "Back then it was pos-
sible for a young musician to move into downtown Manhattan and make a
stand," says Gordon. "My intention was to create art-music compositions
using my vernacular languages—rock and jazz. I wanted to make music
that was hedonistic but also brainy."

Gordon was introduced to Arthur at the Poetry Project at St. Mark's
by Chatham, who realized the two of them would find it easy to strike up
a conversation about pop and minimalism. As Talking Heads (still a trio)
took to the stage for one of their first appearances in New York, Arthur
plunged into a conversation about musical taste and must have realized
he had stumbled onto something rare: a like-minded soul. "We shared an
appreciation for the sweet and sensual elements of pop music, and we both

enjoyed the Muzak-style arrangements of the so-called 'beautiful music' stations," notes Gordon. "Arthur was particularly enamored of the lush strings of the Mystic Moods Orchestra. While others might have perceived this as ironic, we really did enjoy that syrupy stuff." Gordon warmed to Arthur—"He was a gentle sort, very earnest and very funny," he says—and got his first gig in the city when Arthur invited him to play at the Hammond session in March. Then, the following month, Arthur asked him to play in his *Instrumentals* project, a potpourri of art music, pop culture, and Buddhist wonder that combined (in the words of Arthur) the "bright sound and magical qualities of the bubblegum and easy-listening current in American popular song" with "avant-garde musical thought and practice."[41]

Thick with the atmosphere of the West Coast, *Instrumentals* had grown out of Yuko Nonomura's suggestion that Arthur write some music about clouds and illustrate the piece with the Shingon priest's photographic slides. Already intent on taking a West Coast art–meets-pop aesthetic to New York, Arthur went on to develop *Instrumentals* around the basic standard-era chord progressions that had underpinned the popular songs of the 1930s and 1940s, and just like the forerunners of minimalism, who drew on single notes that were tonal, simple, and therefore deemed to be reactionary, he attempted to reenergize his apparently hackneyed material by redeploying it in an innovative structure. That structure was modular in character and included seventy-six lines of chord changes that the conductor could develop in a multitude of directions in order to create "potential voices of harmony in the actual performance." Written with no specific playing order in mind and lasting for a potential forty-eight hours, the lines resembled a postmodern musical maze that would be circuitous and fragmentary even if the conductor and the musicians managed to stay together. To heighten the probability that they wouldn't, Arthur specified that the players could improvise around their melodic lines.

Playing alongside Jonni Sue Bartel (piano), Jon Gibson (soprano saxophone), and Johannes Mager (trombone), and with Nonomura's slides of flowers, landscapes, and skies providing a bright backdrop to the piece, Arthur (amplified cello) led *Instrumentals* for the first time at 1750 Arch Street in Berkeley in January 1975. After that, he began to rehearse for a performance at the Kitchen with Ernie Brooks (electric bass), Rhys Chatham (flute), Jon Gibson (alto and soprano saxophone, flute, and clarinet), Peter

Gordon (piano and organ), Garrett List (trombone), Andy Paley (drums), Jon Sholle (electric guitar), and David Van Tieghem (percussion). Gordon remembers the rehearsals being "centered around waiting for Ernie to arrive, sometimes two hours late, and then announcing he had to go and get something to eat." Once they had settled down, the musicians would try out one of the seventy-six lines, and each time they reached a natural pause, Arthur would rewind a tape recording of the effort and lead a discussion around which parts should be kept for the performance. "There was a fascinating process of repeating different measures or sections and discovering the possibilities of different chord progressions with the harmonic grid Arthur had set up," adds Gordon. "The rehearsals were all about choosing individual measures and looping them, live. It wasn't conducted; we would just feel it. Cage, free jazz, the DJ set — these were parallel energies."

Because the modules contained irregular and unpredictable meters, the musicians found it difficult to improvise without losing their place. "Even though the chords and melodies were quite familiar, this set them apart from the ongoing 4/4 or 3/4 predictability of almost all popular song," Gibson explained a little later. List compared the collective process to assembling a puzzle that "has no model and must be worked out slowly and deliberately to achieve the desired end."[42] The decentralized and democratic format also proved to be draining, and even Arthur felt the rehearsals "turned out to be tedious in some ways." Increasingly agitated, Chatham ended up asking him why he didn't simply write out all the music. "I have a memory of Arthur changing the score a lot during rehearsals and having difficulty articulating what he wanted us to do," says Chatham. "I felt frustrated as a result of this and at times thought he was out of his mind. He'd try out certain things, and they wouldn't work, and we'd do it in a different way. It drove me crazy. I thought it took entirely too long to rehearse." When Chatham asked Gibson if he was equally frustrated, the saxophonist, who was able to draw on a greater reservoir of patience, merely rolled his eyes.

Staged on 27 April 1975, a month after Arthur had unwittingly bungled his opportunity to win a solo recording contract with Columbia, the *Instrumentals* concert delivered an original combination of popular and art sounds. As vibrant melodies and harmonies slipped across the flimsiest of scores, Nonomura's slides of glistening skies and majestic mountain peaks added to the sparkling quality of the evening. The performance was

Instrumentals flyer, 1975.
Designed by Arthur Russell.
Courtesy of Tom Lee.

far from polished: even though the notes and chords were often played "long"—a trait that was still more common in minimalism than pop—the sections regularly imploded after a minute or two, which was the length of time it would take for the musicians to lose their way, or for Arthur to enter into a fateful battle with the feedback that was coming out of his amplified cello.[43] Yet the clipped effect of these sequences inadvertently reinforced the point of the concert. Here was a composed instrumental piece that not only captured the accessibility of pop with its emphasis on repeated phrases, up-tempo drumming, tick-tock woodblocks, and unlikely layers of shimmering maracas, tambourines, and triangles, but also out-popped pop in its pared down, truncated form, with some segments lasting for as little as thirty seconds.

Evoking the frontier compositions of Aaron Copland and Ennio Morricone, Arthur's sunny, almost painterly music hovered in the air as the players regrouped and the respectable audience of fifteen to twenty absorbed the images. Arthur had also wanted the musicians to "accept the color slides as an unconscious input," but the piece demanded too much concentration for them to let their eyes wander from the score. Viewing

Two of the slides that accompanied the performance of *Instrumentals* in
1975. Photographs by Yuko Nonomura. Courtesy of Audika.

the performance from a less demanding vantage point, Philip Glass might
have been the only member of the audience to wonder about the visual dimension. "He told me that the slides were great, but the music stood on its
own," remembers Carlota Schoolman, who had become good friends with
Arthur and operated the projector. "He hoped Arthur realized *Instrumentals* didn't need to be a multimedia piece for it to be interesting to people."
Having allowed his house on East Houston Street to become the rehearsal
space for the assembled musicians, Glass judged that the concert was "im-

portant" and also that it demonstrated Arthur to be "in the vanguard of something very interesting."

The concert's fusion of pop and concert hall instruments, in which an electric bass and drum kit played alongside a cello and a flute, certainly foregrounded Arthur's iconoclastic approach. "He just brought all these different people together," comments Van Tieghem. "It was probably the first time there was a group put together like that." Musicians at Mills College and elsewhere had melded compositional music with pop/rock, but Arthur was the first to stage this kind of exploration in New York, and although the Kitchen's regulars were proud of their open-minded outlook, Arthur's gentle drums, fun-loving tambourines, and clip-clopping percussion appear to have caused some ripples of discontent in the audience. "A lot of people turned off," Arthur told David Toop eleven years later. "They thought that [the concert] was a sign of some new unsophistication—a sign of increasing commercialisation."[44] Glass confirms that Arthur was "too interested in pop" for some people's liking, and that this "might have been threatening to some of the experimental music buffs." Although Chatham, Gibson, and Schoolman can't remember being bothered by Arthur's use of percussion—"Gee, you could bring anything into the Kitchen," says Gibson—Chatham was dismissive of Arthur's "tacky" use of standard-era chord changes, which he regarded as being openly conservative, and says he was "horrified" at his "mixing popular forms with classical music." That would have probably pleased Arthur, and the shifting milieu of compositional music would soon validate his choices.

Rich in melodic layering, Instrumentals was part of the broader downtown movement that, in the words of the critic Carlo McCormick, looked to escape the "reductive language" of minimalism through "more personal and idiosyncratic expressions under the rubric of postminimalism."[45] Inspired by a trip to Ghana and composed in 1971, Drumming marked Steve Reich's breakthrough as a contemporary composer, yet his next major composition, Music for 18 Musicians, which drew on classes he had taken in Balinese gamelan and was first performed in 1976, included a much richer use of instrumentation than had been evident in earlier works. Combining additive techniques with harmonic differentiation, Philip Glass premiered Music in Twelve Parts to critical acclaim in 1974, but then started to compose Einstein on the Beach, which displayed an elaborate instrumental mix and attention to harmony that set it apart from his more rigorous early works. La Monte Young's *The Well-Tuned Piano* from 1973 marked the moment when the composer demonstrated how "traditional harmony . . . can be applied to modern harmony" when developed through complex tuning ratios.[46] And heading toward a similar horizon, Terry Riley began to work on *Shri Camel*, which marked the end of his interest in minimalism, in 1975. There was, in short, a reluctance to simply repeat repetition, and as Paul Hillier notes, by the middle of the 1970s the so-called minimalist composers were "beginning to produce works of such size and stature" that the label was beginning to look "mean-spirited and, worse, misguided."[47]

To varying degrees, Reich, Glass, Young, and Riley were beginning to object to the description of their work as "minimalist." "We didn't think of ourselves as minimalists," explains Glass. "We thought of ourselves as living in a new world of music where composers and performers were one, and where the audiences were in front of us." Their refusal to adhere to any kind of minimalist orthodoxy revealed the deeper importance of these composers, whose music didn't simply introduce an alternative to serialism but also, perhaps more enduringly, opened up the future by breaking the stranglehold of that particular creed.[48] Enjoying the new milieu, Arthur also moved away from minimalism as he developed layers of lush instrumentation within a structure that was always likely to self-implode; the decision seemed right to those who realized that minimalist aesthetics were likely to be less effective in New York than they had been in San Francisco. "Extremely repetitive music made a lot more sense if you were really stoned, and if you were already where you were going instead of on your way somewhere else," comments Ned Sublette. "In New York, people went out to three different places a night."

Having already programmed a Jackson Mac Low poetry performance that utilized audiotape and videotape just before the *Instrumentals* concert, Arthur invited composers such as David Behrman, Chatham, and Gibson to appear during the last couple of months of his directorship. Yet he also refused the safest option available to him, and so it was Robert Stearns, and not Arthur, who booked Reich to present an early version of *Music for 18 Musicians*—titled *Work in Progress for 21 Musicians and Singers*—toward the end of May 1975. "Like a lot of people, Arthur felt that the Kitchen was there for composers who were at the beginning of their career," explains Stearns, who was keen to use the Kitchen's recent history "as a foundation to build a future," as well as to balance out Jim Burton's programming of Philip Glass during the 1973–1974 season, since Glass and Reich had developed followings that were capable of being ungenerous toward each other. "He would have thought that someone like Steve didn't need the Kitchen because he had already got his reputation." Arthur's end-of-season concert took place a month later and featured Nova'billy, an up-front communist outfit led by Henry Flynt, whose wacky take on music and politics wasn't always taken seriously by the serious end of the music scene.[49] Mixing risk with humor, the performance sounded like La Monte Young's take on the blues with an added dash of country, recalls Don Christensen, who played drums. It was a fittingly offbeat way for Arthur to end his eventful year.

Arthur could have made a case for staying on, but lingering tensions made it a good time to step aside. Along with Ernie Brooks, he spent after-hours time in the Kitchen, sometimes to make use of the venue's prized four-track Teac tape recorder, and the bass player remembers that when Stearns approached, Arthur would assume the persona of a naughty schoolboy and comment, "Uh-oh, Bob is coming!"[50] Jill Kroesen also recalls that Arthur "always looked kind of guilty, like he had been a bad boy and we would find out," and while Stearns maintains the boundaries were "pretty stretchable," his communication with Arthur could be halting. "There were thousands of sentences he wouldn't finish," recalls the director. "He would start a thought and then . . . 'Yes, Arthur?!' Then he would look down at his feet and squint. 'Yeees, Arthur?!'" Stearns adds that Arthur would be really on top of things one day and the next it would be, "Arthur, Arthur, where is Arthur?" The 1974–1975 season also turned out to be "a bit of a rough year in terms of logistics," and at one point Stearns says he confronted Arthur about his spacey presence. "What about Carlota?" came the reply. "She's just as spaced as I am. She's *more* spaced out than I am!" Stearns replied that Schoolman "delivers the goods on time."

Arthur's unpredictable presence didn't prevent him from maintaining the Kitchen's experimental trajectory and supporting its neighborhood musicians while removing some of the glass walls that were difficult to detect yet limiting to the venue's potential. Having poured synthesizers, guitars, drums, whistles, computers, video cameras, slides, folk music, melody, and songs into the mix of minimalism and post-minimalism, as well as compositional approaches that didn't fit into either of these rubrics, Kitchen regulars believed they were operating in an environment that was open, democratic, and innovative—where many of the old rules had been cast aside and no new ones inscribed. Yet elements of the cultural elitism that underpinned the serialist regime remained, and Arthur, inspired by Allen Ginsberg's searing critique of snobbery, attempted to loosen up some of these attitudes by introducing popular elements into the venue. If anything, his superficial ineffectiveness helped him get away with more, not less.

"Arthur was equally comfortable with the avant-garde and quirky pop," says Schoolman, who was accustomed to the avant-garde *not* crossing over as a matter of respectability, yet couldn't help but be impressed by the range of Arthur's music program. "I was fascinated that one person could be so interested in so many seemingly different genres." Stearns was also appreciative of Arthur's initiatives and notes that the 1974–1975 season marked the moment when the Kitchen "really started to fly." That meant his music director must have been doing a good job, and even though Arthur could be casual, disorganized, and prickly, he was also fun and enjoyable to work with. "Arthur was very lovable, so everybody would pitch in and help him through the rough spots," remembers Stearns. "Nothing was easy for Arthur—everything was extraordinarily difficult—but he was an absolutely brilliant guy. He did what he needed to do and built a brilliant program."

3 **Alternatives** (1975–1977)

SoHo might have become the fulcrum of the downtown art and music scenes, but its raw industrial spaces rented out at a minimum of three hundred dollars a month. That made SoHo twice as expensive as the East Village, so creative types who were struggling to earn money began to head east, where they reminded themselves that the expansive contours of downtown's lofts weren't essential to their artistic survival and might even blunt their creative edge. Since mean-spirited landlords refused to respect the city's rent-control regulations and deliberately allowed the tenements of the East Village to become run-down, that was about the only comfort available.[1] It was usually a relief when the buildings were converted to co-ops—assuming their former owners didn't burn them down first in an act of nihilistic retribution.

Initially unable to pay his way even in the East Village, where he stayed courtesy of Allen Ginsberg's hospitality, Arthur continued to entertain the idea of moving to Hawaii for several months after Muriel Fujii visited New York during the winter of 1973. He wrote songs about her—songs that were "maybe too sentimental," he confessed in a letter—and called regularly until a $109 phone bill arrived in the mail. But by the time he moved into a cockroach-infested, run-down storefront on East Fourth Street at the beginning of 1975, the letters had slowed to a virtual standstill, and Arthur appeared to have come to terms with his new environment. "It has been nice practicing meditation here," he wrote to Fujii from his new home. "I don't know if I should conceive of the brick walls as real or not. I guess they're real."

The existence of the Puerto Rican kids who walked the neighborhood's streets required less guesswork, especially after they stripped down and vandalized Arthur's VW Beetle. Their presence became more pronounced when a small group of them burgled "the dump" (as Ernie Brooks nicknamed the storefront) and, having tied up Arthur, the raiders grabbed his stereo and money before they started to size up his cello. "Arthur was wriggling around on the floor and said, 'If you take my cello, you're going to have to kill me, otherwise when I get loose I'm going to kill you!'" recalls Brooks. "They didn't take the cello." But although the East Village could be tough, Puerto Ricans also provided the neighborhood with a sense of community that was less readily available in the more gentrified parts of the city. That appealed to many downtowners, as did the burgeoning activity of young Latin musicians, who nurtured their own creative network in venues such as the Nuyorican Poets Café and the New Rican Village — venues that are rarely mentioned in histories of New York City, which tend to ignore all Puerto Ricans but the criminal element.[2]

Arthur's East Village odyssey took a decisive turn in 1975 when he followed Ginsberg to 437 East Twelfth Street, a run-down tenement situated between First Avenue and Avenue A. Ginsberg had moved into the building earlier that spring, after his co-residents in his Tenth Street tenement decided to move to co-op status before he felt ready to buy. When apartment number thirty in the Twelfth Street building became available, he got in touch with Arthur, who invited a bass player acquaintance, Jack Majewski, to take up the second bedroom. The band members of Television, decked out in black polyester suits and dark sunglasses, also moved into the tenement, as did the guitarist Denise Mercedes, while Larry Fagin, John Godfrey, Greg Masters, Simon Pettet, and others fortified the poet contingent. When the critical mass of poets and other creative types outweighed the diminishing presence of older residents, 437 East Twelfth Street became known as "Poet's Building." With an abandoned bus-shelter-turned-crack-house sitting opposite the entrance, the flourishing heroin market controlled by the Mafia stationed on the First Avenue corner of Twelfth Street, and Puerto Rican gangs positioned across the block, they had plenty of gritty urban realism to absorb as they made their way in and out of their home.

Left to right: Allen Ginsberg, Peter Brodsky, and Tom Pickard standing outside Poet's Building on East Twelfth Street, 1981. Photograph by Joanna Voit. Courtesy of Peter Hale.

Arthur would end up living in 437 East Twelfth Street for the rest of his life, but he still hankered after San Francisco, and that might have been on his mind when he met Sydney Murray in a luncheonette café in the East Village early in the spring of 1975. "I had a pin on my jacket that had an image of a Tibetan Buddhist, and Arthur asked about that," recalls Murray, whose blonde hair, warm smile, and inner spiritual calm appear to have activated Arthur's nostalgia for the West Coast. "He asked me if I was a Buddhist. He was pretty active in Buddhism." Arthur and Murray became "sort of" boyfriend and girlfriend, although there were times when it wasn't clear if anything was keeping them together other than love. "We were both people who needed a lot of space and independence," explains Murray, who also lived in the neighborhood. "I didn't really relish the thought of defining myself through a particular relationship."

Murray says she adored the pacing of the *Instrumentals* concert and was also amazed by Arthur's drive. "He could sit down and, almost no matter where he was, pull out this paper" — score paper that he would stuff in his anorak pockets — "and just start writing. Sometimes it seemed like he

Sydney Murray c. 1977–1978. Photograph by Patricia Brennecke.
Courtesy of Sydney Murray.

started with a melody, other times he would begin with a phrase. Song-writing was really important to him, and he wanted his songs to have more exposure." Drawn to jazz and activist politics, neither of which attracted Arthur, Murray never became a cheerleader. But both of them were non-verbal people who discovered they could talk with each other for hours on end, and in the summer of 1975 Arthur invited Murray to move into his new apartment. Of Ginsberg, Murray recalls the poet's "generosity towards Arthur, and his fostering of more self-acceptance on Arthur's part," and she notes this approach contrasted with Arthur's account of his experiences with Ajari Warwick.

By the time Murray moved in, Arthur had started to rent out the apartment's second bedroom to Rhys Chatham, who remembers finding it easy to live with Arthur. With so many cheap restaurants in the neighborhood, the composer-musicians rarely felt the need to cook, and they were also respectfully discreet when the other took a bath in the tub, which was located in the kitchen. Although he was underwhelmed by the attention his roommate was receiving from John Hammond, he was happy enough when the A&R executive sat on a board that awarded a grant to Arthur; then a part-time harpsichord tuner, Chatham had run out of work following the introduction of a new digital tuner, and the Hammond-assisted windfall meant there'd be "no problem with the rent that month." Inasmuch as there were tensions, they emerged around music. While Chatham enjoyed listening to Arthur hook up his cello to a range of effects units that were normally used with guitars, Arthur was so troubled by Chatham's decision to start playing free jazz on a newly acquired saxophone he suggested they begin to rent a rehearsal studio. Pooling their resources with Peter Gordon and Garrett List, they found a basement in Westbeth, a federally regulated artist co-op situated on West Street in the West Village where Merce Cunningham also lived and worked. "That solved the noise problem," notes Chatham.

By 1975, Arthur had developed a network of musician friends who would hang out at the Broome Street Bar, situated across the street from the Kitchen, and Phoebe's, which was located on the Bowery, at the western edge of the East Village. "Phoebe's was an interdisciplinary bar avant la lettre," remembers List, who says that experimental scenesters would go there to hang out with jazz musicians, actors, theater people, and poets. "Ginsberg was a regular and Arthur might have introduced us. The bar workers were mostly gay men and there was also a sprinkling of very pretty, out-of-work actresses. It was fantastic." As he settled into the rhythm of downtown life, Arthur became particularly tight with Gordon, and made a habit of dropping by his railroad apartment on East Fifth Street in order to listen to music and work on songs. "We all lived in close proximity to each other and went to the same breakfast places, bars and performance spaces, which consisted of living lofts as well as alternative art spaces," Chatham told David Toop many years later. "This prompted the sharing of ideas and all manner of cross-experimentation."[3]

During this period the network of musicians who lived in the East Village, as well as in SoHo, TriBeCa, and their surrounds, came to resemble a rhizome—a root structure that grows horizontally rather than vertically and, because it contains no central or hierarchical point of organization, is potentially democratic and egalitarian thanks to its decentralized, multi-nodal structure.[4] The availability of cheap space combined with mazy streets and low-rise architecture made downtown a perfect place for artistic networks to develop and connect into other networks—to develop rhizomatically—and this potential was apparent to Philip Glass when he returned to New York in 1967 and discovered a "supportive environment" in which musicians pursued "the reform of language" in a variety of spontaneous gestures.[5] Since then, organizations such as the Kitchen and figures such as Glass, Reich, and Young had started to establish reputations and visibility that threatened to disturb downtown's flat structure, but they were far from dominant, and their growing prominence was offset by the arrival of so many artists and musicians during the first half of the 1970s. Including Arthur among their ranks, the new arrivals treated established figures and institutions with respect, but were committed primarily to the development of downtown as a lateral, mobile, spontaneous neighborhood that housed the "creative" and the "real." Their purpose was to develop their own projects . . . and to help out friends with their projects . . . and to explore collaborative possibilities . . .[6] "We were a close family playing in each other's bands and Arthur was a pillar in this scene," Chatham added in his conversation with Toop.[7]

Arthur missed the West Coast all the same, and his commitment to the nascent network of downtown musicians received its ultimate test when Murray returned to California in the autumn of 1975. After much debate, he decided to remain in New York and to begin making cross-country journeys in order to keep the relationship alive. "I think there was a part of Arthur that would have liked to go back to California, but he felt he needed to stay in New York for the music," says Murray. "Arthur was extremely focused, while I was extremely unfocused. I think he felt like California might be a better place for someone who didn't have a significant ambition." Arthur had turned to Ernie Brooks for advice. "I said, 'You should go there, you should work it out, that's clearly what you want!'" remembers the ex–Modern Lover. "He would say, 'I can't do it, I don't know how to deal with her!'" Brooks believes Arthur was "intensely happy" with Murray and "would have loved to raise a family" with her, but maintains he "wasn't able to control his desire to go to music all the time." "He let the relationship go because it was demanding. Arthur was just so committed to his music. He was not reliable to do anything else." In the end, he dealt with the transition in the way he knew best—by writing a song. "When you went to California," ran the first verse.

Thoughts like bells rang in my ears each day
Bells hidden in the rooftops
Sunny blue or cloudy gray
But that sky does not determine
The way I think our kisses were
And somehow when I mention you
I always think of her.

On one of his CVs, Arthur says he moved to New York in 1973, but only settled there in 1976.

Sobossek's

Because shows at funded spaces such as the Kitchen only came around once a year or so, even the most successful composer-musicians had to eke out gigs, and having decided to stay on East Twelfth Street, Arthur started to hustle harder than ever. "I'm as broke as when I spoke to you," he wrote to Chuck and Emily in August 1975, "but there is the possibility of making money writing some record reviews." Arthur added that he was approaching an artistic crossroads and needed to move with care. "If I become too much like the conventional singer, I'm sure to alienate my present supporters and dislocate my future acceptance as well. On the other hand, wearing a robe of excesses and useless weirdness as a means of attracting attention would obviously, in the end, be more destructive."

Some middle ground opened up when Chatham invited Arthur to play a regular spot at Sobossek's, a bar located on the Bowery between Fifth Street and Sixth Street. Owned by Stan Sobossek, a visual artist who had made money selling large abstract canvases, the location boasted a wooden interior, a large fireplace, and an unused theater stage. It was the last element that grabbed Chatham's attention when he started to work there as a bartender, and visualizing musicians rather than actors, the former music director of the Kitchen became the unofficial music director of Sobossek's when he made Arthur his first booking. Arthur ended up appearing several times during the spring of 1976, and other downtowners with a popular sensibility, including Gordon and List, were also invited to play. The spirit of the program would only shift when Chatham knew he was going to need to get away early, in which case he would book Gordon to perform his

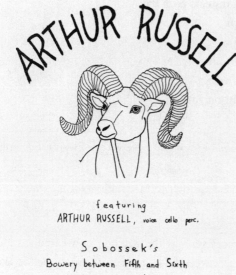

featuring
ARTHUR RUSSELL, voice cello perc.

Sobossek's
Bowery between Fifth and Sixth
Tuesday March 30
9:00 PM
FREE

Sobossek's poster, 1976. Like other downtown musicians, Arthur scratched around for places to perform, and often played in unconventional spaces. When a gig arrived he drew up his own posters, photocopied them on the cheap, and then stuck them up wherever he could. Wheat paste was used as glue. Designed by Arthur Russell. Courtesy of Tom Lee.

uptown-inspired *Atonal Variations*. On one occasion Gordon succeeded in emptying out the bar in five minutes flat.[8]

Switching between guitar and cello, Arthur combined his own material with traditional folk songs from Estil C. Ball, Malvina Reynolds, and Fred McDowell, and if the audience seemed to be unduly focused on eating dinner or ordering drinks, he would tell a few jokes to liven up the atmosphere. "Sometimes it wasn't too funny, but it would really pick up when I got drunk," Arthur noted in a 1987 interview.[9] Wondering how his friend was able to switch between the apparent extremes of compositional music and folk, Chatham was compelled to do some astrological research. "Arthur was twenty-nine degrees fifty-nine minutes Taurus, only one minute of longitude from being a Gemini," he explains. "It is so close I think we can consider Arthur a Gemini, and I know that Arthur certainly thought of himself in this way. His working on a number of different kinds of music at the same time is a Gemini thing. Also, he had Leo rising, which makes sense as Leo rules performance."

Ginsberg

Allen Ginsberg heard Arthur play at Sobossek's and was so impressed he returned to the venue with Steven Hall, a promising young poet who had studied with Larry Fagin while he was still going to high school in Delaware. Hall had met Ginsberg when he traveled to Twelfth Street to see Fagin, and he continued his studies with the beat poet at the Naropa Institute, where he also worked with William S. Burroughs and Chögyam Trungpa — Trungpa being Ginsberg's principal teacher and the guiding force of the school. "Trungpa was rather liberal and wild," recalls Hall, who became one of Ginsberg's boyfriends. "He was accepting of the homo element, which was of the utmost importance to Allen, as well as radical and alternative approaches to writing and the arts in general." At the end of the summer Hall traveled back to New York with Ginsberg, and a couple of months later the beat poet told him about "this guy Arthur Russell." According to Ginsberg, hearing Russell was like hearing William Carlos Williams, the New Jersey poet whose reading at the Guggenheim Museum in 1950 changed his life.

Arthur met Hall in Ginsberg's apartment at a later date and, having initially cut a shy figure, asked him (quite aggressively) if he wanted to go to bed. Although Hall declined, the two of them started socializing, and when Arthur played him "Don't Forget about Me," Hall wondered how anyone could write such a beautiful song. The opening lines ran:

> If you try and wait
> Til we reach each other's arms again
> You might miss the only
> Chance to keep our love alive
> There's no way to stop
> Your feelings sometimes
> It could drive you to be untrue in the end
> It can drive you to be untrue in the end
> And our love could grow so great our cup would
> Overflow with love
> When you're loving me.

As the appeal to stay lingered, the protagonist of the song offered the gift of freedom, asking only for a thought in return.

Steven Hall, 1975. Photographer unknown. Courtesy of Steven Hall.

If he takes your hand and leads you to a quiet place
If he makes you want to be alone with him
Go ahead, because like I said
You know you know you are free
But baby don't forget about me
Don't forget about me.

By the end of the song, Hall realized he had found his "teacher."

Only Ginsberg had realized Arthur might be interested in men. Chuck,

Emily, Kate, and Julie weren't aware that he might have been attracted to boys at school, while Kent Goshorn says there was never more than the faintest suggestion his friend was gay. Arthur's best friends in San Francisco were equally oblivious, as were the girlfriends with whom he had developed physically and emotionally intense relationships. Yet Ginsberg, who was equipped with a set of gay antennae, detected Arthur's penchant for men and later announced he was "the first," having enjoyed a fling with Arthur in a motel in Connecticut.[10] Gleaning some tips from the beat poet, who was prolific as well as persistent when it came to approaching other men, Arthur started trying to pick up guys, and his spurned approach to Hall might have been his first attempt. Following Ginsberg, who in turn was partially channeling Trungpa, Arthur drew on his Buddhist beliefs in order to become open, direct, and spontaneous in his approaches to men, with whom he sought not a binding commitment but a free exchange of energy and pleasure. The practice of cruising brimmed with spiritual purpose.

Talking on the phone, Arthur described his shifting orientation to Allaudin Mathieu as if he were in a therapy session. "Arthur's coming out was a burst, and when he began to regale me with tales of his emerging gay life, I was shocked and fascinated," says the tutor, who footed the bill for the calls. "There was, in fact, a certain mutuality to the conversations: his life was fascinating to me, and to a certain extent, I lived it vicariously through his narratives. He sensed this, I think. He was sincere in asking advice, and I gave it in a heartfelt way, so he knew I was fond of him." Arthur kept other West Coast friends abreast of developments. "When he decided he was gay, he told me flat out, 'Women don't turn me on anymore,' and that was that," recalls Jeff Whittier. Alan Abrams remembers Arthur telling him that he "felt something else happening" when he went to his first gay bar. After that experience, Arthur also began to feel that "women were suddenly more interested in him than he was in them," adds Abrams.

Gay sexuality and Buddhism merged with music when Arthur (cello) joined Steven Hall (guitar), Steven Taylor (guitar), and occasionally Peter Orlovsky (banjo, vocals) and started to perform with Ginsberg around the autumn of 1976. The group played a series of small concerts in New York City and then went on a mini-tour to Boston, which included an appearance at the Stone Soup Gallery. Aware that he was only able to get a concert because of his literary fame, Ginsberg was the first to recognize the limits of his playing and songwriting skills, and he resisted attempts to make his

A year later, Arthur Russell (left) performing with Denise Mercedes, Steven Hall, and Allen Ginsberg at the YMHA in New York City, 1977. Photograph by R. Dulman. Courtesy of Peter Hale.

music more adventurous, choosing instead to make a virtue out of his simplicity. "I have been an adult all of my life, even when I was young, so now it is time for my second childhood—to have fun and be a pop star," he told Hall. Putting Buddhism into action, Ginsberg chanted Tibetan mantras over a simple accompaniment or an improvised drone, and every now and again the musicians would break out into an extended blues jam, at which point the mantras gave way to in-your-face songs such as "Everybody's a Little Homosexual, Whether They Like It or Not." "We got a kick out of playing songs about sucking cock and boys," says Hall. "As a songwriter, Allen became a liberating and political influence on both Arthur and me."

Ginsberg invited Arthur back into the recording studio in March 1976 when he started to work on his next album, *First Blues*. Jon Sholle (bass, mandolin, banjo, electric guitar, harmonizer, ukulele, maracas, drums), David Mansfield (mandolin, bass guitar, pedal steel guitar, violin), and Steven Taylor (congas, recorder, backing vocals) joined Arthur (cello, tambourine), while Ginsberg sang to his heart's content as he squeezed the harmonium and clicked away on a set of song sticks and finger cymbals. Combining country, the blues, and gospel with a dash of Buddhist dharma, the band recorded "Gospel Nobel Truths" and "CIA Dope Calypso" under the customary light-touch production of John Hammond. "I remember Arthur as kind, quiet, and somewhat intense," says Taylor, who would go on to become Ginsberg's main accompanist. "He was a beautiful cat."

Although Arthur also began exchanging ideas with Ginsberg about Buddhism when he relocated to the East Coast, there's no reason to believe Arthur adopted him as a surrogate Yuko Nonomura, and Whittier insists the poet was way behind the Shingon priest when it came to Buddhist learning. "His knowledge of Eastern religion was completely phoney," says Whittier, who tested Ginsberg during a trip to the Tibetan Buddhist Centre in Kensington, California, where Kalu Rinpoche was giving a talk. (Arthur was also in the car.) "From observing Rinpoche, he knew that he was a great man, but his knowledge of Buddhism was pathetic." Yet Hall maintains that Ginsberg boosted the spread of Buddhism in the United States by championing Jack Kerouac's take on the religion and opening the Naropa Institute, and in his conversations with Arthur, he encouraged him to become more self-sufficient in his practice. Trungpa's *The Myth of Freedom and the Way of Meditation* (a Ginsberg recommendation) set out ideas that would become important to Arthur's philosophical outlook: that the moment of inspiration was a heightened moment of poetry; that beauty could lie in the outwardly ordinary; and that expressions of childlike innocence and spontaneity should be treasured. In addition, Ginsberg showed Arthur (in a way that proved to be beyond Nonomura) how Buddhist principles might be expressed in an artistic life. "When I first met him, Arthur and I would talk about using Buddhism as some kind of force in pop music," recalls Hall. "We wanted to write songs that used these ideas. Arthur was really passionate about this." Buddhist-inspired images of the sky and the clouds; of rain, water, and the ocean; of animals, light, and even miracles would go on to suffuse Arthur's songs for the rest of his life.

Nevertheless Arthur didn't follow Ginsberg's political lead. As a teenager, Arthur had resembled a countercultural activist: he grew long hair, he read the beats, he experimented with LSD, he rebelled against his hometown, he lived on a Buddhist commune, he embraced Indian classical music, and he became close with one of the most prominent activists in the countercultural movement—Ginsberg. But in contrast to Ginsberg, Arthur didn't participate in the antiwar protests, and he also remained equally detached from gay liberation politics. It's possible Arthur's conscious dissociation from activist politics during his time in San Francisco was grounded in his over-investment in being different; he had spent a good part of his adolescence wondering if he was unassimilable, and he was only seventeen years old when he arrived on the West Coast. But by the time he arrived in New York, the failure of the countercultural movement to transform society suggested that the moment for a less ambitious, less demonstrative outlook had arrived. "I saw the fallout of the drug scene that resulted in the broken promises of freedom and free love," says Hall. "The heavier drugs such as speed and heroin resulted in a dissipation of creative energies and the deaths of artists and writers. The countercultural movement failed politically because of a loss of focus and lack of long-term vision."

Skepticism about the viability of the countercultural movement had become widespread by the early to mid-1970s, in part because, as Manuel DeLanda has noted, activists "thought they were going to achieve everything within the 60's — and what they wanted was not achievable, period."[11] Having attempted to "break through" too quickly, Arthur turned from LSD to Buddhism, and he continued to engage with the religion not because he was especially devout, but because it provided him with a moral and philosophical framework that coincided with his view of the world. "The desire was to express ourselves through our work," comments Hall. "The radical lifestyles we led were enough, and presenting our lifestyles in our work was our political activity. We had no time for overt political work and a subtle bias against political art, which we felt was compromised by its stridency."

Arthur and Hall didn't so much disagree with Ginsberg's public stand on a range of issues as seek to go about creating a political reality according to a linked set of criteria — criteria that were concerned with working collaboratively, forming a nonhierarchical community, developing an expressive form of art, and enacting a local politics of transformation and liberation. "We thought that we would rather play music and live out the principles Allen taught as a matter of praxis," adds Hall. "To write a song about men having sex was just as political as protesting for freedom of speech. Working as queer songwriters in the macho, straight downtown world was a very radical stance, especially when we encountered the rock and punk elements, and sometimes we were in physical danger as openly gay men. Allen operated within a bubble of fame and was tolerated as an eccentric figure by the establishment; we were in the trenches with no such protection on the streets."

Concerts

Arthur played a key role in the appointment of Garrett List as the next music director of the Kitchen, a position List held for two years. "It certainly wasn't Bob [Stearns] who asked me to do it," says the trombonist. "I was much too radical for Bob." Dedicated to visceral music, List had little time for Philip Glass ("I sat through a performance of *Music in Twelve Parts* and it seemed pretty nice") and no time at all for Steve Reich ("*Drumming* drove me mad"). "The atmosphere at the time was very clean, postmodern, and definitely not 'street,' which is where I was coming from," he explains. "I preferred Arthur, Rhys, Peter Gordon, Anthony Braxton, George Lewis, and, of course, Frederic Rzewski. I was also impressed by the blues-oriented new jazz of the guys who played in my band." Having played on *Instrumentals*, which he "enjoyed very much," List found himself particularly drawn to Arthur. "His music had 'soul' in the sense that we used the word," he notes. "It was completely real and sincere, and it could be listened to without thinking. He had some of his own arrogance—who doesn't?—and artistic pretensions, but his real concern was to find a way to communicate with people by finding a common denominator. In my opinion, that was something that was very much missing in the downtown art music scene. Arthur's was a very noble path."

Not wanting to "break with what had gone before," List programmed downtown composers such as Beth Anderson, Jim Burton, Philip Glass, Peter Gordon, Tom Johnson, Joan La Barbara, Charlemagne Palestine, Richard Peck, and Frederic Rzewski. But following Arthur's example, he also slipped in a new aesthetic. "Arthur and I were both interested in developing an eclectic movement where barriers didn't exist," he notes. "Arthur introduced white pop music into the Kitchen, whereas my own contribution was more to do with introducing new black music." More specifically, List started to program cutting-edge African American jazz, because jazz music, as he would later write, "gave me the permission to enjoy myself and feel comfortable about wanting to simply please the audience, something that has been excluded from the thinking of most composers of 'serious music' today."[12]

Jazz had established a foothold in SoHo when Cecil Taylor and others began to play in lofts in the early 1960s, and the scene was consolidated when Ornette Coleman moved into a loft on Prince Street (later called

Artists House) toward the end of the decade. The so-called "loft jazz" scene took off a couple of years later when the Newport Jazz Festival was staged in New York in 1972, and its director, George Wein, decided to exclude local jazz musicians. "Angered by this exclusivity, trumpeter James DuBois, bassist Juma Sultan and saxophonist Sam Rivers joined a crowd of new-jazz musicians who squeezed into Studio We [one of the earliest jazz lofts] to complain, argue and—finally—to organize a counterfestival that took place in 18 locations," wrote Stanley Crouch in the *New York Times*. "The following year, Wein responded by incorporating many of the new musicians into his festival."[13] Surveying a scene that also included spots such as Studio Rivbea at 24 Bond Street and Ali's Alley at 77 Greene Street, George Gruntz, director of the renowned Berlin Jazz Festival, declared a few years later: "Only here in the lofts is there such exciting music—so many new ideas, such enthusiasm, such control of the instruments. It's the most exciting jazz in town."[14] Writing in the *Village Voice* a few months later, Gary Giddens would note that no coherent style could be associated with the loft jazz network. "Loft jazz is any jazz played in a loft," he stated matter-of-factly.[15] George Lewis of the Association for the Advancement of Creative Musicians (AACM), an important player in the scene, points out that many of the musicians who were involved in the loft period "deeply resented the reduction of the diversity of their approaches to the term 'loft jazz.'"[16]

Jazz had already brushed with minimalism without making a significant impression. La Monte Young played jazz saxophone, although that was hard to detect in his music; Terry Riley and Steve Reich declared modal jazz to be an influence, even though their compositions never sounded like jazz; and jazz outfits such as Karl Berger and Friends and the Peter La Barbara Quartet also appeared at the Kitchen in 1972 (in events that weren't programmed by Chatham). But then came List, who met the black jazz innovator Anthony Braxton in 1972 around the time he debuted at the original Kitchen and was subsequently invited to play at Studio Rivbea, Joe Lee Wilson's Ladies Fort, and Ali's Alley ("the most remarkable jazz loft thus far," in the words of Crouch).[17] List appreciated jazz for its philosophical trajectory as much as its aesthetics; committed to the idea of making music as a social act, he had his doubts about the "lone genius" model that was favored by the European and U.S. avant-garde, and although he enjoyed the power that could come with being a composer, as a musician he understood that "a redistribution of this power might have appreciable benefits." The discovery that this kind of redistribution had already taken place in jazz was a revelation. "While I was mature enough to know that the music that would be 'my voice' was not jazz [...] jazz provided me with a model of an art form that already had achieved several goals that needed to be found in my own creative endeavors," he explains.

Encouraging the downtown compositional and jazz movements to open a dialogue, List programmed Don Cherry, Jack DeJohnette, the Revolutionary Ensemble, and Cecil Taylor, as well as John Paul Amrod and Richard Peck, who combined formal training in composition with an interest in jazz. Then, at the end of his first year as music director, he ran a twelve-night series of jazz concerts (titled the "Jazz Composer's Orchestra Concerts"). "Partly inspired by Arthur's bravery, Garrett felt free to invite all his jazz friends," notes Chatham. "He did this to a much greater extent than Arthur, but only because the scene was ready for it and Arthur had established the precedent. It was very exciting." Noting that the already limited number of available concert dates for compositional music had just become significantly slimmer, a number of neighborhood composers managed to contain their enthusiasm, but there was also an appreciation that, in the words of Robert Stearns, these "were the first true efforts at multicultural programming," which took place long before such efforts "became a requirement" to attract funds. Undertaken at a time when the African American population in the neighborhood was minuscule, the decision to bring jazz into the Kitchen "caused waves," notes Chatham.

List traces his programming outlook back to the moment when, as a young composer aged about eighteen, he went for a drive and started to think about the beauty of Beethoven's Seventh Symphony, only to catch himself whistling an Elvis Presley song. "This wild contradiction (or what seemed to be) was the first inkling of what was really happening in my musical mind, and, although it took a couple more years of intense work to make something out of it, this contradiction became, not two forces working against one another, but a kind of unity," List explained later, in a piece commissioned for the Kitchen's twentieth anniversary.[18] List says that, along with Arthur, he attempted to develop an eclectic agenda in which it was recognized that serious music didn't have to be sophisticated; that practice was more important than theory; that instead of colonizing music from other cultures (as in Reich's use of African rhythms), musicians should play with people from other cultures in order to develop new forms; and that the culture of the time and place in which the musician lived should be the real source of her or his inspiration. "I would have put salsa into the program if I could have found someone to do it the right way," he adds.

The absence of salsa reveals less about possible blind spots in List's program than the degree to which downtown was still marked by segmentation rather than fusion. "Salsa was right over there in the East Village, but there was this disconnect between scenes," comments Ned Sublette, who moved to New York during List's two-year tenure as music director. "From what I could see, the Kitchen made far more of an effort than many to open up to various scenes, but ultimately everybody was in their own little musical town. Even though there were black music directors subsequently, the people at the Kitchen were white folks from middle-class backgrounds, and they didn't necessarily know how to hang in other scenes. I mean, the New Rican Village wasn't going to invite Garrett List in, either." The Kitchen might have been at the forefront of attempts to break down musical and social boundaries, yet downtown remained relatively segregated. "It took a long time for people to get together who should have gotten together much, much sooner," adds Sublette.

As List's program unfolded, the Kitchen changed. Having operated as a fairly relaxed neighborhood space that existed for young, vagabond composers, it became a high-pressure venue. "Whoever got to play at the Kitchen was pretty much sure of getting a review in the *New York Times* and the *Village Voice*, and people were coming from all over, including Europe, to play there," remembers List. "The music director of the Kitchen was a very powerful person." That power increased when Philip Glass staged a work-in-progress performance of his score for Robert Wilson's avant-garde opera *Einstein on the Beach* in the venue. "There was tremendous anticipation for the collaboration between Phil and Bob Wilson," notes Stearns, who was enjoying his last year as director of the venue. An audience of two hundred squeezed into the Kitchen to hear the preview, after which the production traveled around Europe during the summer of 1976 and had its U.S. premiere in November at the Metropolitan Opera—one of the first occasions when downtown trespassed into the dominion of uptown.

Arthur made his first appearance in the Kitchen's 1975–1976 season when he played alongside Kathy Acker, Laurie Anderson, Ernie Brooks, Jim Burton, Rhys Chatham, Philip Glass, Jill Kroesen, Garrett List, Charlie

Peter Gordon performs *Symphony In Four Movements (Music: Words)* at the Kitchen, 4 February 1976. *Left to right*: Garrett List with his back turned to the audience, Arthur Russell, Ernie Brooks, Rhys Chatham, Scott Johnson, Kenneth (then Keshavan) Maslak, and Peter Gordon. Photograph by Teri Slotkin. Courtesy of Robert Stearns.

Morrow, and others in Peter Gordon's *Symphony in Four Movements (Music: Words)*. Staged in February 1976, the performance announced Gordon's tonal and pop-influenced outlook to the downtown scene. At one point Kroesen sang

Don't hurt me baby
Don't do me wrong
I've loved you so long
Can't you see Corporate Violence is killing me?

In the final movement Acker assumed Gordon's persona and delivered a fragment of a song that was never fully realized. As with *Instrumentals*, the concert stirred up some talk. "The use of tonal harmony and melodic fragments was probably part of the same spectrum as *Instrumentals*," says Gordon. "One thing I shared with Arthur was the idea of deconstructing pop-songs down to their basic harmonic and melodic elements, and then reassembling these components over an extended time."

Arthur also played a number of concerts outside the petri dish of the Kitchen, which in the end was only one of a number of important downtown venues. In May 1975 his sparse, ambient composition *Reach One*

(*With Two Fender Rhodes*) was performed on two separate occasions at the Experimental Intermedia Foundation, which had been operating out of Phill Niblock's loft on 224 Centre Street since December 1973.[19] And in February 1976 he made an appearance at the Jolly Monk, situated on Warren Street in TriBeCa, where he sang songs as he played guitar. Other appearances evaporated unrecorded into the sonic stratosphere until Glass, the Kitchen's karmic godfather, invited Arthur to play a piece for cello he had written for the Mabou Mines stage performance of Samuel Beckett's *Cascando*. Glass knew what it was like to struggle for money, and noting that Arthur needed a job, he wrote the *Cascando* score with him in mind. The fact that Beckett had been such an influence on Glass, and that the play was being directed by JoAnne Akalaitis, to whom Glass was married, made the gesture all the more personal.

Glass and Arthur had already developed a friendship based on "mutual admiration." Arthur was drawn to Glass, whose music was more emotional than that of Reich, while Glass thought that Arthur was "very gifted." "I went to a lot of his performances, and I took people to see him," says Glass. "You could go to a concert and find five people there. It was very much underground. But the interesting thing was that Arthur always felt he had the potential to be a popular composer." Sitting in the audience, Glass often wondered if Arthur was playing a piece or fooling around, and says he would "just do things until something would crawl up." Yet Glass remained captivated. "It wasn't that Arthur wore strange clothes, or had overtly odd behavior," he adds. "He was just deeply odd. He would seem like a normal person, but he wasn't. Being odd wasn't an affectation. If anything he tried to pass himself off as a more ordinary person than he actually was. Arthur was a very colorful person to say the least."

The Mabou Mines production of *Cascando* opened to strong reviews at the Public Theater in April 1976,[20] although Glass was left to wonder about what had happened to his composition. "Arthur had changed everything," he recalls. "It was all Arthur Russell! I said, 'It's beautiful!' and Arthur said, 'Do you mind what I did?' I said, 'No, no, I think it's fine.' I thought it was hilariously funny." *Cascando* toured Europe between June and August 1976, stopping off in Berlin (where the company met Beckett), as well as in Nancy, France, and Florence. Arthur headed off on his own at every opportunity, normally returning a few days later. "He had this incredible energy and desire to experience as much as possible," says Sydney Murray, who traveled with Arthur. Back in New York, Mabou Mines (and Arthur) continued to perform *Cascando* from January to March 1977, after which the show moved to Rhode Island. Meanwhile Murray stayed in Amsterdam for a month, after which she returned to New York (with "about twenty-nine cents" in her pocket) and then made her way up to Boston, where she started to waitress. Jerry Harrison, whom she had met through Ernie Brooks, was one of the morning regulars at the café where she worked. Later Murray returned to the West Coast, while Harrison traveled south to join a band called Talking Heads, which was on the lookout for a fourth member and might have even considered Arthur for this role.

Pop and the Flying Hearts

More artists graduated from art schools between 1974 and 1984 than at any time in U.S. history, and as Marvin Taylor notes, the "excitement of what was going on Downtown drew them to New York."[21] On arrival some were disappointed to find that the SoHo gallery scene had become institutionalized and elements of the visual arts had lost their creative edge, and so turned to music, which appeared to be comparatively open. "Performance art and rock performance offered a fresh challenge to many young artists," the *New York Times* critic John Rockwell noted. "Rock entailed fewer technical demands than classical music, and seemed less of a closed craft guild. It provided at least the possibility of self-support. Above all, it was the actual, usual language that people — not 'the people' so much as fellow artists — preferred to speak."[22] According to Simon Frith and Howard Horne, the "most significant art/pop community came together in the Mercer Arts Center," which encouraged "the kinds of collaboration between high and low art staged in the 1960s in [Andy Warhol's] the Factory," and enabled experimental artists such as Laurie Anderson to meet "a new generation of pop-oriented art school graduates."[23]

Arthur became involved musically with Anderson, whom he might have met at Jean Dupuy's "Soup and Tart" evening, or more probably during rehearsals for Peter Gordon's *Symphony in Four Movements (Music: Words)*. "She was kind of set apart from us," remembers Jill Kroesen, "but she was around." Arthur played drums and cello in Anderson's first pop group, the short-lived Fast Food Band, which also included Gordon, Scott Johnson, and Jack Majewski.[24] "I loved his sense of panic, and that he was always much more worried than anybody else," says Anderson. "Your heart kind of goes out to someone who looks like they're going to fall apart. But he was also very, very funny, and dark." Although Arthur played as if he was in "another world," Anderson was fine with that because the band was "pretty loose," and she remained "a big admirer of his work."[25] Gordon has a somewhat contrary recollection: "I think Arthur felt underappreciated by Laurie, which was probably an accurate feeling," he says. Others talk similarly of a vexed relationship. Murray, for example, recalls Arthur being critical of one of Anderson's New York concerts, even though he expressed an interest in the spoken component of the performance. Donald Murk (who worked as Arthur's personal manager during the late 1970s) remembers Arthur wondering about her originality. "At one point he said she was ripping him off, only substituting the violin for his cello," says Murk.

Arthur was more taken with Talking Heads, and he deepened the conversation between art and pop at the Kitchen when he persuaded List to schedule the band in March 1976. "It was in the air to break down these context barriers," comments List, who was happy to go with the flow because Arthur organized the night. In contrast to Jonathan Richman and the Modern Lovers, whose appearances at the Kitchen amounted to a fading echo of an ex-band, David Byrne, Chris Frantz, and Martina Weymouth treated the gig as a serious opportunity and, true to their art-school background, positioned themselves as artists who aimed to explore (as they put it in the program notes) "the commercial accessibility of rock and roll sound and contemporary popular language."[26] Their turn to music was part of a broader trend. "When I came to New York I guess I was very naive," Byrne told a reporter from *Art News*. "I expected the art world to be very pure and noble. I was repulsed by what I saw people putting themselves through, the hustling to try and get anywhere. My natural reaction was to move into a world that had no pretense of nobility. Since I'd always fooled around with a guitar, I formed a rock band."[27]

Introduced to Frantz and Weymouth by Brooks, Arthur edged close to Talking Heads around the time of the Kitchen gig. "When they started out, they were just a trio and they were looking for a fourth member," he commented later. "We became friends but I ended up not joining the band. They were all from art school and were into looking severe and cool. I was never into that. I was from music school and I had long hair at the time."[28] According to the interviewer Frank Owen, Arthur "nearly became the fourth member" during 1976, although Brooks doubts an offer was ever made, and notes the fourth spot went to Jerry Harrison after he introduced his ex-Harvard classmate to Frantz and Weymouth. Byrne, however, was drawn to Arthur. "We were friends," he commented later. "Arthur played cello and he was part of a kind of downtown avant-garde fringe scene, but he had the distinction of also being a great appreciator of pop music. He was a big fan of Abba and of real slick Italian pop stuff, telling me how perfect they were, in terms of song craftsmanship and recording arrangement. I didn't see that at the time." Nevertheless, asked if Arthur had nearly joined the band, Byrne replied, "No."[29]

Arthur had no immediate regrets: shortly before Talking Heads released their debut album on Sire, he took Nicky Siano, the DJ at an influential private dance party called the Gallery, to see them play at CBGB's, and commented they were too straight-faced and ironic for his taste. "They were all wearing Lacoste tennis shirts, and they all had these conservative-looking shag haircuts," remembers Siano. "Arthur told me that David had asked him to be in the group, but that he felt he wasn't mainstream enough for them." Arthur was interested in the band, however, and played cello on "Psycho Killer," only to have his contribution dropped from the version that appeared on Talking Heads: 77, which was released in September 1977.[30] According to Byrne, the cello version "didn't sound that different" and, ultimately, "didn't get enough votes."[31] Brooks adds: "They were interested in involving him, but Arthur was not the easiest person to incorporate into other people's situations."

When it came to pop, Arthur's priority was to work with Brooks, a gifted songwriter whose Ivy League chic and disheveled good looks equipped him to step into the role of a frontman with teen-appeal—something Arthur felt he could never manage thanks to his pockmarked profile. "Arthur had the idea that everybody was capable of taking what he was trying to do to the next level," says the bass player. "He was this odd combination of great confidence and total despair. He had a negative self-image of himself, physically, and it interfered with all sorts of things." Brooks, meanwhile, was drawn to Arthur-the-Corn-Belt-kid, whose "remarkably beautiful lyrics" appeared to come from a font of untrammeled purity and truth — something the ex–Modern Lover felt he might never achieve due to his privileged East Coast upbringing. Compensating for each other's perceived absences, the friends spent more and more time with each other in New

Ernie Brooks, mid-1970s. "Arthur grew up in this small town of Oskaloosa and was obviously a very strange kid in this environment," he says. Photographer unknown. Courtesy of Ernie Brooks.

York, and when Brooks returned to Boston, Arthur started to sing to him on the phone. Soon after they resolved to form a pop band called the Flying Hearts and persuaded David Van Tieghem to play drums, after which they approached Larry Saltzman, a guitarist with the slick pop outfit Desmond Child & Rouge. "They launched into a . . . I hesitate to use the word 'sales pitch,' but that's kind of what it was," remembers Saltzman. "I was completely charmed by what they were doing and knew I had to be part of it." Above all, he remembers thinking Arthur's songwriting was "special and beautiful."

As rehearsals began in January 1977, Arthur presented well-crafted song after well-crafted song to the rest of the lineup, including "The Ballad of the Lights (Part I and Part II)," "Bobby," "I Wish You Were a Girl," "That's What Love Is," "Walk away from That Crowd," "What It's Like," and "You Are My Love." (For his part Brooks contributed "Holding Hands with a Heartbreaker," which he cowrote with Arthur, as well as "I Guess This Must Be the Place," "It's All Up to You," and "Last Look at Love.") Floating above a backdrop of gentle, almost melancholic guitar pop that was inspired by the simple drumming of Fleetwood Mac and the melodic lines of Abba, Arthur's lyrics were tender and simple yet also enigmatic and sophisticated.

In their cerebral allusions to everyday life, they seemed close to Talking Heads, but the contrasting names of the two bands made their different trajectories clear, for whereas Byrne's outfit engaged with the everyday experience of postmodern media culture, the Flying Hearts explored emotions that dipped, soared, and bemused in equal measure. Although he found it easy to hang out with the groundbreaking composers who congregated at the Kitchen, Arthur was also determined to write beautiful songs that were moving. Developing a sound that could extend across this generic spectrum, the light, dreamy sequences of *Instrumentals* could also be heard in the work of the Flying Hearts.

Arthur, Brooks, Saltzman, and Van Tieghem made their stage debut when they opened for Allen Ginsberg at the Other End on Bleeker Street in Greenwich Village at the beginning of March 1977. Mixing intentional casualness and deadpan humor, Arthur mooched about the stage wearing a pair of green vinyl ski gloves while he plugged and unplugged his amplifier in a purposeless manner. During one interlude Arthur read from the Yellow Pages, and a little later he interrupted a long silence with the comment, "Uh, there's a great sign over there and . . . uh . . . Oh well, I guess you'll see it if you go over there."[32] Brooks says he "kind of shared the front duty" with Arthur, which—in translation—means he was even more reluctant to step into the limelight. It was, however, a first gig, and at times Arthur's spontaneous awkwardness was successful. Singing "I would give my life, just to sleep with you one . . . last time," he hesitated at the end of the line as he delivered a nonchalant shrug of unmasked doubt. "The effect," reported the *New Musical Express*, "was magical." Stretching across three nights, the performances "improved 100% at each set," added the newspaper, even if the musicians hadn't quite "gelled as a group" by the end of them.[33]

The Flying Hearts also played at the Lower Manhattan Ocean Club in late March and—featuring Gordon and Peter Zummo (the "Cruise Missiles") on horns—opened for Talking Heads at the Village Gate on 5 and 6 July 1977. "My friends were pretty solid in the idea that we blew them off the stage, and I'm solid about that, too," says Saltzman. "The Talking Heads were great and wonderful and getting to be a big deal. This was the pinnacle for the Flying Hearts." Brooks is less sure that the sweet yet awkward pop of the Flying Hearts eclipsed the lean intellectualism of Talking Heads. "In my inmost soul I felt we were superior in some way," he notes, "but that may have been driven by a bit of jealousy at the amazing level of critical attention they were attracting." Back in the dressing room, the players wondered if they were on the cusp of a breakthrough. "Kenny Kushnick from Sire Records was there," remembers Gordon. "He was describing how they had just decided on a new label for this music. It seemed that 'punk' was too off-putting for the public at large, so they were going to start using the term 'new wave.'"

Originally coined to describe the avant-garde French film movement of the 1960s, the "new wave" label wasn't supposed to replace punk but rather, in the words of Bernard Gendron, "capture in punk bands what the designator 'punk' left out—the arty, avant-gardish, studied, and ironic dimension that accompanied the streetwise, working-class, and raucously 'vulgar' dimension."[34] "More and more," *Time* reported a week after the Village Gate concert, "the punkers find themselves being referred to as members of yet another New Wave . . . [which is] an apt catch-all label for the energetic and varied music that has emerged in recent months from some of the young American bands."[35] Those bands converged at CBGB's, a venue situated on the Bowery that had become an incubator for New York's minimalist rock movement after the Mercer Arts Center closed in the summer of 1973. Television, the Ramones, and Blondie appeared at CBGB's in 1974, and the following spring the Patti Smith Group played alongside Television for two months, after which Talking Heads took to its stage. One of the first industry insiders to venture into the venue, the Sire managing director Seymour Stein signed the Ramones, Richard Hell and the Voidoids (Hell having left Television), and Talking Heads, and the Flying Hearts were also judged to be of interest after Michael Rosenblatt, one of Stein's lieutenants, watched them play an early gig and commissioned Andy Paley to produce a four-song demo in June 1977.

The session didn't lead to a contract, presumably because the tapes didn't resonate with Sire's sensibility. Whereas Talking Heads epitomized the self-conscious sophistication and minimalist speed of new wave, the Flying Hearts remained quizzical and ambivalent—the authors of a sound that wasn't quite sure of itself in a market where confidence was all. "The diffidence of a lot of alternative rock didn't exist then," notes Brooks. "Some new wave was strange, but it was always intense and in your face. Arthur was the opposite." The laid-back aesthetic of the Flying Hearts came to be expressed in Arthur's repeated attempt to persuade Van Tieghem to drag his drums behind the rest of the group. Working as best he could with Arthur's instructions — and he concedes it was often a struggle — Van Tieghem came to wonder if Arthur was the best person to head the band. "He wasn't dancing around or anything like that, and we didn't have a certain style of clothes, or look new-wavey," explains the drummer. "I think we just hoped the sound of the band and the songs would be enough."

That hope didn't appear to be entirely fanciful. Having invited the Flying Hearts to record a demo on 23 March 1977, John Hammond asked the band to return to the studio on 19 July, and in contrast to the earlier incident when Arthur showed up with a "symphony orchestra," this time around the A&R man was gushingly enthusiastic. Versions of "The Ballad of the Lights" (featuring a spoken-word appearance by Allen Ginsberg), "Bobby," "It's All Up to You," "I Wish You Were a Girl," "Last Look at Love," "The Only Usefulness," "That's What Love Is," "Walk Away from That Crowd," and "What It's Like" were laid down, after which Hammond announced, "That's marvelous, Arthur!"[36] Van Tieghem remembers Hammond being "very friendly and enthusiastic about the songs and about Arthur," while Saltzman recalls him taking Arthur to one side and saying, "When they write my legacy, they're going to say, 'John Hammond discovered Billie Holiday, Charlie Christian, George Benson, and then Dylan, Springsteen, and Arthur Russell.'" In a letter to Chuck and Emily, Arthur revealed that Hammond had also declared he would get the Flying Hearts a deal. But Arthur wasn't so sure and remarked that the tapes "didn't come out that good."

Arthur outlined his vision of pop music to Peter Zummo in an interview for the *SoHo Weekly News* that was published on 17 March 1977. It was the first time Arthur's ideas had appeared in print, and Zummo would go on to become one of his most important collaborators. Dry-witted and mustachioed, Zummo had studied with John Cage and Alvin Lucier for his BA and MA in music at Wesleyan University, during which time he played in a rock-jazz fusion band called Sunship and took lessons in the trombone with Daoud Haroun, a bebop player who was crossing into free jazz. Continuing his work on the trombone with the esteemed brass teacher Carmine Caruso, whose primary objective was to demystify the process of playing by analyzing it in terms of physics, Zummo started to try and improvise the tone rows of serial music — at speed and for fun. Then, in the fall of 1975, he moved to New York in order to work as a musician. Struggling to pay his way, Zummo took whatever he was offered and received his most lucrative deal from Charles Morrow, a composer who had developed a profitable sideline in writing commercial jingles and arrangements. "Some people were more pop-minded," says Zummo. "I was not, but I played like that, so it kept coming up."

Gravitating downtown, Zummo performed with his wife, the dancer and choreographer Stephanie Woodard, and Wendy Perron, another dancer, in SoHo's spacious lofts. "I was often the only musician and, being a physical presence in the space, I moved with the dancers," he recalls. "We produced concerts, including solstice and equinox celebrations where we played all night long until the sun came up. No rules of music applied. It was the most freeing musical experience I've ever had." Around the same time, Zummo also took occasional lessons with Roswell Rudd, "possibly the best chromatic improviser in the world."[37] Rudd got Zummo to practice playing the horn without making a tone, holding it in the seventh position (an E) without moving the slide (so effectively turning it into a bugle), playing it in half-steps (moving the slide interval by interval), and finally playing it in whole steps. "Thanks to my training with John Cage, I was quite disposed to doing these exercises for much longer than it was boring," says Zummo. "But I was less interested in learning jazz than I was in playing with this wonderfully abstract system. I'd make recordings of the exercises and play them back at half-speed so they sounded like the ocean with echo."

Arthur and Zummo might have met at the Experimental Intermedia Foundation, where both of them played and liked to hang out; or they might have met at any number of dance events put on by Zummo and Woodard at venues such as La MaMa, the Lincoln Center, and the Dance Theater Workshop; or they might have met on 14 June 1976, when both of them appeared at Sobossek's in the Normal Music Band, which performed songs by Arthur, Jill Kroesen, Kathy Acker, and Peter Gordon under the direction of Gordon. "There were all these fuzzy lines, all these bands, and people were crossing over," says Zummo, whose first clear memory of Arthur is the moment he heard and then saw him yelling on the sidewalk outside his loft, which was situated above a salvage company on West Twenty-second Street by Seventh Avenue. Arthur wanted to talk music. "Sunship toured the Northeast and Canada in clubs and concerts, opened for Steely Dan, and made a record for Capitol," notes Zummo. "I think this was part of what caused Arthur to seek me out."

The conversation continued when Zummo interviewed Arthur for the *SoHo Weekly News*. "Music is a very personal thing," Arthur told Zummo. "How you deal with your music is very closely linked up with how you deal with your life. If you misuse your capacities as a musician you're misusing your capacities as a human being and you're taking humanity in the wrong direction." Refreshingly direct, pop could reach the emotions and bodies of its listeners more directly than experimental art music, and in contrast to the compositional scene, which was dependent on subsidies, it was also commercially self-sufficient. Free from having to justify its existence, pop had the potential to be simple and transcendent, whereas avant-garde compositional music was inevitably caught up in an often-pretentious discussion about value, because it couldn't support itself commercially. "As a kid I always hated this kind of music [pop] because it represented something that I thought was too common," added Arthur. "It was like all the jocks in school in the small town that I grew up in. These were the very people who used to try to beat me up . . . Now I listen to it with great amazement."

Citing Phil Spector's and Brian Wilson's use of echo as an example, Arthur also made a case for pop's aesthetic progressiveness. "In bubble-gum music the notion of pure sound is not a philosophy but rather a reality," he argued. "In this respect, bubble-gum preceded the avant-garde. In the works of Philip Glass or La Monte Young, for example, which are clearly pop-influenced, pure sound became an issue of primary importance, while it had already been a by-product of the commercial process in bubble-gum music." Although pop could seem banal, it also had the ability to be both material and transcendent. "Words can be many things at once, like a mantra," commented Arthur. "Also, people can understand a phrase on a visceral level, and it would mean the same thing that they understand on a spiritual level."[38]

Zummo hadn't warmed to Talking Heads, who "seemed to be art-school people who understood packaging," and considered most art rock to be "bad rock." But he notes that rock artists "who were making music that was more like art—music that wouldn't sell that many records necessarily— that stuff I thought was really cool." Arty while trying to be non-arty, the Flying Hearts (like Lou Reed, the Velvet Underground, and Captain Beefheart) were Zummo's kind of band. "While their music is refreshingly non-derivative in a stylistic sense, the Flying Hearts' affinity with bubble-gum music does manifest itself in ways that are clearly audible," he noted, pointing to the band's ability to sound both conventional and unconventional at the same time.[39]

Pop and the Middle

Although Arthur wanted to record pure pop, he was still drawn to the porous boundaries that separated compositional music from the *Billboard* Hot 100, so he arranged for the Flying Hearts (augmented by a trombone, a saxophone, and an electric piano) to perform *Instrumentals* at the Experimental Intermedia Foundation in early May 1977. As before, harmonic kernels were looped, but in contrast to the earlier Kitchen performance, the musicians were encouraged to generate a full-blown jam while Nonomura's slides clicked away in the background. "Everyone would play parts at the beginning of a section, but as the music went on the drummer would start to push the beat, the guitarist would begin embroidering, and soon other players would be improvising, but not at the cost of the basic structure," reported Robert Palmer in the *New York Times*. "Before long, what had sounded like a minimalist exercise would be rocking along furiously."[40]

During the performance Arthur conducted with nods of his head and cut off the players when they went off track. "The music was difficult to play, and we were a bit under-rehearsed," remembers Larry Saltzman, one of the pop players. "We would start and within three minutes Arthur would look up at somebody and start to give them a signal with his eye, saying 'No, no, you're not in the right place.' When this happened with two or three of us he would wind it down." Palmer, though, was captivated and concluded that "the music of the SoHo minimalists and progressive rock may be compatible [after all]." The *New York Times* critic added: "There have been attempts from both camps to bridge the still very considerable gap between contemporary art music and the wilder shores of popular entertainment, with concerts by Peter Gordon at the Kitchen and some of the work of Brian Eno immediately coming to mind. Mr. Russell's presentation, imperfect though it may have been, suggested not just a furtive embrace, but a real merging."[41]

Gordon, an increasingly influential figure during this time, recalls how

Instrumentals

Arthur Russell

instrumental music by Arthur

performed by The Flying Hearts and other musicians

with color photos by Yuko Nonomura

224 Centre Street

at the Experimental Intermedia Foundation

WEDNESDAY MAY 4 1977 9:00

Flyer from the performance of *Instrumentals* at the Experimental Intermedia Foundation, 4 May 1977. Designed by Arthur Russell. Courtesy of Tom Lee.

"the vitality and sense of common practice which was found in vernacular musics, charged with an intellectual curiosity for the exploration of form and timbre, was something we were all reaching for." Having staged a "Trust in Rock" concert with "Blue" Gene Tyranny at the University Art Museum in Berkeley in 1976, Gordon was invited to put on a benefit for the Performing Artservices in the ballroom of the Hotel Diplomat the following spring, and he ended up asking a not entirely shocking group of performers — Kathy Acker, Ernie Brooks, Ed Friedman, Scott Johnson, Jill Kroesen, Arthur Russell, "Blue" Gene Tyranny, David Van Tieghem, and Peter Zummo — to form the Love of Life Orchestra (or LOLO). The resulting music was underpinned by disco's inclusive rhythm, which invited musicians to exchange parts above its flat structure. "We started to make music you could dance to — a band that would be good for parties in SoHo," notes Van Tieghem, who went on to co-lead the group. "It would be knowledgeable about new music, but not afraid to dance or have a beat. The sound was eclectic, quirky, fun."

LOLO marked the moment when many of the best-known composer-

Peter Gordon (right) performing with "Blue" Gene Tyranny (center) and David Behrman (playing electronics) at the Franklin Street Arts Center, 1977. Photograph by and courtesy of Andy Harris.

musicians from the downtown experimental scene started to play together in a regular ensemble — a kind of downtown big band — instead of asking each other to play in one-off gigs. "LOLO was as much a political statement as a musical one," explains Gordon, who had realized disco was about to establish a "new paradigm" as soon as he heard "Love to Love You, Baby" by Donna Summer. "I was looking to create an ensemble in which musicians coming from a wide range of backgrounds could flourish — a democratization of style. From a composer's perspective, I also wanted to have an ensemble available to play my ideologically populist music." Gordon says he tried to defy genres, yet "always considered LOLO to be an 'art-band,'" even though it sometimes played pop music in pop venues.

When Gordon booked a series of weekend events for June 1977 at the Franklin Street Arts Center, which was situated on Franklin Street in TriBeCa, he invited the Flying Hearts to share the stage with LOLO because the groups were speaking a similar language and, in many instances, employing the same players. "Arthur and I thought that it would be good to split the bill," says Gordon, "so it was a month of dance parties featuring LOLO and the Flying Hearts." Sunday afternoons were dedicated to smaller groups of LOLO members; Gordon shared the first slot with Van Tieghem, after which Tyranny and Zummo covered the second, Kroesen the third, and Arthur the fourth. Returning to *Instrumentals*, Arthur (cello) invited Ernie Brooks (electric bass), Jon Gibson (flute, soprano saxophone, clarinet), Glen Lomaro (keyboards), Bill Ruyle (percussion), Larry Saltzman (electric guitar), Dave Van Tieghem (percussion), and Peter Zummo (trombone) to play with the same kind of upbeat breeziness that had characterized the earlier performance of the piece at the Kitchen, and on this occasion Arthur was unusually happy with the outcome. "Did another version of 'Instrumentals' the other day," he reported to Chuck and Emily a couple of days later. "It was much better than the other time at Experimental Intermedia."[42]

The performance was also better than Ruyle thought probable. This was because when he first met Arthur in the summer of 1974, Arthur had looked him in the eye and, setting pleasantries to one side, asked him if he liked the drummer in the Velvet Underground—and also if he could play like him. A skilled percussionist who had studied at the Manhattan School of Music at the same time as Arthur, Ruyle "didn't find the drummer of the Velvet Underground very interesting," and Arthur didn't pursue the matter until he met Ruyle at Zummo's Franklin Street performance and asked him to perform in the *Instrumentals* concert. When Ruyle asked Arthur what he wanted him to do, Arthur knelt down on the floor and repeated the simple drum beat of the Velvet Underground on Van Tieghem's assorted pieces of plastic, overturned ashtrays and so on. "I'd never heard this piece before, so we started playing, and I was just playing along on the floor on different instruments, and I just heard this most incredible music surround me," remembered Ruyle. "It was just like, 'Wow!'"[43]

If Philip Glass, Steve Reich, and Terry Riley had turned to Ghana, India, and Indonesia (as well as to La Monte Young) in order to escape the closed circuit of serial music, Arthur and Gordon looked to the less exotic source of North American and European popular music, and others followed their example. Impatient with the popular strains of *Instrumentals*, Rhys Chatham had started to get into rock after Gordon took him to see the Ramones play at CBGB's in 1976. (Arthur took Van Tieghem to the same concert in order "to see the new thing that was happening in New York.") "I thought the music that Peter and Arthur were making at that time was almost sacrilege," remembers Chatham. "I wasn't sure I approved of either

The Love of Life Orchestra in an "open rehearsal" at the Franklin Street Arts Center, 1977. *Left to right*: Scott Johnson (guitar), Jill Kroesen (chorus: alto), Peter Gordon (saxophone), Rhys Chatham (flute), Ed Friedman (chorus: poet), Kenny Deifik (harmonica). When LOLO played their Franklin Street Arts Center gigs, Arthur Russell and David Van Tieghem were also in the lineup. Photograph by and courtesy of Andy Harris.

of them. I thought it was tacky! I lumped them together. They were mixing popular forms with ideas coming out of, for want of a better word, art music, because they had this dual background. I mean, Peter took piano lessons with Liberace!" The Ramones provided Chatham with the missing link (and Van Tieghem experienced a similar epiphany): "While hearing them, I realized that, as a minimalist, I had more in common with this music than I thought," the Kitchen's former music director wrote later. "I was attracted by the sheer energy and raw power of the sound as well as chord progressions which were not dissimilar to some of the process [or minimalist] music I had been hearing at the time."[44]

Chatham started to study electric guitar and decided, with a dash of self-confessed arrogance, that it would be easy to play rock. But although he had conquered Pierre Boulez's *Sonatine For Flute and Piano* and could count to four, his playing was stiff—"very stiff," he says—and he had to practice hard, in part because, unlike Arthur and Gordon, he hadn't grown up with pop or folk.[45] In 1977 Chatham wrote and performed *Guitar Trio*, a composition for three electric guitars, electric bass, and drums that explored the realm of timbre. "The melodic content drew upon the musical vocabulary I had worked with on the classical avant-garde scene in

The same rehearsal at the Franklin Street Arts Center, 1977. *Left to right*: Kathy Acker (chorus: soprano), Peter Zummo (trombone), Peter Gordon (saxophone), Rhys Chatham (flute). Ernie Brooks can be spotted playing bass in between the profiles of Gordon and Zummo. Photograph by and courtesy of Andy Harris.

New York and consisted entirely of the overtone series generated by the E string of the electric guitar," explains Chatham, who maintains it was to his knowledge the first composition of its type. "The rhythmic thrust and the way the musicians played together came out of the rock tradition."[46]

Arthur had introduced Chatham to the guitar while they lived together in Poet's Building. "I was very inspired by this," recalls the composer. "Arthur was aware of the rock scene in New York before it really exploded in 1976. Arthur and Peter were responsible for bringing rock to the attention of the art music community and legitimizing it. I would never have thought of mixing minimalist forms with rock had it not been for Arthur, Peter, and Jill." In contrast to Chatham and Gordon, however, Arthur didn't simply aim to write music that nestled between compositional music and pop. He also wanted to record pure pop that didn't have any connection to compositional music, and while the Flying Hearts could be appreciated for their arty streak, Arthur's intention was for the band to produce hummable songs. "The Flying Hearts was pointedly a pop group, and didn't pretend to have any artistic aspirations," notes Gordon. "In fact, Ernie and Arthur repeatedly argued about what would be 'too weird' for pop music."

Surveying the scene, Zummo placed Arthur before his composer peers "in terms of energy, focus, and — more than that — sensibility" when it came to exploring pop, and Philip Glass, who kept a close eye on Arthur, was also impressed. "Arthur was way ahead of other people," he exclaims. "I didn't write overtly popular music. I did later on, but those were busman's holidays. Arthur, though, lived absolutely in the middle of these worlds. His artistic identity was tied up with this. He did it much more directly and intuitively than I ever could, and the way he did it was much more authentic. I was interested in developing my ears. Arthur did it because that was who he was."

Pop Music Journeys

Robert Ziegler, a classically trained musician and the brother of Ellen Ziegler, met Arthur on the West Coast. "He was this odd character — a guy who had turned up from nowhere," says Robert. "We would hang out and we would talk music. He was good fun. He was *definitely* different." Jennifer Warnes was another friend, and when she asked Ziegler to help her move into a new apartment, he persuaded Arthur to lend a hand. "Arthur wanted to talk about pop music most of the time," remembers Warnes. "I had already been out with Leonard Cohen and I wasn't interested in pop music, but he kept directing the conversation to pop. We struck up a nice musician-to-musician conversation. We played this game people play in the music business: *show me what you like.*"

At the beginning of 1977 Warnes scored her first top-ten pop hit, "Right Time of the Night," and soon afterwards Arthur, who didn't let the song's slushiness obscure the quality of the vocal delivery, asked her to record "Keeping Up," "My Tiger, My Timing," "Wild Combination," and "Holding Hands with a Heartbreaker." "He was just sort of, 'I'll send her this song and she'll do it,'" recalls Brooks, who had cowritten "Holding Hands." "He combined reticence with a willingness to be pushy." Ziegler detected a similar ambition. "Arthur realized Jennifer was well known, and that if she sang one of his songs it would be good for him. Jennifer was approached by hundreds of aspiring song writers, but she liked Arthur a lot." As spiritual, solitary souls, Arthur and Warnes were drawn to each other, yet having listened to a tape of the music, Warnes felt uncertain. "Arthur, it's really beautiful, but I don't know where I fit in," she responded. "There's no melody line." Arthur told Warnes he knew exactly what he wanted her to sing and had written out her part, only for Warnes to reply that she couldn't read music. Arthur persisted and said he would give her one phrase at a time.

Arthur and Warnes recorded the songs at the Music Box in Hollywood. "He always loved my parts, whether I thought they were good or not, so I became aware that it was the sound of my voice he wanted—a quintessentially Californian voice." Uncharacteristically, Warnes didn't try to influence the recording process, but instead followed Arthur's instructions, which he delivered with the help of a portable keyboard. "I'm opinionated when people invite me into the studio, but with Arthur I didn't really say a word because his vision was so particular and specific and exacting," she recalls. "It was as if he had to create it this way or he would suffer. If a musician is using music to access parts of themselves, or give birth to their own understanding of themselves, you don't stand in the way." Leonard Cohen had told Warnes: write the song in front of you as passionately as you can so that the song behind it will reveal itself. "Arthur was writing the song in front of his eyes, and I always felt there was a song behind it that would be revealed," she says. "Arthur was writing to find Arthur."

As his decision to approach Warnes about collaborating indicated, the idea of becoming a pop star appealed to Arthur, but his attention rarely drifted from the music. When he went on stage with the Flying Hearts, he normally wore a white, button-down shirt, the classic outfit of the downtown composer, and after John Hammond invited him into the studio, his heart maintained its steady pulse. "When Arthur called me about the session he said, 'John Hammond Senior, you know who he is?'" recalls Larry Saltzman. "'He wants us to come in and record on Tuesday at 10:00 a.m.....' Someone else would have given a sales pitch about Hammond, but there was none of that coming from Arthur." As far as Arthur was concerned, there was no time and no need to dwell on anything other than the playing. "He wasn't focused on fancy clothes or driving a fancy car. It was really about the work, the art. There was no indication he was looking at the next step."

Hammond, however, had become an elder-statesman figure at Columbia, having retired in December 1975, when he turned sixty-five. Although he signed a two-year deal that allowed him to continue to spot talent, the record label had lost confidence in his ability, and with Billy Joel and Meatloaf keeping its manufacturers and distributors busy, the company didn't need to gamble. In a letter to his parents, Arthur acknowledged, "[Hammond] is old and promises more than he has stamina for," though he was unaware that the A&R man was entering the last six months of his two-year extension, and he stopped receiving calls from Hammond after the Flying Hearts completed their second session in July 1977. Chuck and Emily remember something occurring between Hammond and Arthur that their son didn't want to talk about, while Muriel Fujii recalls him telling her that "Hammond had made a decision that it wasn't going to happen, and it was solely because of his appearance."

No contract was ever drawn up and the Flying Hearts, in the words of Saltzman, "ended by osmosis." Heading in different directions, Saltzman focused on building his career as a session musician, Van Tieghem directed his energies toward Steve Reich and LOLO, and Arthur announced he was going to travel to Italy to join the rock group Le Orme. Already frustrated that Warnes hadn't used "Holding Hands with a Heartbreaker" on her debut album for Arista, Brooks became doubly vexed because the Flying Hearts appeared to be on the cusp of a breakthrough, with the Cars having talked about getting the band to open for them on their forthcoming tour. "Arthur was being super-critical of David Van Tieghem's drumming," remembers the bass player. "I said, 'Let's try to make this work,' and he said, 'No, I'm going to Italy!' Something in me said this is not going to work—that I couldn't count on the Flying Hearts as a vehicle if Arthur was going to disappear to Italy." Openly furious, Brooks might have revealed his uncomplimentary feelings about Italian pop music. "Arthur would say, 'You just don't understand, this is incredibly important, this is what I have to do,'" recalls Brooks. "Or he would say, 'Don't worry.'" According to the bass player, Arthur was searching for a synthesis of all the music that was in his mind. "He was looking for something that was of a higher order and essentially difficult to do. I had to respect that, as frustrating as it was given that I was trying to carry on the daily business of organizing a band."

Arthur traveled to Italy as the guest of Le Orme's leader and keyboardist, Toni Pagliuca, who had flown to New York in search of inspiration, and following meetings with Philip Glass and Robert Wilson, was pointed in the direction of Arthur, who was putting on a concert—the June 1977 performance of *Instrumentals*—at the Franklin Street Arts Center. Pagliuca said that the concert was "*molto strano*" (very strange) and "*mi ha colpito molto*" (it really amazed me), and he introduced himself to Arthur during the interval. "When he heard I was in Le Orme he jumped half a meter in the air," remembers the Italian. "He said, 'I was in Italy last summer and I bought one record, 'Canzone D'Amore'—my record—and I said, 'I don't believe you! I want to see this record!'" At the end of the concert, Arthur took Pagliuca back to his apartment. "We partied," remembers the Italian. "It was *bellisimo*." When Arthur told him he had already written two hundred songs, Pagliuca realized his new friend might be able to wean Le Orme away from progressive rock and at the same time help the band *conquistare* the UK and the United States by working as a singer-songwriter alongside Le Orme's vocalist, Aldo Tagliapietra. "I wanted two singers, like Lennon and McCartney," says Pagliuca. "I wanted to discover his world and for him to discover mine."

Philips (Le Orme's label) paid for Arthur to fly to Milan and then to Mestre, Venice, in the autumn, only for the rest of the band to take an instant dislike not so much to Arthur as to the idea of another musician joining the band. "Poor Arthur, he was very upset," remembers Pagliuca. "He was a very sensitive person. *Purtroppo con lui proporio non abbiamo fatto neanche una nota. È stato una tragedia* [Unfortunately we didn't even play a note with him. It was a tragedy.]." Arthur cried. "He didn't understand. He said, 'Tell me why! Tell me why it's not going well! Give me an explanation!' There wasn't a rehearsal where there was a technical problem and they said, 'No, you don't know how to play.' He said, 'Toni, tell me, what's the problem? Why? Why?' I said, 'Arthur, I can't explain it.' It was *terri-bi-le*." In an attempt to rescue the trip, Arthur traveled to Milan, where Philips arranged for him to work with Riccardo Fogli, but that venture also turned sour. "I am sure that you did not enjoy at all the persons and the atmosphere you found here in Italy, especially at the studio we were recording in," Luigi Lopez, one of the group's songwriters, wrote to Arthur the following May. "It was not a good atmosphere and I was as unpleased for it as you probably were, too."

Arthur returned to New York in November 1977 with a black linen suit and a song. Brooks remembers his friend was convinced the suit would transform his life, while the song—"Oh Fernando Why"—was judged by the bass player (as well as Steven Hall) to be one of his best. The opening verse ran:

If I try to be so free that you
Can't remember me

When I come back next fall
I take my time to learn but forget it all
I write myself a letter instead of writing you
See your mind makes faces
See your mind makes faces in the mirror at you.

The chorus looked back to Italy.

Oh Fernando why
Oh Fernando why
The best of me is still alone
Outside the house, outside Milano
Oh Fernando why
Oh Fernando why
Goodbye to Milano
And goodbye to them all.[47]

Writing to Pagliuca while he was still in Italy, Arthur reiterated his be-musement at the Le Orme breakdown, and he penned a similar note after returning to New York. "I continue to work on pop music, but it is difficult to find people who understand the profound meaning of the 'pop sound,'" he recounted. "The ears of 'everyday man' however hear the imperceptible without effort, without thought." He added: "I apologize for my failure to convince Le Orme for the faithfulness of our collaboration, and I apologize for the lateness of this letter to you, my friend. But, I am sure time will see us together again." Arthur never sent the letter, but if he had he might have received a reply from Pagliuca informing him that Le Orme had gone on to drop its progressive rock sound. "We chose the classical road and aban-doned electronics," says Pagliuca. "It was a revolutionary change. We did two records — beautiful records, according to me — with violin, cello, piano, harmonium, clavichord, percussion, vibraphone, and marimba. Arthur con-tributed to the decision."

Back in New York, Arthur mulled over his diminishing pop options. The Flying Hearts had failed to win a contract, while his Italian trip had disin-tegrated into a series of disappointments. Launched by Sire while he was abroad, the debut album by Talking Heads, *Talking Heads: 77*, had received enthusiastic reviews only to bobble along the lowest echelons of the charts, which raised inevitable questions about downtown's potential to break through nationally. Yet Arthur decided to persevere, and at the end of the year, just when his prospects were beginning to look particularly bleak, he called Warnes.

"There was a very strong winter in New York at the time and Arthur was imprisoned in his dismal little flat," remembers the vocalist. "He said, 'When the sky is dark and the snow is high and my mood is grim, the sunny Californian quality of your voice really makes me happy.'" The vocalist believes she had come to represent the missing ingredient in Arthur's life. "If you met Arthur you felt like he would get instantly well if you put him in the sun for a few hours," she comments. "He was addicted to his caves — the caves of his mind and the caves he lived in. He had a dark, hidden, cubbyhole quality to his thinking, and I came from exactly the opposite end of the spectrum — dancing on the beach and that sort of thing. Opposites provide tension and harmony, so he wanted that. He probably had terrible depressions and anything that was light-hearted or sunny brought him to full flower, so I think I represented that for a month or two."

Soon after that, the reverberant sound systems and pulsating dance floors of downtown disco, which had first attracted Arthur a year earlier, took over.

Drawing on Parisian precedent, an exclusive version of disco-theque culture was forged in New York at the beginning of the 1960s. The nascent culture was popularized when Sybil Burton opened her midtown discotheque (coincidentally called Arthur) to the city's emergent breed of young, up-wardly mobile professionals in 1965. Three or four years later, audiences plummeted and venues started to shut down, but the collapse turned out to be a necessary precursor to disco's rebirth. At the beginning of 1970 the Sanctuary (a declining discotheque) and the Loft (an initially nameless rent party) invited a mix of African American, Latino, and white gay men to dance with open-minded straights for the first time. Pre-viously the reserve of heterosexual couples, the dance floor became a space for melting-pot demographics, free-form movement, and turntable experimentation, and as the social ritual of nonstop dancing began to take shape, DJs realized they had to "follow" as well as "lead" their newly-energized crowds. In short, contemporary dance-music culture came into being.[1]

Situated a little to the north of the Broadway Central Hotel, where the original incarnation of the Kitchen had yet to open, the Loft was the wooden-floored home of the Utica-born David Mancuso, whose private-party formula came together for the first time at his "Love Saves the Day" Valen-tine's Day party in 1970. Building his nights around a democratic invite scheme, a free spread of food, and an audiophile sound system, Mancuso was able to stay open long after New York's discotheques were required to close because the Loft wasn't open to the public and alcohol wasn't sold, which enabled the party to operate outside the jurisdiction of the city's licensing authorities. Mancuso accentuated the distinctively festive quality of his setup by decorating his expansive, ex-industrial space with a mirror ball and thousands of balloons, and his willingness to integrate music that ranged from African funk to Latin rock to Philadelphia soul consolidated the party's expansive countercultural ethos. With no bar to distract the flow of the night, the dance ritual at the Loft became the most intense in the city. This was disco, downtown-style.

Inspired by the Loft, the Tenth Floor opened as a private space for a more narrowly defined, white, gay elite in November 1972, and the following February Nicky Siano, who had been a regular at the Loft before he was thrown out for dealing drugs, opened the Gallery as a surrogate private party for straights. At first the Gallery barely registered at all, but when Mancuso traveled to London for the summer of 1973 Siano decided to reopen his venue as the home-away-from-home hangout for Mancuso's predominantly black gay crowd; and by the time the Loft host returned, it had become clear there was enough demand to fill both parties to capacity. Following the collapse of the Broadway Central Hotel, which alerted the authorities to their gray legal presence, the Loft and the Gallery were forced to close in quick succession, but the interruption was brief. Reopening a year ahead of Mancuso in a new location on the corner of Mercer and Houston, the Gallery quickly established itself as the most dynamic party in New York, with Siano the city's most progressive and entertaining DJ. And it was in this setting that Arthur was introduced to disco by a boyfriend, Louis Aquilone, probably toward the end of 1976.

A talented hairdresser and extrovert character, Aquilone dated Arthur for at least three months, maybe even a year, during which time they would begin their weekends at the Kitchen before heading across SoHo's shadowy, cobbled streets to the Gallery. Siano notes that Aquilone must have been serious about Arthur, otherwise he wouldn't have introduced him to the inner sanctum of the Gallery, and he adds that Arthur was transparently "mad" about Aquilone. "I think Arthur wanted to be like Louis," adds Siano. "Louis used to dance really good, and Arthur would try to copy his steps, even though it just wasn't possible." According to the DJ, Arthur

Nicky Siano (left) and Louis Aquilone, mid-1970s. Photographer unknown.
Courtesy of Nicky Siano.

looked "weird" when he danced, but that didn't bother him, and he continued to go to the Gallery after he and Aquilone broke up. "Arthur got the Gallery thing," says Siano. "He was there every week."

It was at the Gallery that Arthur learned about the utopian power of dance culture. Gathering on the floor and generating the fervor of a Baptist congregation, Siano's partygoers gave themselves up to the heady cocktail of sonic rapture and collective motion. Drugs promised to further release inhibitions, especially if participants sipped some of the venue's acid-laced punch, and thanks to the Gallery's private membership policy, regulars got to create an intimate, ecstatic community that subdivided into smaller cells during the week. "I think Arthur was a bit of a loner before he met Louis, and I think Louis offered him something he didn't have, which was a group of friends," says Siano. "There were twenty of us and we had six apartments on the Upper East Side. We would cook and sit down to these huge Italian dinners. I don't think Arthur had been part of anything like that before."

The music must have been equally new, because Siano, as much as any other spinner, was responsible for bringing together the earthy chants, uplifting vocals, soaring strings, and polyrhythmic breaks that made up the sound of early disco. In one moment of intuitive bravado, the Gallery spinner picked up a discarded copy of the Love Unlimited Orchestra's debut album during a private tour of 20th Century Records' basement, and after he started to play "Love's Theme," a track on the LP, the record climbed to the top of the *Billboard* charts. One of the first spinners to perfect the art of seamless beat-mixing, Siano also pioneered the practice of working with three turntables, as well as interrupting a record in mid-flow if the energy of the mix felt right. Above all, the Gallery DJ played with an unparalleled emotional and expressive intensity, and took to sequencing peak songs back-to-back until his dancers lost control of their senses. As one gay male regular put it, "He made you want to put on a skirt and spin."

Arthur's attraction to this formative setting of downtown disco made improbably good sense. He had become interested in repetition at the Ali Akbar College of Music and the Kitchen, and when he went to the Gallery he discovered a parallel scene that was also devoted to repetition—in this case the repetition that lay at the heart of R&B, funk, and early disco. Standing on the floor of the Gallery, Arthur must have wondered how the downtown composers who had studied Indian, African, and Balinese gamelan repetition could have ignored the rhythmic minimalism of James Brown. If that came about because the "ethnomusicological" sounds of Asia and Africa were judged to offer more serious reference points than the popular groove music of the Americas, Arthur didn't let those pretensions prevent him from becoming the first downtown composer to embrace disco, and he absorbed the genre's repetitive variations and textural combinations with unusual attentiveness. "He would stand in the booth at the end of the night and ask, 'What's that record you played that goes so-and-so?' and Louis would tell him the title," remembers Siano. "He started collecting records, and then he started looking at things that I didn't look at, such as the name of the drummer or the bass player."

Drawn to disco's sixties-inspired message of peace, love, tolerance, and strength, Arthur also came to believe in the social possibilities of downtown dance culture. Like his composer peers, he wanted to connect with an audience and had reason to think he might achieve this at venues such as the Experimental Intermedia Foundation and the Kitchen, but the listeners who attended those spots didn't generate anything like the enthusiasm and energy of the Gallery crowd. Instilled with a critical-skeptical outlook that could become stultifying, composer-musicians and their audiences rarely used the word "fabulous," but if Siano dropped to the floor after taking one too many quaaludes only to haul himself up and pull off a heroic last-ditch mix, the children of the Gallery were in no doubt that this was fabulous. Arthur, who was openly sympathetic to the visceral spontaneity of popular music, needed little persuading they were right.

Above all, disco appeared to be more effective than minimalist and post-minimalist compositional music. In his 1980 book *American Minimalist Music*, Wim Mertens would refer to minimalism's ability to create a "hypnotic" or "religious" or "ecstatic state," as well as an "independent libido, freed of all the restrictions of reality." But the analysis seems to better describe the Gallery, where the DJ and the dancers embarked on a trance-inducing journey that would vary according to the shifting planes of intensity generated through Siano's vinyl selections. Mertens would add that repetitive minimalist music "can lead to psychological regression," yet it was on the floor of the Gallery and not the Kitchen that dancers whooped and screamed as they let go of their adult selves under a sky of multicolored balloons. And while Mertens would also argue that the "so-called *religious* experience of repetitive music is in fact a camouflaged erotic experience," it was at the Mercer Street Gallery (and not the Wooster Street Kitchen) that participants generated a kinetic exchange of sensual movement.[2] A haven of social and physical expressivity, the Gallery must have felt like the best medicine ever to Arthur, whose life had been something of a struggle. As he would tell David Toop years later, "[Going to the Gallery] made a big impression on me."[3]

Unable to resist the temptation to make music, Arthur asked Siano if he wanted to work on a record, and the DJ, who had money to spare, agreed to fund a twelve-inch single out of the "Gallery war chest." Siano's decision was in line with music industry developments; DJs had been using their specialist knowledge of the dance-floor dynamic to remix twelve-inch singles for the commercial market since the summer of 1976. And although a deepening heroin habit was eating into his savings, Siano was assured the production "wouldn't cost a lot of money." Having secured Siano's consent, Arthur might have concluded it was easier to flush money out of a carefree party host than any of the uptight arts bodies that financed the competitive and unprofitable sector of compositional music, from whom he had received numerous rejection letters.

Arthur's shift into disco didn't lead him to renounce his earlier interests; he performed *Instrumentals* at the Franklin Street Arts Center in June, and went into the CBS studios with the Flying Hearts and John Hammond in July. But as the summer progressed, his work on the twelve-inch, which he titled "Kiss Me Again," took on an obsessive quality. Lugging his keyboard and cello to Long Island City, where Ernie Brooks had just moved into a loft space above Chris Frantz and Tina Weymouth, Arthur rehearsed the song's funky bass riff until the Talking Heads duo felt compelled to complain. "Arthur was playing it literally eighteen hours a day, and Chris and Tina kept saying, 'What is *wrong* with that guy?'" remembers Brooks.

Maybe Arthur was playing for an absent Aquilone, who was probably an ex by the summer of 1977. Certainly the title of the twelve-inch evoked an erotic mix of absence and desire, which was likely to appeal to the gay dance floor, where the sensation of wistful longing was well understood. Penned for a female vocalist with whom the gay male dancer was ready to identify, the lyrics also appeared to be tailor-made for the new breed of grittily resilient and emotionally expressive divas, who had come to embody the disco sound. Yet behind the song's facade lay an edgy story of sexual addiction and submission that gestured toward a post-disco sensibility while paralleling gay New York's growing fascination with leather and s/m culture. "I need you beside me / The best love that I gave," the song began. "The wind blows, the clouds wave / Am I a woman or a slave?" Later on, the song's protagonist asks, "Ooh baby, is this the woman I want to be?" After repeating the title several times, the lyrics concluded with the line, "I want to be used."

When he returned from Italy, Arthur entered Sundragon Studios with Siano in November 1977. They were joined by a group of musicians who didn't seem to know what was going on, not least because the lineup included two drummers (Yogi Horton and Allan Schwartzberg) and two bass players (Bob Babbitt and Wilbur Bascomb), all of them seasoned, successful professionals. "This was really strange," says Larry Saltzman, who was also hired. "People had used two drummers before, but never two bass players." Assuming someone had made a mistake, Babbitt and Bascomb started to work out who should play until Arthur rushed out of the control room and said, "No, no! I want both of you guys on electric!" Arthur (cello and organ), David Byrne (electric guitar), Sammy Figueroa (percussion), and Frank Owens (piano), plus the familiar faces of Henry Flynt (violin),

Nicky Siano, 1977. Siano was always "in the moment." Photograph by and courtesy of Michael Gomes.

Peter Gordon (saxophone), Larry Saltzman (electric guitar), and Peter Zummo (trombone) completed the lineup. "Arthur went out of the family in terms of hiring the rhythm section," notes Gordon. "He hired proven groove masters."

Arthur, however, didn't invite the groove masters to reproduce their proven styles, and his unconventional methods provoked a degree of disquiet. "Arthur was a very talented musician and his arrangements were very intricate, so the musicians respected him," recalls Siano. "But they were also a little bit like, 'Why do you want to do that there?' Arthur was like, 'No, no, no, it'll work, it'll work! It's really good!' He had to convince a couple of people that that was the way to do it. He was definitely doing some things that were not of the mainstream." Having written a set of startlingly dark lyrics, Arthur had no intention of reproducing the smooth, optimistic sound that was beginning to dominate the *Billboard* Hot 100, so he encouraged the bass players and drummers to bump into each other, after which he added the surreal and somewhat ominous strains of his amplified cello—hardly a common instrument in pop, let alone disco—to the mix. Locking into Arthur's instructions, the rhythm section captured disco's locomotive groove while sounding jumpy and disheveled at the same time, and toward the end of the main take an intensifying crescendo of guitars and drums blended rock dissonance with dance ecstasy. "I remember the musicians being very into it, and the original rough tracks being great," says Siano, who was credited as coproducer, though he says Arthur ran the sessions.

Looking to reproduce the same kind of disturbed energy in the vocal tracks, Arthur invited Myriam Valle, a Latina back-up singer with Desmond Child & Rouge, into the studio. "That was the one point where he let go," remembers Siano, who was asked to coach the vocalist line-by-line and didn't think to ask why his coproducer had decided to relinquish control at that particular moment. Although he wouldn't have admitted as much, Arthur appears to have calculated that the experience of being produced by a saucer-eyed novice would be disconcerting to Valle, whose restrained alarm would complement the rest of the record. Profoundly uncomfortable, Valle did indeed deliver a vocal track that was rough and unstable, and pronounced herself deeply unhappy with the result. Arthur agreed the performance was rough and unstable—and liked it precisely because of that.

Siano played "Kiss Me Again" off reel-to-reel tape at the Gallery, and a small number of acetate records were also pressed up and passed on to the city's most influential DJs. "It was like the biggest record," remembers Siano. "It worked." Arthur, however, wasn't satisfied. "His thing was, 'How do we make it better?' and my thing was, 'Let's get this out!'" adds the spinner. "He was happy, but he still thought there was a lot of work to be done." Byrne's track turned out to be a particular worry, so Arthur called the guitarist back into the studio, and when he realized he had run out of reference discs, he recorded the new take over Valle's vocal track, which he thought was good but also contained room for improvement. Byrne ended up scratching his guitar in a style that was reminiscent of the Afrobeat records that had started to flow into New York during the first half of the 1970s, and Arthur was pleased with the result. But Arthur realized he shouldn't have used the original Valle tape when he attempted to re-record the lead vocals. More composed the second time around, Valle delivered a smoother, richer performance that left Arthur hankering after the nervous instability of her first attempt. Although the new take contained more color, it no longer matched the words of the song.

Dinosaur

As Arthur started work on "Kiss Me Again" he became a bolder presence on the downtown disco circuit where he spent an increasing amount of time at venues such as the Barefoot Boy, the Loft, and the Paradise Garage. Heading out with Steven Hall, he also became a near-nightly regular at the Ninth Circle, a hustler bar situated on West Tenth Street, where Columbia University boys nestled up alongside gay DJs, whose presence made the in-house jukebox a prized showcase. And it was in the Ninth Circle that Arthur met Donald Murk, probably toward the middle of 1977, just as Murk was heading out of the bar. Later on Arthur revealed he had been drawn to Murk's baggy trousers, which demonstrated a certain confidence given that revealingly tight trousers were the ruling fashion, but Murk wasn't immediately sure he wanted to spend the night with Arthur, so he suggested they walk to a distant subway stop in order to buy some time to make up his mind. When they reached the destination, Arthur asked Murk if he wanted to go back to his place, and Murk replied that he did. "By then I was totally charmed," he says.

Having spent his college years listening to orchestral music, after which he immersed himself in English rock, Murk was "amused and a bit superior" when Arthur started to sing folk in his presence, but after he heard the Flying Hearts tapes he "began to see the connection." Strumming and plucking his guitar, his nasal voice rising and dipping in a bluesy slur, Arthur came across as being nervous and awkward, yet he also possessed an inner boldness and never avoided eye contact. "Arthur was such a natural musician that his self-consciousness was transformed into something else when he performed," comments Murk. "He was really intent on communicating, on telling stories, on touching people in some way." Because so many of his songs were unfinished, Arthur would repeat and vary lines, often asking Murk for his opinion as he went along. Murk also remembers feeling aggrieved yet captivated when Arthur played "I Wanna Go All the Way," a song about another man that he had composed in Italy.

The hurt dissipated when Arthur invited Murk to move into Twelfth Street, and Murk recalls blissful mornings when Arthur would get up early and sing, or play the cello to a drone, as the sun streamed into the bedroom and the bells rang out from the church on the other side of the street. Yet there were also times when Arthur and Murk annoyed each other. Sticking a paper clip into his electronic keyboard in order to create a drone, Arthur would move around his sonic anchor until he hit upon a melody that could be transformed into a song, after which he would add and subtract notes as if he was creating a mosaic. "He would repeat something over and over," says Murk. "I would think, 'Jesus Christ, get off that!' But a couple of days later, he would play a song for me on the guitar and I would recognize it." Jam-packed with T-shirts that made for "a very busy visual," Arthur's open closet also irritated Murk, who decided to conceal the clothes by putting up some curtains while Arthur was out one day. "He either liked the visual chaos or didn't see it as that," comments Murk.

Murk's desire to make Arthur more presentable would eventually drive Arthur away, and that parting moment drew closer when Murk started to promote Boston bands in New York, after which Peter Gordon asked him to help stage a LOLO concert at the Kitchen in April 1978. Predisposed to taking unsolicited, unilateral action, Murk borrowed some decorating fabric from Brooks and, going against strict instructions, cut up the material in order to wrap it around the venue's pillars. A short while later, Murk arranged for LOLO to play in Boston, even though the club thought they were getting the Flying Hearts, and having been booed off stage, Gordon ended his relationship with the fledgling promoter. That didn't stop Murk from trying to push the music of his new circle of friends, however, and when he realized Arthur was "talking to a lot to record companies and nothing was happening," he offered to help out. Arthur agreed on the condition that Murk remain "totally frank," and when Murk found out about his boyfriend's misadventure with Columbia, he set up an ultimately fruitless meeting with Hammond. "Knowing how impractical Arthur could be, I naively thought all that was needed was an intermediary between the visionary dreamer and the material world," he comments. "But Hammond lived and worked uptown, and probably felt it was his mission to channel artists into a more practical and commercial sphere. He saw problems with that ever happening with Arthur."

From there Murk started to try to push "Kiss Me Again," and that task took on an added urgency when the tenants of 437 East Twelfth Street, having taken over the building when it was abandoned by its landlord, began to insist that Arthur either pay rent or perform compensatory menial tasks. It fell to Murk (in his capacity as Arthur's personal manager) to offer his services to the building's Polish superintendent two days a week, and although the vodka he was offered at breakfast made the work almost pleasurable, Murk preferred the idea of making his way in music. That possibility began to look more likely when Jerry Wexler at Warner Bros. Records told him "Kiss Me Again" was really "ham and egging"—really happening—but Wexler only offered to fund the finishing touches to the twelve-inch single, after which, if the record sold a certain number of copies, he would provide Arthur with fifty thousand dollars to record an album. There was, in other words, to be none of the up-front cash that Murk needed to settle the rental arrears.

As negotiations with Warner Bros. stalled, Murk began to talk with Michael Rosenblatt at Sire Records, whom he found to be both handsome and knowledgeable. Critical of the approach, Arthur told Murk he was wasting his time because Sire was only interested in punk, and when Rosenblatt heard the record he did indeed let out a predictable "ugh." But Murk coaxed him into admitting that the guitar work was "pretty cool," after which he revealed the guitarist was already signed to Sire. Murk then arranged for Rosenblatt to visit the Paradise Garage, where Larry Levan played "Kiss Me Again" and worked the crowd into a frenzy while dancers lit sparklers and waved luminous swords—having been instructed to do so by Siano at the beginning of the night. "Michael was more used to CBGB's, so he wasn't prepared for this," recalls Murk. "He had no idea it was being done for him. As far as he was concerned, this is what happened whenever 'Kiss Me Again' was played." Intent on maintaining control of Byrne, Seymour Stein ended up offering twenty-five thousand dollars for the rights to the record, but Arthur believed Warner Bros. would market the record more effectively, so he stalled. At that point Murk noted that Warner Bros. would still be involved because they were acting as the distributors of Sire, and he added that the money would come in handy. Somewhat reluctantly, Arthur agreed, after which Murk cut down on his pre-lunch vodka consumption.

Much to the relief of Siano, who believed Arthur had lost control of "Kiss Me Again," Sire's first move was to hire the disco remixer Jimmy Simpson to record additional tracks and rework the record. "Arthur went far beyond what I thought we needed to do," comments the DJ. "The tapes were like patchwork quilts. He just kept on going and going, and making changes where there didn't seem to be a big difference." Having been told he would need to invest four thousand dollars, Siano says he ended up spending more than double that amount, and he also felt that Arthur's thirteen-minute production was about six minutes too long. But when they went into the studio with the remixer in September 1978, Siano was dismayed to hear Arthur insist his original effort should stay intact. "He was right there with Jimmy Simpson saying, 'No, no, no! Do this! No, no, no! Do that!' So Jimmy was just doing what Arthur wanted," recalls Siano. "It was not what the record company or I wanted. But Arthur, even though he was quiet, was very insistent."

It's a wonder Siano can remember anything at all. The Gallery had closed after his brother (who ran the business side of the venture) challenged him to choose between his spiraling drug habit and the venue: Siano chose the drug habit. During this time he landed a spot in a popular gay venue called the Buttermilk Bottom, and carried his pharmaceutical supplies into the remix sessions. "Nicky would sit down, take out his pill bottle, and say, 'Anybody want a quaalude?'" remembers Murk. "According to Arthur, Nicky was very important in the initial thinking about the record, but he wasn't offering anything by this point — unless you wanted some quaaludes." On one occasion the studio gathering took Siano up on his offer, after which the room became rather placid, but the calm was exceptional to the usual atmosphere. One particularly tense battle spiraled around Arthur's deliberate mistuning of one of the bass guitars. When Simpson failed to persuade Arthur to cut the track, he responded by raising its level, which left everyone unhappy. "The bass was still strange," comments Murk, "but not in any kind of productive way."

Arthur cut an unhappy figure during the remix sessions. "He was pessimistic, troubled, always worried, always down and out, always complaining, always feeling like the world was against him," says Siano. "What he was pointing out was true, but my whole thing was, 'Why think about it twenty-four hours a day, seven days a week?'" Yet Murk maintains Arthur's gloominess was caused by Simpson's ineptitude rather than any underlying mindset, and adds that by the end of the process Arthur was almost entirely detached. "Jimmy Simpson thought he was expected to use every track on the master, while Arthur wanted him to pick and choose, discarding the material that didn't fit," adds Murk. "Arthur didn't control the session at all. He thought the remix was obese and far inferior to the raw version that had been successful in the clubs. When it was over, Arthur told me it was not as good as it had been before. I didn't understand why he didn't want it to be successful and he said, 'This *isn't* going to be successful!'"

"Kiss Me Again" was released on 15 November 1978 under the artist name of Dinosaur, which suggested a rejection of disco's growing absorption with the flashy futurism of lasers, mirrors, and technological sheen. "'Kiss Me Again' is a dark, intense avant-garde oddity that sounds like it could become a New York cult item but might prove a bit too heavy, man, for wider audiences," commented the respected disco columnist Vince Aletti in *Record World*. "'My visions are real,' the singer insists and both she and the song have a certain fascination, though perhaps not enough to hold up for the 13-minute Jimmy Simpson mix or the nearly as long variation on the flip side."[4] The twelve-inch made it into the guest chart posted by Larry Levan in *Record World*, and Murk remembers the record being a "crowd pleaser" when he heard it played at the Paradise Garage.[5] But although Sire issued five thousand red vinyl promotional copies of the record, its life outside of the King Street venue was limited. Murk maintains that the appointment of Ray Caviano, the former TK Records disco promoter, to Warner Bros. at the beginning of December might have contributed to its commercial failure, because Caviano was focused on promoting his own records. Disagreeing, Arthur argued that sales were poor because Sire had made the mistake of trying to refashion "Kiss Me Again" after other commercially successful records. "Arthur was miserable and was not surprised when it didn't work," notes Murk. "He said it wasn't very good. He was totally not interested."

Relationships

By this point Arthur had moved into apartment number thirty-eight on the top floor of Poet's Building. Occupying the apartment below, a black drag queen called Cornelius would bang on the heating pipes whenever Arthur played music, and when Arthur responded by turning up the volume, the argument would culminate in a shouting match on the stairwell. One floor down from Cornelius, Allen Ginsberg rented an extra apartment for his lover, Peter Orlovsky. Situated next to Arthur, the Balasko family lived a life of comparative tranquility until their kids turned into minor criminals. Outside on the street, Puerto Ricans from the neighborhood sat on the church steps and blasted salsa, which prompted the Balaskos to aim their huge speakers out of the window and reply with booming opera. "That was quite an interesting sound clash," remembers Bob Rosenthal, Allen Ginsberg's assistant, who had introduced Ginsberg to the building.

Arthur and Ginsberg were still close, and Arthur traveled with the poet to accompany him on the cello during a reading set up by the Gay Student Alliance at the State University of New York, Stony Brook, on Long Island in the spring of 1978. During the visit Arthur met Kevin Killian, a doctoral student and aspiring poet who had planned to sleep with Ginsberg (and in so doing enter into what Ginsberg had described as a line of poetic transmission that involved gay poets making love to one another in a lineage of encounters that went all the way back to Whitman). Killian remembers Ginsberg looking "splendid and fit," while Arthur, who was seated about ten paces behind Ginsberg, wore a "pained scowl" and resembled "the wife of a Mohammedan leader." "On the numbers in which he wasn't asked to play he sat there in what might have been a haze of Buddha, but supple and alert, and in the Blake duets his fingers worked that cello faster than I could see them," recalls Killian, who ended up giving Arthur a lift back to New York City—at Ginsberg's request.[6]

Arthur and Killian went on to enjoy an uncommitted, fleeting relationship that took them to the movies and the Paradise Garage. (Arthur refused to go to Studio 54 because "you couldn't hear the music" there.) Of the Garage, Killian remembers the dancing, the sound, the music, and the mixed crowd, as well as Arthur's eyes blinking in the darkness. "There was what seemed to be an hour-long mix of the Jackson 5 version of 'Forever Came Today,'" adds Killian. "At the same time, the music always threatened to turn into just pure sound, and maybe that's what Arthur liked." Back on Twelfth Street, Killian was struck by the noise of the street, which prompted Arthur to comment how the New York environment made "different composers write as they did" and that "John Cage would have written very differently had he worked in San Francisco." Killian deduced Arthur was speaking of his own musical journey from "the prairies" to San Francisco to New York, which was "drilling syncopation into his head."

Arthur reminded Killian of the raw Antonin Artaud who appeared in *The Passion of Joan of Arc*—"[Arthur] looked like he had been scraped by clamshells, that's how messed up his profile looked"—and Killian also judged Arthur to be "divorced from his body in an interesting way." That didn't stop the Long Island doctoral student from being overawed by what he describes as Arthur's visionary outlook, and every time he arrived in Manhattan he would discover that Arthur "had done some fantastic gig the night before." Nevertheless Killian didn't fall in love with Arthur, and Arthur might have felt equally detached. "At a coffee shop we'd be eating and our table would get filled, one by one, by guys he'd worked with or danced with," recalls Killian, "and I remember having to introduce myself once because he was too high to remember my name."

In addition to the SUNY, Stony Brook, trip Arthur also traveled with Ginsberg to Woodstock in the summer of 1978 to participate in the running of a weeklong Blake workshop at the Creative Music Studio, where students received lessons in improvisation from a mutating roster of musicians.[7] Returning Arthur's generosity, the beat poet was good enough to run a power cable out of his apartment window up to number thirty-eight when Arthur had his electricity supply cut off. But Ginsberg's charity didn't extend to him offering to pay for a phone line, so Arthur would head to the bank of telephones located outside the Gem Spa, a convenience store on the corner of St. Mark's Place and Second Avenue, when he needed to make a phone call. And it was there, by the bank of phones, that he would meet the guy who would become his partner for life.

"Arthur was always on those telephones," remembers Tom Lee, an art college graduate who moved from New Jersey to New York City in the summer of 1978 and spotted Arthur soon after. "I first saw him there coming home one night from Hurrah's [a nightclub], and I started to go back to the same place in the hope that I would see him again." Like Arthur, Lee had dated women but was now focused on men, and he kept an eye on his new interest for a fortnight before he made his first approach. Arthur slipped away on that occasion, but Lee caught sight of him again a few days later, and this time Arthur asked Ernie Brooks (who was on the other end of the line) to write down Lee's phone number. Arthur and Lee went to see Talking Heads and the B-52's play in Central Park, after which Arthur introduced his new boyfriend to the world of gay bars. "We were dating, but also doing things surreptitiously," recalls Lee (who didn't know Arthur was living with Murk). "My excuse is this was all brand new to me, and we weren't living together yet. I wasn't really out before I met Arthur, and going to these gay bars was like going to the candy store."

Arthur was also spending long, lazy days with Steven Hall, whose decision to study poetry at Columbia University didn't interfere with their

Allen Ginsberg looking out from his apartment in Poet's Building, c. 1977.
Photograph by Henry Wang. Courtesy of Peter Hale.

cherished routine of buying grass and getting stoned to the visual backdrop of ambling Latino boys. "We were both total queer potheads," says Hall, "and this is what made us fast friends." Switching to work mode, Arthur and Hall recorded a Japanese version of "Kiss Me Again"—the lyrics were written out for them phonetically—and they also studied records such as "Let's Start the Dance" by Hamilton Bohannon, "You and I" by Rick James, "Got to Be Real" by Cheryl Lynn, "In the Bush" by Musique, "Miss You" by the Rolling Stones, and just about everything by Sylvester in order to calculate how certain effects were achieved.[8] "'You and I' was the track that we used to listen to over and over and over," notes Hall. "We used to dance like white fools to it in Arthur's apartment." In calmer moments, Arthur taught Hall how to play his songs on guitar, and he also gave him an overview of Southern gospel, Middle Eastern music, and Balinese gamelan. When there was time, the two friends also exchanged information about English and

Scottish folk music, and when Peggy Seeger performed in New York, they bought tickets for the concert. "We were entranced by both her playing and singing, and I think in some way Arthur aspired to be not only like her but to be her—a pure folk singer."

Disco was beating more vigorously, however, and Hall notes Arthur's semi-celebrity status in New York's downtown dance scene had turned him into an object of desire. Having become immersed in the largely male gay culture of the Gallery, Arthur discovered that sex was both more straight-forward and more available than ever before. "It became even easier to meet guys of all races and cultures, and Arthur went completely wild," remembers Hall. "At the time, there was no moral or medical issue. It was an explosion of fun, qualified by fellowship. It was not so much a political thing of being free. It was just that everyone was fucking and having a great time. This period was both brief and intense for Arthur." Brooks also recalls Arthur telling him about visits to the "wild world" of sex venues such as the Anvil. "It was irresistible," says the former Flying Heart, "but he realized it was crazy."

Believing Arthur to be "no more homosexual than heterosexual," Brooks concluded his friend had decided over the course of a couple of years to live his life as a gay man, with the disappointment of his breakup with Murray a decisive turning point. "What he really wanted was to be with a woman, and he was denying himself by going with men," argues Brooks. "Arthur would listen to me and say, 'Yes, you're right, you're right, but it's too late! I'm committed to this and I don't want to think about it!'" Brooks wondered if Arthur was being pragmatic, for whereas his relationship with Murray had been demanding, his gay partners were anonymous and fleeting or, when they stuck around, willing to support him and his "passion for music." Hall, however, reckoned that Arthur had been forced to repress his sexuality in his younger years and deduced that Brooks was framing Arthur through his own straight viewfinder. "Arthur had left his world behind to go to San Francisco, and then he crossed the continent again to remake himself," notes Hall. "He was like Kerouac and Ginsberg, who saw the cross-country journey as a metaphor for freedom and escape." New York enabled Arthur to explore not only his music but also his sexuality, and he arrived at a moment when—perhaps more than at any other time in the history of Western civilization—it was cool and exciting to be gay. "That excitement was connected to the excitement in the music, and having Allen as his mentor/teacher/lover opened up not so much that world as the theories that made that world jump," concludes Hall.

Standoff

By 1979 it had become clear that while downtown disco continued to combine alternative social values with innovative aesthetics, midtown disco and out-of-town disco had more or less ceased doing anything of the sort. When it opened in the spring of 1977, Studio 54 had introduced a high-profile, exclusionary door policy that broke with disco culture's inclusive origins, and at the end of that year the figuring of the dance floor as a progressive space was further undermined by the release of *Saturday Night Fever*, which popularized a crass new template that revolved around whiteness, competitiveness, and heterosexuality. A runaway commercial success, the film persuaded New York's previously skeptical major record companies to create dedicated disco departments, which were instructed to insert a four-on-the-floor bass beat under anything that was deemed to have Bee Gees potential. Music buyers, however, along with New York's DJs, became exasperated with the formulaic quality of the new rush of disco releases, and a full-scale backlash against disco gathered momentum as the U.S. economy slipped into recession during the first half of 1979. Citing the countercultural movement of the 1960s as the cause of the nation's difficulties, conservatives began to argue that disco encapsulated the country's lurch into permissive pleasure, and their arguments began to appeal to young white men who had always been uneasy about participating in a culture where women, gay men, and ethnic groups were so conspicuously confident. Suffused with misogyny, racism, and above all, homophobia, the "disco sucks" campaign fabricated a scapegoat for the deteriorating national outlook, and in so doing heralded the economic and political shift to the right that would come to define the 1980s.

The backlash against disco was also pro-rock in orientation. "Death to disco shit!" ran an editorial in *Punk* magazine back in January 1976. "Long live the rock! Kill yourself. Jump off a fuckin' cliff. Drive nails into your head. Become a robot and join the staff at Disneyland. OD. Anything. Just don't listen to disco shit. I've seen that canned crap take real live people and turn them into dogs! And vice versa. The epitome of all that's wrong with Western civilization is disco."⁹ The ensuing "disco sucks" campaign was populated by angry rock fans, and one of them, the talk-radio host and rock DJ Steve Dahl, became the iconic cheerleader of the movement when he blew up forty thousand disco records during the interval of a baseball doubleheader at Comiskey Park in July 1979. That helped persuade the rock-leaning executives of the major labels to close down the disco departments they had just opened and herd the disco moniker into an unmarked grave. Although the debut albums from the Ramones, Blondie, and Richard Hell and the Voidoids hadn't sold well at all and although punk and new wave hadn't come close to matching the commercial success of disco, rock's mutant offshoots escaped the crossfire of blame.

The struggle between disco and rock wasn't simply the invention of fans and executives. In an earlier age, rock musicians had drawn liberally on African American music: the Rolling Stones covered Robert Johnson ("Love in Vain"), the Beatles reworked the Isley Brothers ("Twist and Shout"), and even Led Zeppelin drew on the blues artist Willie Dixon (who wrote most of the lyrics to "Whole Lotta Love"). These covers encouraged rock's more adventurous consumers to explore the R&B origins of the music they were listening to, but the progenitors of punk and new wave split with rock and roll's roots, and their ensuing attempts to create a strain of authentically white popular music could veer into outright discrimination. "Punk / new wave definitely had racist overtones," comments Peter Gordon. "I remember during one of Arthur's recording sessions at Sire, a back-up singer from a semi-famous rock group was going on and on about how she would never have a band with horns again, because too many horn players were 'spades' and the horns attracted a 'spade audience.'" When Brian Eno first arrived downtown, he told Gordon he was campaigning to eliminate funk from pop, and talked proudly of wearing a button that proclaimed "Fight the Funk." At the same time, bands attempted to cultivate an aesthetic of whiteness. "The first part of an audition for joining an established rock group was to pass the 'looks' test," adds Gordon. "For many, the pale, emaciated look was a criterion for hiring musicians. Dark skin just didn't fit in with the de rigueur fashion accessories of the time, i.e., swastikas and the shackles [handcuffs]."

By April 1979 the maverick rock critic Lester Bangs was moved to publish an article titled "The White Noise Supremacists" in the *Village Voice* because "the racism (not to mention the sexism, which is even more pervasive and a whole other piece) on the American New Wave scene" was something he'd "been bothered about for a long time." In it Bangs quotes friends and musicians on their experiences of the casual yet pernicious racism that ran through New York's new-wave scene. "The music editor of this paper has theorized that one of the most important things about New Wave is how much of it is almost purely white music, and what a massive departure that represents from the almost universally blues-derived rock of the past," he writes. "There is at least a grain of truth there — the Contortions' James Brown / Albert Ayler spasms aside, most of the SoHo bands are as white as John Cage, and there's an evolution of sound, rhythm, and stance running from the Velvets through the Stooges to the Ramones and their children that takes us farther and farther from the black-stud postures of Mick Jagger that Lou Reed and Iggy partake in but that Joey Ramone certainly doesn't." Listing examples of the barefaced bigotry expressed by James Chance and the Contortions, the Ramones, Nico, the Rhythm Dukes, Shrapnel, and Teenage Jesus and the Jerks, as well as Sire Records and the Florida punk fanzine *New Order*, Bangs reminds readers of the way in which "most of the greatest, deepest music America has produced has been, when not entirely black, the product of miscegenation." He adds with regret that such an approach hadn't been embraced by the CBGB's bands and *Punk* staff members who had attended one of his house parties and asked him "What're you playing all that nigger disco shit for, Lester?" — and that in response to an Otis Redding record.[10]

The rejection of blackness by punk and new wave, however, was not complete. In his article, Bangs points to the reggae influence that ran through bands such as the Clash, Pere Ubu, the Police, and Public Image Ltd., and other bands could have been added to this list. Mainstream rock acts had ventured into the pan-racial terrain of disco during the 1970s — for example, David Bowie ("Fame"), the Rolling Stones ("Miss You"), and Rod Stewart ("Da' Ya' Think I'm Sexy?") — while new-wave bands advanced into dance and R&B when Blondie released "Heart of Glass" (with its synthesized pulse) and Talking Heads covered "Take Me to the River" (an Al Green song). Blending dissonant rock riffs and edgy vocals with polyrhythmic percussion, funk bass lines, and jazz licks, the Contortions, Defunkt, Lizzy Mercier Descloux, and the Lounge Lizards also contributed to the hybrid mix, and they were soon joined by the Bush Tetras, ESG, Konk, and Liquid Liquid. At the same time, audience responses revealed important nuances; Stewart's dalliance with disco raised the ire of self-proclaimed macho rockers such as Steve Dahl, while downtown new-wavers were more likely to be critical of commercial disco while retaining an interest in the more experimental end of dance. Then again, few new-wavers felt inclined to make this distinction in public, which in turn led downtown dancers to feel defensive.

Of course all of these players would have grown up in a racially divided society, and the challenge of overcoming this separatist heritage in a field as emotive and territorial as music was always going to be substantial. Downtown rock culture's commitment to symbolic shock, in which the wearing of a swastika was more likely to signify a desire to cause offense than a sympathy for Nazism, added to the complexity of the task, and Bangs explores this vexed issue before reaching the conclusion that the effect remained racist all the same.[11] Contributing to the tension, the music industry's preference for originality above honesty discouraged bands from foregrounding their sources, which led disco regulars to remain wary when new-wave musicians ventured into the milieu of seventies dance music only to display symptoms of amnesia.

These and related factors appear to have been on Arthur's mind as he witnessed Talking Heads incorporate a black sensibility into their 1978 album *More Songs about Buildings and Food*; recalling the way Chris Frantz and Tina Weymouth had complained about the incessant funk of the "Kiss Me Again" bass line that percolated through their ceiling during the summer of 1977, Arthur insisted the band should have credited him with their transformation. "Arthur had his paranoid side," notes Brooks. "But although it seemed kind of outrageous, I think he was mostly right." The subsequent release of *Fear of Music* in August 1979 turned out to be even more galling. "This ain't no party / This ain't no disco / This ain't no foolin' around," sang David Byrne on "Life During Wartime." "No time for dancing / Or lovey dovey / I ain't got time for that now." Having made a point of coming out to Byrne, Arthur took offense. "I took [that] as David saying 'Disco Sucks,'" he commented later (even though the second variation of the chorus was similarly dismissive of the Mudd Club and CBGB's). "I took that very personally."[12] In addition, Arthur wondered if he had had a "strong influence" on "I Zimbra," another *Fear of Music* track, and he also believed that the band's reluctance to acknowledge the broader influence of disco was hypocritical. "He thought they were using the energy and cachet of black music without acknowledging it as an influence," notes Steven Hall.[13]

The fact that Talking Heads and Arthur were both signed to Sire exacerbated the ill feeling, and Arthur became deeply bothered by the idea that Byrne's band was getting more attention because of its look. "Talking Heads were coming from a very intellectual context and were very serious, but they were very good at the business side of things, and I think that Arthur thought he would be next, or that he should have happened at the same time," remarks Hall. "He was baffled as to why he didn't become as successful, and became downright jealous of their success." Yet Arthur also contributed to his faltering relations with Sire when, toward the end of 1978, he started to argue with Siano over what was required to complete Dinosaur's second single, which had been recorded at the same time as "Kiss Me Again." "'Dumbo Dumbo' had a slow tempo, like a heartbeat, but it was very, very hot," says Siano. "Arthur could have put it out, but he chose to milk Sire until they dumped him. The record was done, but I left for rehab in California, and I don't think Arthur was able to finish it. There was no one saying, 'This is done!'" "Dancing, dancing, through the night / Waiting 'til the time is right," ran the lyrics, and both Siano and Sire might have wondered when Arthur would decide the time was indeed right. "We had a super deal with Sire," adds Siano. "I fucked it up, and Arthur fucked it up too."

Shortly before these strains came to a head, Arthur traveled to the West Coast to lay down material for what he assumed would be an album for Sire (the contract having stipulated that one would follow the release of the second Dinosaur single). During the trip, which he made in November 1978, Arthur asked his West Coast friends what they thought of his turn to disco and received encouraging replies from Alan Abrams (who saw disco as a place to create iconoclastic, avant-garde music while earning money), Sydney Murray (who appreciated the culture's critical mass of energy), and Jeff Whittier (who saw the move as an outgrowth of Arthur's interest in Indian devotional music). Somewhat less generously, Robert Ziegler declared disco was "crap" because it contained "this beat that drove through everything," while Jennifer Warnes declared she "hated disco" because of the very same "quantified beat." Hurt but not deterred, Arthur called on Abrams, Vince Delgado, and several players from the Ali Akbar College of Music in order to record percussion tracks at Mills College, after which he cut demos of "Tell You (Today)," "Love Dancing," and a handful of other songs at Different Fur Recording Studios in San Francisco. "Arthur had used up all the money from Sire and I was really mad," recalls Donald Murk. "But Arthur didn't think in terms of practical things. As far as he was concerned, the reason for getting money was to record more songs. There would always be sex and drugs and someone to buy you dinner."

The title and lyrics of "Love Dancing"—which was later retitled "Is It All Over My Face?"—had been penned after Murk caught Arthur dancing with another man at the Buttermilk Bottom. "I lost track of Arthur and it was getting to closing time," remembers Murk. "I found Arthur dancing with some cute guy, and there was some communication between Arthur and the guy that made me angry, because I was serially monogamous at the time." Realizing that Arthur and the guy would have gone off together if he hadn't been around, Murk was disturbed. "I insisted we go home then and there. When I said that I knew what was going on he replied, 'I guess it was all over my face.'" Murk recalls that Arthur was "actually very kind to me over all of this, and sort of sad that I was being so narrow." After that the personal manager didn't give the incident any more thought until Arthur played him "Love Dancing" a short while later. The song contained the lyrics:

Is it all over my face?
You caught me love dancing
Is it all over my face?
I'm in love dancin'.

Arthur felt less amorous when it emerged that Sire was planning to ask Larry Levan to "fix" "Kiss Me Again." Levan had established himself as a remixing talent with the release of Instant Funk's "I Got My Mind Made Up" in December 1978, but Arthur either hadn't got wind of the remix or still feared Levan would pull a Jimmy Simpson, because he told Murk it would be "really distasteful" to him if the Paradise Garage DJ received the commission. Believing that if anyone got to remix the record it should be Arthur, Murk got up early one morning, retrieved the masters from Sire, and returned home to place the tapes next to Arthur (who was still asleep). On receiving a "legal call" from Sire half an hour later, Murk insisted the company didn't own the masters, which in turn prompted Michael Rosenblatt to pick up the phone and set up a meeting. The next day Murk walked into the anteroom of the Sire townhouse only to hear Seymour Stein declare over the intercom, "There's a thief in the building!" Several less savory descriptors later, Rosenblatt walked down, apologized for Seymour's expletives, and told Murk he had better leave. "I was sorry we didn't get to negotiate any more money, but the performance from Seymour was really dynamite," says Murk.

Feeling low, Arthur told Murk that if they had gone with Warner Bros. instead of Sire, "Kiss Me Again" would have sold more records and landed him an album deal. Murk replied that following Ray Caviano's appointment as the head of the new disco department, Warner Bros. would have made sure that "Kiss Me Again" failed just the same. For a while there was a standoff between the musician and his companion-manager.

Circus

A pioneering DJ as well as a close friend of David Mancuso, Steve D'Acquisto met Arthur at the Gallery. Impulsive, tempestuous, and dynamic, D'Acquisto remembers thinking Arthur was "incredibly beautiful" despite his "very bad skin." He became even more interested in him when he heard the original reel-to-reel version of "Kiss Me Again," which was one of the most extraordinary recordings he had come across, and he handed a copy of the tape to Richie Kaczor, the principal DJ at Studio 54, where it "got everybody on the dance floor." D'Acquisto was flabbergasted to hear of Arthur's connection with John Hammond, while Arthur was similarly excited to discover D'Acquisto had worked with the groundbreaking remixer Walter Gibbons on the twelve-inch version of Sandi Mercer's "Play with Me," because Arthur loved the rhythm section on that record. Together they started to go to the Ninth Circle to look at boys, but the bar's jukebox kept stealing their attention, and it's possible they already sensed it would soon contain one of their records.

When he didn't know Arthur's whereabouts, D'Acquisto would look for him in the Loft, which had reopened on Prince Street and attracted all sorts of visitors, including Arthur. "Arthur was a human musical instrument," says Mancuso. "He was a very old spirit. He had been around the cosmic circle many times." The Loft host says he and Arthur only got to know each other slowly, in part because both of them were shy, and in part because D'Acquisto tended to dominate social situations. On one occasion at the Loft, D'Acquisto told Arthur about a song he wanted to write about dancing that would include the lyric "Sound now, seek and you shall find," and the next time they met at Prince Street Arthur turned to him and said, "We've written a song." Picking up his acoustic guitar, Arthur sang,

Caught me, caught me, love dancing
Sound now, seek and you will find
Caught me, caught me, love dancing
Sound now, seek and you will find
It's many friends catch the wave, catch the love wave
Feel it up, catch the wave, catch the love wave,
Is it all over my face?
You caught me love dancing
Is it all over my face?
I'm in love dancin'.

Arthur then played "Tell You (Today)," "No Hearts Free," and (in the words of D'Acquisto) "a couple of other amazing songs." "It was then that I realized the talent," says the DJ.

D'Acquisto barely paused before he went to see Mel Cheren at West End Records, played him "Kiss Me Again," and announced he wanted to go into the studio with Arthur. "I sang him 'Love Dancing,'" recalls the spinner. "I said, 'Give me the money and I'll make a record!' Mel gave us a couple of thousand dollars, and then we asked for more money. Eventually we got ten thousand. I was a great salesman!" Working as coproducers, Arthur and D'Acquisto agreed that the first thing to get right was the rhythm section, and that D'Acquisto should track down the Ingram brothers, a family of Philadelphia musicians who had played on numerous disco cuts, including Mercer's "Play with Me." When the Ingrams confirmed they would play, Arthur could hardly contain himself, and he became even more excited when he and D'Acquisto arranged to record the sessions at Blank Tapes, where the engineer Bob Blank had leapfrogged to the top of the disco pile following his work on Musique's debut album, *Keep On Jumpin'*, which included the hit single "In the Bush." That song alone made Blank "a fucking genius," says Steven Hall, and having studied the credits on *Keep On Jumpin'*, Arthur approached the wiry-bodied, bushy-haired engineer and handed him one of his tapes, which Blank found "totally different," "very random," and "very arranged." A short while later, Arthur returned to the studio with Allen Ginsberg, who announced to Blank, "Arthur Russell is an important musician!"

Bob Blank at the console in Blank Tapes Studios, 1982. Photographer unknown.
Courtesy of Bob Blank.

Ginsberg's outlook would go on to hover over the sessions, for although the combination of the Ingram brothers and Blank carried the clear promise of a tight, smooth R&B groove, Arthur planned to record a song that bubbled with the earthy, collective spontaneity of the dance floor—and that was far removed from the calculated sound that had come to dominate disco by the end of 1978. In order to realize this goal, Arthur decided to run the recording sessions as a live mix and knowingly fell back on the philosophy of Chögyam Trungpa and Ginsberg, who argued for the poetic value of unmediated inspiration and lived according the maxim "First thought best thought." "'First thought best thought' came from Kerouac and was adopted by William Carlos Williams as a creed," comments Hall. "This was extremely important to Ginsberg, who saw it as the nexus between Tibetan Buddhist practice and raw, American, in-your-face dynamism—the idea that one should never edit one's own impulses and that the worst thing a writer could do was to pre-edit the very thoughts that preceded putting pen to paper. Hall adds that Arthur read his copy of *William Carlos Williams: Selected Poems* "very carefully."

A boisterous Buddhist who embodied the "first thought best thought" approach, D'Acquisto must have contributed to its adoption given that Arthur had run the "Kiss Me Again" sessions in a more conventional manner. "My whole part was to encourage people to go with the first idea," explains D'Acquisto. "The first idea is the best because it's always the absolute freshest. Ninety-nine out of a hundred times, the first take is the best take, because it's not studied." According to Hall, D'Acquisto resembled a "Brooklyn mafia thug" whose behavior was "punctuated by wild, queeny outbursts" and a "kind of autistic brilliance," and he adds that Arthur would have seen him as an example of the Crazy Wisdom school that was represented by Trungpa and taught by Ginsberg. Drawing a parallel to Ginsberg's relationship with Orlovsky—"Peter was a better writer than Allen, which Allen very well knew, and he helped Allen tap his wild side"—Hall adds that Arthur worked with D'Acquisto in order to "escape his own limited bourgeois background and thus transcend his own ego."

Arthur and D'Acquisto resolved to enhance the energy levels still further by recording the basic tracks on the night of a full moon, which, according to many pre-industrial cultures, is a time of celestial energy, productivity, and ritual. G. S. Sachdev almost certainly would have introduced Arthur to the idea of the full moon's creative potential at the Ali Akbar College, and when Sydney Murray did some research and told Arthur he had been born on a full moon, he might have become more interested in its potential. Yet it was D'Acquisto who persuaded Arthur to run with the plan, and entering the studio on the full moon in February 1979, the coproducers were joined by the Ingram brothers, who made up the rhythm section, and also Blank, who was positioned in the control room. "We were living a stream-of-consciousness existence," recalls D'Acquisto. "We went with the flow. Every penny of the West End money went into recording and mixing."

Setting aside the demos that he had recorded for Sire in San Francisco, Arthur's primary goal was to get the Ingram brothers to play in the right way, which included having the drummer, John Ingram, lag behind the beat—a sacrilegious strategy in the metronomic world of disco, and one that also echoed the sound he had attempted to develop with David Van Tieghem and the Flying Hearts. The ensuing session followed the free-flowing contours of an open-ended jazz workout rather than the carefully structured maneuvers of a disco recording, and as the rhythm section settled down, Arthur picked up his cello, and holding the instrument horizontally, attacked its strings with a coconut shell in order to create a funky, percussive effect. Convinced he was recording the disco equivalent of the Beatles' *White Album*, D'Acquisto egged everybody on.[14] "They just played and I said, 'Keep going, that sounds great!'" recalls the DJ-turned-producer, who had replaced the studio's regular monitors with two of Mancuso's prized Klipschorn loudspeakers in order to replicate the vibrant, live atmosphere that was so closely associated with the Loft. "For me it was always, 'Let's keep that and move on!'" Blank was instructed to just let the tape run.

With the foundations of "Get Down Get Down Get Down," "Love Dancing," "Love Dancing Pt. 2," "No Hearts Free," "Pop Your Funk," "Tell You (Today)," "The Only Usefulness," "Real Nature," and "Don Sonny (Dave Cut You Down)" in place, and additional tracks for "Dumbo Dumbo (Waiting 'Til the Time Is Right)" also laid down, Arthur and D'Acquisto began to prepare for the recording of the vocals, solos, and percussion. Their aim, once again, was to recreate the energy of the downtown dance floor in the recording studio, and in order to do this they invited a group of partygoers from the Prince Street Loft to join them. "Arthur approached me at the Loft while I was playing my shekere [an African percussion instrument] and asked me to record with him the next day," recalls Rome Neal, an aspiring actor and director who worked for the parks department in Brooklyn. "He just loved the sound of the instrument." Robert Green, Leon McElroy, and Melvina Woods, who loved to sing along to the music during Mancuso's parties, were invited in a similar way. "Arthur was very interested in amateur musicians around the disco scene," explains Murk. "He felt that disco proceeded out of some matrix, that something was bubbling away there that resulted in this music, and it needed this background in order to stay vital. Without the milieu, the music wouldn't exist, and it would also be strengthened by connecting with it."

Held on another full moon, the ensuing session began with Hall singing lead vocals, after which he and Arthur doubled up on the chorus, because Arthur was unsure if his voice was rich enough on its own. The mood of focused tranquility continued until D'Acquisto burst into the studio with the partygoers (plus Mancuso) in the early hours of the morning. Overflowing into a small, miked-up lounge located next to the control booth, the new arrivals played percussion instruments and danced while Woods (directed by Arthur) sang in a dementedly off-kilter voice, and Green and McElroy (again directed by Arthur) delivered their lines in a husky, almost absent, monotone chant. As the party intensified, Blank realized there was "a different vibe out there in the trenches" and went with the flow. "It was like a circus," remembers the engineer, who says the session ran for the entire night. "It was really important to let these people, who were regulars at the party, perform with the music, because it was all felt." Although they would have expected to re-record the section that had been interrupted when the phone started to ring, the phone became part of the rhythm, and the Ingram brothers kept their cool. "I know they were unsure of his methodology and were surprised when he told them it was all over," adds the engineer. "They were used to fixing up bad parts."

D'Acquisto remained a significant presence. At one point he whisked Hall to the microphone after he heard him whistling along to "Tell You (Today)" and, in a whirl of energy and fervor, decided to capture the moment on tape. Then, as the session drew to a close, D'Acquisto bounded up to Hall, his fists full of cash, and began to pay him for his vocals (and impromptu whistling) before Arthur grabbed the money and declared, "We need this for the session musicians!" "Steve was amazing," remembers Hall. "His approach was totally mystical. He knew nothing about the technical stuff, but had an ear for the groove. He just felt it in his body and was the advocate of *record now* before the feeling was lost." Hall adds that D'Acquisto considered himself an impresario, with Arthur his Mozart. "The whole idea was to let this guy do whatever crazy thing he wanted to do. He made Arthur start running the tape as soon as they hit the studio. Steve was a great enthusiast and gave Arthur the confidence he lacked at the time. It was a very interesting relationship — very open, intense, and loving."

Enough money remained for Arthur to ask his old friend Kent Goshorn, who was now living on East Fourth Street, to join Woods in the studio for a final overdub. "Arthur would hear a little sound somewhere and say, 'I've got to have it!'" remembers Goshorn, who was asked to "diddle" on a three-stringed electric guitar he had picked out of a garbage can. "He could surround himself with very high caliber professional players, but at the same time he was often flirting with little amateur groups. It was just a little hobby for me, but I ended up in the studio quite a few times to play on things."

By the end of the overdubs, Blank had accumulated an extraordinary fourteen reels of twenty-four-track tape, a quantity that would have led many engineers to conclude that the artist had wasted a whole lot of time and money. But although he was a brash young guy who thought he knew everything there was to know about running a studio, Blank says he learned a thing or two during the sessions. "Arthur showed me that anything is possible, that music is a continuous flow or process," he explains. "Music can evolve out of things. It's not a form that you fit things into." Having always looked to organize material and encourage the ear to go to the parts that were most important, Blank also became less obsessed with symmetry. "Arthur taught me that the off-chance thing going on in the left-hand corner can be as important as what's happening in the middle," he adds.

Cooking

Arthur wasn't in the habit of choosing among genres, so while he recorded disco with D'Acquisto, he also began to prepare for another unlikely night at the Kitchen. Still set on bringing a vernacular voice into his orchestral compositions, Arthur decided to develop a form of "orchestral disco" and present the composite sound at the Wooster Street venue. Suspicious of commercial music, many Kitchen regulars would have been doubly suspicious of disco, which had become a dominant presence in the Hot 100 during 1978. Arthur, though, was drawn to provocative gestures and would have regarded this cautious distrust as an invitation, not a deterrent.

The stakes had become higher at the SoHo performance space during Garrett List's two years as the music director, and when Rhys Chatham reclaimed his old position for the 1977–1978 season, he found the role was much more pressurized than before, with performers "ready to kill" for spots. Chatham responded by introducing a rule that no composer could play more than once every two years. "We went from being a place where composers from the neighborhood could play to being a place where composers would be well paid for playing there, and practically guaranteed exposure in the press," says the music director. "It became a prestigious place to play, and I frankly became scared to pick up my telephone."

Arthur was squeezed into the schedule only after Murk became annoyed "that all these people were playing at the Kitchen, and Arthur was not, in spite of his intimate history with the place." With Arthur's consent, Murk approached Chatham to find out why his partner had been excluded from the program, only to be told that Arthur hadn't requested a slot. "I went to Rhys with an attitude, and left with a gig," recalls Murk. Arthur subsequently asked Chatham if he could stage another section from *Instrumentals*, and in February 1978 the music director replied that he would be prepared to schedule an unpaid performance of the piece. Arthur accepted the offer and turned to a new friend, Julius Eastman, who had become the conductor of the CETA Orchestra, a government-funded body that derived its title from the Changing Education through the Arts program.

A black, flamingly gay baritone who sang experimental opera, Eastman was sometimes described as a walking one-man minority group (although not usually to his face). Raised in Ithaca, New York, he was invited in 1969 to join the Creative Associates, an experimental music group formed by the composer and conductor Lukas Foss and based at SUNY, Buffalo, and he became immersed in contemporary music. Eastman was best known for singing on the Grammy-nominated recording of Peter Maxwell Davies's post-classical opera *Eight Songs for a Mad King* in 1973, and he also wrote avant-garde compositions, including *The Moon's Silent Modulation, Touch Him When, Mumbaphilia, Stay on It, Masculine* and *Femenine* (a matched pair), and *If You're So Smart, Why Aren't You Rich?*[15] Mercurial and intense, Eastman made his inevitable move to New York City in the summer of 1976, and, often dressed in leather and chains, was drawn to the wilder side of gay Manhattan as well as the relatively sober downtown compositional milieu. It was in the latter scene that he crossed paths with Arthur. "Clearly there was some affinity, personally and socially," says Ned Sublette, who became friends with Eastman after joining the PhD program in composition at SUNY, Buffalo, in the fall of 1975. "I'm not implying an intimate connection, but I think they related to each other as gay men."

Sublette had been introduced to Arthur by Peter Gordon, a compositional friend from the University of California, San Diego, whom he bumped into while visiting New York for a weekend toward the beginning of 1976. At the time, Sublette was looking to escape Buffalo, "the grimmest place in the world." "I thought, 'Fuck, he's really doing it, and I'm in this stupid school,'" remembers Sublette. When Gordon introduced Sublette to Arthur, Sublette wrote down the address of his new acquaintance and said, "If you're ever in Buffalo . . . ," at which point Arthur tried not to snicker. After that, Sublette abandoned Buffalo and Eastman followed soon after. "Julius was such a tremendous font of energy," says Sublette. "He was such a thoroughly musical person, and we all liked his edge."

After becoming the conductor of the CETA Orchestra, Eastman got

Julius Eastman composing. Photographer and date unknown. Courtesy of David Borden and Mary Jane Leach. Collection of Frances Eastman.

to work with both Arthur and Sublette when he conducted a selection of works — including *Instrumentals* — at the Kitchen on 10 May 1978. "Aaarrrthuuur, they're waiting out there!" Eastman hissed as his composer-friend became embroiled in the usual tangle of pre-performance detail, but once the concert got going its non-percussive, slow-moving sections resonated with a melancholic calm. Contrasting sharply with previous performances of the composition, the extracts happened to complement the downbeat mood of the CETA Orchestra musicians, who were the epitome of alienated labor. "I had never heard *Instrumentals* before, and I was amazed at how good it sounded with that grumpy group of players, who would rather have been at home watching TV," comments Sublette. "I thought it was a beautiful take on orchestral sonority and structured indeterminacy." Arthur was less enthused, however, and in a letter to a funding body written three days later declared he was "not satisfied" with the CETA performance.

The next time around he wanted, he said, to be able to rehearse the piece "with musicians of my choice."[16]

Convinced that disco, like *Instrumentals*, could be a form of serious music that revolved around shifting, repetitive structures, Arthur went on to invite Mustafa Ahmed (congas), Jeff Berman (drums), Julius Eastman (organ), Peter Gordon (tenor saxophone), Rome Neal (percussion), Larry Saltzman (guitar), and Peter Zummo (trombone) to perform an orchestral disco jam for his next appearance at the Kitchen, which took place on 27–28 April 1979. The musicians improvised around scores in order to create a continuous, evolving groove, while taking their cues from Arthur as he sawed away on his cello. Happiest when asked to take a risk, Zummo says he felt "very free" during the performance, while Neal remembers, "The Kitchen gig gave me a chance to really stretch out on my instrument and jam with the conga player, who was amazing." The result combined frenzied percussion, a raucous guitar, excited drums, and a plummeting trombone, and resembled a cross between Osibisa, the Clash, and the Original Dixieland Jazz Band. At the end of the gig the crowd of people dancing at the back of the venue applauded, while the rest of the audience tried to make sense of what they had witnessed. "There was a schism between the presence of Nicky Siano and the disco crowd, and the new-music people," says Donald Murk. "The new-music people seemed to be fascinated by the strange, disco-ite presence. The atmosphere was one of bemusement."

Convinced the Kitchen audience was "very snobbish about disco," which it judged to be "a 'low' form of music," Hall says the orchestral disco concert was "a very careful, well-staged affront to the Kitchen people and their sensibilities," and he recalls being euphoric at the end of the concert because the idea of presenting orchestral disco as a form of "serious classical music" had "really worked." "Arthur was baffled as to why they would discriminate," notes Hall. "The concert was a very political move on his part, because he was doing this in the Carnegie Hall of downtown." Arthur had already encountered a slice of the growing disdain for disco when he played a Hamilton Bohannon record to a friend, only for the friend to judge it "second-rate music." "That was such a weird thing to say," Arthur commented in a later interview. "I'd never thought of it in those hierarchical terms. It always seems important to me to avoid such value judgements."[17] In a similar vein, Zummo recalls Arthur saying, "If the beat is good enough

Flyer for *24 → 24 Music* at the Kitchen, 1979. Courtesy of Tom Lee.

to move people's bodies, it won't be treated as serious music," and the trombonist adds there was "tension" in the Kitchen during the "orchestral disco" performance.

The Kitchen music program's marked shift toward the sound of rock minimalism might have accentuated the stress. "I was playing minimalist pieces for electric guitar ensembles, and many composers of my generation were working with rock instrumentation, so naturally I programmed all of them," explains Chatham, whose *Guitar Trio*, along with the guitar ensembles of Glenn Branca, exemplified the new sound.[18] Having instigated the venue's shift to rock minimalism, Arthur could have taken some pleasure in its newfound prominence, but as rock's attack on disco gathered momentum during the first half of 1979, he might have doubted if the Kitchen's new converts to rock would be as open-minded when it came to disco. "There was very much a 'disco sucks' feeling by the end of the seventies," notes Chatham. "In retrospect, Arthur was ahead of the curve in that his music was prophetic of the groove-oriented electronic music of the late eighties."

According to Hall, the concert was controversial enough to provoke a feud. "There was a sense that Arthur sold out his so-called 'serious' reputation with disco, and the people running the Kitchen were shocked that he had the audacity to bring this world of sleazy music into this highbrow situation," he explains. "It was very bold of Arthur, and he was very proud of that break." Less certain than Hall that Arthur "intended to flip the bird," Murk remembers Arthur believing there were many Kitchen regulars who thought he was making good money from disco and regarded him as a "traitor to the new music scene." Yet Murk also recalls the orchestral disco audience being more baffled than hostile, and his recollections are in line with those of Arnold Dreyblatt, who had studied media art at Buffalo and composition at Wesleyan before he moved to New York to work with La Monte Young. "Nobody knew what the hell to make of it," notes Dreyblatt. "Rhys and Glenn were high energy and strong overtones, but here was this music that had a disco beat, lovely melodies, strange twists, and bizarre lyrics." Whereas Chatham belted out a clear message of intent, Arthur's wonky groove music seemed to be much more difficult to interpret. "I remember being very surprised, and at first I found it partially unintelligible," continues Dreyblatt. "It wasn't accessible as a statement without somehow knowing Arthur, or knowing more than what was happening in new music. And very few people who were there that night would have known about the alternative disco scene."

Arthur's decision to make music that engaged with black and gay aesthetics and forged intercommunal relations shouldn't be taken for granted; that kind of work wasn't taking place on the periphery of the organized Left during the 1970s, and nobody else was bringing it into downtown with anything like as much gusto. Yet peers such as Jon Gibson, Jill Kroesen, and Carlota Schoolman maintain they weren't offended by Arthur's change of direction, even if disco wasn't their thing, while others edged quite a bit closer to the new dance matrix. "I used to go out disco dancing often when I lived in San Francisco," remembers "Blue" Gene Tyranny, who ended up moving to New York in 1983. "I really liked dancing to a great tune that turned out to have been produced and arranged by Arthur." From afar, Christian Wolff also approved of Arthur's interest in disco, which he preferred to art music's turn to neotonal music. "I knew it was over in the pop world, but I thought it was a really interesting move," he says. "Composers were so tired of having people not like their music they were like, 'To hell with it, I'll give them Schubert!' They were moving into areas where they thought they would give people pleasure, but whereas theirs seemed to be a highly nostalgic and dubious move, Arthur did this by going into something current. There was the idea that people might get into it, but he did this not from a commercial point of view but because it was interesting."

Peter Gordon also tuned into disco, with LOLO's music underpinned by a steady dance beat over which other elements were layered. "I don't recall any unease surrounding Arthur's performance at the Kitchen," he comments. "There was nothing really shocking or startling about orchestral disco. We were all interested in groove and funk music." Gordon was appreciative of the way disco had repopularized the orchestra, and so was Sublette, who had started to get into recordings such as "Young Americans" by David Bowie and "Love Is the Drug" by Roxy Music during his time in Buffalo. "I remember sitting in the car with Julius [Eastman] while we were both living in Buffalo, and Earth, Wind & Fire came on the radio," he recalls. "Julius turned to me and said, 'I've completely lost my ability to discriminate between genres of music.'" Sublette maintains that along with Eastman, Gordon, and others, he was "fascinated by disco." "But Arthur," he notes, "was the one that went out and became effective in it all."

Having developed his production skills with recordings for Sire and West End, Arthur zipped in and out of Blank Tapes to preserve the orchestral disco concept on multitrack tape with an appropriate mix of musicians.[19] Established collaborators included Wilbur Bascum (bass), Julius Eastman (keyboards and vocals), Peter Gordon (tenor saxophone), Kent Goshorn (vocals), Butch Ingram (bass), Jimmy Ingram (keyboards), John Ingram (drums), Timmy Ingram (congas), William Ingram (guitar), Jill Kroesen (vocals), Rome Neal (percussion and vocals), and Peter Zummo (trombone). New faces included Rik Albani, a Zummo collaborator, who played trumpet; Marie-Chantal Martin, a little-known vocalist; Denise Mercedes, a guitarist in the punk outfit the Stimulators and a Poet's Building resident; and Ed Tomney, the moving force behind a new-wave outfit called the Necessaries, who also played guitar. "Arthur was special in his mission of merging the worlds of black music and orchestral music," acknowledges Neal.

Steve D'Acquisto wasn't invited into the studio, and in his absence Arthur sat on top of the studio's Rhodes piano and blew bubbles through a mug of ginseng tea while the musicians acclimated to their surroundings. "Arthur was on a mission, but he was very, very sensitive to the vibe of the people he was working with," says Bob Blank. "He was very concerned with their comfort and their feeling OK around him. It seemed like he was being casual and random, but he was very prepared and had a lot of paperwork with him." The paperwork included conceptual scores filled with staves and colored Cagean parabolas, and he instructed the players to feel out a section of the notated music before developing a decentered, improvised flow, because instead of recording specific songs, he wanted his musicians to lay down shifting combinations of sound. "Arthur came in with this road map, but then had five different pieces going at once," recalls Blank. "He had one of those lateral brains that could hear across all this different material."

Arthur was entering uncharted territory. Whereas "Kiss Me Again" was written before he went into the studio, and the West End jams were organized around a series of songs, the orchestral disco sessions cut the songs altogether—and upped the improvisation that had started to unfold with D'Acquisto. "Arthur might have had a sense of what the finished product would be, but I saw it as a process," says Zummo, who was asked to play in what Arthur called his "chromatic style," setting off the cellist's more tonal mode. "He'd put some music in front of me and I'd say, 'Where do you want me to play from?' He'd say, 'Just play.' I never understood how the score guided the process. It was a very open sound field." A novice in dance music, Zummo saw the sessions as "working with Arthur," who happened to be recording dance. "The Ingram brothers were hot, and because the drummer was so good and the beat was happening, the trombone wasn't an impediment; it could just soar above. It's also true for jazz. Playing the trombone can be a struggle because it's a difficult instrument, but I don't recall finding it difficult to record any of that stuff." One of a number of musicians who were asked to return to the studio to record overdubs, Zummo adds: "Arthur used conceptual bases to go into a recording studio and then proceeded to record funky tracks. I was generally astonished. It was all new."

The vocalists ensured the final cuts would bear only a fleeting resemblance to disco. Martin delivered a series of surreal phrases in a shrill, squeaky voice that mixed French and English. Eastman sang "In the corn belt" as if recording atonal opera with Maxwell Davies, and "Go baaannnggg" as

Left to right: Rik Albani, Peter Zummo, and Bill Ruyle at the Merce Cunningham Studio in 1979. Albani played on the orchestral disco recordings. Ruyle appeared alongside Arthur Russell in an earlier performance of *Instrumentals*. "I was free to do my thing," says Zummo of the orchestral disco sessions. Photograph by Nate Tileston. Courtesy of Peter Zummo.

if that opera had been staged in a gay sex club, like the Anvil or the Mineshaft. And Kroesen sounded like she was halfway through a second bottle of whisky when, depressed and unsteady, she almost wailed out:

Thank you for asking the question
You showed us the face of delusion
To uproot the cause of confusion
I wanna see all my friends at once
I need an armchair to put myself in your shoes
I'm in the mood to ask the question
Ohhh, thank you
Oh, oh, thank you for asking a question
You showed us the face of delusion
To uproot the cause of confusion.

With the tracks laid down and no record company leaning on him, Arthur made a copy of the tape and started to explore the infinite sound combinations that were available to him. "Arthur began bouncing tracks back and forth," remembers Gordon. "He had two twenty-four-track machines that he synched up, and he would find songs by combining these elements." At the end of the process, Arthur labeled the tapes "24 → 24," as if his own presence and that of the musicians had become secondary to the tape-to-tape conversation, which offered not so much a documentary capsule of the sessions as a way of exploring them ad infinitum. "Arthur was playing the studio the same way he would play the cello," adds Gordon. "He tried to capture a certain roughness of performance. The process was getting looser and Arthur was feeling freer. There was almost a sense of him saying, 'I can do this!'"

Along with Gordon, Arthur became one of the first composers to join pop alchemists (George Martin, Phil Spector, and Brian Eno), dub excavators (Lee "Scratch" Perry and King Tubby), and disco remixers (Tom Moulton and Walter Gibbons) in the mission of reinventing the studio as a place where sound wasn't merely reproduced but also created. The move was innovative in the field of compositional music, for while John Cage and Karlheinz Stockhausen had experimented with computers and tape, they also subjected their work to the discipline of rigorously developed scores; others had challenged the totalitarian status of the score without acknowledging that the recording process could be a key aspect of composition. "Scoring moved away from being a precise description of the sound, with every possible parameter notated, to a set of instructions that produced a precisely defined but at times highly variable result," comments Sublette. "But by the 1960s, some of these instruction pieces had gotten very abstract indeed, and consisted even at times of what seemed more like poems in the form of instructions." By the late 1970s, composers began to acknowledge that the recording process could generate sound that existed independently of a score, and in July 1979, just a month or so after the orchestral disco sessions were wrapped up, Brian Eno presented a paper titled "The Recording Studio as Compositional Tool" at the Kitchen. "Arthur was really dealing with the studio as an instrument," notes Gordon. "This approach was something that was in the air, and it was radical."

Refiguring the role of the orchestra and the score, Arthur also took disco though a series of highly original, counterintuitive maneuvers. For the best part of a decade, disco producers such as Alec Costandinos, Kenny Gamble and Leon Huff, Vince Montana, Giorgio Moroder, and Barry White had worked with the sound of the symphony orchestra, and their records imbued disco with a combination of musical complexity and emotional force that, when not treated with care, could also sound excessive and bombastic. Orchestral disco ran the additional risk of eliminating the felt groove out of disco—because the symphony orchestra was too large to allow for this kind of work, and also lacked players who were attuned to this kind of expressiveness. Arthur, however, slimmed down the size of the orchestra and assumed a nonchalant approach to his own score, which his jam-oriented musicians were encouraged to drop whenever they felt the need.

As Arthur refined his method, he distinguished his own use of repetition from the kind of repetition that appeared in earlier minimalist works. "I think the kind of repetition that comes out of me and is in dance music is somewhat different to the repetition of minimalist works of the Sixties and Seventies," he explained in an interview several years later. "Dance music is more improvisatory. It uses an extendable structure which on the one hand is recognisable, and on the other, improvisatory. It's based on hearing what you do while you do it."[20] Convinced the engagement with dance was as important as the exchange between orchestral music and pop, Arthur urged other composers to explore the culture. "I have a recollection of Arthur describing disco clubs as 'temples of music' and evocatively describing the beauty of the bass frequencies coming out of the subwoofers," comments Chatham. "I went to a disco at the old Fillmore East [the Saint] and decided that he was right. I was blown away and had no idea where this music was coming from. But I was so into my own trip I just didn't pursue it. It was Arthur who explored this other exotic area."

Mutant Disco

The seething discontentment of the "disco sucks" movement barely registered at venues such as the Paradise Garage and the Loft. Attracting hardcore dancers who lived for the night, they were never going to suffer a drop in attendance. And while Larry Levan and David Mancuso might have noticed a sudden fall in the number of free records they were receiving, the task of listening to all new disco releases had become time-consuming and often unpleasant, so there was some relief in that. Of more concern was the decline in sales suffered by New York's independent record companies, who had targeted downtown's DJs and were now forced to slash their disco budgets. The number of promotional twelve-inch singles sent out to spinners was cut back, producers were told they had to make do with reduced budgets, and promoters had their expense accounts slashed, or even found themselves without a job. Processed within the micro-economy of West End Records, that meant the studio comings and goings of Arthur soon became an expense that needed to be reined in.

Contemplating the prospect of bankruptcy, Mel Cheren was unnerved when he realized Arthur was spending thousands of dollars recording tracks that amounted to a party jam—and possibly nothing that could be released on vinyl. "Arthur would go and see Mel in his office and play him thirty seconds from a tape," recalls Donald Murk. "Then he would rewind it and play him thirty seconds from another section. There was a lot of rewinding, and Arthur always took the demos away with him. It drove Mel crazy because he couldn't get any idea of the music that was being presented to him." The West End boss became more upbeat when Murk created an acetate pressing of the tapes, but he also continued to wonder about Arthur's ability to turn over a club hit, and teaming up with D'Acquisto, he eventually decided to send a messenger to Blank Tapes to pull the multitracks. "My partner's first reaction was to call Mel and say, 'Yep, you can pick them up. Pay the bill!'" remembers Bob Blank. "Then Steve D'Acquisto called me and cursed and said, 'You are stopping the force of music!' I said, 'Oh, please!'" According to Blank, Cheren and D'Acquisto wanted to go elsewhere to "fix" the tapes, but they were soon faced with an additional opponent. "When Arthur found out about this he freaked because he was under the impression Steve D'Acquisto was going to alter his music, and he was one hundred percent right. It was a big conflict and Arthur, because he was pushed, became very obstinate."

Issued during the holiday season, some ten months after the first recording sessions were laid down, a seven-inch promotional version of "Pop Your Funk" surfaced in a green and red cover designed by Joel Sokolov (a friend of Arthur's from California) and silk-screened by Tom Lee (who was working as the manager of a silk-screen printing shop in SoHo). Murk felt that the seven-inch should be issued under the Dinosaur name in order to generate some product identification. But Arthur, inspired by the dealers who would call out "Loose joints? Loose joints?" as they touted pre-rolled grass in Washington Square Park, successfully argued for it to be released under the name Loose Joints, which would provide it with street-level publicity, as well as evoke the flexi-limbed dancers of the downtown party scene.

Featuring Arthur's taut cello, John Ingram's laid-back drums and spurting synth, and growling, groaning vocals from Leon McElroy, Side A turned out to be a gentle introduction to Side B, where the rhythm pounded along at a frantic 153 beats-per-minute against the backdrop of a shimmering gong. "We sampled ourselves," says D'Acquisto, who maintains that the rhythm section was taken from a sixteen-bar outtake of "Love Dancing." The sounds of the street, which had filtered through a window D'Acquisto and Arthur left wide open during the take, contributed to the scintillating groove, and although Arthur cut his cello from Side B, the high-pitched, oscillating squeaks of the Buchla were left in place. Two minutes and fifteen seconds in, the record started to tremor to the sound of an explosive noise that gradually faded to silence some twenty-five seconds later. Although the record crackled with an offbeat energy, Arthur had wanted the engineer to push the levels higher. "The guy kept saying 'that's too hot' and maybe he was right then and there, but he never tried to set things up to accommodate the vision," recalls Murk. "A great recording was frustrated by an apparatchik." Nevertheless Lee remembers Arthur smiling whenever he heard the seven-inch. "If 'Kiss Me Again' mimicked dance music, that version of 'Pop Your Funk' was an upheaval of it," says Lee. "Nobody expected it. It was like an anarchist dance song."

When the anarchy was slotted into the sought-after jukebox in the Ninth Circle, Arthur smiled some more. "That was a zenith for him," says Steven Hall. "Arthur would go over there to hear the single play and watch the boys gyrate to it." Gordon and Sublette didn't witness that particular scene, but were amazed at their composer friend's ability to get a disco label to fund his experimental flights. "I went to visit Peter and he played me 'Kiss Me Again' and then the forty-five of 'Pop Your Funk,'" recalls Sublette. "I said, 'This is it!' This was what we all wanted to do. It was Arthur jamming on the Buchla. Arthur was being true to his school. He wasn't writing somebody's cliché of what a disco record should be, or what an R&B record should sound like. He was doing his thing in his idiom." David Toop later described "Pop Your Funk" as "one of the craziest 45s ever released."[21]

West End released the twelve-inch version of "Is It All Over My Face?"

Loose Joints poster, 1980. Designed by Leonedis Designs. Courtesy of Steve D'Acquisto.

(the re-titled "Love Dancing") toward the beginning of 1980. Running at nine-and-a-half minutes, which was a good two-and-a-half minutes shorter than the version submitted by Arthur and D'Acquisto, the track opened with several layers of lazy, unfettered percussion, after which standard disco horn phrases and bass lines — in particular, bass octaves, in which bass sequences were interspersed with notes played an octave higher on the offbeat — were introduced around the disheveled groove.[22] Yet D'Acquisto and Arthur didn't get too close to generic disco. Offset by the timid harmony of Arthur and Hall, Robert Green's and Leon McElroy's off-key, gruff, almost absent-minded vocals reinforced the record's post-disco sensibility, and the absence of Melvina Woods contributed to the record's rough, slightly threatening, homoerotic hue. The writers of the record were credited as "Russell, D'Aquisto [sic]".

The B-side featured an extended version of "Pop Your Funk," which was six minutes and thirty-eight seconds long and included the same beats as the A-side of the promo single as well as a distorted guitar that creaked and groaned as it exchanged phrases with Arthur's cello. Mixing oil, gravel, and saliva, McElroy's viscous vocals oozed over this tense, heavy duet. "Pop your funk," ran the opening lines,

Pop your funk
Keep it coming
Pop your funk

You, too
Pop your funk
Ahh, poppp
Poppp
Pump it, baby
Ahh, yeah
Pop that funk
Pop that funk
Pop that funk
Pop that funk
Pop that funk

In contrast to the B-side of the promo seven-inch single, which evoked a frantic, almost blurred climax, there was no rumbling explosion at the end of the twelve-inch version. Throbbing, carnal, and implicitly addressed to another man, McElroy's dirty talk, which earned him a cowriting credit, made that particular metaphor redundant.

The theme of sexual pleasure was hardly new to popular music. Encouraged by male producers, along with a cultural milieu that favored the foregrounding of female pleasure, female vocalists had been mimicking orgasms since at least the 1920s, with Luella Miller ("Rattle Snake Groan," 1927) and Victoria Spivey ("Moanin' the Blues," 1934) among the earliest simulators. Coinciding with the rise of pornographic films, a number of seventies disco records made a similar move, including "More, More, More" by the Andrea True Connection (which featured the adult-movie actor Andrea True); "Love to Love You Baby" by Donna Summer (whose heavy breathing wrapped itself around Giorgio Moroder's phallic bass beat); and "Love Hangover" by Diana Ross (who gasped across the record's slowly accelerating intro). John Corbett and Terri Kapsalis note the popular fascination with the female orgasm: "Men's pleasure is absolute, irrefutable, and often quiet, while women's pleasure is elusive, questionable, and noisy."[23] It was fitting then that Frankie "Half-Pint" Jaxon, who might have been the first male vocalist to simulate an orgasm on vinyl when he recorded "My Daddy Rocks Me (With One Steady Roll)," took on a female role in the song. Yet from the 1950s onwards, the cocktail of popular music, teenage hormones, and black expressiveness led the likes of Little Richard and James Brown to shriek the shrieks of sexual pleasure with increasingly uninhibited gusto.

Working in tandem with D'Acquisto, Arthur continued this exploration of the aural dimension of male sexuality and was one of the first artists to give it an all-male spin. Whereas the Village People ("In the Navy," "Macho Man," and "YMCA") crossed pantomime caricature with gay innuendo, and Sylvester ("You Make Me Feel (Mighty Real)") described the way in which an implied monogamous gay relationship made him "feel real," "Is It All Over My Face?" explored the riskier themes of promiscuous longing and—Arthur's primary meaning, according to Hall—oral sex (in which the *it* of "Is It" left little to the imagination). "With that vocal, I thought to myself: Are they kidding?" remembers Cheren.[24] Although the song can be traced back to the moment Murk caught Arthur dancing with another man, a cursory listen to "Pop Your Funk" suggests Arthur would have been willing to authorize this second interpretation. "When Steve and Arthur worked together they were first and foremost a *gay team*," notes Hall. "They saw themselves as maverick pioneers smashing barriers in both production and the social norm." Only the dark and sinister "Walk the Night" by the leather-clad Skatt Brothers, a cruising anthem released by Casablanca Records in 1979, was remotely comparable in its theme, at least within the disco canon. "Arthur was in this whirlwind, and then trying to produce music that was equivalent to what he was going through," adds Hall. "His songs became very sexual, very aggressive, and very suggestive. Arthur was very much under Allen's influence to be open about his sexuality in his music, and dance was a venue for this expression."

For Arthur, the experience of coming out as a gay man was sexual, social, and political. If straights could write songs about love and sex, then gay men should be able to do the same without fear, and penning suggestive lyrics wasn't so much an alternative to activist politics as a way of putting the liberationist goals of activist politics into practice. Keen to communicate with the gay men he was hanging out with, Arthur developed a language that brimmed with hedonism, hope, and humor, and as he went about his writing he assumed the endearing immaturity of a young boy—something that came easily to him and also chimed with the times. "Arthur and I used to chuckle about 'Is It All Over My Face?' endlessly, and he relished the idea of getting such a dirty lyric into the mainstream," says Hall. "Openness and honesty were integral to our daily practice, and breaking barriers in terms of our sexual and social lives and mores was a heartfelt mission followed through in our work. Arthur was convinced that *nothing* and *everything* was sacred, and that was part of our shared delight."

At the same time, Arthur was careful to make sure his mischievous songs were rooted in innuendo so that straight listeners could dwell on other, safer meanings. As well as dance-floor promiscuity and oral sex, "Is It All Over My Face?" evoked the love train motion of the dance floor ("Is it all over my face? / I'm in love dancing . . . Its many friends catch the wave / Catch the love wave") and the Bible ("Sound now, seek and you will find"), while toying with downtown's penchant for surrealist cool ("And springing out the same / Send one now at seven"). Meanwhile, "Pop Your Funk" was open to a nongay reading, because the song's title referenced the music genres of "pop" and "funk" and seemed to make some kind of statement about music. These subtle insinuations and layers came easily to Arthur, a dexterous writer whose meanings were often difficult to pin down, and this sleight of hand enabled him to continue sending his recordings home to Oskaloosa.[25]

The twelve-inch single received strong reviews. Noting that disco appeared to be returning to the underground, and that dance music was becoming more diverse as it commingled with rock, R&B, reggae, and "everything danceable in between," *Dance Music Report* declared the record exemplified this "anything goes" philosophy, and predicted that it was "destined to be a club monster." On the strength of only a few test pressings, the magazine added, "The street buzz is incredible."[26] *Record World* also gave "Is It All Over My Face?" a strong write-up, describing the release as "off the wall entirely. . . . Strange, and impossible to ignore," while *Billboard* highlighted the record's blending of "new wave rock" and "r&b feeling," and concluded, "Arthur Russell and Steve D'Aquisto [*sic*] show promise with this release."[27] The record didn't sell well, however, and was only played at the Loft when one of Mancuso's dancers requested it. "The concept [of the record] Steve presented was, 'We're going to get the vibe of people coming to the party,'" says Mancuso. "'We'll pick out people who sing on the floor, so it will be a very Lofty experience.' I envisaged a lot of raw, innocent, playful, creative energy, and thought the record would be very free. The concept sounded fabulous. But I thought it could have been done better." The Loft host was particularly concerned about the off-key singing. "It was alright to have some of that, but it was too rough," he adds.

Although he had reservations, Larry Levan played the twelve-inch more willingly, in part because he was faithful to Cheren (who was giving him advance copies of every West End release), and in part because the record's punk-meets-funk aesthetic worked well with other records he was playing (such as ESG's "Moody"). That turned out to be enough for Levan to decide to make a little remix of the record—just for himself, just to play at the Paradise Garage—and because Cheren didn't have enough money to commission the work, Levan grabbed the tapes from West End and walked into Opal Studios, which occupied the same floor as the label's offices at 254 West Fifty-fourth Street. "It was literally done in an hour or two," recalls David DePino, who was tight friends with the DJ. "When Larry heard Mel coming back, he took what he had done and left. Mel got mad because Larry took the tape without asking permission, but that was Larry."

Levan started to play the rough mix, but it was an unfinished piece of work, and one afternoon, while he was hanging out with François Kevorkian at the Garage, he announced that he wanted to finish the job. "It was either twelve or fourteen minutes long and very drawn out," remembers Kevorkian, the in-house mixer at Prelude Records, whose work on Musique's "In the Bush" had established his cutting-edge reputation. "Larry had worked really fast, so there was no echo, no reverb, and no panning." Distilled and with a late-night feel, the new remix opened with a soothing groove, introduced a dreamy synthesizer solo by Arthur after some thirty seconds, and then cut to an unhinged, zigzagging vocal from Melvina Woods at one minute and thirty seconds into the track. Following the introduction of additional layers of percussion and more keyboard work, the recording eased into a spacey equilibrium, after which Arthur's hovering, shy-angel vocal of "Caught me, caught me love dancing / Sound now, seek and you will find" was ushered in. "All I did was follow Larry's directions," comments Kevorkian, who says he turned down Levan's offer of a co-credit because Prelude was beginning to get touchy about his free-lance activities. "It was really Larry's gig, but it was fun. We did it in like three or four hours, and a good edit can take days."

Released as the "Female Vocal" of "Is It All Over My Face?"—the original mix was dubbed the "Male Vocal" and placed on the B-side of the twelve-inch—Levan's remix was so different from the original it appeared as if the Garage DJ had performed an act of alchemy, having transformed a set of tracks (brusque male voices, clattering percussion, choppy cello, and slurring horns) into something that sounded entirely new (a tight, singular, groove-oriented trip-mix). In fact Levan had developed his version out of the previously unused "Part 2" section of the "Love Dancing" tapes that included a series of similar-sounding yet ultimately fresh takes and instrumental combinations, which meant his remix was in part a conceit. In any event, the Garage DJ had plenty of work to get through. "If you hit play with Arthur's music it sounds like the Grateful Dead," explains Bob Blank. "There are moments of brilliance, but you either have to be high or extremely patient, because someone is getting into a groove." Arthur didn't object to the remix, although he reckoned his effort was superior. For their part reviewers preferred Levan's sleazy "Female" version to the brooding homoeroticism of the "Male" original. As *Record World* noted in a representative entry, "It is still quite off beat but somehow more charming."[28]

Hall preferred the "Male Version," in part because Levan's use of an exclusive female voice turned the record "into a boring, straight narrative when it really should have been a gay anthem"—because it was now a woman, and not a man, who was concerned with the "it" on her face. Nevertheless the "Female Vocal" still revolved around a "slack spine," while the discordant freakiness of the Woods vocal remained indelibly strange. Along with "Kiss Me Again" and "Pop Your Funk," both versions of "Is It All Over My Face?" were expressive of what John Rockwell described as the "furious cross-pollination that had come to characterize the lower-Manhattan arts scene by the beginning of the eighties."[29] Extracting dance music from the smooth, commercial sound of late seventies disco, they contributed to the forging of a new, post-disco aesthetic that connected with the streetwise dancers who continued to go out to clubs and needed fiber, as well as sugar, in their musical diet. "Arthur would follow his music wherever it led him," notes Murk. "When his music was played at the Loft or the Garage, the public responded to it because it was raw. It was like their lives." The unlikely figure of a classically trained cellist from Oskaloosa was mapping out the deviant, new-wave, and postpunk-influenced contours of what would come to be known as mutant disco, or disco-not-disco.[30]

Because it was so successful, "Is It All Over My Face?" came to be imitated, although nobody could have imagined that a polished impostor band, appearing under the name Loose Joints, would be brazen enough to tour the Brooklyn discotheque circuit performing the record. According to

Murk, Arthur wasn't fazed when he heard what was going on, but Cheren "thought it was an affront and had to be stamped out," so Arthur responded by going on tour with an approximation of his original lineup that included Robert Green and Leon McElroy, Mustafa Ahmed, and a Japanese stand-in for Melvina Woods. "We would meet at Arthur's apartment beforehand and chant "Is it all over my face?" again and again," recalls Murk, who took on the role of tour manager when Cheren made it clear he didn't want to get involved. "Mustafa would click on a pair of finger symbols, and Arthur would play cello as if it was the guitar. Everybody had to be involved— even the guy who was driving the van." Arthur, adds Murk, was in his element. "In a way Arthur disliked his records because he felt that the performance involved was just one of many possible ways of interpreting the song. Recording was always a drawback because it preserved something, whereas the moment after might be better, so he didn't accept that the vinyl version was something he had to duplicate. He wanted to use the music as a platform to create a sound environment."

The group's performances were mixed. In the run-up to one gig, Murk found out that Arthur was going to be asked to perform in a head-to-head alongside the impostor outfit and thought about canceling, but Arthur liked the idea, and when his band took its turn, the stand-in vocalist lay down, flung her long hair over the edge of the stage, and started to sing—much to the bewildered excitement of the crowd. The counterfeit band turned out to be tight, and Arthur was pleased to hear the reincarnation of his music, but according to Murk he "did think that they sounded like a cover band, and that our group was making music." At a later, less successful performance, Ernie Brooks drove Arthur to a high-tech gay club to perform solo with a backing tape, only for everything to break down. "The tape didn't stop and start properly, and his cello, which he stuffed with paper to stop the feedback, just made this screeching sound," he recalls. "It was an unbelievably comic scene, Arthur in this slick gay club making this screeching noise." At the end of the show, Arthur turned to Brooks and said, "That's it! My career is over!" Reaching a different conclusion, the bass player replied, "This is why we're supposed to have a rock-and-roll band!" But Arthur wasn't willing to break with dance. "No, this is the future," he said.

In terms of New York club play, Levan's remix received a varied response. "It was just too raw and stripped down for [white] gay club appeal," says Robbie Leslie, one of the DJs at the newly opened Saint, a white gay private venue situated on the site of the old Fillmore East. But of course Levan played it several times a night at the Paradise Garage, and his version soon acquired cult status thanks to the fact that the venue's dancers were well practiced in the art of identifying with female divas and took special delight in imagining themselves as Woods.[31] "It was just so *sleazy*," says Jim Feldman, a dance-floor regular. "Everyone knew what the lyrics referred to." Witnessing the record take off from the vantage point of the Garage booth, DePino noted that Arthur was more interested in being creative than commercial. "He always seemed to be thinking, *music, music, music*," he comments. "His versions always needed a remix if they were going to be more commercial. Larry's version was more danceable, more recognizable."

Having heard "Is It All Over My Face?" at the Garage, the influential WBLS DJ Frankie Crocker started to play the remix on his Monday morning show, and the record went on to become a bona fide New York hit. Ned Sublette realized as much when he heard the kids on Avenue B singing the song as they left school, and Peter Gordon remembers the release being "a real turning point." "You would walk down the street and hear it playing on the radio," adds Gordon. Long after it drifted off the airwaves, the record continued to receive play at New York's black gay drag balls. "There are about six or seven hyper-grand-classic vogueing anthems and 'Is It All Over My Face?' is one of them," notes Daniel Wang, a DJ who started to hang out in the ball scene in the early 1990s and made a point of talking to older ballgoers about their history. "That's because the groove is so funky, and also because to be *ovah* ["o-ver"] is gay black slang for being over the top or over the limit, the best of the best of the best. If your face is *ovah*, you are *gorgeous, fabulous*." Wang adds: "The ballgoers would have been amazed to know Arthur was a white, East Village type."

Arthur, however, wasn't happy. Writing to Chuck and Emily in February 1980, he declared that the "quality of life in the city seems to be degenerating." He continued: "The quality of music is also degenerating. It's all I can do to keep an optimistic outlook in this time of cultural decay." Brooks remembers Arthur "going crazy" when, after several weeks of the remix riding high on the *Billboard* dance chart, he received a letter from West End stating that the single had settled at a position just below the point where royalties would have had to be paid out. "It was a huge seller, and that was just bullshit," claims Brooks. Arthur responded by visiting New

York's record stores in order to calculate how many copies of the remix had been sold, and in the autumn he informed his parents, "[I have] found what I think might be reasonable evidence that West End is lying about how many copies they've sold." Seeking concrete proof that he was owed money, Arthur traveled to New Jersey to visit the plant that had manufactured the record, only to be told he'd be beaten up if he didn't go away. Cheren acknowledges the remix "kept us going during a very, very lean period," but maintains it "became a local underground thing" and claims it "didn't sell a couple of hundred thousand copies."

As poor as ever, Arthur took on his first menial job in the late summer of 1980 when he started to work as a courier in a messenger office. "Perhaps you will have seen by the time you get this that Loose Joints has risen to no. 40 with a bullet as well as appearing in the Baltimore-Washington regional chart in *Billboard*," he wrote to his parents between assignments. "Once again, I find my mind's preoccupation with this more and more tiresome. But not as tiresome as waiting here." In another letter he added: "It's hard to admit I should have been a farmer. . . . I suppose you'll have to tell everybody I'm a messenger now and ruin my superstar image, but that's the way it is."

Murk had suggested ways for Arthur to ease the daily struggle of buying food and paying the rent, but the personal manager's willingness to take unsolicited, unilateral action contributed to their breakup toward the end of 1979. Having agreed to disagree about their dealings with Sire and Warner Bros., they had argued again after Murk wrote an impromptu letter to Jennifer Warnes to see if there was anything she could do to promote Arthur's music. Later, when Murk tried to set up a performance of *Instrumentals* at the Walker Art Center in Minneapolis, Arthur remained uncooperative. "I said, 'Let's offer this to various venues and generate some income here, and maybe even record it,' but he didn't like to package anything," recalls Murk (who had moved out of their Twelfth Street apartment by the time he finalized the contractual details for the release of "Is It All Over My Face?"). "Arthur didn't want to be widely regarded as such-and-such if that was only part of what he did." When Murk told Arthur that he had to define himself for people to buy his music, Arthur answered with an emphatic, "*I will not be defined.*"

Arthur wasn't convinced that packaging necessarily made music more commercial, and he also believed that even when it did, the result was still detrimental because it diluted the music's immediacy. Murk accepted the sentiment but not its shaky business foundations, and he drifted further from Arthur when he started to work for Denise Mercedes, the Stimulators guitarist, whose all-consuming personality swallowed him whole. "I became her instrument," says Murk, who was living on Seventh Street between Avenues C and D—he told people he lived between Coke and Dope—before Mercedes dragged him back to Poet's Building, where she lived with her band. "Arthur was amused." Although he had no interest in the Stimulators, Arthur went to see them play at Max's Kansas City, and when Murk left the club during the gig for a breather, he saw his estranged companion standing in the doorway with Tom Lee. That made him "very, very unhappy."

Meanwhile Chuck and Emily continued to subsidize Arthur while encouraging him to become self-sufficient. Earlier, in the summer of 1975, they had given him $150 to launch a secondhand T-shirt business. Then, in 1979, they launched an informal, "buddy-buddy" business called C.A.M.E., or the Charles Arthur Musical Enterprise, and agreed Arthur would repay a sum of loaned money "when his ship came in." Over the years, the Oskaloosan parents estimate they sent Arthur a good $40,000, and on one occasion he sent a small sum back in return. "It wasn't much, but I just about fell off my chair," recalls Chuck. Kate was less amused, and having watched the money flow from Oskaloosa to East Twelfth Street with growing unease, she counseled her parents to stem the stream. "I felt Arthur needed to explore other ways of getting money," she remembers. "I cautioned them that he didn't have the wherewithal to use good judgment." For his part, Arthur believed he was getting no more than his fair deal given that Chuck and Emily had given both of his sisters financial support and a house when they got married. To her later regret, Kate told him he would become more efficient in the studio if he had less money, and notes that after a while she stopped hearing from him.

Communication between Arthur and his parents was detached and unemotional to the point of being professional during this period, according to Lee. "It was almost like he had to prove to them that he was going to do what he said he was going to do." Evidence of Arthur's productiveness didn't always help the relationship: Chuck thought the $24 \longrightarrow 24$ tapes sounded

Arthur Russell and Tom Lee at home, 1980. Photographer unknown. Courtesy of Tom Lee.

like "wood-shedding," while he and Emily could also see why Levan's remix of "Is It All Over My Face?" outsold their son's version. Yet they continued to provide Arthur with money to go into the studio, and never suggested he should compromise his aesthetic judgment in order to sell more records. When Arthur told them the only thing he could think about was money, Chuck advised there was "no sin" in thinking those thoughts so long as they didn't interfere with him staying focused on the "quality" of his work. "The money will come if it's in this order," added Chuck, and that seemed to help Arthur put the financial trauma of the "Is It All Over My Face?" episode behind him. "I'm trying to forget about West End," he wrote a short while later.

By then Lee had started to live with Arthur in Poet's Building, even though the disadvantages were numerous. As far as Lee was concerned, the apartment was too small to share and too grungy for his taste, while the precedence Arthur's music equipment enjoyed over furniture meant it was uncomfortable too. Initially attractive, the prospect of living in the same building as Allen Ginsberg became less appealing when the increasingly gruff poet began to remind Arthur of the need to get his own electricity turned on during chance collisions in the stairwell. Cohabiting also meant

Arthur and Lee were more likely to find out about each other's flings, so that was another drawback. But in the end Lee decided that none of the above really mattered, and he took up residence in time to remember Arthur and Steve D'Acquisto splicing tape like two wired kids on an arts-and-crafts playdate.

Handsome, kind, and calm, Lee would head out every morning to the silk-screen printing shop where he attempted to appease his artist customers. Then at 5:00 p.m., he would stop off to buy some organic produce and prepare a nice supper for his boyfriend. "I was an artist, but never thought I could make it," reminisces Lee. "I liked the vicarious association with Arthur and the thought that I could be the glue that could hold his artistry together. Arthur was working on his music every day and that ended up costing me a lot of money. But here was a guy who was doing something I could only fantasize about." Lee adds: "The person you love is the person you feel the most comfortable with, and Arthur and I were very comfortable together. We would spend hours on the couch. A lot of people saw Arthur as being "one-way, my-way," but I got to see a whole other side to him."

Although he became the recognized breadwinner of the couple, Lee was unable to help Arthur with his every financial need. "I would cringe when he called his parents to ask for money," he recalls. "For me it was a sense of pride. I was paying the way, but Arthur wanted big money—five hundred dollars for the studio and such. His relationship with his parents was very strained, but as long as he spread out his requests he would get it. Chuck and Emily contributed a lot of money." For his part, Arthur was happy with Lee, and the relationship provided him with the stability he needed in order to navigate his sometimes stormy path. "Tom gave Arthur the freedom to do what he wanted," notes Steven Hall. "With Tom he mimicked a conventional relationship, even though they were both men. Arthur got into a situation where he didn't have to worry about money. He had a simple life, but it was very free."

5 **Variations** (1980–1984)

Arthur's wider group of musician friends had never really taken to the social side of downtown disco, and those that did go out dancing tended to head to regular commercial spots rather than the private downtown spaces where the dance ritual was at its most intense and committed. However, along with Glenn Branca (an increasingly influential rock minimalist), some of Arthur's peers became much more interested in a slew of newly opened rock-oriented discotheques such as Hurrah's, the Mudd Club, and Danceteria, because they were self-evidently interesting and also offered them an opportunity to perform live. "By the late seventies, clubs were starting to feature all kinds of avant-manifestations," notes Ned Sublette. "Performance art started happening in nightclubs, and the avant-disco crossover that Arthur pioneered started to become a fact of life. Everybody played wherever they could get a stage and an audience and maybe a little money to pay the musicians. It was necessary to seek out other venues, and New York in those days was pulsating with energy, even though the aspiring performers always outnumbered the available showcases."

Repeating single notes at extreme volume, Rhys Chatham appeared at CBGB's, Max's Kansas City, Tier 3, the Mudd Club, Danceteria, and Interferon, where his singular guitar overtones and harmonics sometimes fooled members of the audience into believing vocalists were performing off-stage. "I didn't want to be a classical composer playing with a rock group in a concert hall," he explains. "It was too safe. I wanted to make sure my music, which I considered art music, also worked as rock." Peter Gordon's shift to the rock-club scene was more predictable—he had, after all, been playing rock gigs ever since he was a teenager—and from the summer of 1978 onward he performed alongside a slimmed-down version of LOLO in venues such as the Rock Lounge, Max's, the Lower Manhattan Ocean Club, Hurrah's, and the Mudd Club. Entering the fray while he worked on his opera *Satyagraha*, Philip Glass also coproduced two albums for the minimalist rock band Polyrock and started to appear in rock clubs, which had evolved into the "most important" and "vital" scene for new music in the city. "I find their approach to their music serious, lively, risky; these guys are doing all the things that artists are supposed to be doing," he told John Rockwell.[1]

A number of downtown composers began to earn unprecedented fees for playing live. "The idea that Rhys or Glenn could get $1,500 to show up with a band and play instrumental work at Danceteria, or that a well-promoted gig at the Mudd Club might send everyone in the band home with one hundred dollars, didn't exist when Rhys started the music series at the Kitchen," adds Sublette, who played alongside both Branca and Chatham. "Some people's music worked better in clubs than others. People doing sensitive, slow, acoustic music went largely unheard. People simulating the sound of World War III had fans." Jon Gibson, one of those whose music barely registered, maintains that Branca's and Chatham's attempts to explore the subtleties of microtuning were lost in the volume. He recalls: "I would literally hold my ears in those environments."

Although many of its onetime fledgling composers were beginning to enjoy the bright lights of flashier venues, the Kitchen managed to consolidate its position in the downtown soundscape when it staged the "New Music New York" festival across nine days in June 1979. Works by Robert Ashley, David Behrman, Philip Glass, Alvin Lucier, Meredith Monk, and Steve Reich were performed, and the nine-day event also featured Laurie Anderson (songs with electric violin), Rhys Chatham (drums and guitar strings), Don Cherry (songs with accompaniment), Jon Gibson (soprano saxophone solo), Peter Gordon (saxophone solo with pre-taped accompaniment), Jill Kroesen (songs), George Lewis (trombone with microcomputer accompaniment), Gordon Mumma (musical saw), Phill Niblock (oboe and bassoon tones), Ned Sublette (an a cappella Western ballad), "Blue" Gene Tyranny (mixed collage of documentary recordings and electronic effects), and David Van Tieghem (toy instruments) among its fifty-three shows.[2]

The quantity and breadth of the performances proclaimed the arrival of a distinctive field of composition, as did the decision to frame the works with a moniker that had been circulating for the best part of a decade. Beginning in November 1970, the Lincoln Center's "New and Newer Music" series had showcased contemporary composers such as Luciano Berio, Pierre Boulez, and Karlheinz Stockhausen, while composers based at the University of California, San Diego, started to use *new music* around the same time to describe their tonal departure from serialism. The discrepant usage of the term continued through to 1975 when Reginald Smith Brindle titled his study of Boulez, Cage, Stockhausen, and Morton Feldman *The New Music*; at the same time Peter Gordon deployed the term liberally in his review of the Modern Lovers.[3] But whereas Smith Brindle used *new music* to signify the avant-garde — and sparingly at that — Gordon joined other composers working in downtown contexts across the United States in employing the term to suggest a departure from both the avant-garde and indeed the idea of a definable category of composition per se. "New Music New York" confirmed that latter usage as the dominant one.

According to Tom Johnson, the event was "a genuine landmark" in the evolution of new music. "Now it suddenly becomes clear that the genre has accumulated quite a bit of support and momentum, that it is becoming organized on a rather broad scale and that, from here on, it will be pretty hard to sweep under the carpet," he noted in the *Village Voice*.[4] Writing in the *New York Times*, John Rockwell went further. "Despite flaws and variabilities of quality, it has been a remarkable affair," he commented. "Above all, it's been an attestation of community on the part of a numerous, highly self-aware group of composers." Rockwell added, "Chief among the ideas that began to emerge in the course of all the music-making and conversation-making was that, just maybe, music is the dominant vanguard art form just now. These things happen in waves, the energy shifting periodically from one art to another: painting was dominant in the 50's and early 60's, dance challenged it later, and now music seems to be having its say."[5]

Assessing the festival, Johnson maintained that "the sheer diversity of the experimental music" left the strongest impression on the audience, but that conclusion was contentious.[6] The event's narrow engagement with multiculturalism prompted questions about the *diversity of the diversity*, and during a panel that included Gavin Bryars, Glass, and Rockwell, Garrett List shouted his way into the proceedings and declared the lineup to be far less eclectic than its organizers and participants imagined. "I said, 'You guys are not looking around you!'" recalls the composer. "'You're not really seeing what's going on!' They said, 'OK, we've heard all of this before, Garrett. Don't you have anything else to say?'" Johnson acknowledged the festival was "clearly weighted toward white musicians," but added: "As I see it the black-dominated loft jazz scene has evolved right alongside the white-dominated experimental scene throughout this decade. Loft jazz has been quite visible and successful in its own way, and for an institution like the Kitchen to attempt to take this genre under its own wing would be far more patronizing than constructive."[7] Rockwell was more openly critical: "Real rock and jazz that also happen to be experimental were underrepresented."[8]

If the multicultural agenda fast-tracked by List during his two years as music director had been edged to the margins of the "New Music New York" festival, it was much more present when the Kitchen staged its tenth anniversary celebration in the spring of 1981, perhaps because the African American composer, trombonist, and member of the Association for the Advancement of Creative Musicians George Lewis led the team that programmed the music. During his tenure as music director, which ran from September 1980 to June 1982, Lewis helped to "shift the debate around border crossing"—as he writes in *A Power Stronger Than Itself*—"to a stage where whiteness-based constructions of American experimentalism were being fundamentally problematized."[9] Lewis notes that his tenure was part of a wider movement across the United States toward multiculturalism, or, as his former student Michael Dessen put it in his 1983 dissertation, toward "decolonizing American art music."[10] The change in direction was evident in Lewis's first curated event, which included John Zorn's "opera" for improvisers, *Jai Alai*, and prompted Johnson to note that the new director was set to "open the door to new forms of improvising and to provide an outlet for performers to present their own programs."[11]

Following "the network—the community" as much as his own preferences, Lewis included improvisers and non-improvisers in a season that featured Muhal Richard Abrams, Robert Ashley, Derek Bailey, Glenn Branca, Anthony Braxton, Rhys Chatham, Defunkt, Arnold Dreyblatt, Julius Eastman, the Ethnic Heritage Ensemble, Douglas Ewart, Diamanda Galás, Tom Hamilton, Julius Hemphill, Rae Imamura, the Jamaican Music Festival, Takehisa Kosugi, Joan La Barbara, Jackson Mac Low, Roscoe Mitchell, Evan Parker, Eliane Radigue, Frederic Rzewski, Carlos Santos, Tona Scherchen-Hsiao, Ned Sublette, Trans Museq, and Bertram Turetzy, in addition to Zorn and others.[12] "Not all the composers were black or jazz-identified," adds Lewis. "I was also able to bring a number of 'new whites' into the process—composers who might well have been excluded for reasons of the intersection of genre, musical methodology, and community membership."

Lewis rejected simplistic distinctions between black and white, low and high, and uptown and downtown, and while he was inclined to introduce more African Americans and improvisers than his predecessor, he insists his program couldn't be subsumed under any generalization about race or genre (including the idea that it featured black people playing jazz). "A frequently asked question in the community during my years at the Kitchen, even by people like Rhys, whom I was able to discuss the matter with at some length, concerned why I felt the need to curate 'those people' because they had 'so many other places to play.' This wasn't necessarily a racial designation, but one of genre. As I saw it, however, blunderbuss genre monikers like 'jazz' didn't figure very prominently in my deliberations. Rather, I saw the work of people like Julius Hemphill as congruent with an expanded notion of experimentalism, which in my understanding was the multi-directional 'genre' that the Kitchen was created to support." Lacking a vocabulary to describe the "new hybridity" of the Kitchen program, commentators fell back on the idea that the venue was concentrating on jazz—"a framing that updated, but ultimately preserved the old racializations," notes Lewis in *A Power Stronger Than Itself*.[13]

Lewis's expanded notion of experimentalism was in evidence when the Kitchen staged its anniversary festival "Aluminum Nights: Ten Years of New Video, Dance and Music" in a cavernous new nightclub situated on Times Square called Bond's on 14–15 June 1981. More explicitly multi-cultural than "New Music New York," "Aluminum Nights" featured Julius Hemphill and Curtis Lyle (poetry and music), Leroy Jenkins (chamber music with improvisation), George Lewis (live electronic music), and Garrett List (trombone improvisation), as well as Fab 5 Freddy, who introduced the borough-based culture of hip-hop to a largely unknowing audience. In addition Philip Glass and Steve Reich represented the "serious composer" side of the Kitchen; Maryanne Amacher contributed an installation; Laura Dean appeared as a dancer-composer; and the increasingly high-profile Laurie Anderson, whose "O Superman" had reached number two in the British pop charts in the autumn of 1980, headed a group of musicians who performed songs from her forthcoming stage work *United States*. Interspersed with dance (Douglas Dunn, Meredith Monk), poetry (John Giorno), acoustic music (Todd Rundgren, Ned Sublette), and video (Robert Ashley, Robert Wilson, Nam June Paik, Brian Eno, and Talking Heads), the event also showcased Branca, Chatham, the Bush Tetras, DNA, the Feelies, Lydia Lunch, the Raybeats, and Red Decade, who took to the stage with drum kits and guitars, yet were set on breaking with rock music's past. "The large number of rock bands on the list might seem surprising to those who regard rock and art as antithetical," reported Rockwell in the *New York Times*. "But in lower Manhattan, art influences rock, and rock influences art."[14] Along with Peter Gordon, Randy Gun, Jill Kroesen, Ned Sublette, David Van Tieghem, Peter Zummo, and others, Arthur appeared on stage with the Love of Life Orchestra.

List appreciated the event's engagement with diversity, which occurred against the backdrop of Lewis's expanded notion of experimentalism, and the inclusion of hip-hop indicated that the black and Latin street culture that had germinated in the boroughs during the 1970s would discover a healthy downtown audience during the 1980s. For his part, Lewis maintains that the incremental impact of his programming at the Kitchen across two years was "much more telling" than "Aluminum Nights," which amounted to "one little festival," and adds that the "move to diversity" was occurring all over the country, not just in New York. That move to diversity didn't simply involve a shift toward a liberal pluralism in which more genres were ushered into venues such as the Kitchen. Rather, it involved a challenge to the very idea of genre itself. "In Hal Foster's memorable phrase, pluralism becomes a location where 'minor deviation is allowed only in order to resist radical change,'" comments Lewis. But, he continues, there *was* a "radical change during this period . . . that a new genre — 'new music' — was being created that valorized diversity of musical practice and was trying to learn to valorize diversity of cultural reference."[15] Well-intended as they were,

Publicity for the Kitchen's tenth anniversary benefit, 1981. Designed by Jo Bonney and Robert Longo. Retrieved from the Vasulka Archive, http://www.vasulka.org/archive/Kitchen.

attempts to account for new music within the confines of already existing genres — new music as minimalism, rock, jazz, and so on — missed the point. "At the time, canons, genres, and the like were unstable and under challenge from without and within," concludes Lewis. "Reality moved beyond the stereotypes."

The new-music agenda was picked up when curators in cities such as Miami, Minneapolis, and Washington ran local versions of "New Music New York," titled "New Music America," while the Kitchen received a significant boost when it started to receive funds to tour the United States and Europe with its most recognized artists — a development that prompted Charles Wuorinen (Arthur's former teacher at the Manhattan School of Music) and his peers to campaign against the siphoning off of monies that had previously been the preserve of uptown. "They could put up with small audiences," comments the downtown composer Mary Jane Leach, "but when they began to 'lose' funding to music that they disdained, that was too much for some of them." Leach applied faithfully to the National Endowment for the Arts for grants — "because I believed that you shouldn't cede that source of funding to the academic scene" — and notes how pre-screenings were used to cull the most "offensive" projects so that the final panel, when the names of short-listed candidates were made public, could appear more open and democratic. "I applied with the same work two years in a row," she recalls of the softening attitude toward the composers of new music. "The first year I didn't make it past the pre-screening panel, and my work was dismissed as 'having no intrinsic musical value.' The next year I got a fellowship with the same music."[16]

However, the economic and political backdrop that began to unfold as new music strengthened its profile was less promising. The election of Ronald Reagan in November 1980 and the assassination of John Lennon in December 1980 forewarned of the rise of economic neoliberalism and the decline of musical utopianism, and as the decade edged forward the degenerate bankruptcy of the 1970s gave way to a darker period of cold-war paranoia, increased military expenditure, tax breaks for the wealthy, and cuts in welfare and arts spending. The pernicious forces of inequality and individualism were felt most brutally in the African American and Latino/a American communities, in which lower-income individuals and families fell deeper into poverty, while the rapid decline of the country's manufacturing base also left white working-class communities fearing for their economic security.[17] When the Reagan government failed to acknowledge the spread of AIDS — the President required several years before he could bring himself to note the existence of the disease — it also became clear that the gay rights movement had suffered major setbacks across the board; activists would have to wind the clock back ten years and begin to argue for their right to full and equal citizenship all over again. As Eric Hobsbawm notes, Reagan's "enemy was liberalism (the 'L-word' [was] used to good effect in presidential election campaigns) as much as communism."[18]

Descending from midtown and ascending from the financial district, the shifting economics of Manhattan had already made their presence felt in SoHo, where the opening of the chic and spacious Dean and DeLuca supermarket in September 1977 marked a turning point in a neighborhood that had previously made do with Da Roma's grocery on West Broadway between Grand and Canal. The most ominous change might have taken place several years earlier when artist-investors bought up the neighborhood's buildings on the cheap with the knowledge that the legislation that had established their artificially low prices would become unenforceable. "The SoHo artists were about real estate, not about art," comments David Mancuso, who faced concerted opposition from the SoHo Artists Association when he attempted to reopen the Loft on Prince Street. "One woman turned to me at my hearing and said, 'David, if I try and sell my space and the buyers look out of their window and see niggers and spicks . . .'" After Charles Leslie of the SoHo Artists Association declared that the Loft's move to Prince Street amounted to "the beginning of an invasion," Mancuso's new landlord came to his defense. "This was an area for people with new ideas, but it's turned into something else," Raymond Zurawin told the *Village Voice.* "I don't see many struggling young artists—just lofts for the rich who are concerned about dog leashes and the crime rate."[19]

Accustomed to operating on the cultural fringe, and maybe reckoning that they lived in a protected enclave, downtowners didn't organize in any kind of cohesive way against the Reagan administration, but there turned out to be a cost, and it was paid for in rent. As property prices began to rise, cash-poor artists and musicians were forced out of lower Manhattan, sometimes through aggressive action. "At one point I played in a music festival in California, and I came back to find that the landlord had beaten holes in the walls and bricks were lying on my bed," remembers List, who shared a loft on John Street in the financial district with Scott Johnson, a composer, and Charlie Moulton, a dancer in the Merce Cunningham Company. "He threw the other two guys out, and when I came back he threw me out too. Like most people, we didn't have a lease, and he tripled the rent as soon as we were gone. We were paying $500 in September, and in October he charged $1,500 and he got it. This was 1979. My landlord was ahead of the game."[20]

The commercialization of property in SoHo was even more marked, yet the pricing out of artists who had failed to invest also prompted a more obviously dispersed, rhizomatic community to come into focus—and this downtown network proved to be more flexible and less centralized than its predecessor thanks to its diminishing dependence on a single, prominent neighborhood. In his introduction to a special section titled "That Downtown Sound . . . From A to Z" in the June 1982 edition of the *New York Rocker,* Tim Carr, director of special projects and domestic touring at the Kitchen, revealed how downtown had become a community and maybe even a movement that was no longer grounded in SoHo: "Those New Yorkers truly involved in the arts and those rockers on the periphery have seen what was once the ideal of an artistic community (perhaps only in legend) transformed into an affluent Disneyland, with two chi-chi novelty shops and three chi-chi eateries for every vestige of 'old Soho.'" He continued, "The generic 'Downtown' is therefore more palatable, and because of the permutations, more correct. Displaced artists, the new noise bands and rock composers are now spread over a wide swatch of lower Manhattan, from Alphabet City to the Fulton Fish Market, NoHo to Tribeca."[21]

Instead of bemoaning the end of a supposedly utopian period in which artists were able to live only with other artists, the protagonists of this expanded downtown began to value the way they shared their buildings and streets with a variety of nonartists (which was a lifestyle that the artist and musician residents of the East Village had espoused all along). And as composers and players in the new-music, rock, and jazz scenes continued to exchange phone numbers and chord progressions, the downtown music scene surged toward its turbo-charged peak. "There is really no definable 'Downtown Sound,'" added Carr, "but rather a spectrum of styles identifiable *en masse* only by their 'defiant non-commerciality,' their willingness to experiment, their desire to go out, outer, outest."[22] Carr and his co-contributors identified Laurie Anderson, Robert Ashley, Avant Squares, Glenn Branca, Eugene Chadbourne and John Zorn, Rhys Chatham, DNA, Dog Eat Dog, EQ'd, Barbara Ess, Friction, the Golden Palominos, I Ride the Bus, Konk, Jill Kroesen, La Guapa Papa, Liquid Liquid, Jeffrey Lohn, the Lounge Lizards, the Love of Life Orchestra, Mofungo, Mon Ton Son, the Off Shoots, Red Dark Sweet, Red Decade, the Social Climbers, The Scene Is Now, Sonic Youth, T-Venus, "Blue" Gene Tyranny, David Van Tieghem, V-Effect, and Zev as significant downtown players, and "That Downtown Sound . . . From A to Z" profiled them all. Extending across ten pages, the piece only mentioned Arthur when it listed his name — along with forty-nine others — as a onetime performer in the Love of Life Orchestra.

Arthur might have been more prominent if he hadn't been quite so eclectic. Although open-mindedness was mandatory among downtown musicians, all of those highlighted in the *New York Rocker* survey could be identified with a project they had stuck with for long enough to get noticed (at least by the left-field press). Arthur had produced enough disco to get recognition in the dance-music press, but dance didn't count as far as downtown's cartographers were concerned, and his other projects turned out to be too varied and thinly spread for them to stand out. Having completed the Loose Joints project in the first half of 1980, Arthur would go on to write a composition for an avant-garde opera; release two orchestral albums; join a new-wave outfit called the Necessaries; continue to play with the Flying Hearts; produce a range of twelve-inch dance singles; work with two of New York's most prominent remixers; release an album of improvised, orchestral dance music; record an electronic ambient piece; pen solo and co-authored songs; join a series of quirky lineups that drew on a range of folk, pop, and experimental modes; explore hip-hop as well as microtonal music; cofound one of the most influential street labels of the decade; and begin work on the voice-cello solo project that would become one of his most enduring statements—all in a three-and-a-half-year period.

In other words, Arthur refused to settle into the comfort zone of genre or the non-generic framework of new music, and he also worked continuously to subvert the idea that music should be organized according to commercial imperatives that came from beyond the musician, because that system amounted to a form of sonic repression. Dividing and subdividing his attentions, Arthur understood his practice was likely to result in a lack of recognition, because independent and major record companies alike would wonder about his lack of focus. Although individual recordings had market potential, label heads would become exasperated at his unwillingness to repeat something that was successful, or to commit himself to developing a coherent identity and following. Arthur amounted to more than a "minor deviation"—to return to Hal Foster's critique of pluralism—because he rejected the commercial record industry's foundational premise: that music has the greatest meaning when it can be converted into a commodity and sold, and that the most effective way of pursuing this goal is for record companies and their artists to forge a recognizable and containable sound. Instead, to borrow again from Foster, Arthur embodied "radical change."[23] Indeed it's possible that even Arthur struggled to grasp the full range of his activity.

Medea

As far as Arthur was concerned, music was capable of rebirthing itself constantly. Notes could be linked in an infinite array of combinations, while a multitude of words, rhythms, and textural effects could contribute to the innate complexity of every choice in the music-making process. The pressures of commodity culture limited the extent to which this immanent democracy of sound could flourish, because artists had to discard all but one variation of a piece of music if they hoped to make some money from selling it. Yet music's will to freedom was hard to contain, and each recording was capable of being reborn—played differently and experienced differently—in an unquantifiable range of settings. Arthur liked this idea, and appreciated the way in which dance music, with its culture of remixing, improvised DJ sets, and finely tuned sound systems, always suggested fresh ways of hearing the same piece. "The final ethical measure of any music is its ability to create new possibilities for life," argues Ronald Bogue, and Arthur, according to Ned Sublette, "couldn't turn his back on the beauty of unexplored possibilities."[24]

Putting this philosophy into practice, Arthur sought to integrate the principles of indeterminacy, reinvention, and freedom of movement in a number of his compositions. Although *Instrumentals* was written down, its possible permutations were boundless, and no recording could come close to capturing its entirety. Organized around an even looser score, the $24 \rightarrow 24$ sessions cultivated the inexhaustible, both because Arthur asked his musicians to improvise, and because he used two sets of twenty-four-track tapes to generate worlds of complexity. And when he purchased his Sony Walkman, which was available in the United States by 1980, it became easier than ever for him to examine different versions of his recordings in painstaking detail before he had to choose one version over all the others. The pursuit of multiplicity could be confusing, however, and there were times when Arthur became embroiled in a cul-de-sac of indecision. Steven Hall remembers that his friend could listen to a set of Side A/Side B mixes so many times "he couldn't hear the difference any more." At that point Arthur would go home, collapse on the sofa, and play the mixes to Tom Lee, who would often decide which one was the best.[25] Lee was often relieved to see Arthur in one piece. "I would worry when he went out running with his Walkman," he explains. "I could imagine him running across all these avenues with a Walkman on, listening to some tape and not paying attention to the cars coming."

Despite his tendency to explore and defer, Arthur drew on previously untapped reservoirs of decisiveness when Robert Wilson, the director and designer of *Einstein on the Beach*, commissioned him to write a score for his next opera production, *Medea*. The project had been offered originally to Philip Glass, but Glass turned it down, having received a commission to write the opera *Satyagraha* as well as a $15,000 Rockefeller Foundation grant in the spring of 1978. Keen to channel Arthur's refractory talent and sprawling ambition, and conscious he didn't want to become too closely identified with Wilson, Glass told the director that "Arthur would be brilliant," which was enough to persuade Wilson to give him the job in October 1980. "It was a big coup," remembers Lee. "Arthur was very pleased, but also very nervous." Handed a $1,500 advance, with the same sum promised on completion, Arthur viewed the job as a life-changing opportunity. After all, *Einstein on the Beach* had established Glass as a high-profile composer, and there was every reason to believe that *Medea* could have an equivalent impact on Arthur's career. "He thought he would achieve the fame and critical acclaim he deserved as a serious composer," confirms Hall.

Making a clean sweep of the apartment, Arthur set up a series of filing shelves, which he divided into parts that correlated to different sections of his piece, and Lee remembers him being much more systematic than ever before. Jon Gibson was invited to work on the composition at La MaMa's rehearsal space and recalls there being "reams and reams of this music," and that although it was recorded in a "huge rush," it "really worked." Unfortunately that didn't prevent the relationship between Arthur and Wilson from deteriorating rapidly, and by January the director had started to fire off terse letters in which he complained that Arthur wasn't providing him with the kind of detail he required, was slipping behind schedule, and was unduly resistant to integrating suggestions. "You will rewrite as necessary," instructed Wilson's assistant in one communication. "I hope we are on our way now." The sentiment turned out to be optimistic. "The direction the music was going in didn't suit Robert Wilson, and Arthur had a stubborn side to him," remembers Peter Zummo. "Arthur felt the project would be better if the music was the way he thought it should be. They couldn't negotiate the future of the music."

Arthur found it difficult to discuss emerging problems with Wilson, whose assistants blocked communication. "Arthur would show up to a rehearsal and would have a question about a passage, but he wouldn't be able to get to Bob," remembers Lee. "Something might then go wrong, maybe around the spacing of the music, and Arthur would end up coming home upset." On the occasions when Arthur and Wilson did get to speak, they usually fought, and after one battle the composer was distraught enough to call his parents for advice. "He said, 'I'm just having an awful time with Robert Wilson,'" recalls Chuck. "'His ideas are not like mine and mine are not like his.'" Chuck told him to compromise, which was difficult for

Arthur to hear because his modus operandi was to try and get away with as much as he could. "I think Arthur and Robert had a lot of respect for each other, but they were both difficult bitches and their clash was inevitable," concludes Hall. "At that point Arthur was very steadfast about his own abilities, and he wasn't willing to compromise."

Conducted by Julius Eastman and recorded in February 1981, Arthur's composition lasted for about seventy minutes and consisted of arrhythmic clusters of sustained notes that generated a medieval sound to evoke the royal setting of Euripides's *Medea* (a play that depicts a court trapped in the throes of power and paranoia, violence and decline). Although the music had little in common with the early performances of *Instrumentals*, which were quirky, rhythmic, and colorful, the score turned out to be quite similar to the CETA Orchestra's later rendition of a more somber section from that piece, and it also reinforced the impression that Arthur could excel in the field of minimal orchestral music (or new music). Having handed the recording to Wilson, Arthur traveled to the Kennedy Center in Washington to see a one-off "workshop" performance of the show (which was probably staged in order to raise more money for the project). "It was a slow-moving Robert Wilson performance," recalls Lee. "I can picture the actors walking slowly across the stage. The music followed the movement of the opera in an interesting way."

Arthur and Wilson parted ways soon after. "I think Arthur was frustrated and disappointed, and I think Bob was frustrated and disappointed," notes Glass. "Neither of them could explain to me what had happened. They just said it didn't work out." Acknowledging Wilson's tendency to deliver at the last minute and with added-on hysteria, Glass reckons a personality clash lay at the root of the conflict. "Maybe two people playing the same game didn't work," he adds. When the fallout came to light, Jon Gibson was taken aback. "I thought it was beautiful theatre music, and I was shocked when I heard that he wasn't using it," he says. A little later, Wilson hired the British minimalist composer Gavin Bryars to write a new score. Bryars maintains that Wilson asked for something he didn't get with Arthur; the possibility of certain passages being sung rather than spoken.[26]

Full of regret, Arthur penned a letter (apparently never sent) to Wilson. "Last night I dreamed we somehow broke the ice again and became friends," he wrote. "Everyone was there and was very angry. You performed a puppet show, I had to go to the bathroom and you thought I was being rude. I know you'll probably tear this up. I never wanted to hurt your show, I was struggling with my inability to go faster. I always thought you would be pleased in the end, but now I'm sorry; you are angry." Arthur's disenchantment was crushing, his moment of probable triumph and elevation having degenerated into an acrimonious argument.

The Moon

As Arthur pursued the big-prize commissions of Loose Joints and *Medea*, he also continued to work with old friends such as Ernie Brooks and Steven Hall, as well as newer ones such as Joyce Bowden. Lacking an advance from a record company or a commission from a theater director, these ventures were intimate and philosophical. Often they involved the players gathering in duos, and occasionally they would culminate in something that resembled a band, but for the most part the formation didn't really seem to matter. The most important thing was to spend time together, and as playing and socializing bled into each other, Arthur, Bowden, Brooks, and Hall worked out their mutual relationships, as well as how their folk/pop sound might one day shape the musical cosmos.

Hall teamed up with Arthur to form a "proto-country band" called the Sailboats that aimed (in the words of Arthur) to "play the mild but penetrating kind of music that the word sailboats evokes."[27] Arthur had explored the tranquil yet potentially strange sound of folk when he began to write songs in San Francisco, and he also had developed a robust form of country when he blended the aesthetic with disco and gospel on the wholesome yet catchy "The Only Usefulness" and "No Hearts Free," which he laid down with Loose Joints. Although that studio lineup turned out to be an ephemeral one, Arthur remained intent on deepening his journey into vernacular folk, and he cherished the way this tradition enabled him to visit the sweeping terrain of middle America without actually having to travel there (like the immigrant who is nostalgic for a home to which she or he might not ultimately want to return). With a Scottish upbringing that connected him to a folk sensibility, Hall became a promising partner for Arthur, and that Hall had been complimented on his "nice voice" by Bob Dylan—he was singing harmony to Allen Ginsberg in Poet's Building when the folk legend uttered those words—didn't exactly harm his credentials.

Like the sailboat Chuck and Emily had purchased after Arthur ran away

Arthur Russell, Tom Lee, and Steven Hall at a *SHINY* Magazine party at the Doug Milford Gallery in the early 1980s. Hall started *SHINY* Magazine after he left Columbia University, where he worked with Kenneth Koch and edited the *Columbia Review*. Photographer unknown. Courtesy of Steven Hall and Johnny Fu.

from home, which Arthur had grown to love during vacations in Minnesota, the new band was built on simple foundational principles: Arthur played guitar and sometimes harmonica, but never cello, because the six flights of stairs in his Twelfth Street apartment assumed particularly cruel proportions when he had to carry his stringed instrument with him; Hall played guitar; and Arthur and Hall agreed to take the lead on their own songs while singing harmony for each other. Public appearances rolled in at a reasonable rate. Ginsberg asked them to perform at some of his concerts, and they also appeared at Max's Kansas City, Tier 3, and Mickey Ruskin's Lower Manhattan Ocean Club. "Mickey Ruskin had an eye for the eccentric genius," says Hall. "He was always surrounded by wild and wildly creative types. He saw something in Arthur." Although country had become one of the most conservative genres in Western popular music, its traditionally safe style was never entirely safe with Arthur and Hall, as the homoerotic "List of Boys" demonstrated. "Arthur had a very fast drum track, and I was instructed to play very fast acoustic guitar along with it," remembers Hall of another (non-Sailboats) proto-country recording. "During the session I improvised a scream and Arthur loved it, so I was instructed to scream over and over. It was as though we were making a new kind of music called speed country."

Brooks, meanwhile, was trying to work out where he stood with Arthur. During the recording of "Kiss Me Again," Arthur had told him that "as a rocker" he would never develop the feel of a disco or funk bass, or understand the instinctual relationship between the bass player and the drummer that was so integral to dance. "I was pissed off because I wanted to do it, but Arthur said, 'No, it's got to be the disco guy,'" recalls Brooks. "I think he wanted the bass to play slightly ahead of the drums, and he thought I was playing behind the drums." Noting that David Van Tieghem was equally upset when he was rejected for similar reasons, Brooks concedes he now thinks Arthur was probably right. "I didn't have experience of that kind of bass playing," he adds. But at the time he was unapologetic about his preference for melody and harmony over rhythm and groove, and he also made it clear he thought Arthur's lionization of certain DJs and remixers was "a bunch of bullshit," as was his reliance on a group of "sterile studio musicians" during the recording of "Kiss Me Again." The tension mounted when Arthur traveled to Sire Records' office in order to push Dinosaur rather than the Flying Hearts. "Seymour thought Arthur was talented but impossible, and dance music certainly confused the issue, Brooks explains." "Arthur was perceived as being committed to the Flying Hearts for only a very brief period, and I think Seymour knew it."

Brooks and Arthur ended up seeing a lot less of each other in 1979, and during that year Russell's interest in the old project of the Flying Hearts dipped so low that Lee only found out about the group when he chanced across one of their tapes. But when the Loose Joints project stumbled to a close, Arthur and Brooks decided to give the Flying Hearts another go. They replaced Van Tieghem with Jesse Chamberlain (a young, energetic drummer whose tight trousers and black ruffled hair got to Arthur) and Larry Saltzman with John Scherman (a skilled guitarist who thought the Flying Hearts tapes possessed an "ineffable quality" that reminded him of the Beatles). A Juilliard dropout who had headlined for a week at Folk City, Joyce Bowden became the third new recruit after Brooks met her at another group's rehearsal (where Scherman happened to be playing). "I remember her listening to the music and wriggling with energy," the bass player recalls. "I liked her a lot." When Brooks found out Bowden possessed a seraphic voice to match her pale features and ringlet curls, he asked Scherman to bring her to a rehearsal—the Flying Hearts having received a couple of bracing rejection letters from Warner Bros. that declared

Arthur's singing was at best "very flat and drab" and at worst "in trouble." Scherman agreed because he wanted to spend as much time with Bowden as possible, and he prepared his path by handing her a tape of the group, as well as warning Brooks to maintain his distance.

"The songs were quite different to anything else that I had heard," recalls Bowden. "The lyrics were full of integrity and honesty, and melodically the songs swooped effortlessly from high to low, and with intervals that were seldom used in pop music. They just ignored the idiom of the day and went with the most beautiful idea of what pop music could be." During the band's next rehearsal, which took place in Arthur's absence, Brooks asked Bowden if she'd like to work with the group. "I thought, 'Wow, OK, that sounds good!'" she remembers. "These guys were very cute and likeable, and the musicianship was fun." When the band met again a week or so later, Bowden thought Arthur seemed "shy and wonderful and sweet," and when he sang "Janine" she decided that she wanted to spend the rest of her life following him.

> It's such a joke
> What he asked you to do
> He must think I'm a fool
> Janine, don't go with those guys
> What's in it for you?
> In another day
> Your dream will appear
> I touched you on the arm
> You were so warm
> Janine, you know I'm your friend
> Whatever they say
> In another day
> Your dream will appear
> I touch you on the arm
> I meant you no harm.

"He begins by speaking to himself, and when he turns to the other the switch is so natural it is hard to even notice," she reminisces. "The song kept switching from the first to the second person until the two seemed to dissolve into one another, as if Arthur had written it while enveloped in a samadhi-like trance. I was floored."

Joyce Bowden photographed
in New York, 1980.
Photographer unknown.
Courtesy of Joyce Bowden.

Bowden was drawn to Arthur's handsome looks, his honesty, and his originality. "He was quiet yet had a wonderful sense of humor," she says. "He always spoke from his center and didn't mind what the effect was going to be on others. He didn't fear himself, or if he did he was a warrior in exposing himself. And his music was extraordinary. He was very easy to fall in love with, basically." A mercurial personality, Bowden advanced toward Arthur, and in a precipitate movement, Arthur invited her back to his apartment in order to practice—because from the very beginning, notes Brooks, he "was attracted to Joyce and wanted to mold her into the kind of singer he envisioned." As Arthur sang and played on his guitar, Bowden sat and melted, after which she took his hand and led him up into his loft bed where they could see the full moon shining into his room. Arthur asked her if she knew he was gay, and she replied, "Yes, but I don't mind that since I figure I like you enough for both of us." After that night, Bowden backed away, having realized she "could no more possess Arthur" than she "could possess the moon." Arthur, she says, "belonged to no one, not even to a particular form."

Bowden joined Brooks and Hall, as well as an amorphous group of other musicians, engineers, producers, remixers, and DJs. "Arthur's aim became more and more to create some sort of virtuous state of mind through his music," says Bowden. "It became a meditation for himself and other people, a process in which to live. I'm not sure he was able to find a person who could match one-on-one everything he wanted, so he developed an unusually intricate, varied, and deep set of musical relationships. He found little pieces of what he wanted in a lot of people." Bowden, Brooks, and Hall regarded Arthur as a superior, ethereal talent, while Arthur came to hold them in especially high regard, even though they could all be frustrating in their own separate ways — because the angelic Bowden lacked direction, Brooks was a gifted songwriter but didn't understand dance, and the talented Hall could be impossible. All three became intimate with Arthur, and they overlapped regularly at rehearsals, gigs, and studio sessions. "We were the viscose, the liquid, to his pigment," comments Bowden. "We all had different flavors, so the color would vary depending on who he was working with." Fluid and interlocking, the relationships remained uncompetitive, even though Bowden, Brooks, and Hall all wanted to edge close to Arthur. "I never felt any rivalry with Steven or Joyce," says Brooks. "Arthur was so committed to music, if you wanted to do something with him he would find the time to do it. I never remember Arthur being unavailable."

As sexual tensions became intertwined with musical energies, Arthur managed to control his crush on Hall as well as his ongoing attraction to Bowden, while he and Hall teamed up to gawk at Brooks. "Ernie enjoyed teasing us by walking around his loft without a shirt, showing off his washboard stomach," remembers Hall. "Arthur and I would shoot knowing glances at each other and giggle like teenage schoolgirls when he paraded around like that. We loved the fact that he was so open and understanding about our queerness." Brooks maintains he had "no inkling" of this, or about who fancied whom, yet he continued to insist Arthur should face up to his "true feelings" for women. A potential recipient, Bowden struggled with her desire for Arthur, but found it relatively easy to handle Brooks, even though he was "something descended from the heavens." As she tracked the argument between Arthur and Brooks, Bowden wondered if the bass player persisted with his theory of lost love not only because he was a poet and a romantic but also because it helped divert attention from "the ethereal movement he had with Arthur," which "floated in the air, wasn't a direct physical challenge, and didn't have to be identified."

In the autumn of 1980, Arthur sent his parents a new tape of Flying

Hearts recordings that included "I Want to Go All the Way," "Don't Make Me Sad Another Day," "Bobby," "Tryin' to Forget You," and "Don't Forget about Me." As musicians joined and left the band, rehearsals were called, but personal diaries and historical circumstances never coincided sufficiently for the group to develop any momentum, and no concerts took place. "Arthur really had a great sense of melody, and at times he would joke that we could be better than Fleetwood Mac," remembers John Scherman. "The Flying Hearts played straight-ahead syncretic folk and pop rock. The sound was almost déclassé. I feel almost defensive."

A new-wave outfit called the Necessaries was notably less vulnerable. Formed toward the beginning of 1978, the band included Ed Tomney (guitar), Jesse Chamberlain (drums), and Randy Gun (guitar), as well as Brooks, who had segued into the group following the breakup of the original Flying Hearts. Initially it looked as though Brooks had made an astute move. The Necessaries played at CBGB's in November 1978, and John Cale, who had been influential in bringing the band together, produced the group's first single, an early release on IRS (International Record Syndicate) Records. But then Tomney (a new-waver) clashed with Gun (a rock-and-roller) over the direction of the band's sound, and when Gun's replacement—the English studio guitarist Chris Spedding—also moved on, Brooks talked about the vacant fourth position with Arthur. "Arthur said, 'I will really commit myself to being in the band,'" remembers Brooks. "He was insistent." Having played on the 24 $\longrightarrow$ 24 sessions, Tomney was skeptical about Arthur's ability to fit in, and his doubts were echoed by Chamberlain, yet Brooks maintained it would work. "They both felt something of his genius, but I think they sensed he was all over the place musically," adds the bass player. "I really forced them to accept him."

According to Donald Murk, who managed the group during its first year or so, Tomney and Chamberlain came around to the idea of integrating Arthur because of his connections with Sire, but tensions soon emerged after Arthur joined them in 1980. Arthur refused to believe the band should exist as a virtually exclusive vehicle for Tomney's songs, and he also objected to its name, which sounded like a pluralized euphemism for the bathroom. Unimpressed, Chamberlain nicknamed Arthur "tardo" (which was short for "retard"). The friction intensified when the musicians went into Blank Tapes to lay down an album for Sire that was scheduled for a UK release. "Arthur was the Neil Young of the group," recalls Bob Blank, who engineered the sessions. "Everyone wanted to make a commercial record, and Arthur was the curmudgeon, the anti-guy. He totally knew what to do musically, and then he would deliberately put people into an awkward position and make them claw their way out." Brooks remembers endless discussions about the tuning of the instruments, some of them conducted through a haze of pot, and during one particularly fraught session Arthur accused Blank of using a hidden vari-speed button to prevent him from tuning his cello (which he played alongside keyboards and the guitar). Attempting to defuse the strained relations, Brooks ricocheted between the control room and the studio floor while pausing whenever possible to reassure an onlooking representative from Sire that everything was OK. "This was Arthur at his wackiest," he recalls.

The Sire subplot thickened when the Necessaries exhausted their budget before the album was complete and nominated Arthur to ask the company for more money—against his will. Convinced that if Stein wanted to do something it was for the wrong reasons, Arthur also suspected the Sire boss was planning to pass his songs to Talking Heads, in part because the group's third album, *Remain in Light*, had featured funk-oriented horn sections and polyrhythmic percussion. As far as Arthur was concerned, the potential for plagiarism was clear—he had written some horn arrangements for Byrne and hadn't been credited. But there's no evidence that these arrangements appeared on the album, and in this instance Brooks believed his friend's suspicions were "absurd" (even if Byrne later said of the arrangements, "[They did] completely reorient my thinking").[28] Visiting the Sire office, Arthur wondered what he was in for when Stein addressed him over the public-address system while he was waiting in the lobby and asked, "What sayeth you, Sir Arthur?" Arthur left with enough money for the Necessaries to complete their album—which they wrapped up at Sundragon Studios—but Stein's comment, which was a sly rather than exasperated reference to his tendency towards preciousness, troubled Arthur deeply and haunted him for years to come.

With the album awaiting release, the Necessaries performed at Danceteria (where R.E.M. opened for them) and again at the 9:30 Club in Washington (where they opened for R.E.M.). "If Danceteria was going to have a pop band it was the Necessaries," says Jim Fouratt, the co-owner of the venue. "I had this night called 'Serious Fun,' which brought in more experimental music. I thought the Necessaries had the potential to be like Scritti

Publicity shot of the Necessaries, 1981. *Left to right*: Arthur Russell, Ernie Brooks, Jesse Chamberlain, and Ed Tomney. "I saw the Necessaries at CBGB's in November 1978 and became instantly devoted," says Paul Waldman. Courtesy of Carrie and Paul Waldman. Photograph by Paul Waldman.

Politti." A breakthrough appeared imminent, but during a subsequent trip to the capital in the spring of 1981 Arthur started to complain about the grinding logistics of the trip, about having to miss another rehearsal in order to travel to D.C., about how a certain song could be improved, and about the band's unfortunate name. As the tour van hit traffic at the mouth of the Holland Tunnel, Arthur realized he wasn't where he wanted to be and, grabbing his cello, opened the door and jumped out. Brooks screamed, "Arthur, you can't do this!"

Arthur appears to have concluded he had no choice, perhaps because the Holland Tunnel represented the dividing line between downtown mobility and a one-way journey into recognizable sound, a life on the road, and a requirement to devote all his energies to a single project. "It'll be good for you!" Arthur called back to the desperate Brooks. "It'll be better to play as a trio!" With unanticipated time on his hands, Arthur walked to the apartment of Ned Sublette, who lived a few blocks away from the Holland Tunnel, and recounted what had happened in a calm voice. Sublette remembers he had "absolutely no idea what to think or say," although what happened next was perfectly eloquent. "Arthur took his cello out of its case, and I picked up my guitar, and we just played instrumental music for the better part of an hour. Then he went on his way."

Back in the van, Chamberlain and Tomney were furious. "Arthur's behavior was outrageous," says Brooks. "Probably all of us wanted to jump out of there at some point, because it wasn't very comfortable. When Arthur jumped out he left the band in disarray." Visiting Brooks a few days after the Necessaries returned from Washington, Arthur immediately made matters worse when he greeted his friend with the words, "I really did the right thing by jumping out." Brooks responded by grabbing Arthur by the waist, picking him up, and throwing him down. "I didn't want to hurt him, but I had to do something physical," he recalls. "If I had wanted to hurt him, I would have punched him. Maybe I wanted to squeeze some sense into him?" As far as Brooks was concerned, a pattern was beginning to emerge. "When Arthur joined the Necessaries the group was very structured and Arthur said that's what he wanted, but then he became the mole boring from within to bring down the building," he explains. "That became my story, in a way. I would get involved with people who would carry on a fairly consistent line of work, and then I would try to integrate Arthur and it would fail." Brooks reasons that an inability to commit "was an absolutely essential part of Arthur's make-up." Yet he also asks: "If Arthur had committed himself would that have limited his creativity? I can't answer that."

Titled *Big Sky*, the debut album of the Necessaries was released in the UK in 1981, but although Brooks, Chamberlain, and Tomney wanted to take the band forward, Sire decided against supporting a tour. Layered over a pre-U2, high decibel, delay-soaked sound, the album's twelve songs were written by Tomney save for "Driving and Talking" (Brooks and Russell), "Detroit Tonight" (Brooks and Russell), and "On the Run" (Tomney and Russell). It was difficult to detect Arthur's quirky voice, playful humor, and poetic loveliness in any of the tracks, including the ones he had co-written, which indicates he wasn't best suited to playing in a new-wave outfit. A year later, the Necessaries released *Event Horizon*, which included five songs from *Big Sky* plus an additional five selections, two of which had been written by Arthur—"The Finish Line" and "More Real." Brooks judged the latter to be the band's most successful attempt at blending "Ed's clearly shaped and muscular guitar and Arthur's softer melodic style." The *New York Rocker* noted that the revised LP contained "some shuffling, some trimming of dead weight, and the setting of real gems in their place (the biggest plus: 'More Real' is easily the prettiest song the Zombies never wrote)." The review continued, "Buy *Event Horizon* and if you really like it, then dig up *Big Sky*, but not the other way around."[29] Yet although downtown composers were impressed that Arthur now had a Sire album to add to his list of releases, the underlying story was one of anticlimax. Tom Lee remembers Arthur saying he didn't want the Necessaries to sound like yet another early eighties new-wave band; the evidence of *Big Sky* suggests he might have failed in that objective.

Arthur's story with Sire almost took another turn when the label proposed that he record a solo album once *Big Sky* was completed. "I thought it would be great," recalls Blank, who had seen Talking Heads and Madonna pass through his studio. "But Arthur wasn't sure that Seymour Stein really understood him." The emergence of Blank as an intermediary might have given Arthur further pause. As requested by Brooks, Chamberlain, and Tomney, the engineer had kept costs to a minimum during the recording of the Necessaries' album in order for them to channel part of their Sire advance into living expenses, and Blank believes Arthur "probably smelled a rat" when about half of the money ended up being siphoned away from the studio. Accustomed to spending every last dime on the recording process, Arthur might have wondered if the engineer was planning to conspire with the record company to produce his solo album on the cheap. Blank says that his unqualified enthusiasm to do the deal, combined with his failure to reassure Arthur about the all-important details, could have contributed to the musician's decision to "back off." Pointing out that Stein and Michael Rosenblatt were concerned about Arthur's neurotic temperament, Brooks questions the theory that it was Arthur rather than Sire who backed away from the putative deal, but the bass player concedes, "It's possible Bob could have got Sire to do the deal," and adds that "there was definitely a breakdown of trust between Bob and Arthur."

The list of disappointments was growing: Arthur had fallen out with West End, the label that was supposed to forward his dance career and maybe even release an album; the impasse with Wilson had dashed his hopes of becoming a significant composer in new music; and now he had missed what would turn out to be his last chance of striking an album deal with a major label. Arthur might have wondered if the common element in these relationships — Arthur — had anything to do with the sequence of disappointments. Sensitive, creative, and prone to dogmatism, Arthur could be singularly intransigent when it came to making compromises. Then again, the music industry was full of people who wanted to tame his music until it became a recognizable commodity, and he was never likely to be happy with the profit-oriented prerogatives of a commercial label. "Arthur probably felt that unless he had budgetary control, he wouldn't have got the results and studio freedom he wanted," concludes Blank. "Certainly a major record deal would have constrained his method of operation, which was to go in and do whatever he felt, rework it as needed, and then have ownership over what he had created. He would have been answerable to me and an A&R guy, and would have also been subjected to the endless remixing that was just beginning to take hold of the music industry."

The Necessaries were the last signed-up band to feature Arthur as part of their regular lineup, which was another disappointment. Arthur cherished the idea of working with a group and made it clear to anyone who was confused that Dinosaur, Loose Joints, the Flying Hearts, and the Necessaries were meaningful collective entities — not subterfuge fronts for his solo work. Yet Arthur was too awkward, eccentric, and opinionated to survive for long in a settled lineup, especially one with a fixed sound. Although Brooks had taken on the challenging role of mediator, the grinding tours, claustrophobic dynamics, and limiting aesthetics that were part and parcel of being in a band were too much for Arthur, who preferred to record music to the rhythm of his own idiosyncrasies, putting together ephemeral lineups that matched close musician friends with talented newcomers. As harrowing as it had been, at least the experience of working with the Necessaries had clarified Arthur's future.

Absolutely Unconcerned with Identity

A common agenda could still be detected in the Kitchen's ranks during the late 1970s and early 1980s. Works and performances avoided climax, or the portrayal of conflict that could be resolved; tonality was more popular than atonality; and although a certain level of musicianship was required, virtuoso skill was rarely necessary. As they had done throughout, composers played their own pieces and called on friends to make up the numbers, and

Arnold Dreyblatt, 1980.
Courtesy of Arnold Dreyblatt.

many also notated their music, because this practice was, ultimately, their most distinguishing feature. Along with peers such as Arnold Dreyblatt, however, Arthur was drifting away from the conventions of composition and, perhaps more significantly, showed no interest in capitalizing on the cachet that came with the formal title of "composer."

Unable to play a traditional musical instrument or notate music in a recognized manner, Dreyblatt appreciated Arthur for his entirely non-judgmental relationship to the compositional process, as well as his lack of enthusiasm for traditional compositional routes. Dreyblatt had started to hang out at the Experimental Intermedia Foundation and the Kitchen while he was working for La Monte Young, and he later formed the Orchestra of Excited Strings, where he played a heavily amplified double bass strung with unwound piano wires that he would beat with a bow, as well as other unusual instruments, including a modified, miniature, acoustic upright piano and a hurdy-gurdy. His band included musicians who were trained and untrained, and although Dreyblatt says the music was necessarily reduced in structure because of his nonmusical background, he adds he was trying to be serious. Others weren't convinced. "I was coming from a background in visual media and wasn't really a musician-type, so I didn't fit into the Kitchen's music scene," he says. "Arthur was one of the few who embraced me. He gave me some cello lessons and invited me to play some gigs. I learned a tremendous amount just from hanging out with him."

Dreyblatt was taken with Arthur's sensibility, which he describes as "a lightness that could appear non-serious to some," as well as his ability to move between the disparate clusters of the downtown music scene. He also appreciated Arthur's lack of concern with establishing a definitive artistic identity, even though he existed in a competitive network that seemed to require precisely that kind of self-representation. "Someone like Rhys Chatham had new-music credentials and developed a composed music with the electric guitar, maintaining all along that he was first and foremost a composer," notes Dreyblatt. "Arthur, though, was absolutely unconcerned with identity—with projecting 'I am just this.' Rhys was standing there saying we are composers, whereas Arthur didn't need to do that at all. That loss of identity—the loss of the I-genius—can be very threatening to the new-music world, but that was Arthur."

As he worked on dance with Loose Joints, new music with Robert Wilson, and new wave with the Necessaries, often shuttling between these disconnected worlds on a daily basis, Arthur also started to find out more about Dreyblatt's specialty "little black boxes," which generated electronic sine tones, and took a particular liking to a digital model that could produce a tone that was (in the words of its inventor) "absolutely clear and stable." Having played around with the equipment, Arthur composed an experimental track titled *Sketch for "Face of Helen,"* which evoked musique concrète in its use of the ambient sounds of wind, water, and birdcalls. The recording didn't sound like anything Arthur had recorded previously, so in that respect (and in that respect alone) it was entirely predictable.

Arthur developed two longer versions of *Sketch*. The first stretched the sound effects across a slowed-down, eighteen-minute edit of his *Medea* recording, while the second removed the *Medea* backdrop in order to give extra emphasis to the undulating stream of muted sound effects, including the slow groan of a depressed tugboat. On this second version, a continuous hiss generated a saturating humidity while simple synth lines darted in and out of the stream-like collage, and at one point these notes started to fall like electronic raindrops onto a xylophone, bringing hope into the ascendant mood of mournful wistfulness and claustrophobic anxiousness. Arthur mastered the longer versions of *Sketch* and, pairing them with *Reach One (With Two Fender Rhodes)*, manufactured test pressings of a debut solo album, *Instrumentals: Volume 1*, which he pressed up at Chatham Square,

Ned Sublette, 1986. Publicity photograph by
Marsha Resnick. Courtesy of Ned Sublette.

Philip Glass's label.[30] Having completed the hard work, Arthur proceeded
to shelve the album, although a short edit of *Sketch* was released in 1981
when the Belgian label Les Disques du Crépuscule asked him to contribute
a track to the album *The Fruit of the Original Sin* in 1981.[31]

Arthur worked with a wide range of experimental musicians in the early
1980s, and one of them, Ned Sublette, had become a little uneasy about the
direction of the downtown scene. "My objection to the rock thing in new
music was not that I objected to rock in new music," says Sublette. "It was
that if you didn't do it, you didn't count. If you didn't do punk rock, people
wouldn't listen to your music." He adds: "I found the downtown rock scene
at least as snobbish as any other scene."

Sublette had come to realize he was mostly into songwriting and singing and, having spent most of 1979 back in New Mexico where he grew
up, he started to write songs about the West. One of them, "Cowboys are
Frequently Secretly (Fond of Each Other)," was penned in 1981 as a rebuke
to the urban-cowboy plague and its representative film, *Urban Cowboy*. As
Sublette wrote,

There's many a strange impulse out on the plains of West Texas
There's many a young boy who feels things he don't comprehend
Well, the small town don't like it when somebody falls between sexes
No, the small town don't like it when a cowboy has feelings for men.

Sublette felt good about "Cowboys," which brought together his Texan and New York sensibilities, and wanted to play it to Arthur. Concerned the song might be misinterpreted as making fun of gay men, he also thought his friend would be a good judge of its content. "I figured if someone as sensitive as Arthur liked it, I was OK," recalls Sublette. "He got it and was supportive. Once Arthur had given me the seal of approval, I knew it was OK to sing the song." Accompanied by George Lewis on sousaphone (a type of tuba), Sublette performed "Cowboys" for the first time in the summer of 1981 at a small performance space called Inroads and opened the show with a voice-and-sousaphone version of "Is It All Over My Face?" With Arthur on drums and Peter Gordon on synthesizer, Sublette went on to perform "Cowboys" during his debut gig at CBGB's in June 1982, and the song became a cult anthem soon after. "Cowboys" was rejected by the makers of the gay cowboy film *Brokeback Mountain*—"The word I got was that it was too funny for a tear-jerkin' movie," comments Sublette—but it was recorded and released in 2006 by Willie Nelson, a longtime fan of the song.

A number of experimental musician-composers fed Arthur bits and pieces of work in the early 1980s. Jill Kroesen asked him to perform cello on the single "I Really Want to Bomb You," which was released in 1980, as well as "Fay Shism Blues," which appeared on the 1982 album *Stop Vicious Cycles*. "I was like, how can I possibly do a record without Arthur on it?" says Kroesen, who channeled her punkish political satire through a deep, dark voice and, more often than not, a mustachioed mouth. "We weren't really close in terms of hanging out, but if I needed a cello played, I would call him." Arthur also appeared at the seventieth birthday tribute for John Cage held at the Symphony Space on Ninety-fifth Street and Broadway in March 1982, as well as the memorial service for Cornelius Cardew in June of that year, where he performed two of Cardew's songs in tandem with Sublette.[32] And later that year he took to the stage with his cello in Bill's Friends, a short-lived group led by Tim Schellenbaum that performed disjointed rock at the Kitchen.[33]

It's likely there were other appearances, but Arthur wasn't focused on getting occasional work, even at a cutting-edge venue like Danceteria, which would have been easy to negotiate. "Arthur never asked me if he could play," remembers Jim Fouratt, who was in charge of booking bands and DJs at the venue and became close with Arthur during this period. "He would bring me these tapes, which I thought were absolutely beautiful. I realized my role was to be supportive of him, because most of the music he would bring me was a work in progress. I felt that what he wanted from me was an honest critique of what he was doing." On the lookout for a group of players with whom he could develop a profound musical relationship, Arthur also started to work more closely with Mustafa Ahmed, Elodie Lauten, and Peter Zummo. In contrast to his pop-driven collaborations with Bowden, Brooks, and Hall, these musical relationships tended to be more experimental and never flirted with the fantasy of pop fame.

Zummo had left New York in the autumn of 1979 when his wife, Stephanie Woodard, was offered a professorial position at Oberlin College in Ohio. Arthur visited the college to perform music for *Big Game*, an athletic dance event directed by Woodard, and when Zummo returned to Manhattan a couple of years later he played trombone on "Sahara" (one of the songs on *Big Sky*), split the cost of renting a rehearsal studio with Arthur in Westbeth (the West Village artist co-op), and joined John Lurie's Lounge Lizards. "We played at the Mudd Club," remembers Zummo, who was a cool player but not an especially cool dresser. "I was carrying my horn and I still had a hard time getting in." Zummo notes that while Arthur and Gordon had a "conscious focus on pop or art rock," he "didn't have the focus" to make this kind of music by himself. Instead Zummo liked to compose music by collecting things he had heard—a fragment of sound, a bar of notes, or a catchy lyric. "Sometimes I would just play an interval, two notes, and they would jump out at me, and I would think, well, today's a pretty hip day, so I'm writing!"

Toward the end of August 1981, Zummo invited Arthur, along with Rik Albani (trumpet) and Bill Ruyle (marimba), to record his piece *Instruments* in the Greene Street loft of the choreographer Risa Jaroslow. The windows at the far end of the room were open when Arthur showed up with a Nagra

Peter Zummo dancing with Stephanie Woodard during a free Lincoln Center Out of Doors concert staged in Damrosch Park (also known as the Guggenheim Band Shell) in the late 1970s. Behind Zummo and Woodard, Bill Ruyle plays the talking drum. Tucked away, Arthur Russell plays the cello—horizontally—behind the amp. "Maybe he was getting some good tone or feedback," suggests Zummo. Photograph by Wendy Perron. Courtesy of Peter Zummo.

reel-to-reel tape recorder—a high-end Swiss machine—and the trombonist left them that way in order to accentuate the phantom, low-frequency rhythms that were likely to emerge when the musicians, playing at their own tempi, produced combinations of notes that weren't controlled. The setup was perfect for Arthur. "He was very soulful but completely unpredictable, and every once in a while I'd be playing along and hear Arthur and think, 'Am I really hearing that? What am I hearing?'" Ruyle recalled later. "I would think 'Is he really doing that?' and look over and, *'Yes, he's really doing that,'* and [I would] quieten down to listen and he'd stop doing it. He was a very rare kind of musician and player."[34] Zummo was pleased with the contribution of Arthur. "The piece was based on repeating phrases at your own rate and within the limits of the group," explains the trombonist. "I told Arthur this and he took it at a pace that made it almost impossible to play. My reaction was, 'The music has changed, I like it now!'" Arthur was adding energy, which was typical, says Zummo. "He would take an instruction and push it two orders of magnitude further. The nature of the times was to think, well, that's the way he plays, so that's how we're doing it now."[35]

For his part, Arthur hoped to glean additional energy from Ahmed, who was recording the *Rhythm of Life* album with James Mason at Downtown Sound on Christopher Street—around the corner from the Westbeth rehearsal space—when Arthur passed by to check out the studio one day. "He liked what I was doing and invited me to work with him," remembers Ahmed, who had grown up in the Bronx and breathed the sensibility of pan-African culture. "He told me he was looking for a funk sound and that was his new direction." Arthur invited Ahmed to play congas during his orchestral disco concert at the Kitchen in order to introduce him "to the 'scene,'" and although Rome Neal was leading the percussion that night, Arthur started to call on Ahmed more and more until he finally stopped calling Neal altogether. Ruthless when it came to choosing which musicians he wanted to work with, Arthur must have decided Ahmed was the superior player. An aspiring actor and director, Neal hardly felt let down, having achieved a major breakthrough when Arthur suggested he audition for *Medea*. Neal landed the role of Aegeus, the king of Athens, and acquired an equity card in the process.

Ahmed and Arthur formed a "fairly intense" relationship right away. "Arthur lived in the Lower East Side, where the community was heavily Latin and black," notes the percussionist, who had worked as a counselor before becoming a full-time musician. "He wanted access into the thinking and feeling of black musicianship, and through his association with me he was able to bring something that was clearly identifiable as being ethnic into his music." As with his suggestive lyric writing, Arthur was more interested in enacting a form of cultural politics that revolved around aesthetics and collaborations than engaging in a form of campaigning activism, and Ahmed was willing to see where the relationship might go. "Because I was not this macho, hostile person, but was a little bit more urbane, sophisticated, and political, I was more open than the younger hip-hop guys, who were ten years younger. The Afrika Bambaataas were probably a bit more intimidating." Ahmed was in a good position to make this judgment, having counseled Bambaataa while he was in the Black Spades, and hanging out in Poet's Building, he and Arthur would play music until the late afternoon, at which point they would turn on the TV to watch Video Jukebox, one of the first programs to screen hip-hop videos. "Arthur was fascinated by hip-hop," notes Ahmed. "We would sit down and talk about it. The music was very aggressive and very black. Arthur was very interested in beats." In return, Arthur became Ahmed's first white musician friend, and he revealed to Ahmed not only an alternative aesthetic consciousness but also an alternative way of being. "James Mason was openly ambitious and imagined himself with big cars and bling. I was also hanging out with Grandmaster Flash and the Furious Five, who acted like stars. Arthur didn't have any of those pretensions. He was very humble and always about the music."

Meanwhile Arthur and Elodie Lauten bumped into each other again in 1981, having lived together in Allen Ginsberg's apartment during the summer of 1975. The daughter of a Paris-based jazz musician, Lauten had played with the experimental rock band Flaming Youth and became friends with Ginsberg, from whom she learned to appreciate the value of living in the East Village, where "you didn't have the social pressure of having to behave in a certain way." Lauten and Arthur didn't spend much time together that summer, but they started to develop a close musical relationship six years later. "He remembered he liked my singing and asked me to sing [his song] 'Go Bang!,'" recalls Lauten, who recorded the vocals with Arthur at Sorcerer Sound a couple of weeks later. Arthur doesn't appear to have used the tracks, but Lauten remembers the session being a watershed. "We really connected musically," she says.

Arthur shared spiritual ground with Lauten (she was also a Buddhist and they would discuss their beliefs), and he appreciated Lauten's quirky sense of humor (he chuckled when she placed her keyboard on top of an ironing board at an Experimental Intermedia Foundation concert). Lauten was also a formidable intellect, and Arthur was soon drawn to her questioning of equal temperament tuning, the standard tuning system, which uses equal semi-tone intervals between notes on the octave to tune instruments. The equal temperament system has been used by Western musicians since the late nineteenth century and is convenient for large orchestras because it simplifies the tuning process. But it also results in some out-of-tune intervals that, in the words of Lauten, "call for a more subtle division of the octave" in order to achieve a natural harmony, and although they are barely audible in Western orchestral music, these peculiarities become more audible in music that uses sustained notes and repetitions—including non-

Arthur Russell in rural Iowa in the mid-1980s. Photograph by Charles Arthur Russell Sr. Courtesy of Audika.

Western music and new music. Spearheaded by La Monte Young and Terry Riley, the return to the microtonal system of just intonation enabled the re-introduction of the non-Western colors that had gone missing from Western music, and Lauten adopted this outlook, much to Arthur's interest. "We wouldn't intellectualize it," she recalls. "Arthur would say, 'You've got a good ear for tuning,' and that was it. It was a very intuitive approach. I was trying to work with my ears, and so was Arthur."

Arthur formed the Singing Tractors with Ahmed, Lauten, and Zummo in March 1982—he came up with the name during a trip to Iowa—and for the most part the group worked with scraps of paper on which Arthur had scribbled a few melodic lines. "We would rehearse, get a set list out of Arthur, go on stage, and have no idea what was happening," recalls Zummo. "There was just no way to tell whether we were playing the songs in the order they were indicated on the set list or not. He would just start going and you would have to make a decision, but it would be a difficult time to make a decision. That happened *all the time*." Contributing to the chaos, Lauten (on a Casio keyboard) only played the parts "loosely," because she wasn't in the habit of playing other people's music. Lauten adds that Arthur liked to participate in instinctual, idiosyncratic performances, and he also liked to develop musical relationships that were sophisticated and cerebral.

Featuring occasional appearances from Steven Hall and Ned Sublette, the Singing Tractors also played at Wesleyan University's World Music Hall and the Tibetan Institute in New York, as well as CBGB's, where Arnold

Dreyblatt did duty on the Casio. According to Dreyblatt, Arthur wasn't in the least bit fazed by the fact that he and some of the other musicians were unsure what to do: "Arthur said, 'Just play F-sharp.' I replied, 'Which note is that?'" Dreyblatt remembers, "Personality-wise he really had trouble being a dictator, which is forgivable, even if you need some of that to be a band leader. But it was not in his character. He preferred to allow things to happen with musicians he respected." Struggling to control a secondhand pedal steel guitar, Sublette played at the CBGB's and Experimental Intermedia Foundation concerts. "It was a lot of fun and I thought the music was lovely," he recalls. "I wasn't too troubled by the fact that I had very little idea what I was supposed to be doing. I figured the main thing was just to play. I loved being a Singing Tractor."

Such a group could have provoked catcalls of disapproval from the judgmental audiences of downtown New York, but instead they tapped into a zeitgeist in which musicians teased out the strangeness that lay dormant in unfashionable roots. "Turning up a rich loam of musical sensibilities," ran one Singing Tractors flyer, quoting a spoof review from the *Farm Quarterly*. Arthur developed his Midwestern theme when he started to wear the rustic uniform of a farmer's cap and a plaid farmer's shirt, as if he had just stepped off his tractor. "He came from an upper-middle-class family, but he cultivated a Woody Guthrie kind of thing," says Hall. "It wasn't cool then, so it was very leftfield." Dressed in his country getup, Arthur couldn't have been more New York if he had tried.

Sleeping Bag

Arthur identified with the natural world. His handmade flyers featured childlike sketches of birds and antelopes; he stuck a cutout cardboard rabbit onto the front of his cello; he carried stuffed animals onto stage with him during performances; and songs such as "Eli" developed animal themes. In assuming the Dinosaur moniker when he released "Kiss Me Again," he took up the cause of the extinct, and his subsequent use of the name "Killer Whale" would create an alliance with the endangered. And as he set about establishing his own label following the falling-out with West End, he started to nestle up close to a cuddly koala bear.

Arthur met his label partner at the Loft. The stocky son of one of Mancuso's lawyers, Will Socolov met Steve D'Acquisto and then Arthur, after which he asked his father to provide the Loose Joints producers with a loan to enable them to complete their sessions. Realizing he had been drawn into a "fucked up situation," Socolov turned against D'Acquisto — who had "no right being in the studio" and "bossed Arthur around constantly" — and told him to "fuck off." Socolov drifted until a chance collision with Arthur on West Broadway resulted in Arthur asking him to form a partnership and open a record company. Backed by Socolov's father and an old-time record promoter called Juggy Gayles, the label acquired a name when James Brown's "Papa's Got a Brand New Bag" started to play over the radio, which prompted Socolov to joke that he could forget about buying a brand new bag — he was still going to bed in a sleeping bag. Arthur seized on the throwaway remark, and Socolov agreed that "Sleeping Bag" sounded like a good name. "It was supposed to be a reaction to the disco era and to make fun of that," he notes. "Arthur and the rest of us were, 'Fuck the cool way! We're not going to be wearing designer suits!'" Emphasizing the label's alternative, idiosyncratic intentions, Arthur proposed that they also use a picture of a koala bear sitting in a sleeping bag as their logo.

Socolov's entrance encouraged Arthur to move away from D'Acquisto. An important enabler and an inspirational presence, D'Acquisto's relentless championing of Arthur's ingeniousness had provided the self-doubting Oskaloosan with a valuable dose of self-belief. Yet the Loose Joints co-producer also required a return for his big-heartedness, and when Arthur chose not to follow a particular piece of advice, a more confrontational side emerged. Having lent Arthur money to record the $24 \rightarrow 24$ tapes — it's not clear how much — D'Acquisto assumed they were part of an ongoing production team, but Arthur had become less sure about that, and the emergence of Socolov and Sleeping Bag Records encouraged him to think laterally. Whatever his stake, D'Acquisto hadn't managed to engineer a release for the $24 \rightarrow 24$ tapes, and given that eighteen months had passed since they were recorded, Arthur had no qualms about taking them to Sleeping Bag. D'Acquisto was devastated. "Arthur was basically a bit of an opportunist," he says. "He was an artist who needed to work and he would go anywhere if somebody promised him money."

With D'Acquisto out of the picture and the $24 \rightarrow 24$ tapes lined up to appear as Sleeping Bag's debut album, Arthur returned to the studio to record additional tracks with Lola Blank, a backing singer with James Brown who was married to Bob Blank. In possession of a powerful, gospel-

Original silkscreened
mock-up artwork for the
cover of *24 → 24 Music*,
1981. Designed by
Tom Lee. Courtesy
of David Hill.

trained voice, the vocalist had to unlearn everything she knew. "I had just come off the road with James, and I said, 'Arthur's great! He's *funky*!'" she recalls. "He was this very quiet, non-descript person who would sit and watch, and the next thing you knew, he'd create this funky music! He was one of the most creative, innovative, and off-beat producers and composers I'd worked with." "Bang go-bang-bang go-bang-go," she sang in a crazed, little-girl voice that made it sound like she had escaped from a psychiatric hospital in a helium balloon. "Go bang bang bang go-bang it back." "Most of the R&B singers are gospel," adds Lola, whose voice was augmented with echo in the studio. "You've heard one, you've heard them all. For me, recording with Arthur was a time when I could be creative and fun. It was a time when I could go a bit crazy. I could sing anything and he'd make it work." Bob looked on open-mouthed. "I hadn't seen that side to her," he explains. "Arthur brought that out of her."

Wrapped in a silkscreen cover designed by Tom Lee that featured a gray print of a marauding dinosaur plus a cluster of bright red, floating "24"s and arrows in the top left corner, *24 → 24 Music* by Dinosaur L was released on Sleeping Bag at the end of 1981. (Arthur had added the "L" to provide the artist name with a more powerful numerological value.) Discordant and manic, "You're Gonna Be Clean on Your Bean" opened Side A with sharp beats and a repeated Peter Gordon saxophone refrain, after which a rhythm guitar and a synthesizer underscored a barrage of high-pitched, hysterical yelps delivered in a female voice's Franglais, and a recurring rap-chant of "You gonna be clean on your bean" in male voices that sounded deadpan yet quizzical. "No, Thank You" continued the stumbling-out-of-the-asylum ambience, with Zummo's chromatic trombone skipping over echoey keyboard notes as a female voice intoned in a pained, desperate near-shriek, "I said, 'No thank you.' I meant, 'No thank you, please.'" "In the Corn Belt" featured Arthur's descending cello lines and Zummo's zigzagging trombone, as well as a surreal operatic cameo by Julius Eastman, who sang, "In the corn belt, CORN, COOORRRNNN." "Get Set" interspersed its merry-go-round sound clash of instrumental riffs and longer solos with a range of percussive effects. And "#7" consisted of a live take from the orchestral disco performance at the Kitchen — the night when Arthur's weird, funky, art-house jam began to take shape.

That jam found its ultimate expression on the album's second track, "Go Bang!," which opened with John Ingram's tight, sibilant drums, Eastman's faint keyboard, and Jill Kroesen's slurry, unstable vocals. Judging by the tone of her voice, Kroesen wasn't in a fit state to buy a pint of milk, let alone "uproot the cause of confusion," which was one of her stated goals, yet the musical backdrop provided an outlet from the chaos when it shifted to a toughened beat pattern that incorporated Eastman's keyboard and Timmy Ingram's congas along with Arthur's twangy, pizzicato cello. Running for several minutes, the groove was interspersed with Eastman's faint orgasmic cries of "I want to go baaannnggg" (which began at a subterranean register before scaling three-and-a-half octaves to end on an orgasmic high) and, a little later on, the sound of a sustained, discordant, undulating cluster of notes (as if Eastman had taken a few swigs of whatever Kroesen was drinking and ended up crashing on the keyboard). While layers of percussion washed in and out, a group of male vocalists — probably Arthur, Rome Neal, and Kent Goshorn — blurted out:

I wanna see all my friends at once
I'd do anything to get the chance to go bang
I wanna go bang
I wanna go bang

I wanna see all my friends at once
I'd do anything to get the chance to go bang
I wanna go bang.

A cluster of scrunched-up guitar and trombone lines prefigured the close of the track, which concludes at seven minutes and fifty-two seconds.

In a nod toward the nonlinear underpinnings of the tracks, which had been spliced from tapes of tapes of tapes, the album's six tracks were given new numbered titles and listed in a jumbled-up sequence—"#1 (You're Gonna Be Clean on Your Bean)," "#5 (Go Bang!)," "#2 (No, Thank You)," "#7," "#3 (In the Corn Belt)," and "#6 (Get Set)." The studio had become the space of searching and madness, where tapes overflowed onto the floor and the splice reigned supreme. "Arthur didn't say, 'I've got a song called 'Go Bang!,' let's record it,'" notes Gordon. "It was more like discovering the song in the raw material." As the molecular composition of sound was explored, knowledge didn't so much accumulate as disintegrate, and although most of the tracks were given names, these were bracketed and provisional, suggesting that they were unfinished and might (or perhaps even should) continue to evolve after their initial release. Music can unravel under this kind of scrutiny, and the unraveling that took place on 24 —> 24 Music was reflected in Arthur's sound, which often seemed to slur as the instruments and vocals were slowed down or sped up to the point where their waves didn't produce any kind of meaning.

Nevertheless, 24 —> 24 Music wasn't so much illegible as unpredictable, with its shaky jams and counterintuitive patterns taking up residence on the precipice of implosion. Drawing on the solo workout of jazz, the spatial awareness of dub, the raucousness of rock, and the insistent drive of funk and disco, the album's instrumentation and claustrophobic edits depicted a universe that consisted of tangents and coincidences. Yet the album also flirted with structure, with its rhythms searching for a sustained groove and its songs hinting at the possibility of organized form. Refusing to gloss over the complexities of the world, the album sounded surreal but was actually very real, as well as foreign while being grounded in a neighborhood where disco, jazz, rock, new music, and Latin music seeped out onto the streets. Presenting a strangely coherent, left-field sound that hinted at genre yet remained steadfastly unnameable, 24 —> 24 Music could only have been developed by an artist who was embedded in the full range of downtown's diverse music scenes—which is to say, it sounded like an Arthur Russell album.

The album confirmed Arthur as a significant writing talent. "Kiss Me Again," "Pop Your Funk," and "Is It All Over My Face?" had provided snapshots of his ability to come up with memorable hooks, and with the release of 24 —> 24 *Music* he demonstrated that he could come up with vividly expressive lines with ease. (The Flying Hearts material would have done the same if it had ever appeared on vinyl.) The track "#3 (In the Corn Belt)" harked back to the earthiness of his home state, while "#1 (You're Gonna Be Clean on Your Bean)" and "#5 (Go Bang!)" were laced with the same kind of witty sexual innuendo as "Pop Your Funk" and "Is It All Over My Face?" Yet as far as Arthur was concerned, this was all very unremarkable. Ever since his time in San Francisco, he had penned lyrics that combined vernacular language and evocative imagery at a phenomenal rate, and Lee points out that the popular appeal of his lyrics was deliberate. "Arthur saw them as catch-phrases," he explains. "As serious as he was, he wanted people to respond to his music. He wanted his lyrics to be anthemic."

Arthur also wanted his lyrics to appeal beyond a gay male listenership, and "#5 (Go Bang!)" remains indicative of his oeuvre. The record contained obvious homoerotic undertones, with Eastman's vocals simulating the moment of male orgasm with startling expressiveness, and the lyric "I want to see all my friends at once, go bang" suggested a male orgy. Indeed it's even plausible that Lola Blank's contribution was cut from the final mix in order to emphasize the all-male thrust of the lyrics. Yet the line "I want to see all my friends at once, go bang" also evoked the better-than-sex moment of the dance floor when the DJ worked a mix with sublime dexterity or caught the mood of the floor, and the crowd responded with energized moves and jubilant screams. "Arthur's lyrics were more sexual than homosexual," comments Steven Hall. "'Go Bang!' is about having all my friends in one place, which is more like a hippie ideal of everyone making out together. Arthur was inclusive in a way that even some early gay pride pioneers were not in terms of straight sexuality, and he was also informed by his experiences with women. It is limiting to think of his music through the gay prism."

Although "#5 (Go Bang!)" was the likeliest dance cut on 24 —> 24 *Music*, most of the DJs who had got into "Kiss Me Again" and "Is It All Over My Face?" were unnerved by its spider's web structure, in which threads of instrumentation were woven together into a springy, mucoid mesh. Larry

Levan persevered with the record, and so did David Mancuso, but most thought it was too difficult for dancers, so when album sales ground to a halt at the two thousand mark, Socolov gave Arthur the green light to ask François Kevorkian to remix the record. The Prelude Records mixer agreed, even though he hadn't warmed to "Kiss Me Again." "There was something in the hook, in the songwriting, in the germ of it that meant it could never become one of the great songs," he comments. "There were parts that were really intense—the tom toms at the end of one mix—but they lasted for a minute and then they were gone." Because it was "extremely complex, disorganized, and uncompromising," "#5 (Go Bang!)" presented a different kind of challenge, but Kevorkian reckoned it was something he could work with. "There are people who think the original version is a work of genius, which I'm not going to disclaim, because Arthur had his own vision of things, which was very peculiar and very much genius-like," he says. "But sometimes genius works are hard to play at parties."

Asked to deliver the remix for as little money as possible, Kevorkian went into Right Track Studios, worked through the night, and emerged the next morning unhappy with his effort, which was "not to the point at all." Kevorkian came from a jazz-rock background and was familiar with the chaotic beauty of Sun Ra, Pharoah Sanders, and Cecil Taylor, yet none of their music prepared him for the Byzantine complexity of Arthur's studio work. "The multitrack was an absolute, utter, and total mess," he recalls. "The way all the elements were thrown in there seemed to be gratuitous. It was just so *thick*. There were all these great ideas, but every thirty seconds there would be a change of direction. There were at least twenty songs that could have been put together from those tapes." Having studied the tapes track by track in order to create a "master score" map, Kevorkian ended up spending so much time on this task that he failed to "absorb all the data and make sense of it." Adamant he wasn't willing to hand over the remix, he insisted that Socolov allow him to go back into the studio and work on it for an extra day—even if he had to pay for the studio time himself. "There was some arguing back and forth," recalls the mixer. "Finally we came to an understanding."

Kevorkian returned to the studio intent on providing the diffuse if compelling original with a more streamlined and structured focus. First off, he plucked out a Zummo trombone phrase from the depths of the multitracks and positioned it as an avant-garde fanfare that opened the remix. After that, he created a streamlined groove in which instrumental phases were signaled with greater clarity. Key parts, such as Eastman's sound-swarm synthesizer, were chopped into recognizable shape, soaked in echo and reverb, and given a curatorial position above the driving track. In addition, two vocal quotes—Eastman's operatic orgasm, which was hazy and submerged in the album mix, and Lola Blank's off-kilter, little-girl utterances, which hadn't been used at all—were transformed into vivid motifs that regulated the tense drama of the mix. "Lola and Julius Eastman were outstanding in their unique and quirky way," reflects Kevorkian. "The rest was the icing on the cake."

With the studio work completed, Kevorkian cut an acetate of the remix and handed it to Mancuso, who played it at the first opportunity. "The whole thing took fire right away," says Kevorkian. "It was one of those instant records. There was nothing like it and you couldn't forget it. From the Loft perspective, the record was all about *baaannnggg*." But when Arthur went to the Loft with Socolov the following weekend, he was disappointed with what he heard. "After David played it Arthur came up to me and said, 'I can't believe it! François is trying to sabotage me!'" recalls Socolov. "I thought he was going to say, 'Man, it's fucking great, I'm really happy,' because that was the first time he heard it in a big venue, so I was surprised." Socolov asked for clarification. "I said, 'Arthur, what are you talking about?' And Arthur replied, 'François is trying to ruin me! The drums are muddy! They're not the way they're supposed to be!'" Arthur wanted the drums to be pounding, perhaps after Bohannon, who was one of his favorite percussionists and producers, but Socolov just laughed. "I said, 'You're out of your mind! The people went crazy! It sounded great!' I think he agreed afterwards. But he still felt the drums could have been EQ-ed [equalized] differently."

Convinced Arthur was way ahead of his time, Mancuso made a point of hanging onto his album copy of "#5 (Go Bang!)," which contained so much information and so many nuances it reminded him of John Coltrane. But the Loft host also thought that Kevorkian's remix was "very, very good," and because the remix was tailor-made for the circus-like climax of his parties, Mancuso started to play the album version as the party was warming up and the twelve-inch during its peak. The remix would also become Levan's favorite record of all time, and Arthur made a point of traveling to King Street to hear it thunder out of the world's most powerful sound sys-

SLEEPING BAG RECORDS
P.O. Box 613
Canal St. Station
N.Y., N.Y. 10013

Sleeping Bag's koala twelve-inch record-mailer envelope. Designed by Tom Lee and Arthur Russell. Courtesy of David Hill.

tem while some two thousand black gay men responded in an explosion of energy. When a spandex-clad Lola Blank and a tuxedoed Wendell Morrison (a session vocalist with Inner Life) performed "Go Bang!" at the Paradise Garage, the song's lyrics were so effective in generating their utopian objective, the performers were drowned out in the din. "When Wendel went 'Go baaa . . .' you couldn't hear the record any more," remembers Bob Blank, who looked on from Levan's booth. "It was amazing to see the reaction. I had no clue."

Featuring an echo-laden Kevorkian remix of "Clean on Your Bean" on Side B, the twelve-inch remix of "#5 (Go Bang!)"—now titled "Go Bang! #5"—was released in the spring of 1982. It was picked up in no time at all by Frankie Crocker, a regular at the Garage who would take a peek over Levan's shoulder whenever a record caught his ear, and the WBLS DJ started to rotate the twelve-inch immediately. "We heard 'Go Bang!' on the radio and on the street," says Lee. "The whole idea of it getting played was a big boost." Enthusiastic reviews increased the record's momentum: *Billboard* described it as "progressive jazz"; *New Musical Express* named it as "a strange new fascination, a jazzy sensation"; *Dance Music Report* hailed it as "an instant 'underground classic'"; and *New York Rocker* noted that "with its electric piano and congas, it sounds almost Nigerian."[36] The author of the *New York Rocker* piece, Steven Harvey, was an unlikely convert given that he was a member of the experimental rock group Youthinasia, yet he found himself drawn to Arthur's combination of dub and repetitive rhythms—elements that the journalist-musician would later identify as being the most salient feature of downtown dance music in the early 1980s. "Arthur was really hip to that in the way he mixed his music," notes Harvey. "I got to know him, but it was completely around the music. Arthur struck me as being very ambitious about his music and he worked hard at getting it over, but he was shut down, slightly strange, and emotionally cool."

Composed by Arthur and refined by Kevorkian, the "Go Bang! #5" twelve-inch uncovered fresh territory for both experimental music and disco. Zummo, who actively sought out difficult music, was wary of the process that resulted in the record becoming "presentable," yet still appreciated the remix, while Gordon (who received a coproduction credit for finding the male rappers who performed on "Clean on Your Bean") felt that Kevorkian's disciplining handiwork "revealed another side of Arthur's music." The mixer, meanwhile, believed the twelve-inch was one of his finest to date. "It sounded really special," he notes. "It brought all these different elements into a flow that is so natural you'd think it was recorded like that, when it fact it was the opposite." Having expressed concern about Kevorkian's use of the drums, Arthur came to appreciate the mixer's work, which he valued above Jimmy Simpson's version of "Kiss Me Again" and Levan's reworking of "Is It All Over My Face?" "It was very different from the album version, but that was never a problem for Arthur," comments Lee. "The song was still his basic idea and he was thrilled with what François did." Arthur, adds Kevorkian, was also excited to see his record "become a major-league contender."

Mustafa Ahmed heard "Go Bang! #5" play on the radio the night his wife went into labor with their first child. "She was experiencing discomfort and was having a hard time going to sleep," he remembers. "We turned on the radio to WBLS, which was the only station that played primarily 'black' music at the time, and a little after 3:00 a.m. the DJ said, 'Listen, I've got something really different that I want to play for you. Give me a call and tell me what you think.'" "Go Bang!" started to play on the radio. "I was excited to tell my wife that this was the guy I was telling her about. That was October 16, 1982." They started to talk about the music; Ahmed's wife fell asleep; and five hours later she gave birth.

Even though the Singing Tractors didn't rehearse or perform a great deal, Arthur always seemed to end up playing with Ahmed, Lauten, and Zummo. When Dinosaur L was invited to perform alongside Allen Ginsberg, Afrika Bambaataa, and the Rock Steady Crew at the Mudd Club's "Beatwaveoldwavenewwave" night in June 1982, Arthur asked his Singing Tractor co-musicians to join him. And around this period, when Ahmed, Lauten, and maybe Zummo were practicing with Arthur one day, Lauten came up with a line for a song, "In the Light of the Miracle," and Arthur latched on to the Buddhist-themed idea in the hope that it could take the transcendent impact of "Go Bang! #5" to its logical musical-spiritual conclusion. The recording session burst into life when Ahmed brought out an agogo bell (the sound of which is ubiquitous in Brazilian samba) and some cowbells. "Up to this point, Arthur's music had the drums and the congas, but percussion-wise it was still what I would call linear. It was kind of flat. But with the addition of the agogo bell or mambo cowbells it was *percolating*." Subsequent sessions were less dynamic. "We would record material again and again and again until we had a zillion versions of it," recalls Lauten, who cowrote and coproduced the song. "We could never get copies of the tracks, and after a while I got really frustrated, because I just didn't see where it was going."

Several versions were recorded. One opened with Arthur repeating the refrain "Living in the light" alongside Ahmed's percussion and Zummo's trombone, after which Arthur sang duet while Lauten repeated the lines:

> Holding in the light
> In the pouring rain
> Holding in the light
> In the thunder.

Another began with Lauten's repeated refrain, "Living in the light," after which Arthur hummed in a vocoder voice,

> Pony loves the sun
> To touch her back
> And see her run

Pony loves the milky way
Before the sky
Turns into day.

He then repeated the phrases in Spanish. Julius Eastman turned in a cameo appearance, although this time his lung-busting delivery sounded misplaced, while Arthur intoned additional lines such as,

Since everything as far as I see
Is part of you and that's all
Since everything is it turns out to be
Just another part of you
You know that you are with me
And that's all (living in the light)
Every part of me
Is from your last call (living in the light)
You know that you are with me
And then I see you (living in the light).

Reverberating with delay and echo, Arthur's guitar, Lauten's keyboards, and Zummo's trombone wove swirling, ethereal patterns around each other, while Ahmed's bright, multilayered percussion led the song across different planes of intensity. Built around shifting flows and sparkling textures, and showing no interest whatsoever in development, "In the Light of the Miracle" floated above the constrictions of form.[37]

The song formed a point of spiritual contact for Arthur and Lauten, who were drawn to the Buddhist theme of light, and believed that music could embody a form of Buddhist practice by inducing an experience (rather than a rationalization) of spirituality. Since moving to New York, Arthur had stayed in touch with Yuko Nonomura; he had defended baby cockroaches from the unsentimental shoe heel of Donald Murk; he had searched out meetings and visited spiritual centers; and a Buddhist outlook continued to permeate his method. "Arthur spoke of the importance of using music as a tool to strive for a heightened awareness beyond the normal state of ego," explains Joyce Bowden. "He advocated using a continuous, unified flow of attention until the movement of sound would become more vivid and fewer abstractions would occur. His point was to wait until the music became a meeting point between the finite and the infinite. This happened more often than not, and sometimes it would become an enlightened moment, with the music unfolding or revealing itself to us in a magical way." Lauten adds that Arthur had two sides to him: "He had his experimental side, which is the kind of music Peter and I would get into, and then he had his pop side. He wanted to write Buddhist pop music, because he felt it would be karmically better to reach out to as many people as possible. I think he was hoping to make some money with it too."

Although the release of 24 ⟶ 24 Music had been smooth, and Arthur had given Socolov the surprise gift of a coproduction credit on the twelve-inch of "Go Bang! #5," the final monetary goal turned out to be unrealistic, for while Arthur wanted Sleeping Bag to function as a vehicle for his left-field music, Socolov was looking to create a street-oriented company that sold boxes of records, because that was what was required to survive. "Frankie Crocker played 'Go Bang!' for a week, and it started to sell like crazy," recalls Socolov. "Then he dropped it. I guess it was too weird. It wasn't a commercial hit. It was an underground classic." Having assumed the drifting role of in-house artist-impresario, Arthur came under pressure to help with the day-to-day running of the company, which left him wondering if Socolov understood how his talents could be best utilized. By the time he handed over "In the Light of the Miracle"—an act that might have involved him submitting a succession of demos and asking for feedback— Socolov was searching for a dance record that would make some money. A straight-talking New Yorker, Socolov doesn't remember the particulars of the exchange, but he was unlikely to have thought the lulling chimes of the song sufficiently pragmatic. "Arthur worked forever on 'In the Light of the Miracle,'" says Tom Lee. "He loved that song and I loved it, too. We both thought that it was brilliant and that Will would put it out, but there were these other distractions."

Socolov had already revealed his market sensibility when he released a Larry Levan mix of Class Action's "Weekend" as the follow-up twelve-inch to "Go Bang! #5." Originally recorded on Atlantic Records by Phreek, a studio outfit led by Patrick Adams that featured Christine Wilshire on vocals, "Weekend" never made it beyond the promo stage, but the record was rotated heavily by Levan, and when dancers discovered they couldn't buy the track, its popularity was enhanced by its commercial unavailability. Socolov responded by inviting Levan to mix a new version of the song, and the Garage DJ's effort was released under the name Class Action toward the beginning of 1983 (some ten months after "Go Bang! #5"). "There was a big fight over 'Weekend,'" recalls Bob Blank, who engineered and coproduced the record. "It was very commercial and a success in New York—much more so than 'Go Bang!'—but it wasn't the kind of thing that Arthur wanted to release."

Arthur failed to get another label to run with "In the Light of the Miracle," but he still had "Tell You (Today)," an unashamedly sweet and optimistic Loose Joints twelve-inch single that was built around the standard major-minor-major steps of pop. Written before the eighties consumer boom swept through the Western world, the song told a humble story of material possession.

> Walking down the street
> I knew it was my chance
> A chance today
> New shoes on my feet
> They thought that they could dance
> Dance away
> Makes me come alive
> I remember the look of sadness on your face
> That was before
> I want to tell you today
> I want to tell you today.

As far as Arthur was concerned, owning something as basic as a new pair of shoes could be experienced as a form of joyful rebirth, and when Socolov agreed to put some money into the record, Arthur returned to the studio to integrate fresh vocals with Bowden and Steven Hall, as well as Hall's cheerful whistling from the original Loose Joints sessions.

Working alongside Eddie Garcia and Robert Morety, Levan mixed "Tell You (Today)," apparently to nobody's satisfaction. "Arthur wanted to come up with a record that was more commercial than 'Go Bang!,' and he said, 'Let's do something with Larry!'" recalls Socolov. "But I didn't think it was one of Larry's great jobs, and Arthur thought the same. I don't even know if Larry was happy with it. It was a record that just never clicked." In the end Socolov sold the mix to the Island Records subsidiary Fourth and Broad-way, which released the twelve-inch in the summer of 1983. "Fourth ate it up because it was Larry Levan and Arthur Russell," says Socolov. "They were our international licensee and they really went on it." Produced by Killer Whale (Arthur Russell) and the now absent Steve D'Acquisto, "Tell You (Today)" breezed past New York's club zeitgeist of twisted hooks, rumbling dub, and murky sex, and perhaps because of that, it didn't sell at all well.

A short while later Levan received another Arthur-related commission from Sleeping Bag when he was invited to remix "#3 (In the Corn Belt)" from *24 → 24 Music*, but the project got off to a problematic start when he failed to show up for the first two-and-a-half days of the three-day studio session. Stripping the song of its coordinated chaos and bringing the beats and the bass to the fore, the Garage DJ thinned the instrumental parts, introduced a gentle dub treatment, and extended Eastman's slightly terrifying vocals, but Socolov decided that mix wasn't fit for release. "Larry did a lot of mixes that were terrible," he explains. "He was getting high a lot, and I don't know if he did better mixes when he was stoned or straight." By this point Levan and Arthur weren't seeing eye to eye as much as they had in the past. "At times Larry was a lot of work, and Arthur was not a good enough politician," adds Socolov. "Arthur didn't have the patience for bullshit, and Larry was just a bullshitter, getting stoned and being the empress of dance music."

For his next dance release, "Tiger Stripes," Arthur teamed up again with Nicky Siano, who had persuaded the father of a girlfriend to fund the venture. Arthur wrote the lyrics and Siano remembers the basic tracks being "phenomenal," but problems emerged when Arthur began to tire of Siano's hyperactive presence and incessant stream of life-changing ideas, while the former Gallery DJ became exasperated with his collaborator's constant tampering and money-is-no-object approach to the studio. The feuding came to a crescendo when Arthur attempted to introduce a drum machine into the mix (because the drummer hadn't kept time) and ended up having to scrap the original tracks, including the Evelyn Thomas vocal. Urged on by his girlfriend, Siano assumed the role of lead vocalist, which persuaded Arthur he had no choice but to quit. Siano maintains that by this point he "was just looking to save money," but Socolov believes he might have started to eye the lead vocal role before the drum machine became a factor. "Arthur predicted beforehand that Nicky would fire the singer," says the Sleeping Bag boss. "But Nicky was stoned a lot of the time and he was paying. He wanted the record to be a vehicle for himself. Arthur was appalled at how bad Nicky sounded. His vocals were terrible." Siano admits: "I wanted to sing and I was going out with this girl who said, 'Sing, sing, sing!'"

Featuring Siano alongside newly recorded backing vocals by Maxine Bell, "Tiger Stripes" was released in 1984 on Splash Records, a subsidiary of Sleeping Bag. On the record Siano was credited as the artist and sole producer, while a disillusioned Arthur, who didn't want to be associated with the release, agreed to be credited as the writer under his Killer Whale alias. A little later, Sleeping Bag issued a promotional copy of "Tiger Stripes" that featured Bell as the sole vocalist with a new song, "You Can't Hold Me Down," on the B-side. Running under the artist name of Felix (at Arthur's suggestion), the promo credited Hipolio Torales and Killer Whale as the respective mixers of Side A and Side B, and also listed Killer Whale as the writer of both songs.

"Up and down your back / Orange and black / I can see your tiger stripes," ran the lyrics to "Tiger Stripes."

Since you are a tiger
Since you are a tiger
You can find your tiger spot
Moving through the trees at night
Looking for your tiger spot
You can move
You can move
You can move
You can move.

"There may have been a better record in Arthur's head, but the record that we all got to hear was great," remembers Ned Sublette. "It wasn't, uh, a typical clubland lyric. I went to the Loft with Will one night and heard David Mancuso put it on his marvelous system." Socolov, however, wasn't satisfied. "Originally Nicky thought the record was going to be a huge hit and would need to come out on a bigger label than Sleeping Bag," he notes. "But when he played the record to everyone and got a bad reaction he came to me. It was never a serious release for Sleeping Bag."

By this point Socolov had persuaded Arthur to cede directorial control

Arthur Russell at home, c. 1983. Photograph by and courtesy of Tom Lee.

of the company to him. The failure to maintain the early momentum of "Go Bang! #5" and "Weekend" on subsequent releases such as Symeran's "Tonight (I'm Gonna Have You)," Sounds of JHS 126 Brooklyn's "Chill Pill" (which included a trippy Arthur mix), Jamaica Girls' "Need Somebody New," and Urban Blight's "A Nite Out" had paved the way for the change of power. When Levan's "Cornbelt" failed to end the disappointing sequence, Socolov turned to Arthur toward the end of 1983 and argued that Sleeping Bag would fare better without his managerial input.[38] Initially unsure, Arthur agreed to the proposal, perhaps having calculated that Socolov's more commercial ear would enable the label to subsidize further forays into the studio. Given that the company was more or less worthless, Arthur didn't appear to be risking much, but he had waived his formal influence, and that counted for quite a lot.

A shift in the balance of power between the Loft and the Paradise Garage exacerbated Arthur's struggle to be heard. Following the closure of the Gallery, Mancuso's party space had become his favorite hangout, and the venue's combination of beauty, poise, and privacy suited his temperament. Consisting of warm Klipschorn loudspeakers, luminescent Koetsu cartridges, and Mark Levinson's audiophile amplifiers, the Loft's sound system complemented Arthur's life-affirming, esoteric sensibility, and the fact that Mancuso was a like-minded soul with whom Arthur could swap knowing glances meant he felt comfortable handing the party host his latest recordings and checking his new material on the most musical system in the city. Yet by the early 1980s the Paradise Garage had overtaken the Loft as the preeminent venue for breaking dance music, and Arthur started to spend more time at the King Street venue, because when Levan played his records they were also heard by label promoters, recording artists, and radio DJs. Sporting the most powerful sound system and talented DJ in New York, as well as a stage upon which artists would perform in front of three thousand dancers, the Garage nevertheless remained a challenging place for a genteel soul like Arthur to hang out, and the setup didn't favor his offbeat aesthetic.

Arthur's nocturnal escapades became less frequent, especially after the Loft moved from Prince Street to Third Street and Avenue C, where Mancuso became embroiled in a series of intractable problems. Tom Lee remembers spotting nice-looking guys with Arthur at the Mudd Club and trying to guess who they might be with, or which one of them they might be eyeing up, but for the most part Arthur would head out alone in order to gauge the latest club sound, use his Walkman to sneak a recording of a track he was interested in, or hand an acetate to a DJ and wait to see the crowd's reaction when it was played. Once he had achieved his goal, he would hang around for a respectable length of time before slipping out.[39] Distant were the nights in the mid-seventies when he would throw himself into the bouncing shadow of Louis Aquilone. Going out had become research.

Lee was a restive presence when he accompanied Arthur on these outings. He didn't like to dance (something he shared with Arthur) and wasn't drawn to club music (which set them apart). "I thought Arthur made dance music because he could be commercially successful at it," says Lee. "But I remember him telling me that there were lots of singer-songwriter wannabes and that he didn't want to be another person in that world." Although there was no danger of that happening, the experience of seeing "In the Light of the Miracle," "Cornbelt," "Tell You (Today)," and "Tiger Stripes" crash in relatively quick succession was discouraging. From this point on, it was to songs—innocent songs, twisted songs, even funky songs—that Arthur would turn with increasing regularity.

Songs

In his report on the "New Music New York" festival of 1979, Tom Johnson noted the emergence of a distinct generation gap within experimental music. "The older group derived much from Cage and almost nothing from popular culture, while the younger group almost reverses these priorities," he wrote. "While the song form is almost never used by the older composers, it occurred several times in works by the younger ones."[40] Singing "Eli" at the Kitchen in 1974, Arthur had been an early exponent of the idea that compositional music and the song form could go hand in hand, and he went on to develop a repertoire that included pure pop, oddball folk, and lyrical dance. "I don't think Arthur's songs were ever appreciated as songs," says Peter Gordon. "He was a beautiful songwriter and this side of his work was not recognized. He was never able to realize the same visibility with his songs as he got with his dance releases. But he was a real poet, and I think that that's where his heart was—in his songs."

Arthur's lyrics revealed an outlook that was sensitive and touching, or, when the mood grabbed him, as it did with "Is It All Over My Face?," "Pop Your Funk," "#5 (Go Bang!)," and "Clean on Your Bean," witty and subversive. Drawing on the great pop themes of romance, love, and sex, Arthur somehow managed to bypass cliché and make them interesting thanks to his ability to express subtle, perceptive insights through a writing aesthetic that was both grounded and oddball at the same time. He could write about gender ambiguity in "I Wish You Were a Girl," unrequited desire in "Kiss Me Again," feeling happy in "Tell You (Today)," and relationships in "Oh Fernando Why?" without coming across as being hackneyed or sentimental. Released in 1984, "Heaven Knows I'm Miserable Now" by the Smiths revealed the way indie pop groups were also beginning to engage with emotions other than anger and frustration, yet in contrast to Arthur's weightless, quirky observations, many of these songs came across as being whiny and self-absorbed. "Arthur's songs were lovely and lyrical, and he was a very lyrical sort of guy," notes Robert Ziegler, who would stay on East Twelfth Street whenever he visited New York. "Arthur was a sort of indie songwriter before that style proliferated."

Perhaps because he had experienced a series of setbacks in orchestral music and dance, Arthur's interest in songwriting intensified in the mid-eighties, and composing songs with the accompaniment of a newly acquired Yamaha DX7 synthesizer, he began to work regularly with Joyce Bowden. "The keyboard had a little pitch tone bar, and he created whole melodies with it, creating this weee-eee-eee," recalls the vocalist. "It was like a wah-wah pedal on a guitar and people didn't often use it, but Arthur used it to sing his melodic content. His melodies were all over the place, but they were quite classically oriented. There was an Indian influence in the tonal quality. He was going places where people in the West wouldn't normally go." Bowden came to half-expect Arthur to call her on the night of a full moon in order to arrange a last-minute studio rendezvous, and the sessions would often begin with Arthur asking her to sing something, after which he'd provide directions through the headphones. As Bowden acclimatized to Arthur's decentered approach, she began to notice he would stop the tape at unexpected moments, and came to realize this was Arthur's way of marking a peak moment in the recording. "He loved the sound of rewinding tape, and I learned to love that sound too," says Bowden. "I figured he may have been splicing together the best parts for the future and re-using the rest of the tape."

Certain tensions—tensions that could cause confusion, even if they sparked energy—lingered between Arthur and Bowden. "Arthur had made it clear that he wanted to live his life as a gay man, and was quite clear about this from the beginning," says Bowden. "After our first night together I learned how to let the love I felt in his presence move through the music he would reveal to me. But for my part there would always be the sense of having something unanswered between us." When Bowden showed up late for the recording of "My Tiger, My Timing" she was greeted with an admonishing "Oh well, at least you look good" that left her crushed. But Alan Abrams remembers Arthur being completely taken with the redheaded vocalist. "It wasn't about being homosexual or bisexual or anything like that," he says. "You could just see Arthur was totally devastated by her. It wasn't just sexual; it was also emotional. She sang like an angel, she was gorgeous, and she was spiritual. She was holding her heart while she sang, and Arthur didn't know what to make of it. He said, 'Is she for real or not, Alan?'"[41]

Hoping that Bowden's bright soul would offset his own melancholic voice, Arthur invited her to also contribute to "Hop on Down," "Keeping Up," "Losing My Taste for the Nightlife," "Lucky Cloud," and "See through

Love," as well as "I'll Be Outside," "It's a Boy," "Mr. Problems," "Over the Line," "Sunshine Lover," "The Letter," and "Wild Combination."[42] "We would start with the main melodic phrase of the music or groove, and I'd overdub a part onto that, after which Arthur would open up another track and run the tape again, and I'd overdub on top of that as well," she recalls. "There might end up being four or five levels for him to sort through later. Some parts would be discarded and others would end up being a main theme." Although Arthur's songs were filled with melodic somersaults and vocal phrasings that could seem lazy, Bowden came to appreciate that they were in fact rigorously devised. "If I got a nuance wrong it could affect the whole balance of the song," recalls Bowden, who would regularly ask for a demonstration. "Arthur was quite an architect of structure. He knew about balance and the *je ne sais quoi* of style. His ideas were not just random. He could work for hours, days, on a little phrase, and if one came in and discounted it, or just thought of it as a random glissando, it would be wrong. These glissandos were quite specific, and although they had to be treated randomly, they weren't random at all."

Arthur respected Bowden and he might have thought his plan to add her vocals to two songs he had recorded with Jennifer Warnes, "Keeping Up" and "My Tiger, My Timing," would have been interpreted as a compliment. "Here was someone with a beautiful voice who wanted to work with Arthur, and that opened up a lot of possibilities," notes Lee. But Bowden threw up her hands when, during a difficult session, Arthur turned to her and said, "Why can't you sing like Jennifer? Why can't you do that?" The questions tore into Bowden. "On the one hand, I was jealous of the deferential treatment Arthur seemed to display toward Jennifer in sending her copies of music weeks before the session so that she knew exactly what he wanted from her," explains the vocalist. "On the other hand, the beauty of the work they created together was undeniably exquisite. The parts I'd come up with originally for the song didn't compare with the beauty of the parts Jennifer created for Arthur. This was something that made me want to quit singing altogether." Bowden persevered with the recording of the long-distance duets with Warnes and, looking back, believes she was wrong to be jealous. "Arthur aimed to take musical form out of conventional grooves into a state that was beyond groove, and I think this was his way of pursuing freedom of spirit. Although he missed many worldly connections that would have brought him more notoriety, it was rare that he missed a chance to tran-

Arthur Russell in the basement at Westbeth in the mid-1980s. "That's my RE20 microphone and Arthur's SM57, so we were recording and rehearsing," says Peter Zummo. Photograph by Tom Lee. Courtesy of Audika.

scend himself within music. He was purely attracted to brilliance." Bowden adds, "It was a different process. But I also loved Arthur for saying, 'Why can't you do that?'"

Featuring his own voice and cello, Arthur continued to work with song when he recorded "A Little Lost" with Steven Hall, whose sunny guitar went with the song's jazz-folk aesthetic. The first verse, its complex phrasing made simple by Arthur's mobile, languid voice, ran:

I'm a little lost without you
That could be an understatement
Now I hope that I have paid the cost
To let a day go by and not
Call on you
'Cause I'm so busy, so busy
Thinking about kissing you
Now I won't do that
Without entertaining another thought.

Crooning sweet words in a wispy, naked voice, Arthur concluded,

It's so unfinished
Our love affair
A voice in me
Is telling me to
Run away
I hope your feeling isn't diminished
I hope you need someone in your life
Someone like me.

Hooking up his cello to an amp, Arthur also recorded "This Is How We Walk on the Moon" with Mustafa Ahmed, Peter Zummo, and Rik Albani. "Every step is moving me up," ran the lyrics to this song of innocence and awe.

I'm so far away
One moment there
Moving me up
Every step is moving me up
One moment there
One tiny, tiny move
It's all I need and I jump over.

Performed solo, "Lucky Cloud" was just as delicately perceptive. "Lucky cloud in your sky," sang Arthur. "A little rain / A lot of fun / One, yeah, kiss and I go overboard."[43]

On his own Arthur penned "Hold On to Your Dreams" for François Kevorkian, who had parted company with Prelude Records, and was working with Jah Wobble, the Edge, and Holger Czukay on his first production, an EP titled Snake Charmer. Having laid down an atmospheric instrumental that featured wafting keyboards and echo-laden guitar, Kevorkian came up with the title and asked Arthur to write some lyrics for the piece. Arthur responded with an ecstatic daydream of a song. "Didn't I get to see what you can do," ran the opening lines.

Totally sure it is you
Feeling coming up another time
I'll never be the same without you

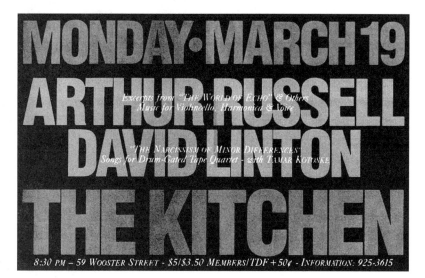

Poster for *World of Echo* at the Kitchen, 19 March 1984. Courtesy of Tom Lee.

Putting out a feeling when you go
Now I hurry up to see you
Seeing is believing, baby
And I believe in you
And this feeling too.

"Arthur had an uncanny talent," remembers Kevorkian, whose record was released on Island Records in 1983. "He wrote the lyrics very quickly. I think he was quite happy with the way it went."

An amplified cello and harmonica performance in the Pass Concert Series of solo works by composers, which was curated by Elodie Lauten and staged in the New York Theatre on East Fourth Street in October 1983, might have been the moment when Arthur decided to spend more time working on solo voice-cello pieces. Six months later, he premiered (in his words) "portions of a new composition-in-progress titled WORLD OF ECHO" at the Kitchen.[44] Accompanied by five musicians, Arthur played amplified cello and occasional harmonica in a set that, according to Jon Pareles in the *New York Times*, "at best evoked such Americana as square dances, church sing-alongs, and one-chord garage bands." Pareles added, "The average Neil Young song is more evocative and more concise."[45] Un-

Arthur Russell (right) and co-musicians play portions of his composition-in-progress at the Kitchen, 19 March 1984. Photograph by Teri Bloom. Courtesy of the Kitchen, New York City.

deterred, Arthur returned to the voice-cello solo format when he performed *Sketch for World of Echo* at the Experimental Intermedia Foundation in June 1984. "He was in himself, a bit introverted but very concentrated," remembers Arnold Dreyblatt. "He had some beautiful wispy phrases on the cello where he barely touched the string near the bridge. He seemed totally in control."

Studios

Arthur did whatever he could to scratch out studio time, so when Bob Blank offered him three thousand dollars for the 1951 Chevrolet his father had lent to him, Arthur took the money and then gave it straight back to Blank. "There were many 2:00 a.m. sessions with Arthur," recalls the engineer. "He would bring in some cash, or he would work it out after a couple of days. I would often comp the session — write it off — because I was the owner of the studio, and I could do whatever I wanted to do."

Arthur would head to Blank Tapes whenever possible because he appreciated Blank's unrivalled skill at producing a consistent, fat drum beat, his nuanced understanding of the groove, his ability to move across the black/white musical divide, his readiness to roll tape, and his breathtaking speed, which meant the moment of musical inspiration could always be caught and studio time was never wasted. In turn, Blank was willing to stretch the rules of the studio for Arthur because he valued his tirelessly innovative approach to musicianship and the recording process. "Arthur was always creating in the studio," says the engineer. "We would do a project and I would be like, 'This is amazing,' and I'd never hear of it again. Arthur would have five different songs going on at once. He had one of those lateral brains that could hear across all this different material." But the relationship became complicated when a disagreement with Will Socolov resulted in Blank being cut from the credits on 24 —> 24 *Music*, and Arthur's meager cash flow led him to work more and more on "spec time," which became messy. "I remember there were times when he would start something with Bob but couldn't finish it because Arthur couldn't pay him," says Mustafa Ahmed. "Bob wouldn't give him access. He would hold on to the tapes. There were periods when that was very frustrating."

Seeking out an alternative studio owner who was less focused on balancing the books, Arthur stumbled into Mark Freedman, the son of an established real estate developer who could pour as much money as he liked into his hobby studio, Battery Sound, which operated out of one of his father's buildings. The contrast between the privileged Freedman and the self-made Blank must have appealed to Arthur. With Freedman, Arthur didn't need to feel guilty as his pile of IOUs stacked up high, and having spent so much time working with Blank, who was always wired, Arthur might have also appreciated the way in which Freedman would get stoned on the job, especially because the haze didn't interfere with the studio owner's ability to realize that Arthur could provide him with something that he lacked—credibility. Situated at 90 West Street, around the corner from the Deutsche Bank building, from where it enjoyed a luxurious penthouse view of the World Trade Center, Battery Sound was extremely comfortable and loaded with all the equipment money could buy. But Freedman was inexperienced and needed to develop a relationship with a respected musician in order to add gravitas and momentum to his studio. Arthur fitted perfectly.

"Bob [Blank] recognized that Arthur was a genius, and their collaboration was loving and contentious," says Steven Hall. "But whereas Bob was

Arthur Russell recording music at Battery Sound in the early 1980s. Eric Muiderman, a student of Peter Zummo and apprentice of Arthur, stands on the right. Mark Freedman works in the adjoining room. Photograph by and courtesy of Peter Zummo.

a businessman, Mark truly supported Arthur and simply gave him the key to the studio, which was like giving him the key to a wonderful city or to his heart. He let him work all night long, alone and undisturbed, and he supported any wild or weird thing Arthur wanted to do, so the music recorded at Battery tended to be deeper and more relaxed." Arthur also learned to appreciate the way Freedman's lack of organization could inspire new approaches. "Mark was a tech-toy freak and was always trying out the latest gadgets and devices," adds Hall. "He was able to get a magical, deep sound and often left things set up in a particular way for Arthur when he left him alone in the studio all night."

Arthur went to Battery Sound with the putative Flying Hearts as well as the lineup that performed on "In the Light of the Miracle," but for the most part he went into the studio with one or maybe two players from his inner circle, or even by himself. He started to lead a twilight existence, walking down to Battery Sound late at night and spending hours upon hours in the studio, where he would set up, tweak equipment, and try to get the right sound. Treading softly and taking all the time he needed, Arthur immersed himself in recording equipment and electromagnetic tape in a way that had never been possible previously. Then, when he became too tired to carry on, he would find a place to curl up and go to sleep, comfortable in the knowledge that he could record right away if he woke with an idea running through his head.

Comfortable and free, Arthur started to lay down his *World of Echo* material with Freedman and Eric Liljestrand, an engineering assistant who exchanged his labor for slices of studio time. "Arthur was an odd sort of guy," remembers Liljestrand. "He was very, very soft spoken, so you really had to listen when you were talking with him. It took me a long time to get inside his head as to where he was going musically, but I thought his style on the cello, with the fuzz box and echo and percussive tapping and various bow techniques, was great." Because Freedman didn't like staying up late, and had enough money to go to bed whenever he liked, Liljestrand assisted on the all-night sessions, and ended up working with Arthur on pretty much every full moon between August 1983 and August 1986. The *World of Echo* songs combined complex structures with strange melodies that veered into muted pop, and featured lyrics that were increasingly abstract. Fed through a set of digital delays, the results sounded like the songs Arthur had played to Allaudin Mathieu in San Francisco channeled through ten years of living in New York.

Every Imaginable Perspective

Whenever Philip Glass bumped into Arthur and Tom Lee, usually around brunchtime on a Saturday or a Sunday, he made a point of urging Arthur to release one of his orchestral compositions and repeatedly offered to press up an album on his own Chatham Square label. "Arthur really wanted to be a popular composer, but he didn't do anything to make that happen except write brilliant music," says Glass. "He didn't have a plan to make that happen in the way Frank Zappa had that plan or I had that plan. He just seemed to feel that the music *should* be popular. I was very interested in helping him." Glass had been criticized following the release of *Glassworks*, which some judged to be too commercial, but Arthur couldn't have been less fazed and toyed with the idea of giving Glass his as yet unpublished *Instrumentals: Volume 1* collection, which he had pressed to acetate himself, before he handed him the *Medea* recording instead. After all, Glass had set that disaster rolling when he introduced Arthur to Wilson, so perhaps he could provide it with some sort of closure. "I said, 'You have to have a record because the radio stations won't play tapes,'" remembers Glass. "I coached him on the business aspect of how to put a record together. He kind of followed my lead in that way."

Having retitled the composition *Temple of Meaning* when it was picked up by the choreographer and dancer John Bernd in May 1983, Arthur chose the name *Tower of Meaning* for the Glass release. "We worked on it forever, although that was true of just about everything I ended up doing with Arthur," says Liljestrand. "I often felt that Arthur would hit the magic moment and then go sailing right past it and keep on working. It was really hard to know what was on his mind, what he was reaching for." Because Arthur was predisposed to working on several aspects of the multitrack at a time, Liljestrand had to be ultra-organized, ambidextrous, and patient, and he also came to learn that peaceful relations were enhanced when he played the role of the obedient technician while the tape was being organized, after which Arthur would take control of the mixing board. "It seemed like the creative process was really private," adds Liljestrand, who was left with the unconfirmed impression that Arthur was happy with the final edit.

Released on Chatham Square in 1983, *Tower of Meaning* consisted of six shorter sections and one longer section, which totaled forty-four minutes. Like the 1978 performance of *Instrumentals*, much of the music was elegiac and beautiful, yet the piece also featured dissonant tone clusters in which a range of instrumental combinations were repeated in no discernible pattern. Arthur's musical procession, gaunt and faltering, moved so slowly that tempo became a distant memory, and toward the end of the album the music plunged into a dark, circular existence. Moving beyond the intended setting of the Wilson stage show, the composition took on new meanings of its own, but none of these were suggestive of the humorous, mystical, idiosyncratic sensibility that ran through so much of Arthur's other work. The music contained an ominous peacefulness that precluded peace, like a lake where somebody has drowned.

Jon Gibson, who had contributed to the album but who had not warmed to Arthur's "funny little tunes" for voice-cello, was enthusiastic about the result.[46] "I liked *Tower of Meaning*," he says. "It does tend to go on, but that could be said about a lot of pieces that were released during that period." Having added her Casio keyboard to the recording, Elodie Lauten says she began to appreciate Arthur's compositional skill. "It's a very beautiful piece," she says. "Arthur had a voice as a classical composer. It's definitely spiritual and it has a strange flavor. There's definitely an edge to it." Glass, who covered the cost of pressing 320 copies, remembers Arthur being "very proud" of the result.

As *Tower of Meaning* came together, Arthur also handed the jigsaw of his instrumental recordings—the *Instrumentals* performances (1975 at the Kitchen, 1977 at the Franklin Street Art Center, and 1978 at the Kitchen), *Reach One (With Two Fender Rhodes)*, and a version of *Sketch for "Face of Helen"*—to Les Disques du Crépuscule. The Belgian label worked on assembling the pieces during 1983, and at some point Arthur became agitated enough for a label rep to write in November, "Don't despair, be pissed off, etc.—we believe this is a long-lasting record." In the end the label dropped the 1975 recording of *Instrumentals*, along with *Reach One* and *Sketch for "Face of Helen*," and released the remaining material as *Instrumentals (1974—Volume 2)* on a subsidiary, Another Side, in 1984. Side One opened with a clip from the Franklin Street performance, which evoked a bright and dreamy landscape in which melodic chord progressions welled up while a fairly frantic David Van Tieghem tapped and shook seemingly every percussion instrument he could lay his hands on. The rest of the side was filled with a much more obviously orchestrated section from the 1978 performance at the Kitchen that featured horns and strings playing notes in unison, while Side Two contained a longer clip from the same, slow-paced concert.

Arthur can't have been pleased. The decision to omit the entire 1975 Kitchen performance of *Instrumentals* was hard to comprehend, for while many of the sections had broken down after a relatively short period of time, the more successful takes were both lovely and intriguing (and also provided a historical document of an important concert). Farcically, music that was already of longer duration than many could comfortably listen to became twice as long again when Les Disques Du Crépuscule / Another Thought made a hash of the transfer and recorded the second side at half-speed. "It was a mess," says the Audika boss Steve Knutson, who studied the tapes when he released *First Thought Best Thought* (2006), which includes the 1975 *Instrumentals* performance, along with *Reach One, Sketch for the Face of Helen*, and the correct-speed version of the 1978 *Instrumentals* concert.

Instrumentals (1974 — *Volume 2*) doesn't appear to have been reviewed in the English-language press, but the media response to *Tower of Meaning* revealed that Arthur was beginning to make a gentle impression on the contemporary classical-record market. *Sound Choice* noted that the album consisted of "enchanting and desolate music that seems to stand a bit outside the supposed continuum of Western music and yet, at the same time, be informed by a blur of many past and present practices. . . . The integrity of this music shines through." The *Washington Post* even described the album as "gentle and cloud-like, recalling [Olivier] Messaien but without the severity."[47] Indeed the *Post* positioned its discussion of *Tower of Meaning* at the end of an article that also reviewed new recordings by Glass (*Mishima*), Terry Riley (*Cadenza on the Night Plain* and *Other String Quartets*), John Adams (*Light over Water*), and Steve Reich (*The Desert Music*), and although nobody would have argued that Arthur should have been placed ahead of these other composers in terms of seniority or generic impact, his presence alongside such a hallowed lineup suggested he was now a composer of rising significance. Arthur might have been particularly pleased to have appeared alongside Glass and Riley, if only in print, given that he made a point of attending their concerts whenever the opportunity arose.

It seems likely Arthur's profile would have continued to rise if he hadn't abandoned his orchestral ambitions after *Medea*. But the experience of working with Wilson shattered his belief that he could make it in the world of composition, and because of this, the release of *Tower of Meaning* and *Instrumentals* (1974 — *Volume 2*) amounted to a closure rather than a beginning. More committed to exploring oblique angles and interconnections than bolstering his reputation as a composer, Arthur was unlikely to have been overly concerned about this lost opportunity, and as he moved between the musical worlds of downtown New York, a coded legacy began to form in the slipstream of his lateral movements. That legacy epitomized the evolving sound of perhaps the most influential music city in the Western world during one of its most vibrant eras, for as Arthur worked on *Tower*

Arthur Russell on the rooftop of 437 East Twelfth Street in the mid-1980s. He could see across downtown. Photograph by Tom Lee. Courtesy of Audika.

of Meaning and his *Instrumentals* album, he also recorded pop, new wave, and mutant disco, as well as a series of dub-inflected folk songs that he performed while playing cello. "Mozart was described as a genius because of mental capacity, such as his ability to complete his last three symphonies in his head," says Peter Zummo. "Arthur was one genius I worked with, because he had the ability to work in so many areas at once and bring them to fruition."

Arthur's range was breathtakingly broad and outlandishly ambitious to the point of being counterintuitive, or maybe even irrational, and because of this, Arthur's way of making music suggested an unconscious sonic, or an approach to making music that resembled the unconscious. The least accessible part of the mind, where desires and fears run free, the "unconscious system," as Freud noted, "is not governed by laws of logic, especially not by the law of contradiction."[48] The psychoanalyst concluded that the unconscious is therefore a space of psychic mobility, and there were times when Arthur seemed to float around genre with the ease of a dream. Some sort of unconscious state seemed to govern Arthur, for as he went about his work he set aside the constraints of everyday reality: styles of musicianship that were supposed to be perfected, genres that demanded aesthetic and ideological obedience, cultural hierarchies that ascribed differing values to differing sounds, social settings that necessitated networking expertise, and outfits and postures that required insider knowledge. For Arthur, the act of pursuing so many sounds wasn't contradictory because their properties bled into each other. Indeed if anything was contradictory, it was the idea that music had to be contained, or that musicians had to make a choice. And although the challenge of working across so many scenes could be overwhelming, Arthur survived the moment in the early 1980s when the courier job seemed to mark the failure of his utopian project. He had followed his ear in order to live out an ambition that evoked the sublime chaos of the inner psyche—or a dream that resembled a dream.

Despite the setbacks with Socolov and Wilson, Arthur would continue to develop dance music and compositional music. And although the experience with the Necessaries reminded him to avoid joining another new-wave band, he would carry on writing songs, because that was how he felt most comfortable. "If I was to reduce Arthur's musical principles to a single idea it would be his willingness to look at things from every imaginable perspective," comments Ned Sublette. "Yet Arthur was also a songwriter. His words and his music were equally important. The sonic clothes would change, but the lyrics always had a similar sensibility. Arthur the lyricist was as important as Arthur the composer." Performed on his cello or a sparse electronic setup, as well as at increasingly rare Flying Hearts sessions, Arthur's songs could barely be heard amidst the angular noise and pulsating rhythms that continued to swirl around downtown. But as rising property prices, public spending cuts, and the AIDS epidemic converged, Arthur stood his ground and continued to provide an alternative account of the world. His songs were little lanterns that carried the promise of hope in a darkening terrain.

6 **Reverberations** (1984–1987)

New wealth arrived in New York after the stock exchange began its high climb in 1983, but the benefits were only felt by a small number of artists, while the funding that sustained many of the organizations through which artists exhibited and played was slashed by Ronald Reagan's administration. Developing a more obviously market-driven program, the Kitchen attempted to hold on to its reputation for innovation by programming fewer composers — composition having become dated in the downtown music scene — but it weakened its distinctiveness in the process. "I went to a concert at the Kitchen that seemed like a variety show," remembers Rhys Chatham. "When Arthur, Garrett or I booked a jazz or a rock group, it was to show a 'connection' with what was going on in art music at the time. By the mid-eighties, the music directors were clueless as to what they were supposed to be doing." Meanwhile, composers who might have previously regarded the Wooster Street venue as the preeminent performance space in Manhattan continued to gravitate to the alternative club scene. "Times had changed," says Ned Sublette, who started to drift away from the experimental scene and became a "confirmed salsa-holic" in 1985. "Although it continued, the Kitchen was no longer as significant a part of the scene."

SoHo's infrastructure and demographics underwent a simultaneous transformation. As the once-abandoned district became a magnet for fashionable boutiques and rising rents, land-lords began to put commercial buildings to residential use with increasing disregard for the law, and although the New York government responded to what it described as an "emergency" by introducing the Loft Law, the attempt to clamp down on the flow of nonartists into spaces designated for artist use proved to be unenforceable.[1] As the beneficiaries of the Wall Street boom moved into the neighborhoods of SoHo and TriBeCa, prop-erty prices skyrocketed in line with the five-figure prices being paid for the paintings of Jean-Michel Basquiat and Keith Haring. "Mainstream America is fascinated with the idea of a scene in which seemingly every-one is an artist, musician, designer or 'beauty engineer' (i.e., hairdresser) and keeps such unusual office hours—from dusk to dawn," wrote Michael Musto in his book *Downtown* in 1986. "In fact, downtown's so chic it's not downtown anymore. It's a feeling, a style, a sensibility that's invaded popu-lar culture."[2]

Having made the most of a twenty-year blip that began when light industry left New York, downtown's artistic population divided and dis-persed. "We were forced to move away from each other, thus destroying the sense of community we had together," notes Chatham, who relocated to France.[3] Moving out of "a hole" on Elizabeth Street, Garrett List also set off to Europe, convinced that the Kitchen had become too corporate. "I couldn't stand the city anymore," he says. "I was happy to go." Arnold Dreyblatt traveled in the same direction, in part because the downtown scene had become "more image-oriented," and he recalls feeling liberated as soon as he landed in Berlin. "The scene in New York was so paranoid I was afraid to use percussion," he explains. "Arthur said, 'Just put in a snare drum. Not a bass drum, a snare drum.' As soon as I came to Europe that's immediately what I did." Heading to Brooklyn with his collaborator and wife, the video artist Kit Fitzgerald, Peter Gordon also moved out. "Those empty SoHo lofts became co-ops, affordable only by the gainfully em-ployed," he says. "The cheap rehearsal rooms and galleries disappeared. Those with commercial leases were sunk."[4] Jill Kroesen exited the art scene during the same period. "I was intensely creative and then all of a sudden I had this nervous breakdown," she recalls. "My father was supporting me a little and he pulled that support, and the art world changed. The whole thing stopped. It just stopped."

For all of the pernicious external forces, however, downtown also unraveled from within. As Musto comments in his book from 1986, "When you're alone and life is making you lonely, you can always go downtown . . . if you're on the list. (Preferably the 'A' list.)" He continues: "Oh sure, anyone can hop into a Porsche—or a Sherman tank—and drive through the chicest rubble in town to gape and gawk at New York's young, gifted and broke, but to go beyond touristy and be welcomed into the downtown elite, you have to observe a few thousand rules." Musto's tongue-in-cheek hyperbole aside, an ethos of insider trendiness had taken over significant parts of lower Manhattan's art scene, where a series of codes were supposed to keep outsiders at a distance. Musto outlines them: "First, realize that there *are* not rules; you just look and do as you feel. Second, be incredibly rebellious and angry, but not to the point where it might hurt your career. Walk around with a huge chip on your shoulder, but only if the chip looks fabulous. Feel a constant, driving creativity—rather than throw out a beer can, you should feel the urge to make an earring out of it. Above all, get bored so easily that by the time a trend you started becomes accepted, you should be willing to let someone else cash in on it just so you can move on to the next three trends."[5] In his contribution to *New York Noise: Art and Music from the New York Underground, 1978–88*, Bill T. Jones concurs: "It was a time of many cliques and clans of affinity, extremely competitive and the notion of community was a dubious one as careerism was rampant."[6]

A number of downtown musicians thrived in the new milieu. Performed in front of a packed Brooklyn Academy of Music in 1983, Laurie Anderson's two-night debut of the eight-hour *United States* indicated that experimental music could appeal to a wider audience. Talking Heads, their very name an ironic take on media culture, continued to deliver quizzical lyrics about the search for meaning in the decentered and disjointed culture of postmodernity on their commercially successful albums *Speaking in Tongues* and *Little Creatures*. A regular at venues such as Danceteria and the Paradise Garage, Madonna released her eponymous dance-oriented debut album in 1983, and became downtown's most recognizable icon following the international success of *Like a Virgin* and the offbeat film *Desperately Seeking Susan*, which was set in lower Manhattan. Meanwhile the Beastie Boys performed as a teenage, pre–hip-hop outfit alongside Sublette's band at the Kitchen in December 1983 before Madonna booked them to play on her 1985 Virgin tour, and the following year the band released *Licensed to Ill*, the best-selling rap album of the 1980s. However, although the route between downtown experimentalism and midtown commercialism had become clearer than anyone could have imagined in the middle of the 1970s, New York's record companies became less amenable to releasing experimental music, and many downtown musicians discovered that their prospects had actually worsened. "After 1985," notes Kyle Gann, "commercial pressures were about as difficult to avoid in Downtown Manhattan as rhinoceroses."[7]

Arthur wanted to be successful on his own terms — as a collaborative artist who worked across several styles — and as the prospect of working with a major company receded, he handed Will Socolov two completed albums at the beginning of 1985. The first, recorded with Steven Hall, was submitted under the artist name of Bright and Early — the two friends having adopted and then set aside other names, including the Sailboats, Blue Green, and Palo (after Palo Alto). "It was a constant word game," says Hall. "But to us it was all the same thing — me and Arthur trying to create pop together." Featuring Hall on Side X ("Fresh Feeling," "Special Weakness," and "Triangularize") and Arthur on Side O ("Planted a Thought," "Apple to the Orange," "Love Is Overtaking Me," "Follow You," and "Every Face in Every Window"), the songs sounded airy and sweet, while the simple instrumentation carried echoes of the Flying Hearts, even if "Fresh Feeling," which featured Hall singing five songs over Arthur's continuous drumming, was very un-pop.[8] The cover of the test pressing — labeled TLX 2-X and TLX 2-O — was designed by Hall's Chinese boyfriend, Johnny Fu, and featured the Chinese character for "bright," which resembled a stick man, but the album never came out. "It wasn't Will's fault because Will was patiently supportive," explains Hall. "Arthur was being difficult about deciding if things were ready and ambivalent about promoting me."

As Bright and Early unfolded and then folded, Arthur worked on his own solo album, which was noticeably more electronic than his previous recordings, especially in its use of Mustafa Ahmed's drum machine. Like many percussionists, Ahmed had resisted the new technology, initially because the first wave of analog drum machines didn't sound like drums, and then, when digital technology improved the lifelikeness of the sound, because the equipment threatened to replace live players. But Arthur wanted Ahmed to adapt, in part because he believed the equipment wasn't going to go away, in part because it might enhance the percussionist's range, and in part because he wanted to engage with the syncopated strains of elec-

Arthur Russell and Steven Hall at the Ted Greenwald Gallery, c. 1984.
Photographer unknown. Courtesy of Steven Hall and Johnny Fu.

tronic hip-hop. "He wanted me, as his percussionist, to be as proficient and knowledgeable on this machine as he was," remembers Ahmed. "He also felt if I learned how to use it I would be able to program rhythms that were my own, and that that would be more exciting for him."

There were times when Arthur's sense of rhythm was challenging for the African American drummer. Whereas a musician like Peter Zummo was invited to come into the studio and play free-floating lines, Ahmed was often asked to lock into an odd, stuttering meter that might have been no more than a vague suggestion in Arthur's mind. "It would always take Mustafa a while to get into Arthur's groove, because Arthur put the beat in an odd place," recalls Eric Liljestrand. "They seemed to argue a lot. But once Mustafa heard what he needed to hear to lock in, he had a fantastic feel." If the beats still sounded too static, Arthur would ask his percussionist to record an overdub of live congas, or to rub his hands together to create the sound of friction, or to play the drum machine live. "We got a new toy and we went home and we played with it together," notes Ahmed, who maintains there were no more than a handful of other downtown musicians playing live against electronic drums at the time.

During late 1984 and 1985, Arthur recorded approximately twenty tracks for his solo album and, having struggled to settle on a final version, presented the results on three separate test pressings. "Working with Arthur was not easy and not typical," remembers Ahmed, a major player on the project. "I worked for hours on tracks but never got the sense we were finished because of his constant editing. Anyone who collaborated with Arthur would tell you this was the most frustrating aspect about working with him. He never seemed to finish anything. Arthur was never satisfied." Socolov came to regard his ex-partner as a procrastinator. "Arthur wasn't happy with anything he did, so he ended up with all of these alternative mixes for the same thing," notes the Sleeping Bag boss. "He would EQ things a million times and then he would ask me to listen to the tapes. There were times when I could distinguish between them, but I didn't know what was better, and he just went on and on." Socolov says Arthur "went crazy" over his recordings. "He didn't want to be dependent on François or Larry Levan, but he ended up questioning his own mixes constantly. He had such tremendous insecurities. I said, 'Arthur, just give me a record to put out!'"

Presented under the artist name Indian Ocean, the test pressings for the solo album *Corn* included "See My Brother, He's Jumping Out," "The Deer in the Forest—Part I," "Hiding Your Present from You," "Calling out of Context," "The Platform on the Ocean," "You Have Did the Right Thing When You Put that Skylight In," "The Deer in the Forest—Part II," "Keeping Up," "Corn," "They and Their Friends," and "I Like You!"[9] Emphasizing the snare drum rather than the bass drum, the dry and sparse rhythm of the album suggested the arid, flat terrain of the Midwest that gave *Corn* its name. Ahmed's pitter-patter congas softened the rhythm while highlighting its angularity, and the instrumental parts were completed by Arthur's harsh keyboards and coarse cello, plus Zummo's slurry trombone. Featuring no bass, a suggestive void hovered at the center of the album, while a static, serrated buzz added to the atmosphere of tension and gentle claustrophobia. Low-key even when up-tempo, Arthur's funky yet awkward minimalist pop pointed to a dance floor that was both near and very far away.

The album's lyrics spun a web of contrasting scenes that explored the affective range of everyday life, articulating a perceptive sensibility that would soon become standard in Anglo-American indie pop/rock (although years would pass before the resolutely white bands of this scene would think about black funk). "See My Brother, He's Jumping Out" contained the

Arthur Russell in an Iowan cornfield, July 1985. Photograph by Charles Arthur Russell Sr. Courtesy of Charles Arthur Russell Sr. and Emily Russell.

line "Let's go swimming," a call to childlike spontaneity and the pursuit of pleasure. "You Have Did the Right Thing When You Put That Skylight In" acknowledged the moment when Alan Abrams installed a skylight in his room in San Francisco, as well as Arthur's subsequent advice to Ernie Brooks to do the same in his Long Island loft. "Hiding Your Present from You" painted a picture of the domestic game played between two lovers (or a parent and a child) that laced tenderness with tension. In "The Platform on the Ocean," Arthur sang about seeing fish and hearing the sound of the whitecaps. And in "Calling out of Context" he delivered a series of loosely connected tableaux, which linked together seamlessly even if their meaning was elusive. "Calling out of context," ran the lyrics,

> Just to see her
> Falling out of sunset
> Into your blue sky
> Just to see her

Just to see her
Just to see her
I see your light is shining
Where there was no face
I see what it's defining
From another space
From another space
From another space.

Exploring nuanced rhythms and unexpected notes, Arthur's voice, just like the musical backdrop, brought a black sensibility into a white format.

The final test pressing of *Corn* (Sleeping Bag code TLX 3) was too avant-garde and strange as far as Socolov was concerned. "My taste was much more commercial than Arthur's," says the label boss. "Arthur loved dance music, but he was developing this large body of work that had nothing to do with dance music, and Sleeping Bag was primarily a dance label." Along with a few thousand downtown dance aficionados, Socolov was waiting for Arthur's next twelve-inch smash, and he tried to engineer that outcome by introducing Arthur to up-and-coming performers such as Dena Valcek, the lead singer of Konk (one of the bands that straddled downtown's disco and postpunk scenes), and Kurtis Mantronik, one half of an unreleased hip-hop act named Mantronix. "Neither of them worked out," notes Socolov. "Arthur would ask Kurtis how he would get certain sounds. Arthur would make an interesting remark and Kurtis would agree. But Kurtis was into being a hip-hop head and Arthur was into doing all different kinds of music. Kurtis respected Arthur, but he also thought he was weird."

Arthur's and Socolov's positions were hardening. Arthur wanted to put out a seductively strange form of electronic pop that followed his artistic convictions rather than any imagined formula of what might sell, and he fought for the right to work on his music until the sound was right. Socolov, meanwhile, felt he had a better sense of the sound of the street, as well as how that sound could be channeled into a company that made enough money to stay afloat (and maybe even move its office out of his apartment). "I think Arthur could see Will's point of view," notes Tom Lee, who remembers a lot of yelling, screaming, and frustration. "But music was like heroin to him. He just needed it to keep on doing it. It was all about the immediate satisfaction of going into the studio that night and getting the five hundred dollars that would enable him to do that. But Will wanted the guarantees."

Arthur and Socolov discovered some common ground when Sleeping Bag released "Five Minutes" by Bonzo Goes to Washington, a collaboration between Bootsy Collins and Jerry Harrison that sampled and lampooned Ronald Reagan's alarming joke that the United States would outlaw the then-communist Soviet Union forever and begin bombing in five minutes. Arthur contributed two edits to the Bonzo twelve-inch, and his rapprochement with Socolov seemed set to deepen when he offered him the rights to his track "Wax the Van," which contained a knowing reference to a product called Sex Wax and had good club potential. (Steven Hall comments that Californian surfers used a product called Sex Wax to make their boards more adhesive, and that the surfers were gay icons.) Socolov was tempted but backed away when Arthur started to work on the record with Bob Blank, Lola Blank, and their seven-year-old, Kenny Blank. "Bob wanted to promote Lola, and she really wasn't a good singer," says Socolov. "'Wax the Van' was Arthur paying Bob to use the studio. I told him it was a major mistake."

Released on Jump Street Records in 1985, "Wax the Van" was built on a strong drum track and a pulsating bass line, around which Lola, Kenny, and Arthur created a chorus of soulful, squeaky, and spoken voices. Having signed a riddle of a contract that required him to "compose lyrics and music for the existing composition," Arthur shared a cowriting credit with Lola and a credit for the keyboard tracks with Kenny. Lola now says that Arthur "wrote the song," and it is indeed difficult to imagine anyone else coming up with a line like "Wax the Van." Yet Bob Blank notes that the musician received all the compensation and credit that had been agreed upon in advance, and adds that his wife "contributed a lot to the music." Arthur appears to have been happy with the division of labor and attribution, and was also pleased with the final release. "It's not really my record, but I did the music," he commented later. "I worked really hard on it."[10] For his part, Socolov felt vindicated when New York's DJs sidestepped the twelve-inch.

Back at Sleeping Bag, Arthur concluded that his position at the record label had become untenable when he read about the creation of Fresh Records, a Sleeping Bag subsidiary, in *Billboard* toward the end of May 1985. "For the last 18 months you have stonewalled any progress from my part of our company and financed and nurtured only projects emanating from yourself," Arthur wrote to Socolov soon after reading the piece. "I am taken by an indefinable frustration." Arthur also claimed that, if anything, the label's financial difficulties had worsened since Socolov acquired sole responsibility for the catalogue. "When, during these 'crises,' I persisted in my own work, instead of magically reversing the situation created by you, you were outraged frequently, saying 'we're just trying to make some money,' and even tried to act as though I was guilty of some kind of mismanagement by not being more involved," Arthur declared. "Not even a few hundred dollars was available to release the Bright and Early project, though thousands were spent elsewhere. Now time has passed and the claim is still made by you that I am merely selfish in looking for an outlet for my work."

Although the specifics of the Bright and Early episode remain hazy — was Socolov as patiently supportive as Hall says he was, or did he withhold financial support for the release, as Arthur asserts in his letter, or were both responses jumbled together? — a much more straightforwardly ferocious argument between Socolov and Mark Freedman hastened the end of the original Sleeping Bag partnership. "Mark manipulated Arthur and there were things I ended up paying for," remembers Socolov. "It became a fight between Mark and myself. We were screaming at each other. Arthur was very embarrassed about it and he was also pragmatic. He said, 'That's the place I record at, I can't find a place that's that cheap.' He needed Mark Freedman and I wanted to punch him in the face. I just said, 'Arthur, we're going in different directions.' I said, 'Keep the music you recorded at Battery [Sound], keep your relationship with Mark, I'll take Sleeping Bag.' At the time our money was very tight, and Arthur had to make his deal with the devil.'" Arthur headed off with his tapes while Socolov kept the label. "I was becoming an entrepreneur, and Arthur was an artist," reasons Socolov. "I wanted to run a record company, and he wanted to create all of these different types of music."

From a financial point of view, Arthur's exit was poorly timed. He recorded "Tiger Stripes," Sleeping Bag's eighth twelve-inch single, and then was gone by the time the very next release — "Your Life" by Konk — began to make money. A short while later Mantronix's "Fresh Is the Word," which was recorded at home on a semiprofessional, half-inch eight-track machine and cost less than a thousand dollars to put out, clocked up sales of more than seventy thousand.[11] Blank believes Arthur was "iced out of the company"; Lee feels Socolov "just left Arthur in the dust"; Hall remembers Arthur feeling "horribly betrayed." But Hall also notes that "Arthur did have a tendency to feel neglected and betrayed" and remains mindful of his friend's obstruction of the Bright and Early release. Left-field in his sensibility, hungry for expensive studio time, and reluctant to finalize his recordings, Arthur was always likely to fall out with the entrepreneurial, matter-of-fact Socolov, but although the recriminations lingered, their fight was underlaid with mutual affection and respect. "I think Arthur harbored a couple of things against me, but he and I saw each other after we split up and he told me he wanted to do records," says Socolov. Lee confirms there was "frustration, not animosity or hatred."

Let's Go Swimming

When creative differences emerged between Arthur and Hall, they allowed themselves to be raw and passionate. "Sometimes Arthur would call me up in the middle of the night and accuse me of stealing melodies from him, or would be paranoid about some vague kind of psychic battle that he perceived was being waged between us as equals and competitors," says Hall. "He was scared that I would take the principles of what we were developing—the power of Buddhism and Eastern ideas ensconced in pop music, and access to certain special musicians and studios—and become a big pop star without him." Their spats had the "timbre of fights between brothers" and on one occasion Arthur's competitive streak got the better of him when, having produced a solo album for Hall and arranged for it to be released on Sleeping Bag, he pulled his friend out of the clinch meeting with Socolov and begged him not to sign. Such disputes were normally resolved when Arthur offered a sheepish apology, says Hall, who believes Arthur's consumption of grass contributed to his "paranoid arcs."

Arthur liked to joke that his paranoia was often "justifiable," because his royalties struck him as being lower than they might have been, and also because his ideas sometimes seemed to appear on other people's records. Yet he was also susceptible to naked jealousy, and shards of envy began to fly in the direction of another musical soul mate when Peter Gordon's career took off just as Arthur's began to dip during the first half of the 1980s. "I remember Arthur being frustrated by not being able to play in certain places, or things not working out as he hoped," remembers Arnold Dreyblatt.

"He was a little uncomfortable about Peter's success." Gordon detected a paradox. "Arthur was very charismatic on a one-to-one basis, but he had a hard time projecting that to an audience," he notes. "He was also naturally self-effacing, and had some sort of innate dislike of self-promotion, which ended up being self-defeating."

Having once run parallel to the mutating *Instrumentals* collective, Gordon's Love of Life Orchestra performed gigs and released records, and as Arthur quarreled with Robert Wilson, Gordon was invited to compose ambitious scores for dance, theatre, film, and video projects. *Secret Pastures*, a modern dance performance choreographed by Bill T. Jones and Arnie Zane, and featuring sets by Keith Haring, costumes by Willi Smith, and a live score by Gordon, premiered at the Brooklyn Academy of Music's Next Wave festival in 1984 and won the Dance Theater Workshop's Bessie Award the following year. And although the saxophonist's work for Richard Foreman and Kathy Acker on the modern opera *Birth of the Poet* received mixed reviews when it was staged at the Brooklyn Academy of Music, Gordon's composition for the production of *Otello* by the Neapolitan theater group Falso Movimento won the *Village Voice* Obie Award in 1985. "Arthur was probably jealous that I got more critical attention than him at the time," says Gordon. "We probably envied traits in each other. When everyone is scuffling and trying to have their voice heard, it's easy for frustration to give way to envy."

Gordon had already performed on a number of Arthur's projects, and he returned the favor by asking Arthur to cowrite a dance-oriented movement for the score of *Secret Pastures*. They came up with "That Hat," which featured dense electric cello, programmed beats, and vocals by Arthur; percussion (congas, cowbell, and whistle) by Mustafa Ahmed; and additional vocals by David Johansen of the New York Dolls and Rebecca Armstrong of the Steve Reich Ensemble. Produced by Gordon and Arthur, an edit of the *Secret Pastures* version of "That Hat" was released as part of the cassette edition of the score, and Gordon notes it featured some "great performances by Arthur." "Some people say Arthur wrote 'That Hat' about me," says Ahmed, who would always wear a baseball cap or a beret. "It was another one of those tunes that had this really interesting little hop to it."

Another version of "That Hat" was laid down when Gordon signed a contract—precisely the kind of contract that had eluded Arthur—to write

Secret Pastures collaborators in Keith Haring's studio, 1984. *Left to right*: Peter Gordon (composer), Bill T. Jones and Arnie Zane (choreographers), Keith Haring (sets), Willi Smith (costumes). Photograph by and courtesy of Paula Court. ©Paula Court.

and coproduce a solo album for CBS Records in June 1985. Written, recorded, and mixed between June and September, the new version of "That Hat" included more saxophone, while Johanson's growl was replaced by Arthur's free-floating yet precisely placed vocals. "The two versions couldn't have been more different," recalls Eric Liljestrand, who engineered the sessions. "Arthur's version was very smooth and ethereal, while the David Johanson version was really aggressive." Arthur became unhappy with the record during the mixing process, however, and judged the sample and drum-heavy promotional single, which was mixed by Doug DeFranco of Double Dee and Steinski, to be even worse. "The promo was one of those classic record-company debacles that left both Arthur and me disappointed," explains Gordon. "Arthur always chided me for letting that happen, but since it was a 'promotional' product rather than a 'creative' product, Arthur and I were excluded from the process by the record company."

That irritation aside, Arthur owed Gordon a word of thanks, because it was during a studio session for "That Hat" that he met Gary Lucas, a gifted guitarist and Yale graduate who had worked in the advertising department at CBS since 1977. "In 1980–81 I took vacation time and several leaves of absence to record with Captain Beefheart and the Magic Band and tour with him in Europe and the U.S.," recalls Lucas. "But I held on to that day job throughout my Beefheart years." When Lucas was promised a production role if he brought CBS Masterworks (a subsidiary of CBS Records) "the next Philip Glass," he approached Gordon, whom he had seen lead LOLO during a concert at Hurrah's, and he became the coproducer of Gordon's album, *Innocent*. Lucas went on to meet Arthur while "That Hat" was being mixed at Bearsville Studios in Woodstock. "Arthur breezed in for the mix with his long-time companion Tom Lee, and proceeded to turn the session topsy-turvy with his manic obsessiveness," Lucas recalled later. "At one point he demanded that we all drop outside the studio into the corridor for a playback because, he insisted, the tune 'sounded slower' out there, and he asked why didn't we remix it accordingly."[12] Lucas adjusted his A&R antennae. He recalls, "I said to myself, 'Peter is great, but I really want to work with Arthur.' My heart was in championing the underdog and Arthur was deserving of more breaks. I transferred my Van Vliet / Beefheart affections to Arthur."

In need of a new place to hang out following his spat with Will Socolov, Arthur started to visit Lucas at CBS, and the two of them became (in the words of Lucas) "as tight as a straight person and a gay person can get without having sex." Lucas had admired the seductive vocals, heavy bass line, and unexpected accents on "That Hat," and as Arthur plied him with gifts of vinyl pressings and demo tapes each time he visited, he came to fall in love with his "spooky, jazzy voice, inner-child sense of wonder and eternally great music." As Lucas would later write, "Arthur Russell could musically deliver the kind of quirky goods that simultaneously melted your heart and forced you to listen to music in a new way—and do it all with a sense of high-spirited panache and good humor."[13] The idea that Arthur could do this while being what Lucas describes as a "free-spirited, secretive, awkward and stubborn trickster figure, a wilful creative force of nature, who fought the system yet also tried to embrace it," made him all the more intriguing.

While work continued on *Innocent*, Lucas set up Upside Records with Barry Feldman, who had become bored with his job at PolyGram, and started to push for the label to release music by his new friend. "Arthur started bringing projects to me and Gary encouraged it," confirms Feldman, who took up the day-to-day running of Upside while Lucas assumed a creative role. "Gary was a fan. *Arthur Russell Arthur Russell Arthur Russell.* I give Gary all the credit for that." Arthur started to spend time in Upside's tiny, two-room office on Lafayette Street, and he soon handed over a copy of "See My Brother, He's Jumping Out," one of the outstanding tracks from *Corn*, which he wanted to release under the new title of "Let's Go Swimming." "It was pretty much done," recalls Feldman, who paid Arthur four thousand dollars and released the record on Logorhythm, Upside's dance subsidiary. "But I had to pay for the mastering, and Arthur also wanted to bring in Walter to do some work on it."

A pioneering club DJ, Walter Gibbons had more or less invented the art of mixing between the percussive breaks of two records. (He did this in conjunction with DJ Kool Herc, who unknowingly worked the same technique in the Bronx.) Gibbons also remixed the first commercial twelve-inch single when Salsoul invited him to cut and splice "Ten Percent" by Double Exposure, and he became the first DJ to be trusted with the multi-tracks during a remix project (Salsoul having asked him to rework Loleatta Holloway's "Hit and Run"). If Tom Moulton pioneered the concept of the disco remix, it was Gibbons who explored the aesthetic potential of the new format, and Gibbons remained in demand until he became a born-again Christian while wrapping up a remix of Instant Funk's "I Got My Mind Made Up"—again for Salsoul—at the end of 1978. Disenchanted with that record's frisky vocals, Gibbons agreed to have Larry Levan put the finishing touches to the remix, after which the Paradise Garage DJ burst onto the remixing map while Gibbons embarked on a wholly unsuccessful battle against the use of profane lyrics in dance music.[14] As the commissions started to dry up, Gibbons took to working behind the counter at the store Rock and Soul, where he sold records and dished out sermons with equal gusto. When Arthur handed him a copy of "That Hat," which featured "The Day the Devil Comes to Getcha" (written by Laurie Anderson) on the B-side, he was subjected to a fiery tirade.

Arthur had become interested in Gibbons after he heard his mix of Sandi Mercer's "Play with Me," and the two of them eventually met at West End Records, where Gibbons was completing a mesmerizing remix of Bettye LaVette's "Doin' the Best That I Can."[15] Nothing came of that encounter, but in 1984 Arthur heard the moody, trance-inducing syncopation of "Set It Off" by Strafe, an out-of-the-blue Gibbons production of stunning origi-

Walter Gibbons in Blank Tapes Studios. Photographer unknown.
Courtesy of François Kevorkian.

nality, and realized he needed to team up with the Rock and Soul salesman. "Strafe changed our lives," reminisces Hall. "It would play in the black gay clubs on the waterfront, and people would abandon themselves in a kind of Bacchanalian trance. The record gave Arthur a new idea about how to use trancelike states in dance music to achieve the kind of open-vista Buddhist mind he was striving for."

Arthur and Gibbons worked on "Let's Go Swimming" at Battery Sound, where they would meet at eleven at night and carry on until eight the next morning. "There were incredible scenes of screaming and fights," recalls Lucas. "Arthur was shrieking and tearing his hair out, raging around the studio like a psychotic bat, while Walter was calmly snipping and pasting the tape as if it was macramé. Arthur would say, 'You're ruining my fucking vision! This isn't what I had in mind! What are you doing? This is my big shot!' And Walter would reply, 'Arthur, Arthur, calm down!'" Lucas sat back and watched the drama unfold, while Liljestrand, who had been stationed in the studio in order to make sure that nothing was broken, did his best to keep out of the control room because Gibbons worked with the volume deafeningly loud. "There was a lot of back and forth between the three of them," says the engineer. "It seemed argumentative, but Arthur would often defer to Walter, and I don't remember him deferring to anybody else." Liljestrand says he can't recall how many speaker fuses he replaced that day.

Assuming the imperative mode of "Kiss Me Again," "Pop Your Funk," "#5 (Go Bang!)," and "Clean on Your Bean," "Let's Go Swimming" depicted the water as a great place to go and have fun with a friend or two. Flipping between the contained ripples of the swimming pool, the ebb and flow of the ocean, and the swirling effects of a whirlpool, the instrumentation underscored Arthur's liquid intent. Ahmed's percussive effects lurched from beat to beat in an unpredictable stream of dislocated rhythmic combinations, creating a platform for Arthur's harsh, manic synth stabs and rumbling cello, while Arthur's voice took on the quality of a light, inky liquid that was swept up in the maelstrom. The lyrics ran:

Every morning I climb
Down a hillside
And walk wherever
I can see a road to walk on
Where the sky is clear and blue
And it's good for swimming
Let's go swimming
Let's go swimming
Let's go swimming
Let's go swimming
Let's go.

The song concluded with a further variation of its recurring verse.

To the warm
Part of that
That country I am swimming to
'Cause where you've been I go
That's where I always go
I'm banging on your door
Up in the big blue
Up in the big blue sky

I'm banging on your door
All set
Let's go swimming
All set
All set to go
Let's go swimming.

Released in the summer of 1986 under Arthur's name, the "Let's Go Swimming" twelve-inch included three mixes. Arthur's "Gulf Stream Dub" and the "Puppy Surf Dub" appeared on Side A, while Side B showcased the "Coastal Dub," Gibbons's mix, which at seven minutes and fifty-eight seconds was significantly longer than both of Arthur's efforts. Less song-oriented and more conceptual than the "Gulf Stream Dub" and the "Puppy Surf Dub," the "Coastal Dub" included an opening instrumental section that built to a crescendo before it broke down, as well as an extended outro that rose out of a gurgling sound effect before Ahmed's congas locked into a groove alongside Arthur's cello. "Walter created a visionary, psychedelic soundscape for the song," says Lucas. "He sort of out-avant-garded Arthur and took the song out to the stratosphere. There was a kind of one-upmanship as to who could be more far out—like Zappa and Beefheart." Despite the studio drama, Arthur was pleased with the contribution of Gibbons. "If you try and do something different in dance music, you just get branded as an eccentric," he told Toop. "A lot of DJs take the tapes I make and try to make them into something more ordinary. 'Let's Go Swimming' was supposed to be a futuristic summer record. Some DJs said that nobody would ever, ever play that. I think eventually that kind of thing will be commonplace."[16] Toop would later state that "Let's Go Swimming" sounded "like nothing in the history of disco."[17]

Coproduced by Mark Freedman and Arthur Russell—Freedman contributed by donating studio time and tape—"Let's Go Swimming" told the coded tale of Arthur's childhood holidays by the lakes of Minnesota, his odyssey from the landlocked terrain of the Midwest to the mountainous shores of San Francisco and the island of New York City, and his devotion to the state of Maine, where he traveled every year to see his sisters and also go whale-watching. "There's something about water that does it to me," he would tell Frank Owen of *Melody Maker* in 1987. "I have to live near water. I couldn't live in the centre of the continent. I go to see the Hudson River

Arthur Russell by the water in Iowa in the mid-1980s. Photograph by Charles Arthur Russell Sr. Courtesy of Audika.

nearly every day."[18] Growing up in Oskaloosa, water was exotic to Arthur: when he traveled with his family to Minnesota for their summer vacations, he would go swimming as soon as he arrived; he started to collect fish, lining his bedroom with several tanks of darting neon tetras and illuminated reefs; one of his earliest career ambitions was to work as an ichthyologist; and after reading Jules Verne's *Twenty Thousand Leagues Under the Sea*, he set about designing his own visionary submarine. Arthur was more drawn to Mount Shasta than to the Bay when he lived in San Francisco, but in New York he installed a fish tank in the living room, placed a picture of a surfacing whale on the mantelpiece, and put up Hall's "found poem" gift of a poster of tropical fish in the bathroom. "In the gentle undersea rhythms of a coral reef," ran the caption, "the Blue Tang displays his dreamy coloration."

Arthur's music was geological as well as aquatic in its themes. *Instrumentals (1974 — Volume 2)* and *Tower of Meaning* evoked the rolling planes of the Midwest and the mountains of San Francisco, his country-folk guitar outings carried the smell of freshly turned soil, and the scratchy, bumpy

Arthur Russell on Jones Beach, Long Island, summer 1986, around the time
"Let's Go Swimming" was released. Photograph by and courtesy of Tom Lee.

instrumentation of "Kiss Me Again," "Is It All Over My Face?," and *24* ⟶
24 Music conjured up the dust and friction of downtown New York. Yet
an oozing fluidity also flowed beneath the surface of these records, and
this inner aquatic quality was drawn out by Larry Levan (who highlighted
Arthur's dreamy, liquid synth solo on the "Female Vocal" of "Is It All Over
My Face?") and François Kevorkian (whose remix of "Go Bang! #5" was
streamlined in the interests of dance-floor flow). Later on, Arthur named
one of his groups the Sailboats, chose "Indian Ocean" as his artist name for
Corn, and adopted the moniker of Killer Whale on "Tell You (Today)" and
"You Can't Hold Me Down," as well as on his "Under Water Mix" of "Chill
Pill." He also penned the song "The Platform on the Ocean." For "Let's Go
Swimming" he used the Killer Whale name again and this time developed
lyrics to match his musical theme. And when Gibbons gave Arthur a homemade aquarium video that opened with TV edits of an octopus-like crea-
ture moving through the seabed in time with the record, the cellist could
hardly contain his joy.

Barry Feldman says he had "a beef with some of Arthur's equalization," which he thought was "a little too crash," or trebly, but he also "loved the record." The reviewers were even more enthusiastic. "Arthur Russell is nothing short of a genius," declared *Record Mirror*. "Mixing African, electro, hip hop, house, soul, pop and a touch of the avants into a wholly danceable suite, he'll create mayhem on the dance floor."[19] *New Musical Express* described "Let's Go Swimming" as a "genuine oddity" and added, "thank God for something that strays off the beaten path."[20] In another article, *Record Mirror* noted, "Like his earlier Dinosaur L underground classic, ["Let's Go Swimming"] really will need time to mature and become as widely accepted as it deserves. Right now it'll be classed as 'house,' although it's far deeper."[21] Writing in *Melody Maker*, Simon Reynolds noted, "This is an *impossible* dance music, jumbling your urges, making you want to move in ways not yet invented, confounding your body as it provokes it. In its tipsy mix, I seem to hear Can, Peech Boys, Thomas Leer, Weather Report, hip hop, but really this is unique, original, a work of genius."[22]

As work on "Let's Go Swimming" progressed, Arthur also asked Gibbons to apply his unorthodox touch to "School Bell / Treehouse," which he had written for his *World of Echo* project. Financed by Peter Zummo, who received a coproduction credit for his support, the resulting twelve-inch replaced the oscillating flows of "Let's Go Swimming" with a recognizable groove that revolved around Ahmed's jagged congas and skipping hi-hats. Scratchy cello and discordant synth patterns (from Arthur) along with spacey trombone passages (from Zummo) wrapped themselves around this prickly structure, while Arthur's echo-laden voice evoked a childlike world of innocence and play that was darkened by the record's awkwardly aggressive groove. When the percussion accelerated over the last couple of minutes, "School Bell / Treehouse" began to sound like a proto-house track, although the rhythm was too organic and peculiar to suggest anything more than a passing proximity to the Roland-generated rhythms of mid-1980s Chicago house music. Instead the recording was closer to the hypnotic groove that might have been generated if Ali Akbar Khan, James Brown, Fela Kuti, and Neil Young had busked together in Grand Central Station.

Arthur and Socolov were on good enough terms for "School Bell / Treehouse" to be released under Arthur's Indian Ocean moniker on Sleeping Bag Records. "I told him, 'Arthur, it's not commercial, but it's a really interesting record,'" recalls Socolov. The Sleeping Bag boss appears to have told a different story to others, and in so doing expressed a view that was becoming increasingly prevalent in New York dance circles. "I told Will Socolov how much I loved 'School Bell' when Walter [Gibbons] gave it to me, and Will said he wasn't pleased with it," remembers Steve Knutson, who was working at Tommy Boy Records at the time. "He said he needed Arthur to make great club records, and he doesn't do that anymore. Everyone at Tommy Boy was a big disco expert and they were like, 'Do you like that shit ["School Bell/ Treehouse"]? Arthur's never made a good record except 'Go Bang!'"

Running with the ten-minute "School Bell / Treehouse" on the B-side and a shorter version, "Treehouse / School Bell," on the A-side, the twelve-inch received good reviews. "It's got the same jazzy inflections as 'Go Bang' but, if anything, it's more weird with this mutated cello moaning in the background," Frank Owen wrote in *Melody Maker*. "Art funk hasn't got the best of reputations back in Britain. I remember one particularly dodgy band, whose name I've long since forgotten, who specialized in doing pale imitations of Brass Construction while chanting 'Image/Music/Text/Mythology' over the top. 'Schoolbells' [sic] is exactly the opposite. Its art is firmly rooted in its funk. You can't hear the join because there's no join to hear."[23] *New Musical Express* also gave the twelve-inch a strong write-up. "Possibly a bit too esoteric for current dance tastes, this will undoubtedly be a collector's item in about three years time," wrote Jay Strongman.[24] Evaluating "School Bell / Treehouse" and "Let's Go Swimming" for *Spin*, John Leland wrote, "Neither record makes any goddamn sense, but they entice and invite you in."[25]

During this period Arthur started to visit Gibbons at Rock and Soul, and, having learned to tread carefully around the question of religion, he began to receive invitations to the Saturday night parties Gibbons put on in his basement apartment in Queens. "It was like being in a high school rec room or a teenager's den," recalls Tom Lee. "There would be soda and chips, and Walter also had these colored lights. Religious icons were dotted around, and he played pre-made tapes on a reel-to-reel." Only a few people danced, yet while Lee would drift around, wondering if he might end up in a conversation with one of the host's more religiously resolute friends, Arthur didn't bother with such niceties. "Arthur's goal was to talk with Walter," says Lee. "He'd wait for his opportunity to chat with Walter

Logarhythm's press picture of Arthur Russell, sitting on the roof of Poet's Building on Twelfth Street in the mid-1980s. Photograph by Tom Lee. Courtesy of the Kitchen, New York City.

about some project they were working on. Arthur was all business in that regard."

In Gibbons, Arthur found an ideal collaborator with whom he could make left-field dance music, as well as a friend who, like himself, was intensely creative, soft-spoken, and unremittingly intense. Socolov remembers Gibbons being obsessed with the nuances of musical texture—the former Galaxy 21 DJ would lure him into discussions about sound that he could barely follow and never had time for—and notes that the only other person who liked to analyze sound in such microscopic detail was Arthur. Their collaborations weren't always successful; when Gibbons remixed "#5 (Go Bang!)" during scrambled-together hours at Blank Tapes, the taut, stretched-out result lacked the dramatic dynamism of Kevorkian's mix and was never officially released. (A bootleg version appeared in Japan some twenty years later.) Other records, such as the sparse and funky "C-Thru," remained unfinished. Yet the more or less simultaneous release of "Let's Go Swimming" and "School Bell / Treehouse" confirmed their intention to supplant the mutant disco of "Is It All Over My Face?" and "Go Bang! #5" with a new form of jittery, wonky dance music. Steven Hall confirms that Arthur respected Gibbons more than anyone. "Everyone knew that Walter Gibbons was the real thing," he comments. "He was not just a mixer but a musician and an alchemist. He could turn a good groove into gold or mercury. Arthur and Walter were totally soul mates."

According to Hall, who dated him briefly, Kirk Winslow was "breathtakingly beautiful" and "high-strung like a racehorse." He was also the "only other major romantic figure in Arthur's life," although he was never "any threat to Arthur and Tom's marriage." Arthur met Winslow before he met Lee and employed him later as an assistant during the production of *Medea*. They became close. Winslow accompanied Arthur to miscellaneous rehearsals, sometimes showing up in a pair of silver spray-painted boots, and Arthur consulted with him about astrology and numerology. "Kirk approved the name of every group that Arthur and I played together in," notes Hall. "Arthur would adjust or change titles of works according to Kirk's suggestions. A simple letter change in a word or group of words would make that title and by extrapolation the work itself more powerful and effective. This consultation was of key importance to him — as much as recording on the full moon and editing on the new moon."

Winslow also catalyzed Arthur's connection to avant-garde dance, having introduced the cellist to Merce Cunningham and John Bernd. Arthur played for Cunningham, but forged a much closer relationship with Bernd, who developed the modern dance performance of *Little America* in May 1983 around his score for *Medea*, and who also asked him to provide the music for the improvised choreography of Ishmael Houston-Jones at the Cooper-Hewitt Museum in June 1984.[26] Arthur and Bernd worked together again when Hall staged the performance art piece *Turbo Sporty* at the Piezo Electric Gallery for two weeks in August 1984. Hiding from the audience, in part because he wanted to watch the Olympic swimming and diving events on TV, Arthur played languid cello over a keyboard drone while, on various nights, Hall read his two-word poems, Johnny Fu filled the gallery with giant, pornographic calligraphy, and Bernd improvised solo dances.[27] When Bernd developed AIDS, he teamed up with Winslow (slide projector) and Arthur (cello) for a series of breathtaking performances in which he danced naked, revealing a body smitten with psoriasis. "They [Bernd, Winslow, Russell, and the performance artist and writer Tim Miller] were the coolest of the cool, and also the sexiest and most confrontational," says Hall. "Everyone in the East Village was following their progress. The music Arthur played with them was his most ethereal and shimmering."

Modern dance appealed to Arthur because its kaleidoscopic show of muscular limbs and lithe movements opened up a medium in which desire and physicality could be expressed without recourse to categories and choices. Arthur was happy to live his life as a gay man and would often be drawn to the male dancers, yet he also showed interest in female dancers and on one occasion told Peter Zummo he was a "closet heterosexual." Echoing his interest in the pitches that existed between the standard tunings of European art music, which were assumed to be natural even though they were randomly asserted, contemporary dance offered Arthur a sensual, nonprescriptive space in which he could explore the lacunae that rested between the either/or institutions of homosexuality and heterosexuality. "He was mesmerized by abstract dance," comments Zummo. "I think he looked forward to coming to rehearsal."

Arthur received further contemporary dance commissions from Zummo and his wife, Stephanie Woodard, and in September 1985 he teamed up with the Peter Zummo Orchestra — Mustafa Ahmed (percussion), Guy Klucevsek (accordion), Bill Ruyle (marimba), and Peter Zummo (trombone) — to play at the performance of Tricia Brown's *Lateral Pass*. Brown had commissioned Zummo to write a suite of compositions for the show, and one of the pieces, *Song IV*, which featured Arthur singing and playing cello alongside Ruyle and Zummo, was released on Zummo's album *Zummo With An X* later that same year. Before that came about, the musicians flew to the Walker Art Center in Minneapolis, and during their stay Arthur developed a heavy crush on Stephen Petronio, one of Brown's dancers. "Stephen was a big problem for Arthur," remembers Zummo. "It was a case of unrequited love. They housed us at this motel in Minneapolis for a week, and Arthur was falling over himself because of Stephen. I think Stephen was trying to fend him off most of the time."

Staying in the room next to Arthur's, Ahmed expected the two of them to spend time working on joint music projects in between rehearsals and was particularly eager to wrap up "Let's Go Swimming," which they had been working on for a while. "'Let's Go Swimming' is the song that epitomized the way—excuse my French—Arthur could never fucking finish a song," says Ahmed. "I would go home with a hot mix and come back a week later, and he would be doing something else with it, or have changed it, and that was a characteristic. It seemed like we recorded for ever." Ahmed persevered and recorded a series of conga and bongo overdubs for the record that Arthur promised to wrap up during their free time in Minneapolis. "They were extremely hot," recalls Ahmed. "Those mixes were the closest Arthur ever came to that elusive black/salsa dance scene he wanted to be part of." During the trip Arthur plunged into a weird, impenetrable mood, however, and when Ahmed asked Zummo if he knew what was going on, he was given the lowdown on Petronio. "I was clueless," says Ahmed, who had managed to work with Arthur for several years without clocking his sexual identity. "Coming from where I was coming from, a gay person was a flaming fag. Arthur didn't behave that way. All the time that we were together he was a gay man living a gay life, and I didn't know anything about it."

Ahmed and Arthur almost fell out over Arthur's failure to work on "Let's Go Swimming" in Minneapolis, and tension continued to mount when Ahmed heard the final version of the track. "It was the one song I really connected with, but when I heard the released version I was very disappointed," he says. "It didn't capture the bright energy of the mixes that I'd worked on with Arthur." Ahmed was also frustrated the final mix included so many counterintuitive hops and skips. "One of the things that was left unresolved was whether the way I heard 'Let's Go Swimming' would have provided Arthur with a commercial hit," says Ahmed. "I thought my interpretation of the record would have been right up Will Socolov's street, but Arthur insisted he wasn't going to do things the easy way. He would introduce some little hitch or syncopation that took the record out of dance. A simple four-on-the-floor would have been just fine, but Arthur had to have something different. He kept on experimenting and experimenting." Ahmed only heard the finished version of "School Bell / Treehouse" when,

touring with Peter Gordon in Italy, he visited a club where a DJ was spin-
ning the record. "Other folks might have felt snubbed under similar circumstances, but I didn't feel that way," he remembers. "I was in Italy, having a
great time with fabulous musicians, thanks in large part to Arthur."

World of Echo

> The Lama Ngawang Kalzang had been meditating for twelve years in
> various caves and retreats in the wilderness of the mountains of South-
> ern Tibet. Nobody knew him, nobody had heard of him. He was one of
> the many thousands of unknown monks who had received his higher
> education in one of the great monastic universities in the vicinity of
> Lhasa, and though he had acquired the title of *Géshé* (i.e. Doctor of
> Divinity), he had come to the conclusion that realisation can only be
> found in the stillness and solitude of nature, as far away from the noisy
> crowds of market-places as from the monkish routine of big monasteries
> and the intellectual atmosphere of famous colleges. The world had for-
> gotten him, and he had forgotten the world. This was not the outcome
> of indifference on his part but, on the contrary, because he had ceased
> to make a distinction between himself and the world. What actually he
> had forgotten was not the world but his own self, because the 'world' is
> something that exists only in contrast to one's ego.
>
> Lama Anagarika Govinda, *The Way of the White Clouds*[28]

Having filmed Sun Ra in the late 1960s, Phill Niblock decided he didn't
want to repeat the exercise with anyone else, but Arthur's not-quite-of-
this-world persona gave Niblock second thoughts, and he ended up film-
ing Arthur performing a selection of his voice-cello *World of Echo* songs at
the Experimental Intermedia Foundation on two separate occasions in the
autumn of 1985 — both times without an audience. "Arthur had this strange
lighting setup with a bunch of cheap lamps and filters and a dimmer board
that Steven Hall was manipulating," Niblock recalls. "The lighting changed
dramatically from moment to moment, so it was all quite interesting."[29]
Shot on a single camera and without breaks, the first video was marred by
interference while the second ran smoothly. As far as Niblock knew, Arthur
was planning to release the second performance, provisionally titled "Terrace of Unintelligibility," in a video-only format, but the filmmaker had

come to appreciate there was little point asking Arthur what he was going to do with the tapes.[30]

Arthur continued to perform songs from his solo, voice-cello *World of Echo* project during 1985, more often than not at the Experimental Intermedia Foundation, where cheap wine could normally be found in a corner. "Phill's loft was a much more relaxed hangout than the Kitchen," notes Arnold Dreyblatt. "Phill may have been less critically curatorial than some of the directors of the Kitchen, and it's true that he did not present some of the more provocative acts that appeared at the Kitchen, but it is not an accident that Arthur became friends with Phill and ended up performing at this very off-the-mainstream space." Arthur also liked the audio tracks of Niblock's videos so much he resolved to release a *World of Echo* album. "We would start at eight or nine in the evening and go on at least until 3:00 a.m.," recalls Eric Liljestrand, who confirms the songs were recorded almost always at night. "Arthur always tried to maximize the time, so we did everything in a rush. It's not like Arthur did endless takes of the same thing, but the tape was continually running and the sessions were pretty blurry to me."

Because he was the only instrumentalist in the sessions, Arthur realized he could break with the standard practice of playing in a quiet, isolated room, and so he set himself up in the control booth in order to hear exactly what the engineer was hearing and tweak the sound according to his own taste as he played directly into the mixing board. Then, when he was done with singing or playing, he would cut, re-equalize, and manipulate the recordings, weaving them together as if he were a time-traveling tapestry artist. During these sessions it became standard for Arthur to splice together separate tapes, and he would regularly grab a track from one tape and fly it into the multitrack of another while his onlooking engineer tried to stay calm. "We would be mixing on a piece of tape, and I would see a splice go by," recalls Liljestrand. "It was all very confusing. I could never really tell what we were working on until it was done." The ghostly accidents that arose from Arthur's insistence that they re-record over old tape became an integral part of the sonic fabric. "There would be leakage of an old track into a new track, which drove me bonkers," explains the engineer. "But it didn't seem to bother Arthur." Arthur was more concerned with Liljestrand's habit of double-checking every time Arthur instructed him to record over an old multitrack, and on one occasion he "got really mad," re-

Experimental Intermedia Foundation. Photograph by Maria Blondeel.
Courtesy of Phill Niblock and Maria Blondeel.

members the engineer. But as their working relationship deepened, Arthur relaxed and took to standing over Liljestrand's shoulder, clenching his fists and rocking backwards and forwards in a virtually imperceptible motion as the material was played back to him. "It was almost like he was dancing inside, and only a little bit was coming out."

Working into the early hours, Arthur and Liljestrand studied a series of recordings that showcased the startling complexity of Arthur's amplified cello—an instrument that, in terms of Arthur's releases, had been restricted to playing orchestral scores and making cameo appearances on twelve-inch singles. Arthur had started to amplify the instrument in San Francisco, but it was only when he combined an MXR Graphic Equalizer with the Mutron Biphase box (a hundred-dollar piece of equipment that generated resonance by combining the technology of phase modulation with the wah-wah pedal) that the electric cello sounded (as he put it) "really beautiful." "The result is that a very new road is opened to me with the cello bringing it a long way from its traditional orchestral role," Arthur wrote to Chuck and Emily in 1977. "I don't think anyone plays this instrument this way, amplified with such a clear sound." Arthur went on to acquire a bewildering number of other effects boxes, which he would combine as he searched for a "deep and shifting feeling" that resembled an "undertow current" (in the words of Hall). "He took his cues from heavy-metal guitars, and was looking for the same depth of sound and impact," notes Hall. "He was fascinated by their huge, monolithic soundprints and studied various metal guitarists in his quest."

Arthur's playing was directed toward sonic range rather than virtuosic skill. When his fingers flew up and down his cello's neck in darting, athletic movements the instrument twanged like a funk bass, yet when he bounced his bow on its strings or tapped out rhythms on its wooden body, the sound was percussive. On some songs Arthur's cello reverberated with electrostatic intensity as the bow screeched over the instrument's strings, while on others it rumbled deep and threatening, or generated a modulated bleep-like signal, or even shifted between a series of affects. "Echoing the chance operations of John Cage and Jackson Mac Low, he loved constant, random modulation," adds Hall. Indeed the cello only sounded like a cello when Arthur played pizzicato, sending off gentle, acoustic sounds of such subtle detail that even the movement of the air around the strings seemed to be audible. And although feedback was an ongoing curse that could result in chaos, by the time of the *World of Echo* recordings Arthur had come to describe these untameable waves as "feedback harmonies."

Arthur's voice discovered a similar freedom during these insomniac sessions. Having taken vocal lessons at the Ali Akbar College of Music, where he let go of the objective of clear pronunciation and started to slur his vowels, Arthur continued his studies in New York with the vocalist and composer Joan La Barbara, who taught him how to utilize the bones in his nose to get a droning, nasal sound. "Arthur was a dedicated musician with lots of ideas," recalls La Barbara. "His time at the Kitchen was very rich and meaningful for the downtown music community." As with all her students, La Barbara went through her basic physical warm-up exercises with Arthur, "because a good singer is like an athlete and sings with the entire body." Then she ran through tongue exercises, because, as La Barbara notes, the back of the tongue is connected to the vocal cords, and the exercises help bring blood directly into the area and warm it up in preparation for singing. Finally La Barbara moved on to working with vocal sound. "I always do a lot with resonance and with placement of the sound in specific areas in the face and head, focusing on specific bones such as cheek bones, the fore-

Arthur Russell playing cello during an interview and performance at WUSB Stony Brook, New York, in 1987. He developed his voice-cello oeuvre with *World of Echo*. Photograph by John Rosenfelder. Courtesy of Charles Arthur Russell Sr. and Emily Russell.

head, and, of course, the wonderful nasal resonances where one can make extreme sounds."

On the *World of Echo* recordings, Arthur's languid voice discovered a freedom of movement that had not been available in the comparatively formal settings occupied by the Flying Hearts, Loose Joints, Dinosaur L, and the Necessaries. Suspended between the musical traditions of India, Brazil, and North America, Arthur whispered and moaned, glided between notes, and explored unexpected directions as he moved through a series of seemingly impossible maneuvers. Like a kite, he combined tension with darting movement as he switched across a range of barely fathomable time signatures, yet the energy expended on maintaining his poise and flow didn't result in a loss of range and evocativeness. At times he sounded as though he was about to swallow his mike, while on other occasions he might as well have been singing on a ferry bound for Staten Island. And as his words blurred into each other to the point of being indistinguishable, Arthur edged away from the obligation of verbal communication and relaxed into an economy of phantasmagorical sounds. "After listening to tapes of *World of Echo* as well as foreign language singing," Arthur wrote in a later set of program notes, "I've enjoyed the musical effect of words as sounds, but where the meaning is not totally withdrawn."[31]

Evoking textures in infinite detail as they helped each other to discover their full expressive range, Arthur's voice and cello moved with a subtle dexterity as they headed into a Delta Lab 2 delay box, which generated echo and reinforced the illusion of disappearing sound. Yet whereas most dub producers sought out murkiness, Arthur hoped to create an echo that was scintillating rather than muted. "I like the bright sound, I like compression," Arthur wrote in a letter to the mastering engineer of the tapes. "Please make it as loud as possible." Arthur asked friends if they thought he was using too much reverb, and Ernie Brooks, who placed a high value on hearing the words of a song, told him that he was. Persevering, Arthur created a chorus of voices that combined in a flickering, spectral harmony. A shimmering, mystical celebration of vowel sounds, "Tone Bone Kone," which would become the opening song on the album, expressed itself as textural sensation rather than textual meaning, while other songs evolved in meandering, mesmerizing threads, fluttering about in tender butterfly movements that were impossible to predict and would have been terrible to contain or discipline. "When I have written songs, the functions of verse and chorus seem to be reversed for some unknown reason," Arthur wrote in a set of accompanying, unpublished notes. "The idiomatic style I ended up using is not immediately reference-able."

Arthur's decision to blend all of the songs into one continuous track contributed to the unraveling of structure, while his acoustic reworkings of "Let's Go Swimming," "School Bell / Treehouse," and "Wax the Van" illustrated the way his songs could discover an even greater degree of elasticity when they weren't required to follow the pulse of a drum. "It's the same song just different instrumentation," Arthur said of "Tree House" (as it was renamed on the album) in an interview with Frank Owen published in September 1986. "I think, ultimately, you'll be able to make dance records without using any drums at all." Songs without beats, Arthur added, would be the source of "the most vivid rhythmic reality."[32] In his unpublished jottings, Arthur also noted that his aim was to "redefine 'songs' from the point of view of instrumental music, in the hope of liquefying a raw material where concert music and popular song can criss-cross." That made *World of Echo* the song-oriented successor to *Instrumentals (1974 — Volume 2)*, which introduced popular forms into compositional music, and *24 → 24 Music*, which channeled orchestral improvisations through disco.

Along with the music's hushed, late-night atmosphere, the re-recording of older songs in an acoustic/dub format suggested that songs contain their own echoes — their own ability to discover a reincarnated form that's both the same and different. The self-referential twist suggested an introspective mind-set, and the use of sonic space, in which Arthur's voice and cello bounced around the three-dimensional contours of the mix, bolstered the impression that the recordings amounted to an internal, multidimensional play area that could be explored ad infinitum. At times Arthur appeared to be playing a game of existential hide-and-seek with his own shadow: his schizophrenic edits resulted in the multitrack tapes shifting between contrasting sonic environments — flat or hissy, spacious or closed, muffled or clear, dry or wet, populated or empty — in rapid succession; and because the voice-cello setup was so sparse, disappearance and loss were continually evoked as Arthur's feathery voice floated away, or a scratchy strike on his cello reverberated into thin air, and nothingness was met by the next word or note. Sounds moved across the multitrack tape like the gentle, recurrent movement of the seashore, where a receding wave would begin to reveal the sand underneath, only for the next wave to fold over the escaping undercurrent.

Channeling the jams of the Mantric Sun Band, the drones of the Ali Akbar College, and the meditative chanting of Ginsberg through the deserted downtown space of the Battery Sound studios, *World of Echo* was Arthur's latest attempt to blend West Coast spirituality with the East Coast avant-garde. Devotional and ethereal, the songs were delivered as twilight prayers as Arthur lost track of the distinction between himself and the world — perhaps like the Lama Ngawang Kalzang following twelve years of his cave- and mountain-bound meditation. John Hull notes that "Sound places one within a world," because the auditory is experienced inside the body of the listener (in contrast to the visual, which is experienced as a separate scene to be observed).[33] Yet in *World of Echo* Arthur appears to have transcended this state, as well as the mind/body divide (the notion that the physical and the nonphysical are always separate and opposed), because the recording worked as a form of abstract materialism in its illustration of the way movement isn't just physical but is also about potential. Stripping music down to its bare essence—to simple sequences of notes and friction and air—Arthur revealed the infinite quality of sound and existence.

As a rule, Arthur didn't get along with label bosses. When relations with the decision-makers at Sire and West End deteriorated, he cofounded his own label, and even this move simply became the precursor to his falling-out with his partner. But things seemed to be different at Upside, where he felt comfortable with Gary Lucas and Barry Feldman. "Arthur had this great résumé, but everyone in the scene treated him like shit—like, 'Fuck you, Arthur!'" says Feldman. "This would go on all the time, and he just seemed beaten down by all of it. I think he liked me because I wasn't very judgmental. Respectful of Feldman's background—the label boss grew up with jazz and could play compositions by Ornette Coleman, Charlie Parker, and others—Arthur began to call Feldman up and wait for him to start a conversation, or drop by the Upside office to share musical obsessions and low humor. And at some point during the second half of 1986, he decided that things were going well enough for him to entrust Feldman with *World of Echo*.

The album contained fourteen tracks, two of which were live takes recorded at the Experimental Intermedia Foundation.[34] "He blurted out, 'Barry, I think you really should release this record,' and then practically ran out the door," recalls Feldman. "The album was completely done. If he had proposed it and asked for money, I would have probably said, 'No.'" The Upside boss reasoned that if he gave Arthur one thousand dollars he'd have one problem, whereas if he gave him three thousand dollars he'd have three problems, but Arthur wasn't asking for money, and although Feldman wasn't a big fan of the record, he paid Arthur a token sum and crossed his fingers he would break even. "By that point there were so many problems with cash flow the idea of making a lot of money went out of my head," he says. "But I was like, 'Fuck it! I'm not making any money, I might as well put out a cool record!'"

Aside from a persnickety review in *New Musical Express*, the album received strong press.[35] *Billboard* declared it to be "one of the finest avant-garde pop albums in some time," while Frank Owen described the album as being "mournful, mysterious, intimate, understated, indeterminate and altogether beautiful."[36] Writing in *Melody Maker*, David Stubbs was even more adulatory. "This is what is left when the Beat has eaten itself, when the crunch of hip-hop has crunched itself to dust," he wrote. "'World Of Echo' is an orbit of resonance, a giant, subterranean repository of Dub. . . . It *works*, as a fuzz, a blur, a ric, throbbing pulse, a signal in space. . . . I imagine that, at some point in the future, it will be possible to dance quickly and furiously to 'World Of Echo,' once the rust-marks of the beat-grid have made a sufficiently indelible mark on the folk-memory, enabling the listener to refer to his ancient instincts to know what to do with his feet."[37] *Melody Maker* went on to list the album at number twenty-two in its chart of the top thirty releases for 1987, but sales were disappointing. "I was getting great press, but the stores barely took it," says Feldman. "I think I pressed up 1,200 copies and sold 900 at the most." As the movement in the stores faded, Arthur asked Feldman if he would place a football-shaped sticker on the cover that contained a single word: *Unintelligible*. "It was Arthur's way of saying to people, 'Don't expect to get it the first time, or the second time. Don't listen to it that way.' The sticker became a running joke."

Arthur appeared to be in good humor. Although his Flying Hearts, Bright and Early, and *Corn* recordings remained unreleased, he now had four albums to his name in addition to the two he had recorded with the Necessaries, and that was good going for any artist, let alone a compulsive procrastinator. "The next album might be a bit more of the same, except with drums," he told the *Oskaloosa Herald* in December 1986. "Or there may be a country album, because I like that a lot. Playing in a country band would have been perfect for me."[38] A few months later, in April 1987, he talked of the Upside LP as being a "sketch version" rather than a "complete version" of *World of Echo*. "I want to do the full version which will have brass bands and orchestras playing outdoors in parks with those band-stands that project echo," he commented. "I also want to have Casio keyboards on sail boats."[39] Arthur was still planning, still dreaming.

Drums

Arthur dug rap music. He studied the recordings of Afrika Bambaataa, Grandmaster Flash and the Furious Five, and the Sugarhill Gang with Mustafa Ahmed, and he also hooked up with Will Socolov when the Sleeping

Gary Lucas, 1990. Arthur Russell told him he looked happiest when he was with his guitar. Photograph by Marion Rosendahl. Courtesy of Gary Lucas.

Bag boss went to hear Bambaataa, Afrika Islam, Jazzy Jay, and others spin at the Roxy, the "first really major downtown club that had like a legitimately mixed scene," in the words of Fab 5 Freddy.[40] "Arthur said, 'This is going to be the music of the future!'" recalls Peter Zummo. "I thought, 'Are you kidding?'" In September 1986 Frank Owen asked Arthur if his "classical background" left him "disturbed by the radical lack of any trace of melody or harmony" in contemporary hip-hop. "It doesn't bother me at all," replied Arthur. "I grew up with atonality so it's nothing unusual to me."[41]

Although Tom Lee says his partner was never enthused about the project, Arthur attempted to produce a straight-up hip-hop track when Gary Lucas introduced him to a young rapper called Mark Sinclair as work on *World of Echo* drew to a close. "Mark was this mixed race guy who lived in Westbeth and worked at Minter's Ice Cream Store on Hudson Street, right around the corner from where I was living in the West Village," recalls Lucas. "He used to rap and breakdance in front of the store when things were slow, so I thought, 'Ha! This is pop! Mark and Arthur could be a genius collaboration!'" The ensuing studio session was a disaster because Sinclair was used to rapping a cappella, and Arthur selected a particularly difficult rhythm track. "Arthur used a tape of one of his patented avant-garde irregular beat grooves," remembers Lucas. "The 'one' [downbeat] kept drifting all over the place, and the staggered off-beats were overly high in the mix. Arthur also kept starting and stopping the tape at random places for each aborted take. It was no wonder Mark Sinclair had difficulty rapping. The groove kept getting yanked out from under him."

Arthur struggled to stay calm — "You really have to sing on the beat, Mark!" he instructed. Eric Liljestrand shared Arthur's frustration. "This guy just could not find the beat," remembers the engineer. "Then he started hitting David Van Tieghem's marimba with a hammer. The session was full of please-don't-do-that moments. I just wanted to put a gun to my head." Already fed up with his long hours and low pay, Liljestrand called Mark Freedman and quit when Arthur called it a night at 3:30 a.m. Sinclair would go on to be reborn as the buffed-up Hollywood action hero Vin Diesel, and the surviving tape of his studio work with Arthur suggests he chose his career path wisely. Yet the recording session was not without significance; a seemingly innocuous aside made during the course of the stop-start evening became its lasting legacy. "Arthur told me, 'You should be making music full-time, as you're happiest with a guitar in your hands,'" remembers Lucas. "This hardened my ambition to leave CBS to do music full-time and became a turning point for me."

During this period, Arthur started to talk with the London-based post-punk label Rough Trade, having been introduced to the label's owner, Geoff Travis, by Lucas. "I shopped tapes of Arthur's music to Geoff twice — once during my honeymoon in the summer of 1985 and again about a year later," says the guitarist. "Reinforced by his friends in the UK club scene, and also by various writers in the British music press who were all very pro-Arthur, Geoff finally came round to the opinion that Arthur was an artist worthy of signing." Although he had developed a reputation for releasing cutting-edge rock, a trip to the Paradise Garage in the early 1980s had left Travis wondering how he could bridge the two worlds, and Arthur provided him with a solution. "I liked the idea of doing dance, but it existed in a different time frame to the world of bands and live gigs, and I couldn't do both," he says. "Then Arthur came along and started to tell me about this unsung hero called Walter Gibbons. Arthur believed the remix would take the record ["Let's Go Swimming"] into the mainstream. He talked me into licensing it."

The "Let's Go Swimming" twelve-inch caught Travis by surprise. "I was mildly disappointed you couldn't dance to it, but I really loved it. You could dance to it in your head, as Ornette Coleman put it. It didn't sell well, but it got ecstatic reviews." Travis went on to release *World of Echo*, which he judged to be "a quite beautiful series of fragments and miniatures," in the spring of 1987. "Arthur appealed," adds Travis. "He fused all these different sensibilities, and I loved his word-sound poetry. There was something very rock 'n' roll about that. But it can't be overestimated what a small ripple *World of Echo* made in the vast pond of pop culture." Convinced the album wouldn't sell, Travis had persuaded Feldman to hand him the rights to release *World of Echo* for nothing, but in the aftermath of its release, and spurred on by the remixer Dave Lee, Travis decided to hand Arthur a ten-thousand-dollar advance (a sizeable chunk of money for an independent label) to record another album. "I found Arthur to be very intriguing," remembers Travis. "I loved his music and his sound, and I also liked him as a person. He was hilarious and had this fantastic enthusiasm. He always presented a relatively upbeat face."

Arthur's music also appealed to David Toop, who wrote a short feature about him for the *Face*, a cutting-edge UK fashion magazine, in the run-up to the release of *World of Echo*. "Russell is a man engaged in the seemingly hopeless task of crossing the great divide between contemporary composition and disco imperatives," wrote Toop. "On the one hand you have the sombre minimalism of 'Instrumentals,' recorded at The Kitchen and absolutely undanceable; alternatively you have 'Let's Go Swimming' and Indian Ocean's 'School Bell / Treehouse' which are sort of danceable.'"[42] Arthur told Toop about his vision for music without drums—something he had touched on during his interview with Frank Owen. "I like music with no drums . . . partly, I guess, from listening to drums so much," he said. "When you hear something with no drums it seems very exciting. I always thought that music with no drums is successive to music with drums. . . . In outer space you can't take your drums—you take your mind."[43] Running alongside a photo of Arthur wearing a newspaper hat, the piece acknowledged the difficulties the musician had faced in his attempt to straddle the worlds of composition and dance. "Do you have any unreleased material that nobody will touch?" Toop asked. Arthur laughed and laughed.[44]

A Sudden Chill

Arthur kept his distance from his family, but he stayed in touch and even visited from time to time. Emotionally distant and wrapped up in his music when he made these trips, Arthur seemed to think of Oskaloosa and Maine as peaceful outposts where he could get on with the business of writing new songs or listening to old tape. "It was hard to talk with him in those days," remembers Julie. "He was very withdrawn and into his music. I also found it difficult to be around people, but I was better at making a show of being normal—at being sociable and pleasant with people. Arthur wasn't into niceties. His message to me was: Be yourself." Kate also felt detached. "When he visited us up here he was gone," she says. "I always thought the reason he came here was not to see me or my sister or my folks, but to be in his own world, and also to have Beau to listen to his music."

Kate's son Beau had started to play with pots and pans when he was four, and the following year his parents bought him a drum set. A little while later Arthur started to talk music with his nephew, although his motivation was research-oriented rather than pedagogical, and related to his desire to develop an innocent aesthetic that registered with children as well as adults. "Arthur became obsessed with Beau's opinion of his music," recalls Kate. "He didn't really want to play music with him or coach him. He wanted his input as a young person who might have his finger on the pulse of something." When Beau took to the hard rock of Van Halen, Arthur became dispirited. "It was as if Arthur thought he was doing something wrong if Beau didn't like what he liked. I said, 'Arthur, he's *eight*!'"

Arthur's relationship with his parents improved as his career took off. "They started to mend fences when he reported back about 'Kiss Me Again' and 'Go Bang!' because he wasn't just the guy who needed to be bailed out," explains Tom Lee. "Chuck and Emily hung on to this. It was something concrete." The Russells were proud of *Instrumentals (1974 — Volume 2)* and *Tower Of Meaning*, and they were also fond of "Tell You (Today)," but when their Oskaloosan friends asked them how their son was doing, they struggled to reply because they were never quite sure "what phase he was in" (as they told the *Des Moines Register* years later).[45] Arthur, meanwhile, kept his relationship with Lee in the background, and Lee would hastily pass the phone to his partner whenever he happened to answer one of Chuck's and Emily's calls. "Arthur was careful about what he said to them,"

Arthur Russell and Tom Lee, c. 1985. Photographer unknown. Courtesy of Tom Lee.

remembers Lee. "He would say that Will was a pain, but that Sleeping Bag might release something, and could he have some money to go into the studio or buy some equipment. It depended on when he had last asked for money. Chuck and Emily wouldn't send money every month." When Arthur visited Oskaloosa, he would call Lee often and told his parents that he was "the feller living in the place." "We should have known he was gay, but didn't," says Chuck.

Julie was the first to find out about Arthur's relationship and Kate came next. Then, in 1985, Julie's husband told Emily that it "sure was good" how she and Chuck were tolerant of their son's homosexuality, at which point he realized he had inadvertently outed his brother-in-law. Arthur called his mother immediately and told her that "this was what he was," after which he added he had been "so much happier" since he had starting dating men. His words were only mildly reassuring. "Chuck and I have always had the same feeling about gay people," says Emily. "We are tolerant and were fond of people we knew were gay. But I have to admit it made a big difference that it was Charley. Who wants that? It's not an easy lifestyle." Emily was aware of the hazards. "One of the first things I said was, 'Have you had a test for AIDS?'" she recalls. "He said, 'No, I don't want to.'" Having with-held from her husband the news of Arthur's sexuality, Emily traveled to

Arthur Russell on the family sailboat, July 1985. "Have you ever been on a sailboat?" says Arthur Russell. "It's so quiet, all you hear is wind and sea" (quoted in Frank Owen, "Echo Beach," *Melody Maker*, 11 April 1987). Photograph by Charles Arthur Russell Sr. Courtesy of Charles Arthur Russell Sr. and Emily Russell.

New York with Chuck in 1986, after which they went on a car journey with Arthur to Canada. "I remember he was boring the devil out of us with one piece," says Chuck. "He had twenty-five versions of it and he kept playing them. I liked his music, but not that much. When he was done playing those tunes he saw an opening and he said, 'You know, Chuck, I'm gay.' I said, 'Are you sure?' He said, 'I'm sure.' I said, 'OK.'"

Later that same year, Arthur started to feel unusually tired, and the cause of his malaise was revealed when he went for a checkup and was asked to take an HIV test. "At some point he fooled around with the wrong person," says Lee. "He pinpointed it to a guy he had sex with in San Francisco in the early 1980s." Arthur told the same story to Ernie Brooks, who says that Arthur had become "horrified" with sex clubs such as the Anvil before this point, and he also recounted a more specific version to Bob Rosenthal, Allen Ginsberg's assistant. But the fling hadn't loomed large in his consciousness, and when he went for the health check, he had barely considered he might be HIV-positive. "The test confirmed he really was sick—that his fatigue had a basis in reality," says Lee. "He almost needed to hear that. I thought he was tired because he didn't have a regular job, so of course he couldn't get motivated. He didn't want to think he had HIV, and he would have been more at peace with another diagnosis, but he at least knew why he couldn't get going in the morning."

Arthur had become sick when knowledge of HIV and AIDS was still in its infancy. Deprived of support from Ronald Reagan, who had only acknowledged the existence of HIV/AIDS following the high-profile passing of Rock Hudson, researchers were coming to realize that the virus functioned by attacking the immune system, but no effective medication existed and six thousand AIDS-related deaths had already occurred. "We didn't know what to think because you're not dying when you get the notice of the virus, but it was also a death notice," recalls Lee. "We talked about other people having AIDS, especially John Bernd, because John was profoundly ill, and it didn't feel like Arthur was in that camp at all. All of these horrible things were happening to other people, and because Arthur was in the second wave of the disease, he was separate from all of those people in the news. It felt surreal." The opening lines of "A Sudden Chill," which was recorded by Arthur in 1986, might have been written with the test in mind.

A sudden chill broke the dream
He leans away from where he is
He laughs or tries to laugh
And thinks to himself
That's the very reason
I have opened this
You reminded me
I responded in the other way.[46]

With *World of Echo* now sounding as though it had been recorded by someone who knew he was sick—a retrospective reading that was incorrect—Arthur decided to move fast. "I'm working on a new album for Rough Trade, which should be done maybe in the next month," he told WUSB Stony Brook's *Music for Modern Ears* program in April 1987. Noting that some of the songs would be drawn from *World of Echo*, this time with the drums "turned on," he added, "It should be a pretty good dance record." A little later in the interview Arthur referenced a series of other forthcoming projects before he mentioned his plans for the summer. "I'm going to make very certain plans of an uncertain nature," he said. "Have a good time, I mean."[47]

Arthur lost his bonhomie when he played at the opening of the "Music:

Poster for the "Music: It's The Ocean" concert series at the Kitchen, 1987. Courtesy of Tom Lee.

It's the Ocean" series at the Kitchen later that same month, and he punctuated the concert by pacing the floorboards as well as plugging and unplugging his array of gadgets. "If these sketches seem anxious and impatient on record, Russell makes them sound terrorized and tormented in person," wrote Jonh Wilde in a review for *Melody Maker*. "Coarse and dissonant at one end, calm and beatific at the other, Russell's sideshow veers from abrasive scratchings to pastoral reveries, never less than cathartic." After the show, Wilde turned to a "stunned" Rolo McGinty, the lead vocalist of the Woodentops, who were also signed to Rough Trade, and discussed the applicability of the word "genius."[48] Robert Palmer, writing for the *New York Times*, was similarly dazzled. The concert, he wrote, "called up mental images that were insistently aquatic. . . . Mr. Russell alone on a sailboat, singing into the wind." Arthur's music, added Palmer, was "ethereal but never bland," his singing "fragile, liquid, long on vowels and short on consonants, apparently casual but with superb intonation."[49]

Arthur's casualness was also beginning to look eccentric in the increasingly rigorous and professionalized world of the New York avant-garde, and the musician was criticized for this when the *Village Voice* critic Kyle Gann reviewed his contribution to the Christian Wolff retrospective, which was staged at the Clocktower, again in April. Having applauded the contributions of John Zorn, Peter Zummo, and others, who were "utterly convincing," "entirely in line with Wolff's proletarian aesthetic," "unforgettable," "creative," "timbrally fascinating," "refreshingly different," and "spirited," Gann turned to Arthur. "There's a fine line between a casual performance attitude (to which Wolff's music conduces) and seeming to not give a damn, and only Arthur Russell stepped over it," he wrote. "He sang some Wolff *Songs* from '73–74, accompanying himself on cello in a lethargic deadpan that somehow suits his own music, but which rendered Wolff's all-important political text unintelligible."[50] Wolff read the review and disagreed. "I didn't buy it and I was sorry that Arthur was singled out in that way," he says. "I had no problem whatsoever with how he played."

Arthur had been developing an aesthetic of *intentional slackness* for some time. In *Instrumentals* he virtually encouraged his musicians to implode during the performance, and when he performed with the Flying Hearts he harangued David Van Tieghem for playing too tight. Arthur had better luck explaining to John Ingram how to play behind the beat during the Loose Joints sessions, but the Necessaries turned out to be more disciplined than he liked. Back in charge of his own music, Arthur captured a slurry, draggy sound on *24 —> 24 Music*, while the diffuse, undulating textures of "Let's Go Swimming" and "School Bell / Treehouse" contributed further to his oeuvre of irregularity. But while Arthur was often enthralling and disconcerting when he performed his own music, a similar approach to the interpretation of someone else's music ran the risk of sounding disrespectful. Outwardly stubborn but inwardly delicate, Arthur was probably distressed by Gann's review.

In an interview with *Blitz* the following month, Arthur began to talk about the way in which he was becoming more solitary in his practice, although no mention was made of his illness. "I used to work with huge groups of people in the past, thinking that more meant more," he said. "I suppose the emphasis has changed with all the technology. Now I can make more noise just by myself." Questioned about his evasive marketing strategy, Arthur commented: "I've used these different names because, to me, it's just like poetry. When a name is printed on a record label, it becomes a poem. The real struggle is to make clear the things that I would like to do." Noting how Arthur's music seemed to "blur all edges and follow its own wanton instincts," the interviewer asked Arthur if he wanted to do everything. "Eclecticism *per se* has never been the big issue for me," he replied. "It's not a word that has been thrown at me a lot but, no doubt, it will be. Maybe I'm willing to embrace it more. Fusion, though, is a word that interested me more, or it would if it hadn't been used to describe a Seventies trend. Fusion could literally be the understanding of the common denominators of two musical styles."[51]

"Fusion" seemed to be a pretty good description of Arthur's outlook. He had never attempted to blend dance, pop, folk, dub, and orchestral music into a single piece, and there were times when he looked to explore difference rather than break it down. Yet his work was always alive to the way in which supposedly discrete styles could drift into one another, and he undersold his outlook when he suggested to the *Blitz* interviewer that it was akin to the merging of two styles because he engaged with a greater number of sounds than that. For Arthur, there was no cachet to being eclectic. Rather, he played across genre because it would have required a colossal and entirely counterproductive effort on his part to stick to one sound, and during late 1986 and early 1987 his wide-ranging artistry began to receive recognition in print—largely by journalists based in the UK. Drifting into an ethereal, gravity-defying zone, Arthur had come to embody the interconnectivity of music. In a poignant twist that nobody could anticipate, the records that had so impressed— "Let's Go Swimming," "School Bell / Treehouse," and *World of Echo*—would turn out to be the last material released by Arthur during his lifetime.

7 Tangents (1987–1992)

By the beginning of 1987 Arthur had every reason to pursue a path of musical introspection and isolation. Thanks to his shy, oddball personality, collaborative work had always been a little awkward for him, and his HIV-positive status virtually ushered him toward a more self-absorbed future. If Arthur wondered what sound might complement his condition, *World of Echo* suggested a melancholic plateau upon which he could float above his body and exist in a barely-perceptible dimension. But instead of shutting himself off, he continued to work intensely with close musician friends such as Mustafa Ahmed, Elodie Lauten, and Peter Zummo. (Joyce Bowden, Ernie Brooks, and Steven Hall, who were touring or out of the country altogether, were not around as much as the 1980s drew to a close.) And instead of deepening the solitary aesthetic of *World of Echo*, he moved in unpredictable ways, returning to instruments that he seemed to have discarded (such as the drums), and playing with groups that seemed to have broken up (such as the Flying Hearts). In order to protect the normalcy of his day-to-day working relationships, Arthur even made a point of concealing his medical condition.

The backdrop to Arthur's musical practice changed irrevocably during this period. Since moving to New York, Arthur had been acutely aware of his relationship to downtown's evolving soundscape and, secondarily, to the major record companies of midtown, but those contexts began to fade as he became absorbed with his medical condition, as well as what would happen to his music after he died. "Arthur was very anxious about his health after he was diagnosed," recalls Tom Lee. "There was no calming him down. It was like he was always trying to ward off what was about to happen next. The approach of the specialists was, 'This is going to happen, so we're going to try to give you all of these medicines to make sure it doesn't happen,' and then they would say, 'Whoops, it's happened!' So it was a constant scramble, and Arthur was totally in that scramble." Visiting the Community Health Project, which housed the first community-based HIV clinic in the United States, Arthur became close with an adviser named Anne Milano. "She thought Arthur was very quirky," recalls Lee. "She was like, 'Who is this guy? What do you mean he's worried about people taking advantage of him and his music after he dies?' She was a wonderful and understanding person, but to her he wasn't anybody important in terms of the music world."

Laid Back and Loose

Grasping for everyday normality, Arthur asked Ahmed, Hall, Lauten, "Blue" Gene Tyranny, and Zummo to perform with him at the Walker Art Center in Minneapolis in November 1987. "The songs were gentle and they were also filled with various kinds of moving and non-moving drones," remembers Tyranny. The same lineup minus Tyranny appeared as the Singing Tractors at the Institute of Contemporary Art in Boston in May 1988, and a few days later Arthur played amplified cello "in both solo and group settings" with Ahmed, Hall, Lauten, and Zummo at the Alternative Museum in New York. Appearing at the second annual New Music Festival at La MaMa in May 1989, he staged an "avant-disco cult jam" of material from his forthcoming Rough Trade album, which he provisionally titled *1 — 800 — Dinosaur*, and asked a number of his musician friends to join him once again.[1] "Most of the songs used a rhythm box, yet rhythmic edges were so softened that you couldn't always tell if the ensemble was together," Kyle Gann wrote of the Alternative Museum gig. "Far from seeming sloppy, though, it created a feeling of independent but parallel involvement as though, like monks, each player were focused on his own task, and all the lines had been composed to fit together no matter what happened. Each song didn't so much end as disintegrate when the players ran out of material, and the pieces were so similar that even the starting and stopping seemed arbitrary. Floating beneath this nebulous surface were some fetching pop tunes based on simple motifs."[2]

Calling whenever an opportunity arose, Zummo asked Arthur to play in his *Zummo with An X* concert at the Bessie Schönberg Theater in 1986 and at the Alternative Museum the following year, after which they played each other's translucent, gentle compositions at the New Music Festival in 1989. The trombonist also invited Arthur to help compose music for Stephen Petronio, who had requested a dance score that was "leaning over into pop." "I thought if I brought Arthur into the project it'd be cool recording this kind of rhythm in the studio," says Zummo. "Arthur then put too much energy into it and kind of took over. He was getting me to do things that were not leading toward a resolution. There was a deadline and I had no way of bringing it in for a landing, because Arthur had sent me in so many directions. We had all this material that wasn't adding up." As the deadline approached, Zummo and Arthur traveled to Connecticut, where Bob Blank had built a new twenty-four-track studio, but the plan was wrecked when Arthur had a huge argument with the engineer before the session began. "After that there was no way we could finish it on time," recalls Zummo. "Arthur turned to me and said, 'Well, I've really gotten you in too deep this time, haven't I?' He was conscious of just pushing any situation to the edge, and I wondered if he pushed everything to the edge in ways that just didn't jive with any practical way of conducting business or being responsible in the world, because he knew his time was finite — that he could go for broke because he wasn't going to have to answer for it."

Meanwhile Arthur played and sang on Lauten's operatic album, *The Death of Don Juan*, in 1985; he accompanied her when she performed one of her compositions for the Serious Fun series at the Lincoln Center; he formed part of her duo at the opening of *Remembrance of Things Past*, a Proustian sound installation developed by Lauten and her architect husband; and he accompanied her on *Music for the Trine* — the "trine" being Lauten's homemade amplified lyre — at La MaMa in 1987 and again in 1988. "The beauty of the trine is that you could tune everything in natural tuning, and it had more potential than the guitar because you could create these true harmonics," says Lauten. "I built it because I wanted to have an instrument I could easily tune to non-standard tunings. It is very difficult

Elodie Lauten, 1988.
Photograph by Daniel
Sussman. Courtesy of
Elodie Lauten.

to do that with the piano, and at the time synthesizers didn't have all these presets with alternative tunings. Because the trine has twenty-one strings, I could also have two simultaneous tunings on the same instrument, which meant I could experiment with tuning and obtain very subtle and unusual harmonies. Arthur loved the trine." Reviewing the 1988 La MaMa performance for the *New York Times*, an unmoved Peter Watrous remarked that Lauten "managed to pull slight harmonic changes out of her instrument," but Gann was captivated by her attempt to capture the *anahatta*, or the "unuttered sound," of Buddhism.[3] "The music was a delicate continuum of heard and half-heard sounds," noted the *Village Voice* critic. "Lauten's hazy melodic patterns are never quite decipherable, and once the left brain quits straining to define what's going on, the right is seduced by her feathery strumming." Gann added: "Russell, whose ultra–low key presence made a perfect match, droned on delicate single notes."[4]

Along with Zummo and Bill Ruyle, Arthur was also part of the core trio that played on Zummo's *Experimenting with Household Chemicals* and performed gigs at La MaMa in January and May 1989, the Snug Harbor Cultural Center in June 1989, and the Knitting Factory in September 1989. (Zummo's band became a quartet with Ahmed on percussion, a quintet with Jon Gibson on soprano saxophone, and a septet with Joseph Kubera on organ and synthesizer plus Dennis Masuzzo on contrabass.)[5] "It was a project that didn't make any sense that I just kept doing as if I knew what I was doing," recalls Zummo. "It involved having all these musicians dealing with some information that I presented, but taking it off on their own and letting the whole thing mix and meld in the airwaves." The notation rarely included rhythmic directions, and also allowed the musicians to play notes moving forwards, backwards, and even diagonally across the page. "Arthur started reading aloud some of the notation," remembers Ruyle. "He did it completely seriously, as though it were a vocal part, as though this were a totally sensible way of interpreting the piece. And it was."[6] Arthur liked to play laid-back and loose in groups that were already laid-back and loose, and Zummo's outfit was perfect. "Although Arthur didn't fit into a lot of ensemble situations, this one suited him well," notes the trombonist.

Milwaukee

"When Arthur was working with Elodie Lauten, he kind of said he'd found a singer that he liked working with," remembers Joyce Bowden. "It wasn't Jennifer Warnes, and it wasn't me. I wasn't there enough." After working on Broadway, Bowden had turned to acting, got married, and then returned to school to study cognitive science. "I needed something more predictable to hang on to and tried to deny the part of myself that needed to be an artist," she adds. "I think Arthur wanted me to be more courageously serious than I was willing to be." He also hoped Bowden would find her voice. "A lot of things came easily to Joyce, so you didn't know what was really her," explains Ernie Brooks. "Was she a country singer or a soul singer? At one point she had an incarnation as a heavy-metal priestess at CBGB's with the Trashaholics. Joyce was protean—she was able to do a lot of things—and the question was always, 'What direction would she go in?' But it was also unfair because Arthur would say, 'Oh, you're just the person we want,' but when she did it he would say, 'It's not right.' He could be merciless with her." That didn't stop Bowden from agreeing that she wasn't always producing her best work, especially when she was swept up by people who could pay her good money, and Arthur ended up turning to Lauten instead. "I remember being quite crushed when I heard about it," recalls Bowden. "I was like, 'What do you mean? What do you mean?'" She adds: "It also made perfect sense. Elodie is a performer of great merit."

Bowden still went into the studio with Arthur every now and again, and on one snowy night in 1987 Brooks asked her to travel down to the

Hit Factory where he and Jerry Harrison were recording "A Perfect Lie," a song Arthur had cowritten with Brooks for *Casual Gods*, which is varyingly listed as being either Harrison's second solo album (after 1981's *The Red and the Black*) or the debut album of the Casual Gods. "They wanted me to sing parallel harmonies to Arthur's wonderfully amorphous melody," says Bowden. "It was a meandering river of a melody that didn't really rest on one point, and it was quite difficult to sing." Bowden also helped defuse tensions that were running through the studio. "I think Jerry was freaked out by Arthur, and he didn't find a lot of Arthur-isms charming, especially because he was on deadline to finish that night. Of course Ernie and I did find them charming, and maybe Ernie brought me in to be a second voice in favor of this brilliance that was Arthur that Jerry wasn't quite getting. In the end, critics hailed the song as one of the best on the album."

Having worked less with Russell over the last few years, Brooks was also pleased with the result. "Because Jerry was such an old friend of mine, he trusted me about Arthur, even though he was wary. It was opening a can of worms bringing Arthur in, but it's one of the best songs on the album." The bass player also remembers looking on fondly as Arthur instructed Bernie Worrell (of Parliament/Funkadelic) on how to "get the rhythmic quirks" of the funky keyboard line he had written for the song. But instead of dwelling on the success of his participation, Arthur turned to Bowden and communicated an urgent message. "That night Arthur told me, 'Joyce, if I were you I'd be working on my voice all day long,'" she remembers. "'If I had a voice like you, I wouldn't want to do anything else.' He was a serious musician, and he didn't have much time for people who were being wasteful with their talent. He was quite upfront about this. I think one of the things that drew us all to him so deeply was he was so honest about other people's weaknesses. If you had a problem expressing yourself, you might get a phone call later from Arthur."

The following year, Arthur, Bowden, and Brooks returned to the studio during a trip to Milwaukee, where Harrison was about to get married. Having recently turned down the opportunity to record an album with Arthur and Will Socolov—she had been "put off by rumors of bad blood between Arthur and Will"—Bowden paid for Arthur's travel and took him as her "date," and as they prepared for the big day, Arthur, Bowden, and Brooks resurrected the Flying Hearts and invited Rick Jaeger (drums) and Jason Klagstad (guitar) to join them in the studio. Produced by Harrison,

Arthur Russell and Ernie Brooks in Ernie's Long Island City loft, c. late 1980s.
Photograph by Paul Waldman. Courtesy of Ernie Brooks.

Joyce Bowden and Ernie Brooks at Jerry Harrison's wedding, Milwaukee, December 1988.
Photograph by Arthur Russell. Courtesy of Joyce Bowden.

Arthur Russell and Joyce Bowden, Milwaukee, December 1988.
Photograph by Ernie Brooks. Courtesy of Joyce Bowden.

the group recorded "Don't Forget about Me," "Over the Line," "I Saw How Lucky I Was," and "Laying by Your Lover," with Bowden delivering the vocals. "Arthur sang 'Don't Forget about Me' in Milwaukee in order to get me to sing it in a certain way, and that was the definitive version of the song," she says. "His voice was right there on that song. It actually sounded best when he sang it."[7]

Arthur didn't tell any of his friends that he was sick, and there were moments when he appeared to be in denial. "I believe in maximum enjoyment, constant sex and fun all the time as well as not losing any years," he had told the *New York City Paper* in November 1987. In the same interview Arthur also criticized the way musicians "tend to talk about ideas" rather than things they're "afraid of" before he hastily added, "not that I'm afraid of anything in particular."[8] From 1986 to 1987, there were few outward signs of his malady, but by 1988 the disease had become manifest. Arthur chose to keep the information to himself as best he could, even though Sylvester had become one the first celebrities with AIDS to confront his condition in public.[9] "We were going to drive to Milwaukee, but he had a problem sitting for long periods of time," remembers Bowden. "It was something that would come and go, and it was really uncomfortable." Arthur didn't address the question directly. "He didn't ever talk about it. He didn't bring it up. It was the elephant in the middle of the living room."

This withholding of information was uncharacteristic of Arthur, who rarely overlooked an opportunity to dare people to think differently. But he feared the revelation of his illness might interfere with his ability to make music, and worried his trusted collaborators would treat him differently once they found out. "He did not want AIDS to affect how people worked with him or how he might be considered in the recording studio or at performance venues," explains Tom Lee. Then again, maybe the Milwaukee rendition of "Don't Forget about Me"—an old song that had acquired a new resonance—was Arthur's way of gently relaying the news.

Rough Trade

With no pressing orchestral or dance works to deliver, Arthur pushed on with his songs and in April 1987 announced that his new album for Rough Trade would be ready that summer. It's possible he was being serious. The *Corn* material was available for recycling, and during 1985 and 1986 he had worked on numbers such as "Another Thought," "Hollow Tree," "Home away from Home," "Just a Blip," and "See through Love" at Battery Sound, so he had plenty of material in place.[10] However, Arthur didn't submit any tapes to Geoff Travis in the autumn of 1987, and by the autumn of 1991 Travis was still waiting for the delivery. "Arthur made me wait for years," recalls the Rough Trade boss. "It was frustrating, but I knew he needed my support to keep financing his music."

Between 1986 and 1990, Arthur also worked on "Arm around You," "Calling All Kids," "Get Around to It," "Hop on Down," "Make 1, 2," "My Tiger, My Timing," "That's Us / Wild Combination," and "You Can Make Me Feel Bad."[11] For "My Tiger, My Timing" and "That's Us / Wild Combination," he traveled to the West Coast to record extra sessions with Jennifer Warnes, who had just performed "(I've Had) the Time of My Life" at the Academy Awards ceremony, where it won in the "Best Song" category. Stopping off in Oskaloosa, Arthur wrote the final version of the lyrics on a brown paper grocery bag and posted them to Warnes so that they would arrive ahead of the session, which took place in April 1988. "He sent the final mix to me for my approval," remembers Warnes, who appreciated Arthur's no-flourishes-beyond-the-music approach. "I didn't understand it [the musical aesthetic] and I still don't understand it, because I come from plainer tastes."

Ahmed became Arthur's most important collaborator during the Rough Trade recordings. "There were times when Arthur would explore these new boxes and these new machines, and I would just sit there and watch him try and get these sounds," recalls the percussionist. "On other occasions I would figure out ways to assign different drum sounds to different locations that would make them easier to play and get a better feel. It was like we were in a laboratory—experimenting, writing down formulas, testing hypotheses." Ahmed had his reservations about World of Echo—he found it too melancholic for his taste, and he also thought it symbolized the way in which Arthur was becoming "more and more isolated" from the musicians he normally worked with—but he appreciated the rhythmic, dynamic thrust of the Rough Trade recordings. "I could hear my influence," he says. "They're busier, they're intense in a way, they're more linear, they're more grounded, they're more four-on-the-floor. This is certainly where Arthur was going."

Growing out of the Corn recordings, Arthur's new songs forged a distinctive strain of alternative dance-pop. After playing such a prominent

Mustafa Ahmed playing congas, c. 1987. Photographer unknown.
Courtesy of Mustafa Ahmed.

role on *World of Echo*, the cello returned to its former role of background instrument, save for the recording of "You Can Make Me Feel Bad," where it scraped up a heavily amplified, almost screeching sound. Gone, too, were the atmosphere-bending edits of *World of Echo*, perhaps because their presence would have interfered with the corporeal objectives of this more overtly popular project. In their place, Arthur's keyboards veered between a lush, warm hum ("That's Us") and a dinky, playful groove ("Hop on Down"), while the undulating, crisscrossing rhythms of "Let's Go Swimming" were supplanted with drum-machine beats that were raw, steady, and funky. In describing his performance at La MaMa in 1989, Arthur maintained that "minimalism and progressive pop [could] fuse into an exciting experience," and it was on his Rough Trade recordings that he developed this sound most fully.[12]

Retreating from the sometimes unintelligible lyrical content of *World of Echo*, Arthur wrote songs that ranged between the themes of vernacular love, childhood games, and summer holidays. The lyrics in "Arm around You" explored the tender moment of a loving exchange.

I'm sad and I can't talk about it
All alone and right next to you
[. . .]
Got to put my arm around you
Got to put one arm around you
I'll touch the other side, side of your face.

"Get Around to It" developed the theme of sexual initiation.

Show me what the girl does to the boy
If you can get around to it
Show me what to do, you most enjoy
If you can get around to it.

Remixed by Walter Gibbons, "Calling All Kids" doubled up as a manifesto for young people.

Calling all kids, calling all kids
Entering in binocular mode
Calling all kids, calling all kids
Grown-ups are crazy, crazy, crazy.

And "That's Us / Wild Combination" evoked the times when, having set out at night in order to avoid the daytime heat, the Russell family would jump out of the car at sunrise for a memento snapshot while driving to the Minnesota lakes.

That's us before we got there
That's morning time before we got there
That's you, me, on self-timer
We're leaving at five in the morning
We could get better mileage
That's you, in the pool, you're a swimmer.

If anything, Arthur's voice was even stronger on these songs than it had been on *World of Echo*. "Arthur would play me Side A and Side B of these cassettes, and they sounded almost identical," recalls Peter Zummo, who was a prominent collaborator on the recordings. "I said, 'Could you tell me what I'm listening for?' He said, 'It's EQ.' I said, 'The vocal sounds good, you should keep that.' He said, 'Forget the vocal, I can do that anytime.'"

Zummo was impressed. "His singing just got better and better," he notes. "He had more different voices to call on. Lines like "Get around to it" didn't go where you would think in terms of articulation. He had a real sense of phrasing and melody that was hip. I could see why his music worked in black circles."

As he worked on these songs, however, Arthur's relationship with Mark Freedman deteriorated. Although he had given the Battery Sound owner a generous coproduction credit on "Let's Go Swimming," the gesture hardly balanced out the amount of free studio time he received, and as he continued to struggle for money, Arthur became quite resentful when Freedman asked him to pay for a session. At one point Arthur tried to redress the accumulation of favors by offering to work as a session musician on tracks such as "Lost Tribe" by Powerman (Powerman being Freedman's artist alias). But Freedman was constantly stoned, and the studio's slipshod records exacerbated the confusion, while the vacuum created by Eric Liljestrand's departure heightened tensions over the engineering process. "There were some very testing times," recalls Ahmed. "When Arthur didn't like the way something was recorded, I would be the peacemaker."

Arthur started to seek out alternative studios and ended up spending two or three days a week at Bob Blank's Connecticut setup. "I would give Arthur the key to the studio and let him get on with it," remembers the engineer. "Peter Zummo would come up, Arthur would put up a tape, and they would play for hours and hours. Who knows what happened to this music?" At least one of the recordings, a track called "Anti-Gravity Soup," which echoed the "speed country" song Arthur recorded with Steven Hall earlier in the decade, remains unreleased. "It's a manic, thrash drum-machine track that speeds up and slows down," explains Steve Knutson. "A pulsing electronic keyboard bubbles, fast, and there's a slapping cello that's similar to the cello in 'School Bell / Treehouse.' Someone yells 'Hey! Hey! Hey!' and there are groans as well as cowboy hootin' and hollering. The track was recorded on seven synched Song Video 8 Cartridges and is unfinished. It's one of the weirdest things I've ever heard."

Because Arthur could rarely afford to pay for the Connecticut sessions, Blank would either give him free time or strike a deal and ask him to do some work — such as to record an album's worth of material for Lola Blank, or record odd projects with his son, Kenny. (Arthur had already worked on "I Need More," Lola's follow-up single to "Wax the Van," which was released on Vinylmania in 1985, and Blank says "Let's Go Swimming" was originally intended for his son.) Will Socolov continued to argue that Blank was taking advantage of Arthur, but others were less quick to condemn. "Arthur would accuse Bob of all sorts of things, and Bob could be a pretty ferocious businessman," says Ernie Brooks. "But I don't think Bob really exploited him." Hall also believes the engineer acted reasonably. "Arthur bartered himself as a songwriter / session player and that caused him to get upset and feel exploited. But he let himself be exploited because all he cared about was getting *more studio time*."

Drawing heavily on his Rough Trade advance, Arthur satisfied his dependency on the recording process by building his own home studio. He set up his mini-facility in the living room, where one wall was already groaning under the weight of audiotape, and stacking his keyboards, drum machines, and electronic processors high, he left a little opening that was large enough for him to slip into his makeshift rig, sit on a perch, and have everything at his fingertips (an essential feature as he became increasingly weak). When everything was in place, Arthur started to play into the early hours, recording take after take, relieved that he had an outlet if Blank's or Freedman's price—artistic, financial, or emotional—turned out to be too high. "Arthur's home set-up gave him total autonomy," notes Brooks. "He could work all day long on a particular passage to get the right blend. That's what he continued to do until his death."

Travis, meanwhile, met up with Arthur whenever he visited New York. "We would listen to mixes on the Staten Island Ferry, or while I was walking frantically down the street going from one meeting to the next," says the Rough Trade boss. "I was always on the run when I was in New York." During their meetings Arthur would play snippets of songs, and when an opening arrived—such as the moment he played "Wild Combination," which Travis loved—he would hit him for more money. "The songs weren't as abstract as *World of Echo*," says Travis, who ended up paying Arthur between fifteen and twenty thousand pounds. "I think he was striving for a fusion of sounds. I think he thought that this fusion would eventually come to him." In between, Travis would call to see how things were going, and Arthur would tell him that things were going great, which was enough to persuade the Rough Trade boss to keep on sending the money.

Having OK'd the idea with Travis, Arthur also set up a label called Teen Tal Records and made progress with plans to release a recording by Jackson

Arthur Russell performing with Steven Hall at the Experimental Intermedia Foundation in 1989. Video still by Phill Niblock. Courtesy of Matt Wolf.

Mac Low, whom he admired greatly. Anne Tardos, who worked and lived with Mac Low between 1978 and 2004, remembers Mac Low held Arthur "in great regard," and that Arthur visited the house. But the Teen Tal project was never completed, and none of Arthur's tapes were presented to Rough Trade. "I didn't put him on the spot," says Travis. "I was quite gentle and patient with him, and he appreciated that. There aren't that many other people in the music industry who would have indulged him so completely." Travis adds, "It cost me a king's ransom over quite a few years, but I considered Arthur to be someone very special and have no regrets."

Label interest in Arthur's work doubled when Philip Glass asked him to record an album some time around 1989. Glass had continued to follow Arthur's movements and was still enough of an enthusiast to take the teenage composer John Moran to hear one of his performances in the mid-1980s. "There were about three of us at the concert, including Phil and I," recalls Moran, who went on to receive commissions from venues such as Lincoln Center for the Performing Arts and La MaMa in the 1990s. "Arthur showed a video of a bunny and a baby chick while he did his thing. His music was both alien and catchy at the same time. The concert changed my life." Fascinated by Arthur's oeuvre, Glass believed Arthur's recordings were becoming more mature and focused, more assured and eloquent, and that their blend was quite unique. "His music was quite unlike anything anyone else was recording," says the composer. "When I listened to Arthur's music, I heard the music of a cosmopolitan New Yorker living in the latter part of the twentieth century."

Arthur was sufficiently flattered (and enough of a realist) to know that he should say yes to Glass's offer. After all, Upside Records had gone out of business a year after the release of *World of Echo*, so he needed to be flexible in his allegiances, and the Milwaukee tapes had also come to rest at the top of his homemade magnetic mountain, which reiterated the need for him to cooperate with anyone who was willing. Asked if he would object to the Glass proposal, Travis confirmed he was happy for his relationship with Arthur to be "non-exclusive," and was reassured by Arthur's promise that he would develop a distinctive, acoustic style for the Point Music album. Contracts weren't drawn up between Arthur and Glass, however, and it's not clear if Arthur ever recorded any new material for the project. When Glass (accompanied by Moran) bumped into him in the Kiev Restaurant on Second Avenue some time later, a stalemate was quickly reached. "Arthur barely bothered to remove his headphones while Phil urged him to stop laboring over the same pieces for so long," remembers Moran. "Arthur just looked at the floor and said, 'Yeaaahhh, well . . .' I remember wondering why he didn't want to be more public. He seemed so far away most of the time."

Dance/dance

Charged by the enduring adrenalin rush of the 1970s, many gay men were in denial about the threat of AIDS during the first half of the 1980s, but by the middle of the decade that outlook was no longer sustainable. If disco had become an emblem of gay liberation, as well as an illustration of the profound impact gay men could cast over popular culture, by the late 1980s it embodied the dangers of gay decadence. The Paradise Garage closed in September 1987 after its owner, Michael Brody, tested positive and decided against renewing the venue's lease. Cast out of his cathedral and increasingly strung out, Larry Levan went into free fall, while Brody passed away just a couple of months after the venue closed. The Saint, which had provided AIDS with the early nickname of "Saint's disease" (the etymological roots lay in the venue's seductive balconies), was hit even harder, and a little while later insiders started to refer to their space as "the AIDS factory."[13] When the eerily empty dance floor became too much to bear, the club shut it its doors in the spring of 1988.

By then Arthur had more or less stopped going out to clubs. Although *World of Echo* didn't address AIDS explicitly, its delicate lyricism and turn from drums signaled a post-party sensibility, and by the late 1980s Arthur started to believe that dance culture was becoming more conservative. He defended the scene in his interview with WUSB in April 1987 when he noted it "engenders a certain perception of social interaction that is pretty inter-esting," but in his interview with *Blitz* the following month he reflected on the way he was expected to produce dance records, even though that was only a small part of what he did.[14] Distraught when he discovered Walter Gibbons was also sick, Arthur was now recording music that suggested dance but wasn't obviously danceable, and he started to cut down on the number of nights he would stay out late in order to lead a healthier lifestyle. On the rare occasions he went to a club, he would become bored if the DJ rotated a record for too long or veered into a repetitive four-on-the-floor cycle. "We started to work together on this song called 'I'm Losing My Taste for the Night Life' in the early 1980s," remembers Joyce Bowden. "Working on it again in the late 1980s was a different thing entirely. It had a different resonance."

The spread of sampling technology in the second half of the 1980s con-tributed to the impression that the idealistic thread of the 1970s had worn thin. Capable of isolating short snatches of music and transplanting them into another recording, the sampler was of no immediate use to Arthur, because he could produce his own sounds or call on the goodwill of friends to give him what he wanted. But when he discovered the equipment was being used to extract quotations from his own recordings, invariably with-out his permission, he was deeply upset. To the neutral listener, this was simply the latest stage in the nascent history of remixing, a messy process of artistic creation, ownership, and attribution that Arthur had turned to and even enjoyed on several occasions. Yet the proliferation of the sampler also marked the moment when remixing seeped beyond the parameters of the law, and Arthur wasn't quite ready for the cavalier attitude shown by New York's new breed of streetwise alchemists.

Todd Terry became the first producer to sample Arthur's music when he released "Bango (To the Batmobile)" on Fresh Records in 1988. "I loved a lot of Arthur Russell's music," comments Terry. "He had a great organic touch. His sound was great for me to get snippets from." Although it was often assumed to be an uncreative act of thievery, sampling was an art form that required producers and remixers to exercise a sharp ear and a lateral mindset in order to isolate and then recontextualize sounds, and by 1988 Terry had earned the nickname "Todd the God" thanks to his impressive ability to combine driving beats with catchy fragments.[15] On "Bango" the producer singled out Lola Blank's female vocal from "Go Bang! #5." "Arthur Russell always had a lot of parts to deal with," he adds. "His records wouldn't always come together, so it made it easier for me to bring them together."

Arthur might have replied that "Bango" came together too quickly, the record being reliant on an exciting yet ultimately ephemeral beats-plus-sample adrenalin-rush. But his primary concern was for justice to be administered, and the rip-off element of "Bango" was always likely to come to his attention given that Fresh Records was a subsidiary of Sleeping Bag, and the song's title was a barefaced inversion of "Go Bang! #5." Terry ended up meeting with Arthur and cutting him a deal in order to settle the dispute. "I don't know if he was too keen about the record," says the producer, "but he got *half of the publishing*." Later that year, Terry trumpeted his opinion that Arthur and others should be grateful for his existence. "I feel it [sampling] helps the old artists," he told the *Face*. "They can be sitting at home and hear themselves used on the radio, and say, 'Oh, that's terrible!' Next thing they know, somebody's calling them up for a show."[16]

A year later, a young Dominican American spinner called Roger Sanchez also drew on one of Arthur's earlier recordings. "'Go Bang!' had this very SoHo / East Village sound," says Sanchez. "It's one of my favorite tunes of all time. Arthur always had a way of coming up with infectious bass lines, and I tried to emulate that feeling with 'Luv Dancin'." Equally enthusiastic about "Is It All Over My Face?" — "the sheer force of that groove is brilliant" — Sanchez layered the spaced-out phrasing of the Loose Joints release over a dense, moody, jazz-inflected house track, and when Gladys Pizarro of the Strictly Rhythm label heard the record, she took it straight to Tony Humphries at the Zanzibar, an influential New Jersey club that had been modeled on the Paradise Garage. "Tony loved it," recalls Pizarro. "He played it three or four times. A lot of industry people were there. The next day all the record companies were calling." Having scored one significant

Arthur Russell in black leather jacket, 1990. Photograph by and courtesy of Tom Lee.

club hit, Strictly Rhythm cleared the Loose Joints sample with West End and went on to sell some fifty thousand copies of the record.

Arthur was enjoying something of a revival in dance music, and on the occasions they realized Arthur was around, spinners would play "Bango" or "Luv Dancin.'" That might have felt like he was being kissed and slapped at the same time, and Arthur might have also regretted the way in which young producers were mining his catalogue at the very moment he hoped one of them would give a contemporary edge to the four hours of unfinished tracks he had just recorded—William Orbit and 808 State being his favored candidates. Titled *Springfield*, the tracks on the rough mix spliced hypnotic electro with thick synthesizer, gravelly cello, wafting voice, and Peter Zummo's poignant trombone. "'Springfield' . . . is a jacuzzi, percussion bubbling, as weird as Ricardo Villalobos at his most maximalist and haunted by ghosts of the late '80s, right down to the corroded AOR brass (shades of near-death Miles Davis) and house pianos," Jess Harvell wrote when the recordings were finally released in 2006. "Russell's falsetto and love of smeary reverb means you only hear every other word of what he's singing, but it's more about the *way* he sighs 'never been kissed.'"[17] Collaborative offers still came Arthur's way, and at one point Will Socolov tried to set him up with the producers of Crystal Waters, who had scored a *Billboard* Hot 100 success with "Gypsy Woman" in 1991, but it never materialized into anything substantial.

Arthur had become more interested in contemporary dance, which provided him with an outlet to play his songs as well as to develop longer compositions for cello. He worked on Daniel McIntosh's *Mindset* at P.S. 122 in September 1987 (a fortnight before the last night party at the Paradise Garage), and he also played "husky" and "elusive" songs (in the words of the *New York Times*) for Diane Madden's *Answer Me* at the Dance Theater Workshop at the beginning of 1988.[18] "Madden's ability to balance smooth strength against delicate and extremely subtle movement makes her always fascinating to watch," wrote Deborah Jowitt in the *Village Voice*. "I also read vulnerability and anxiety, but the dance is so loosely woven that I keep seeing air between its strands."[19] The performance appeared to evolve out of Arthur's music. "Quietly sung words that composer-performer Arthur Russell drops into his fine and variegated live-and-electronic score may be the crux of it," added Jowitt.

As his interest in modern dance deepened, Arthur spent more and more time working with Alison Salzinger, a choreographer who had studied with Stephanie Woodard at Oberlin College. Having traveled to Oberlin when Zummo invited him to play in the production of Woodard's *Big Game* back in the early 1980s, Arthur met Salzinger later on in the college's Hi-NRG disco, but he didn't succeed in catching her eye—because Salzinger was (as she puts it) eighteen years old and focused on the dance floor. They crossed paths again when Tom Lee approached Salzinger at the end of one of her shows, after which the dancer went over to Twelfth Street to listen to Arthur's music. "He would play stuff and I would say what I liked," remembers Salzinger. "He was interested in the fact I was young. He kept saying he was too old to know what was cool."

Salzinger's interest in creating a "deliberately clumsy, funky, anti-dance" matched Arthur's ongoing fascination with amateur aesthetics and disjointed rhythms, and they worked together on a number of productions, including *Like You, Forever Newcomers*, and *Lifestyle*.[20] As reluctant as ever to perform on a stage, Arthur ducked out of the limelight whenever he could, and during one show he played amplified cello from the back of the room. A little later, when they returned to Oberlin to perform in the

Warner Center, Arthur spent a good part of the trip explaining how he had been rejected by the college. "The whole time we were there he was like, 'Oh, they didn't want me,'" says the dancer. "Arthur was humble and very insecure. He would play a song for me and it would keep changing. I would say, 'You've gone through five different versions. Why are you throwing away all the early material?' He edited himself so much. Arthur was so insecure he didn't seem to realize what he had."

Omens

Arthur began to work again with Joyce Bowden, the vocalist having insisted her ideas be taken more seriously until he "capitulated." "This was around the time he was trying to do something with Philip Glass, which was the late 1980s or the early 1990s," says Bowden. "It's interesting when you try to force a collaboration with someone!" But she inadvertently provoked Arthur when she performed at a Casual Gods concert in May 1989. "Why did you dance like that on stage?" Arthur asked at the end of the performance. "Aren't you repelled by the image of the sexy dancing girl?" Bowden didn't think that she was dancing in that kind of way and allowed herself to be flattered until Arthur's righteous anger overruled the possibility that he found her presence alluring. "He was quite bothered by it and thought I should be bothered by it as well." Bowden was forced to confront Arthur's illness for the first time when they went to a coffee shop on Avenue A, between Fifth and Sixth, after the show. "He had developed the Kaposi's sarcoma face," she remembers. "He had never talked about being sick, but when I saw his face I knew."

Acne had plagued Arthur all his life, but now a different order of facial sore advertised his fatal condition. "I started talking about death and life in an abstract way, and he seemed to be relieved to be able to talk about that," recalls Bowden. "It seemed as if a weight was lifted from his shoulders." As their conversation deepened, Arthur and Bowden agreed that the dividing line that runs between one's body-bound existence and its aftermath should be quite easy to navigate, like "a smooth train stop," because they were two equal states. After that, Arthur revealed he might have only a couple of years left, and admitted to being afraid. "He needed to work with the scariness and get the kinks out of the scariness so that he could focus on knowing what he already knew—about the continuation of life in death," adds Bowden. "The conversation was a point of love and understanding, without need of anything else. I always thought it was his hello and good-bye, a sweet solace, and testimony to his innate kindness, that he should be concerned with the effect his departure would have on the world around him."

Arthur's lesions healed, but John Bernd died of complications arising from AIDS in 1988, while Julius Eastman and Keith Haring passed away under similar circumstances in 1990. When Arthur was diagnosed with cancer that same year, it became clear the virus had scored a decisive victory over his immune system. "I remember getting the phone call at work, and it left me with such a horrible feeling," says Tom Lee. "I didn't know what to do or what to say." On his way home, Lee went to Tower Records and purchased *Robert Johnson: The Complete Recordings.* "I thought, 'How do I commemorate this horrible thing? What better way to honor this diagnosis than the blues?'" Arthur's reaction was muted. "We both cried. There was just a real sadness. Then we listened to one of the cassettes and talked."

Along with Lee, Arthur was always on the lookout for new treatments. He applied to join an AZT trial in Washington, but was rejected on the grounds that doctors wanted to test the drug on patients whose symptoms were less developed. He also began to look beyond the domestic health system when he arranged for Johnny Fu to send him the Chinese medicine his mother had taken to combat a different condition. New dietary regimes and therapy combinations were also tried, although Lee notes that Arthur would question any medical advice that came his way. "He was a wise patient in that regard," Lee wrote a few years later. "I wanted to trust that everyone was united in our struggle. Arthur knew that it was his job to be as attentive as possible."[21]

Because he was prepared to divulge more information than his boyfriend, Lee became the key point of contact for Chuck, Emily, Kate, and Julie. "It went from me passing the phone to Arthur to them asking me how things were going," Lee remembers. During the same period a form of reconciliation took place between Arthur and his family. Beginning in 1989, Kate and Julie made three successive pre-Christmas trips to New York, and on one occasion Chuck and Emily (who found out about their son's illness a year after he was diagnosed) traveled to the city to meet up with their children. Arthur also spent time with his family in Maine, and during the summer of 1990 they went on a group outing to Baker Island—Arthur's

Arthur Russell listening to his Walkman during an earlier trip to Wonderland, Mount Desert Island, Maine, c. 1987. Photograph by Charles Arthur Russell Sr. Courtesy of Charles Arthur Russell Sr. and Emily Russell.

favorite place to record the sound of the sea. The forty-five minute speed-boat journey turned out to be more grueling than any of them had foreseen, and the task of carrying Arthur from the boat to the land was hazardous. "Arthur got very angry, but once we got him ashore he had a great time," remembers Kate. "He spent some quiet time alone. He was rocking and singing and just feeling the energy from the water."

A rather uncomfortable form of fence-mending also occurred between Arthur and Kent Goshorn, whose friendship had become increasingly tenuous until one day in 1990, just as Goshorn was fuming about "the many things Arthur had said and done over the years that had pissed me off and left me feeling used and betrayed as a friend," Arthur called. "I told him what was on my mind and he apologized," recalls Goshorn. "Then he said,

'By the way, I have AIDS.' Suddenly I felt a little embarrassed about what I had said. The phone call was an awkward, if not telepathic, moment." Arthur told Goshorn he was doing fine, but when they met up later that autumn Goshorn was left with a different impression. "Arthur was still working away at his music, but the disease was obviously pretty well developed."

Having traveled to France to play music with Rhys Chatham and Elliott Murphy, Brooks heard about his friend's illness over the phone. "I remember being angry that he hadn't told me," he says. "I was upset that he was sick and that I didn't know." Like Bowden, Brooks had started to wonder about Arthur's health some time earlier, and had even asked him if he was sick when they met up during the mix of *Walk on Water* (1990) — either Jerry Harrison's third solo album, or the second album of the Casual Gods.[22] Looking tired and gaunt, Arthur told Brooks he was fine. When the bass player's suspicions were confirmed a little later, he was asked to hunt down a retroviral drug that was available in France but not the United States. "Arthur told me about this drug," he recalls. "It took me a while to find it, and by the time I got it to him he thought it was part of some kind of plot."

Arthur told Hall about his diagnosis face-to-face, just when it looked like they would never make music together again. Their collaborations had already become less frequent: in 1986 Hall staged a poetry reading ("Johnny Eagle starring in Black Watch") in which Arthur played background accompaniment while Johnny Fu showed slides; in 1988 Hall put on a fashion show ("Plastic Clothes") at the Elizabeth McDonald Gallery in SoHo and invited Arthur to play cello; and around the same time Hall also contributed background vocals to "My Tiger, My Timing." Hall went on to publish his poetry book *Black Watch* in 1991, after which the Zuni Icosahedron experimental theater group invited him to travel to Hong Kong. That became the trigger for Arthur to tell him about his illness, and also make it clear he was unhappy about his imminent departure. "Arthur returned several twenty-four track tapes and DAT masters of the Bright and Early project and other unfinished projects to me as a goodbye gift, as he knew we might not meet again," says Hall. "He was a control freak and was afraid that while he was alive I would betray him and leave him for commercial success. He only gave the tapes up when it was too late to worry about that." The two friends maintained occasional contact. "I've been lax

Steven Hall in Allen
Ginsberg's kitchen
on Twelfth Street in
the early 1990s.
Photograph by Allen
Ginsberg. Courtesy
of Peter Hall.

in communicating, haven't I?" Arthur wrote in one letter. "Your life sounds
so wonderful. I imagine you're David Bowie by now." He added, "Sounds
like you have a very good deal. I think you should pursue it. I say this still
hoping for your return." At the end he declared, "I love Allen I love Phil
Glass I love you I love Terry Riley I also like this group Bassomatic."

A month later, in June 1991, Arthur, who now weighed about eighty
pounds, made a farewell trip to the West Coast, where he told Allaudin
Mathieu he was saying goodbye to a few friends and spent time recording
ambient sounds with voice-overs. "He looked baleful, but also inwardly
pleased," recalls the music teacher. The inward pleasure was wiped away
by Yuko Nonomura, who refused to meet up with Arthur. "Yuko was afraid
of AIDS, pure and simple," says Jeff Whittier, who saw Arthur immediately
after the rebuff. "He would scarcely talk to Arthur. Yuko's rejection was
tremendously hard for Arthur to take." Hanging out, Arthur and Whittier
talked Buddhism and agreed to disagree about the meaning of the *Tibetan
Book of the Dead*. "I think of it as being symbolic," says Whittier. "But
Arthur was thinking of preparing himself for the death process in light of
this book. He definitely believed in reincarnation."

Back in New York, Arthur visited Barry Feldman on an almost weekly

Arthur Russell on a beach
in San Francisco, 1991.
Photographs by and courtesy
of William Allaudin Mathieu.

basis. "We talked all the time," says Feldman, who was now working at CBS Records. "We talked about music, stuff. We were just friends. He got sick very quickly." Arthur also got in touch with Gary Lucas, although their one-off meeting was rather tense. "I saw Arthur and said, 'Where's your record?'" recalls Lucas, who had no idea his friend was sick. "Arthur replied, 'I don't want to turn it in.'" Then, when Lucas played some of the music he had been recording, Arthur became suspicious. "He said, 'Unless you're really serious about music you shouldn't do it, because you'll take up space from those who are serious about it,'" recalls Lucas. "He was acting pissy." The guitarist was upset. Following Arthur's advice that he should devote himself full-time to his music, Lucas had given up his job at CBS in 1990, and his first album, *Skeleton at the Feast*, went on to receive strong reviews. But now Arthur appeared to be envious of his success. "I was like, 'Bullshit! It's a big market! Life's too short!'" Although he was a little sad, Lucas also left with a good feeling, and encouraged Arthur to finish his album, because it seemed he was reluctant to tie things up. "He was like Penelope at her loom, waiting for Ulysses," notes Lucas. "He was afraid that if it came out it would fail, and he would not get another deal."

Dozens of other friends found out about Arthur's illness and did their best to offer solace while coming to terms with their own powerlessness. When Ellen Ziegler heard the news from friends she sent Arthur a talisman and told him (countering the advice of one health adviser) that eating citrus fruits wouldn't worsen his condition. "I said, 'Arthur, you're dying. It's OK to have orange juice.'" The D Train provided the setting for "Blue" Gene Tyranny's last encounter with his downtown collaborator. "I asked Arthur how he was doing, and he told me that he had AIDS. I didn't know what to say except, 'Oh Arthur.' I sat with him until we had to part." Donald Murk found out his ex-companion was sick during a chance encounter in Poet's Building one winter's day. "I asked him if he was OK, and he answered that he had AIDS and it was very cold in his apartment," remembers Murk. "He said nothing more about his situation, and I didn't ask him to, as bringing me up to speed couldn't have been a priority for him, and anyway I felt I knew what I needed to know. I was extremely upset." Murk took Arthur into his second-floor apartment, wrapped him up in some blankets, sat him in front of an electric heater, and made him a cup of tea. After about an hour, during which time there was no further mention of his condition,

Arthur said he had to go home. "There was some music that needed his attention," remembers Murk.

Arthur also told Peter Gordon his news. It had been a while since they had worked on music together, in part because an argument between Gordon and Lucas had made it awkward for them to collaborate; in part because Gordon was also busy working on projects such as *Return of the Native*, which premiered at the Brooklyn Academy of Music in 1988 and subsequently traveled to Rio de Janeiro and Amsterdam; and in part because spontaneous get-togethers became less frequent after Gordon moved to Brooklyn. But they made a point of staying in touch and visiting each other, and when Arthur told Gordon his medical news, Gordon asked: "How long?" After that they went out to the opera on a couple of occasions before seeing each other for the last time toward the end of 1991. A little later, Gordon traveled to Tokyo and had his fortune read in the Asakusa Temple. Refusing to translate its contents, a Japanese friend would only reveal that the omens were bad.

Arthur continued to visit Bob Blank's home in Connecticut during 1990 and, in exchange for studio time, recorded "Birthday" and "In the Can" with Lola. Another song, "Problem Child," was rejected by the husband-and-wife team. "He didn't share he had AIDS with me," says Blank, who noticed nothing other than an intensified bitterness in Arthur's demeanor. Some time later Arthur called the engineer and said, "I'm sick and I'm going to have to get all my material back." Blank says he had "tons of stuff" at the studio, including a cello. "Bob was having Arthur create enough songs for me to do an album," remembers Lola. "The last song he was working on before he made his transition was about not wanting to go to school."

As traveling became more and more tiring, Arthur continued to build up his own home studio. A royalty payment for $451.50 from the producers of the documentary film *Paris Is Burning*, which told the story of New York's drag queen scene and included a sequence that featured "Is It All Over My Face?," helped him with his expenses. But for the most part he borrowed and begged from Geoff Travis and Philip Glass as well as his parents whenever he needed a cash injection to buy the latest drum machine, effects box, or keyboard. Others were approached for more specific favors. "In 1991 Arthur asked me to give him sample sets—a library of sounds on disc," recalls François Kevorkian. "I gave him my best sounds, basses, percussion, so he could work from home with his Akai sampler."

Arthur Russell in his home studio, 1990. "He built himself a little lotus loft where he could sit all day," recalls Joyce Bowden. "The mikes were set up so that he could just sit there and record. He was trying to make it as easy as possible for him to not move. I think the walls were made of tape." Photograph by Tom Lee. Courtesy of Charles Arthur Russell Sr. and Emily Russell.

Instead of narrowing his ambitions until they cohered with his inevitable end, Arthur grasped at every opportunity to record music. He played cello on *Naked*, the final Talking Heads album. He told Will Socolov he wanted to lay down one or two records for Sleeping Bag. And he worked on his LP for Glass, which was "patterned on *World Of Echo*" (as he put it to Steven Hall). "Arthur told me he was sick," recalls Glass. "I thought he meant he had a cold, so I said, 'Oh well, make sure you're wrapped up properly.' He said, 'No, no, no, I'm *sick*.'" Arthur continued to take his material to the Point Music office, and in the spring of 1991 he arrived all excited, only to discover his tape contained no material. As Arthur struggled to come to terms with what had happened, one of the producers at Point declared the cellist was losing his grip on reality, which contributed to his crumbling sense of well-being. Arthur persevered because he had grasped one of the fundamental truths of life: that sound indicates activity, whereas silence suggests that something has died or disappeared.[23]

Arthur also worked at a "whirlwind pace" (in the words of Peter

Arthur Russell, 5 April 1991. Photograph by Allen Ginsberg. Courtesy of Peter Hale.

Zummo) on his Rough Trade album, and during a meeting with Travis urged him to release Hall's LP, *Active Driveway*, which he had produced. Maintaining he would struggle to sell more than a couple of hundred copies, Travis turned down the offer. "Unfortunately the situation with you has made me look like a goof," Arthur reported back to Hall. "I don't mind." Hall was flattered his friend had been so supportive, while Travis remained philosophical. "He was trying to help Steven and just hoped I would go for it," says the Rough Trade boss. As for Arthur's album, Travis began to wonder if the process of invention rather than the final edit had become the main purpose, and he also speculated that the delayed ending allowed Arthur to hold on to the dream that he might one day become a mainstream artist. "It was a blessing and a curse having me as a patron," says Travis, implying that a tougher overlord might have forced Arthur to deliver an end product.

Others became more openly frustrated. Ahmed recalls saying of the same set of recordings, "Arthur, it's like you're not finishing! Some of this stuff is really good! Let's wrap this up!" As the sessions dragged on, the percussionist began to wonder if the specificities of the drum machine — its sheer usability and its economical use of space on a multitrack — was

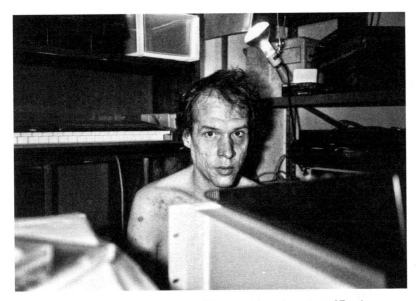

Arthur Russell in his home studio, July 1991. Photograph by and courtesy of Tom Lee.

encouraging Arthur in his tendency to over-record, but Arthur remained indifferent to his prompts. "He wasn't particularly defensive," says Ahmed. "He seemed to be very self-assured. It was like he was on a different plane, as if he had some understanding, and that it was all going to work out. He just had to find the right person, the right partner, the right engineer, the right studio."

Although his immune system was unraveling, Arthur continued to obsess about the barely perceptible shades of difference that existed between one version of a song and another, and as he played Side A and Side B to his friends and family, old frustrations took on an added urgency. "I would say, 'For Christ's sake, Arthur, just choose one of them!'" recalls Kate, who would listen to her brother's demos over the phone. "'You've got these people in England, and you've got to get something off to them!'" Back in London, Travis deduced why Arthur was entering into a seemingly endless cycle of fine-tuning. "I began to understand that his being ill was one reason it was taking him so long," says the Rough Trade owner. "It gave him a reason to live, and I was glad about this."

Performing live whenever he could, which wasn't often, Arthur appeared with Ahmed and Jon Gibson at a Zummo gig in McGraw-Hill Park that took place in July 1990; the other musicians were in full flow by the time he showed up, exhausted, with his Yamaha DX7 synthesizer, cello, and amp toward the end of the second movement. At another Zummo gig that took place at Roulette, an important venue for downtown musicians since its opening in 1978, Arthur ended up playing on the floor, supported by some cushions. "He was quite ill at that point," remembers Zummo. "I thought that the best thing was to let the guy play, not take him for dead." The music never really got off the ground and was, says the trombonist, "a very dead event." Zummo stayed with the situation. "It was real. It may not have been satisfying musically, and I don't know if Arthur would have rather not played, but it was out there as a performance concept. It did nothing to please the presenters who had approached me with such conviction, but I stand by it." At the end of the concert, Arthur came close to telling Zummo he was sick. Zummo recalls, "He borrowed my harmonica and when he gave it back to me he said, 'You might want to wash it.'" The trombonist didn't flinch. "My oeuvre is suffering," he reflects.

Arthur didn't say anything to Ahmed and Elodie Lauten, even though he was slowing down and the "awkward moments" (in the words of Lauten) were on the increase. Ahmed eventually asked Lauten if she knew why Arthur was being so moody and rude, and when she explained, he says he was "dumbstruck" but also "amazed at Arthur's dignity and the respect that those close to him had for his privacy." Arthur continued to press the outer limits of live musicianship and, during a concert at the Experimental Intermedia Foundation in March 1991, encouraged Lauten to pursue her free-spirited approach by having her play her Casio keyboard in a tent. "It turned out to be a strange experience," says Lauten. "Everyone wondered about the significance of the tent." Lauten's and Arthur's last co-performance—a "crazy harpsichord-cello gig"—took place at the Knitting Factory in the summer of 1991. "My reaction to Arthur being sick was to treat him exactly the same way as I treated him when he was well," remembers Lauten. "I asked him if he wanted to do the gig and he said, 'Yes.' It was a very good gig and a lot of fun, but Arthur was tired, really tired. I was left with a sadness in me."

Even when he had been healthy, Arthur would battle with his equipment as he attempted to fine-tune everything to his satisfaction, and this often led to his performances starting late. Now that he was frail with AIDS, his audience witnessed his heart-rending struggle to continue as if nothing had changed. "It's low-key stuff, but Russell has a charming way of whisking a bow across his cello and crooning softly to himself that makes you think you're picking up pop music from Neptune," wrote Kyle Gann in a March 1991 preview performance review that managed to avoid saying just how low-key Arthur had become.[24] Six months later he performed in the vaulted caverns and chambers of the Anchorage, a venue situated under the Brooklyn Bridge. "[Arthur Russell's] style is gently poetic, and combines a steadfast tonal orientation with a graceful exoticism," reported the *New York Times*. "Some of his pieces revolve around a drone, as Indian music does; some bear a resemblance to Paul Simon's 'Graceland'-era glosses on African vocal styles."[25] The article avoided mention of the stark reality that was striking to everyone in the audience; that Arthur was so ill he could barely make it to the end of the concert.

A little less than two months later, Arthur accepted Rhys Chatham's invitation to play solo at the Kitchen's high-profile twenty-year retrospective, "Five Generations of Composers at the Kitchen, 1971–1991." The appearance marked a kind of closure, in part because Arthur had been omitted from the tenth anniversary lineup, and in part because his contribution to the downtown new-music scene had been overlooked in Tom Johnson's *The Voice of New Music*, which was published in 1989. (While peers such as Glenn Branca, Chatham, Peter Gordon, and Garrett List received respectable coverage in Johnson's account, Arthur's appearance was limited to a fleeting mention of his presence at a Christian Wolff performance in 1974.)[26] Wearing a red long-sleeved shirt, dark trousers, red socks, and no shoes as he edged into the show, Arthur started, stopped, and then started again, scratching and plucking his strings while he looked distractedly into the air. When he opened his mouth to sing "Innocent Fun," barely a croak came out, and as the concert continued his playing degenerated to such an extent he seemed to be breathing his last breaths. Whereas the union between voice and cello had once been complete, now it was broken. The concert was harrowing. Nobody who saw it could have believed they would see Arthur play again.

Tom Lee was Arthur's constant, devoted, and tender caregiver during his final years and months, and he also listened as his lover played him whatever song he was working on. "Arthur was frustrated and tired, yet he

Arthur Russell and
Tom Lee, July 1991.
Photographer unknown.
Courtesy of Tom Lee.

kept trying to make music," recalls Lee. "All I could do was console him at the end of the day, but he was tough on himself and worried a great deal about how people in the music business considered him." There were times when Lee became vexed at the amount of time Arthur would spend in his makeshift recording studio, because those sessions came at the expense of them sitting together on the sofa. But Arthur thought that Lee understood his need to write, and of course Lee did understand, however painful that process of creation might have become. Arthur tried to make it up by penning a song for Lee — "Love Comes Back" — which spoke of the preciousness of their remaining time together, as well as the melancholic mood that was descending on their upstairs apartment. "Put your little hand in mine, once you know that love is back, and being sad is not a crime."[27]

By the spring of 1991 dementia started to set in. "I worked in a picture-framing shop in SoHo, and Arthur would come by to see me," remembers Lee. "He would be in a fog. He would have his Walkman with him, but he wouldn't know what he was listening to. It was extremely, extremely sad." As he left the shop Arthur might say he was going to Canal Street to buy some cassettes, but when Lee returned home three hours later, he would still be out. "I'd be very worried," says Lee. "I didn't trust he could make his way back home. He didn't seem to be aware of the severity of his condition." Arthur still wore the Walkman as if it was an appendage of his body, but the task of comparing edits had become impossible, and he was no longer certain he could navigate the streets he had walked a thousand times. "I just wanted Arthur to be at home and protected," adds Lee. "I was worried about him being out and about."

Lee says he would have welcomed more help, but Arthur's closest friends weren't around as much as they had been in the past. "Instead of walking into the fire, I walked away a little bit," confesses Joyce Bowden, who met up with Arthur once a month or so during this twilight period. "There were reasons Ernie and Steven were out of the country too—because this was a huge, huge event, and the idea of Arthur not being around for us was unimaginable, unfathomable. I think for me, and I think for Steven and Ernie too, something shut down. We shut our eyes, clenched our fists, and shook our heads back and forth." On one occasion Bowden accompanied Arthur on a doctor's visit, and as they sat in the waiting room, Arthur poured himself a glass of water, took a sip from the cup, and then passed it to her. "I had just had my wisdom teeth pulled and my mouth was full of open sores, yet I drank after him because I wasn't quite sure if this was really going to kill me or not, but I knew that it was going to kill Arthur if I didn't drink after him," she says. "'Are we blood brothers? Do you love me? Do you trust me? Are you going on this journey with me? Are you abandoning me? Am I OK? Am I a leper? Am I untouchable? Am I alone in the world?' I just thought his wanting me to drink after him, which he clearly wanted me to do, was all of that. I think he felt isolated, marginalized, and frightened."

Brooks felt bad that he had not been around to play music with Arthur and help Lee with the chores, and when he saw his friend again in the spring of 1991 he was shocked at his deterioration. "He was wearing this cheap leather motorcycle jacket that I bought in France, and it was hung on him like he was a skeleton," remembers Brooks. When Arthur played "Love Comes Back," the bass player was deeply moved. "'Love Comes Back' was probably the best song Arthur ever wrote," he says. "I didn't know anybody who was writing songs that were this good. It was a new order of songwriting. They [his new songs] made me think of John Lennon, whose best songs were on his solo album, Imagine. Arthur's best work didn't have to be solo, but that was where he was, in his apartment, weak, and writing songs that were getting better and better. He was pursuing this beautiful sound, and he never stopped doing that." Staying with Brooks's mother for a couple of days, Arthur and Brooks went to work on some songs in Bob Blank's Connecticut studio, including vocals for another version of "Oh Fernando Why?." That was the last time the two of them saw each other.

Having drifted from Arthur during the mid-1980s, Allen Ginsberg stepped into the semi-vacuum that was left by close but absent friends. Contact had been maintained, with the poet-activist calling on Arthur whenever he needed him to play cello, such as in 1981, when he recorded "Father Death Blues," and in 1984, when he played on a New Year's Day PBS Broadcast ("Good Morning, Mr. Orwell") organized by Nam June Paik. During these and other collaborations it became clear that Arthur had become less willing to go with Ginsberg's flow, and some time later Ginsberg would note that Arthur had "developed a cello form which was more scratchy and much more avant-garde than the sort of mellow-yellow that I was interested in." Ginsberg added: "We actually had a fight whether he would play unison or whether he would be doing some avant-garde number on my simple-minded Blake lyrics. I don't think I was very understanding about that." [28] Yet in the sleeve notes to *First Blues*, which was released in 1983, Ginsberg commented that "the bulk of the music was notated by Buddhist pop star Arthur Russell," and toward the end of the 1980s they started to spend more time with each other again. [29]

Climbing up the stairwell dressed in his pajamas, Ginsberg would talk poetry with Arthur — Lee recalls the poet found Arthur's *World of Echo* lyrics to be rather abstract — and when Arthur became sick, Ginsberg showed no shyness when it came to confronting (and photographing) his condition. The old friends meditated together, and Ginsberg also introduced Arthur to the Tibetan lama Gehlek Rinpoche, who filled part of the void left by Yuko Nonomura. "Arthur came downstairs a few times and talked with Gehlek, and the main subject of the talks within this twelve-month period was, 'What do you do with your mind at the moment of death? Where do you place your mind, and how do you relate to it?'" Ginsberg recalled later. "The suggestion was to cultivate a sense of sympathy or compassion toward all sentient beings in the universe at that moment, some sense of openness or emptiness, and to revert to whatever meditation practice you are most familiar with . . . because it's too late by that time to rearrange your bookshelf or to complete ordering your tapes." [30]

When Arthur became extremely sick, Ginsberg tried to persuade his close musical collaborator Steven Taylor to look at Arthur's legs, which

Twelfth Street, 1987. Photograph by Allen Ginsberg. Courtesy of Peter Hale.

had swollen up. "Allen had a morbid, Buddhist fascination with physical suffering and death, and he wanted me to face it," remembers Taylor. "He saw himself as the guru showing horror to the naive kid, but the way he proposed the visit, although not callous or mean in any way, put me off. I felt I was being asked to witness some kind of spectacle, and that it was disrespectful of Arthur's situation, so I declined to join him." Ginsberg also urged John Moran to visit. "Arthur was dying and Allen tried to convince me to say, 'Goodbye,'" he recalls. "I kept telling Allen that I didn't know Arthur well enough, that I just loved his music. Allen kept insisting, but I chickened out in the end. It was a huge mistake and I think about it often."

Meanwhile the Russell family began to wonder if it might be better to have Arthur cared for in Maine or Oskaloosa, although they rarely held on to the idea of taking him away from New York for long. During a trip to Maine in the summer of 1990, for example, Arthur became concerned that his T-cell count was plummeting and made a number of visits to the hospital, but when Julie and Kate offered to take him into their care, Tom said that he and Arthur believed the best treatment was available in New York, and that was where they wanted to live. When the family returned to Maine for a muted reunion over Thanksgiving in 1991, Chuck and Emily asked if it would help if they took Arthur back to Oskaloosa, but were confronted with the distasteful thought that there might be local doctors who would refuse to treat their son. "When we mentioned the idea of bringing him home, Tom broke up," recalls Emily. "Tom was absolutely marvelous. We can't say enough about how wonderful he was." Although his dementia had progressed by the time they made that trip, Arthur still hoped to be able to work. "He took his equipment with him—the Casio, the Walkman—but he was doing nothing with it," recalls Lee. "He just didn't have the strength." But when Julie and Kate traveled to New York the following month, Arthur persuaded Julie to lay down some vocals for "Hop on Down." By that point a nurse had moved into Twelfth Street to assist Lee. "Arthur was just sitting, barely remembering to eat," he says. "He was like a ninety-year-old man."

Friends said their goodbyes, in person or on the phone. Jon Gibson received a wooden flute from Arthur as they traveled together on the Staten Island Ferry following a rehearsal with Peter Zummo. Geoff Travis saw Arthur a couple of months before he died and was shocked at his state. Will Socolov met up with his old partner to discuss his planned albums, but says Arthur deteriorated too quickly for them to get anything going. "It was just so painful," recalls the Sleeping Bag boss. Kent Goshorn's last encounter with Arthur left him feeling empty. "His mind was finally going, and yet he was still sitting there alone, doggedly working on a project involving a techno-machine sound with Peter Zummo," he recalls. "I tried to give him a hug, but he just stood there limply, surrounded by recording equipment." Ned Sublette was out when Arthur phoned him on Christmas Day 1991, so Arthur spoke with Constance, Sublette's wife, instead. "All I recall with absolute clarity is his anger and incoherence, and that there was no end to it," says Constance, who was on the phone with Arthur for at least an hour. When Sublette called back later, Arthur told him what he had already guessed. "I felt him being shyer than ever," says Sublette, "but it seemed to me he was being as brave as anyone could be." By the time Hall returned to New York in February 1992, Arthur had contracted cancer of the throat— "the most torturous disease to strike a singer," notes Hall—and was barely able to sing. Returning from another trip to Hong Kong, Hall remembers that although the dementia had progressed, Arthur "had lacunae where he was quite lucid and graceful." Brooks phoned regularly, but the conversations became harder and harder until, during his last month, "Arthur was incommunicado."

Arthur spent his final weeks in the Memorial Sloan-Kettering Cancer Center. When Bill Ruyle visited he recounted the time Arthur had demonstrated some chord formations on a guitar, to which Arthur replied, "I did it all wrong." "I had the impression he was referring to more than guitar chords," says Ruyle. "I told him that he had certainly showed me all of the right chords and that he had made beautiful, beautiful music, and that I loved it so much. He said, 'Thank you.'" Zummo visited, too, and found it difficult. "We probably communicated on a musical level very well, although we may not have communicated so well on some other levels." When Phill Niblock dropped by, he was left with some regrets. "Arthur was always quite thin, but he had bloated up and was not able to speak," he recalls. "It was unclear if he recognized me. It was fairly horrifying." By the time Bowden traveled up from North Carolina for a week in March 1992, Arthur was in a stupor and, having cut her hair short and dyed it dark, she wondered if he would recognize her when he came around. "I was taking my shift because Tom didn't want Arthur to be alone at all," she remembers. "I was just singing to him and looking at him, and he looked up and said, 'I can't believe it!'"

Chuck and Emily saw Arthur for the last time toward the beginning of March. By that point his hair was falling out, and as Chuck started to comb it he told him, "Charley, you're a good sport." Arthur opened his eyes and said, "Are you sure I'm a good sport?" Chuck, who had sometimes made a point of telling his son he was a poor sport as he was growing up, said he was sure. A few days later, Chuck, Emily, Julie, and Kate (plus Beau) traveled to the hospital and, along with Tom, whose status as Arthur's partner wasn't recognized by U.S. law, instructed the doctors that they shouldn't take any extreme measures to prolong Arthur's life. "He was in and out of consciousness," remembers Kate. "We would just sit and wait for him to come around and be able to talk."

Arthur had slipped into a haze toward the end of March. "It was so sad because he couldn't recognize anyone," says Elodie Lauten. "Tom was there everyday, spoon-feeding him. He was so devoted it was incredible." Mustafa Ahmed also traveled to the hospital and read out a letter that he had intended to send until Lee called him in to deliver it in person. "Arthur was barely conscious and only his closest friends were present," says the percussionist. "Tom whispered in Arthur's ear to let him know I was there. Somehow I managed to read the letter aloud. Everyone was crying." When Sublette called on Arthur he found him asleep and alone, with no member of staff in sight. "A radio was playing commercial easy-listening music quietly by the bed," remembers Sublette. "I wondered, 'Can Arthur hear this? Who chose this station? Should I change it? Or is this what he wants to hear?' I did nothing." Sublette sat quietly and after a while heard himself say, "Goodbye, Arthur." Returning later he found Arthur semiconscious and Lee by his bedside. *"Arthur!"* Tom called out. *"Was Ned here? Do you remember Ned coming in?"* Also dropping by, Alan Abrams experienced a flashback to the scene at the end of *2001: A Space Odyssey*, in which the last surviving astronaut on the centerpiece spaceship faces himself as an old man and then goes on to be reborn as a supernatural star child—an embryo encased in a bubble of light. "I kept thinking about the end of the movie," says Abrams, who held prayer beads, as did Arthur. "It gave me something."

On the gray, quiet afternoon of Sunday, 29 March, Lee visited Arthur in Sloan-Kettering and remembers him being largely sentient as they watched *West Side Story* on television. "I remember it being a very peaceful time between the two of us," he says. "It felt like Arthur was looking at the TV screen; he was not speaking, but he seemed to be aware. Sitting on the edge of the bed together, it felt tender to me, clinging to this moment. There were no other visitors for a number of hours." The following Friday Lee left the hospital at 9:30 p.m. and was "pretty shocked" to see Ginsberg arrive as he made his way out. "I thought it was unusual for someone to come to the hospital that late at night," he says.

The next morning, on 4 April 1992, Lee received a phone call at 8:00 a.m. saying that Arthur's blood pressure was low and that he was unlikely to live for much longer. Lee traveled to the hospital and was with his partner when he passed away around 10:30 a.m. "I walked home in disbelief," says Lee. "I remember saying to myself that I would visit the hospital forever if it meant that he didn't die. I got so accustomed to going every day, and although he wasn't responding to me, it still felt like it was exactly the place I wanted to be. I never thought I would get over my sadness." Lee recalls thinking it was a good thing Ginsberg had grabbed the chance to see Arthur the previous evening. He adds that he should have realized the end was coming when Arthur stopped listening to his Walkman, comparing Side A and Side B of the same recording.

A private memorial event was held at the Experimental Intermedia Foundation on 12 April 1992. Having traveled from Oskaloosa and Maine, Chuck, Emily, Julie, and Kate Russell tried to match the unfamiliar faces to the tapes Arthur had sent them over the years, and others were also bemused by the range of people who traveled to Phill Niblock's loft that day. Everyone knew people from their own musical circle, and some had previously encountered musicians from adjacent clans, but for most of them the service was the moment when they grasped the range of Arthur's explorations and collaborations, which spanned poetry, folk, pop, rock, progressive composition, and disco/dance—because people from all these fields had come to pay their respects. "Arthur's new-music friends were there, and some dance people who came from a completely different world were there, and Allen Ginsberg was there with his friends," says Arnold Dreyblatt. "All of these different worlds were colliding. It was only then that the full diversity of Arthur's world became apparent to me."

Organized by Lee, the memorial was loosely structured. A tape recording of *Instrumentals* played in tandem with Yuko Nonomura's slides as friends and family made their way into the event, after which spoken and musical contributions were interspersed with other selections, including "Go Bang! #5" (François Kevorkian remix), "More Real," "A Little Lost," "Big Moon," "That's Us / Wild Combination," "Let's Go Swimming," "Tell You (Today)," and a couple of tracks from *World of Echo*. Each record told a story. "More Real" and "Tell You (Today)" were selected because Arthur had been unusually pleased with them; "Go Bang! #5" was picked because it had been his biggest hit; the *World of Echo* selections showcased his vocal range; "Let's Go Swimming" was intended as a joyful and celebratory antidote to the reigning mood; and "That's Us / Wild Combination" provided a taste of all the recordings that had never been released. "Arthur just had so many songs to listen to," Lee told the gathering as he moved between cassettes.

A number of guests said a few words. Alan Abrams described the importance of Arthur's relationship with Nonomura. Ned Sublette read a haiku poem Peter Gordon had faxed from Japan and spoke of his own admiration for Arthur's poetic sensibility. Mustafa Ahmed spoke of Arthur's openness, generosity, and sense of musical adventure, and reflected on the way he had taken him (and others) on a fascinating journey into sound and friendship. Kent Goshorn reminisced about his time growing up with Arthur. And Alison Salzinger remembered how Arthur "always seemed to reside simultaneously in some mystical and erudite musical plane and down on the ground among the teenagers, MTV, and drum machines." Salzinger added: "At P.S. 122 we performed together. After the show everyone wanted to know, 'Who played that beautiful music?' They hadn't even noticed Arthur, sitting behind the audience, inside the usual cloud of amplification and echo devices. He hadn't wanted to be seen, but the music spoke for him."

Allen Ginsberg spoke longest of all. "I sort of had a crush on Arthur," he revealed as he remembered the time they spent together in San Francisco. "There was something that he exuded that was both delicate and exquisite-minded and youthful and at the same time oddly reticent, and I was really curious about him." Ginsberg spoke of his subsequent collaborations with Arthur, who was always a "quick and sympathetic" accompanist, and also of Arthur's musical vision. "What I was amazed at was his modesty, always, and his ambition seemed to be to write popular music, or bubblegum music, but Buddhist bubblegum; to transmit the dharma through the most elemental form, or transmit some sense of illumination," noted the poet. "That was a constant preoccupation." Ginsberg recounted how Arthur would pop downstairs to discuss poetry and song lyrics, even though the poet "didn't understand what he was doing with music" and had almost no idea of the scope of his upstairs neighbor's work. "I knew him better as a pop musician and a neighbor and a Buddhist more than anything else," said Ginsberg. "I also knew him as someone who was completely perfectionistic and indecisive or hesitant or timorous in a way, unable to conclude sometimes even a sentence or a lyric or a composition, but very strong-minded about it."

Having flown in for the service, Ernie Brooks played "The Ballad of the Lights," at the end of which he choked out the words, "Arthur's . . . light . . . was . . . bright . . . indeed." A little later Joyce Bowden sang a new composition titled "Expanding Song for Arthur"; Peter Zummo provided trombone background to Ahmed's address and then added a wistful solo coda; Bill Ruyle played a marimba piece that had been inspired by Arthur; Elodie Lau-

Score by Arthur Russell. "In 1981, to get a jump on building up a repertoire to sing, and to see what my friends might come up with, I asked a few people to write songs for me," says Ned Sublette. "Arthur responded with a one-page notated song. Short though it was, it was a complete thought, with a strong tune precisely notated and lyrics precisely punctuated. It would have propped up a long instrumental piece well, but I always sang it concisely. There was no title, but I always called it 'Out by the Porch.'" Scanned by and courtesy of Ned Sublette.

ten recited a Buddhist poem followed by an extract from *Tower of Meaning*; and Ned Sublette sang "Is It All Over My Face?" and "Out by the Porch." Gary Lucas, who would dedicate his *Gods and Monsters* album to Arthur, also attended the service, as did Johnny Fu, Meredith Monk, Donald Murk, Phill Niblock, Bob Rosenthal, and Carlota Schoolman, while a withered-looking Walter Gibbons stood as a stark reminder of the traumatic link that had been forged between downtown dance, gay culture, and AIDS during the 1980s. "I don't think I was inclined to speak," recalls Zummo, who sat next to Bowden and tried to make sense of what was happening. "I'm not too good with memorials or wakes." The service closed with the screening of a video of one of Arthur's voice-cello performances, after which everyone was handed a river rock as they left the room. "It was very sad," says Brooks. "There was this sense of possibility that was no longer there."

Steven Hall was in Hong Kong when he received the news that Arthur had passed away, and he was unable to fly back for the service. "I had no idea he would get so sick so quickly," he says. "I wrote a poem about Arthur, which I faxed to Phill Niblock to be read at the ceremony, but it was lost and never read." Peter Gordon was also out of the country, working in Japan, when Sublette sent him a fax with the news. Gordon froze when he realized Arthur had passed away on the fourth day of the fourth month of the fourth year of the current Japanese emperor. In Japan, the number four symbolizes death.

On 14 April 1992, the *New York Times* ran an obituary of Arthur Russell. The piece described him as "a cellist, vocalist and composer who was known for his fusion of classical and popular music," and provided a concise précis of his life.[31] The brevity was of little concern to Arthur's circle, and in particular Chuck and Emily, who read it as a validation of his artistic significance. A few days later, *Billboard* declared that Arthur had been "on the cutting edge of New York's downtown music scene," and a week or so after that, Kyle Gann published an elegant tribute in the *Village Voice*.[32] "In a monotonously loud and commercial decade, Arthur Russell was a quiet, introverted voice," he wrote. "His early ensemble music was minimalist, but peculiarly soulful in its hummable melodies and playful harmonic surprises. Later, most often at Phill Niblock's loft concerts, he moved toward solo work with subdued pop elements, playing his cello while singing almost inaudibly. . . . His recent performances had been so infrequent due to illness, his songs were so personal, that it seems as though he simply vanished into his music."[33] Anne Milano, Arthur's friend and adviser at the Community Health Project, called Tom Lee after reading the notices. "She said, 'Tom, I had no idea he was so important,'" recalls Lee. "'Now I get it. Now I understand why he was so anxious about what would happen after he died.'" Many more would have missed the tributes altogether. "There was a time when you were afraid to read the obituaries, because someone you knew would be in there," notes Peter Zummo. "A lot of dancers died, too."

〜 〜 〜

In August 1992 Allen Ginsberg wrote "The Charnel Ground," a poem about life on Twelfth Street, which contained the lines: "While the artistic Buddhist composer / On sixth floor lay spaced out feet swollen with water / Dying slowly of AIDS over a year . . ." Ginsberg continued to live on Twelfth Street until he completed a move to Thirteenth Street just a couple of months before he died in 1997. "Allen was most involved with Arthur when he was ill," says Bob Rosenthal. "Allen really loved Arthur."

〜 〜 〜 〜

A public memorial took place when Mustafa Ahmed, Joyce Bowden, Ernie Brooks, Rhys Chatham, Jon Gibson, Peter Gordon, Kent Goshorn, Steven Hall, Gary Lucas, Bill Ruyle, Larry Saltzman, John Scherman, Jon Sholle, Ned Sublette, "Blue" Gene Tyranny, David Van Tieghem, Peter Zummo, and others participated in "A Tribute to Arthur Russell." Curated by Andy Lyman, the event was staged in the Winter Garden, an acoustically diffuse atrium connected to the World Financial Center, on 19–20 May 1993.

The first night of the memorial was organized around Arthur's ensemble works, including *Instrumentals* and *Tower of Meaning,* as well as pieces by the Singing Tractors. "It was amazing being there, with Arthur's music bouncing around in that huge cavern of hard surfaces, this soft music floating amongst all that glass and marble, wondering what Arthur was thinking of the whole thing," recalls Bowden. "I think he would have liked it." As the evening unfolded, Chatham had an epiphany: when he had performed *Instrumentals* in 1975, he approached it from within the context of contemporary compositional music, and dismissed the piece, but having gone on to practice jazz improvisation for ten years he was now able to "appreciate" the composition. "Arthur tapped into the hipness of these standard-era changes way back in the middle-seventies and put them together in a way that nobody had done before," he notes.

The second night featured Arthur's songs, which were delivered by groups of musicians and vocalists. Sublette teamed up with Tyranny to play "Out by the Porch"; Ahmed, Bowden, Brooks, and Lucas delivered "Tell You (Today)" and "Let's Go Swimming"; Bowden, Brooks, and Hall performed "Don't Forget about Me," "List of Boys," and "Lost in Thought" ("Lost" being a song Hall had cowritten with Arthur); Ahmed, Bowden, and Scherman sang "Love Comes Back" and "It's a Boy" (with Jonathan Best); Bowden and Scherman appeared with Brooks to play "Oh Fernando Why"; Bowden, Brooks, and Scherman (with Best) recited "Big Blue Bus"; and Brooks returned to the stage with his old Flying Hearts collaborators Saltzman and Van Tieghem to perform "Bobby." Alternative lineups also played "Let's See / Time to Go Home Now," "Me for Real / Home away from Home / Lucky Cloud," "Soon-to-Be-Innocent-Fun," and "What It's Like." During the rendition of "List of Boys" — "I'm not on your list of boys / I'm not in your hand / I'm only your friend" — Hall started to scream at the top of his voice. "It was an early song of Arthur's, and we had performed it together many times," he explains. "I had prepared a DAT tape of music to perform solo, but I had not planned to do the scream. It just came out." Arthur might have gone, but he continued to course through the veins of everyone who had heard his music.

~ ~ ~ ~ ~

By the time of the tribute, Arthur Russell was floating in waters choppy and still, having set off from Baker Island in the late summer of 1992. He drifted along the coast of Maine, after which he might have floated down to New York and the piers that ran along the Hudson River, his favorite backdrop for listening to music on his Walkman. None of his friends on the West Coast would have been surprised if he hitched a subsequent lift with a slipstream that was heading to the coastline of San Francisco.

Tom Lee and the Russell family had been trying to think of a way to commemorate Arthur. Julie and Kate liked the idea of contributing to the AIDS Memorial Quilt, and said that they could include images of water, fish, and light, but Chuck and Emily weren't sure. As an alternative, Chuck proposed they take Arthur's ashes to Baker Island, where Arthur and his family had made their last outing together. "Chuck said it was a special place for Arthur and that the trip had been important," recalls Lee. "I had taken ownership of Arthur's health and the memorial service, and I wanted Chuck and Emily to be able to decide where the ashes should go. Chuck's idea just made a lot of sense to me."

The Russell family and Lee set out with the ashes on a bright and breezy day in late August. The presence of two young nieces lightened the somewhat somber atmosphere, and at the end of the boat ride, the family and the lover walked across the uninhabited island until they reached its exposed shore, where ocean waves were crashing against huge boulders. Having found the right spot, they scattered Arthur's ashes in a tide pool, after which they sat and waited for the water to come in. Eventually the Atlantic Ocean touched the pool, took the ashes into its midst, and dispersed them far and wide. At long last, Arthur was free to go swimming.

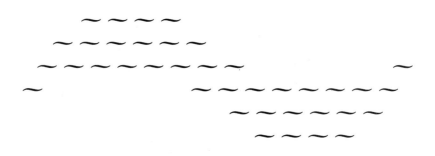

Epilogue

"There are people who are boring and there are people who are not," says Steven Harvey, who wrote pieces about downtown music for the *New York Rocker* and *Collusion* during the first half of the 1980s. "There is something that remains interesting in Arthur to this day." Delicately balancing his commitments to downtown's varied music scenes like a plate-spinner, Arthur Russell was hard to capture, but his heterogeneity and complexity have made his legacy durable. The subdued loneliness of his voice-cello songs ended up resonating with the height of the AIDS crisis during the first half of the 1990s; his mutant disco recordings became required listening for dance fans who started to excavate the post-disco canon during the second half of the 1990s; his off-kilter dance tracks from the mid-1980s caught the imagination of the early followers of broken beat during the late 1990s and early 2000s; and in the early to mid-2000s, his unreleased recordings for Sleeping Bag and Rough Trade sounded premonitory to those who became fascinated by the recycling of the electronic-pop canon of the first half of the 1980s. "If I listen to Marvin Gaye I'm still compelled," adds Harvey. "You hear a great singer and their work retains its relevance. Arthur's music has that. His music still sounds contemporary."

Russell's unwavering eclecticism suggests he deserves to be considered alongside Captain Beefheart, John Cage,

Charles Ives, Harry Partch, Steve Reich, La Monte Young, Frank Zappa, and others who have contributed to the robust tradition of maverick music writing in North America. Although the maverick sensibility isn't peculiar to the United States, there is something in the country's historical make-up — the frontier tradition, the abundance of choice, the emphasis on free speech — that conspires to produce such an outlook, and Russell could be viewed as part of this lineage inasmuch as it's difficult to imagine him acquiring the same degree of independence and diversity if he had grown up in another part of the world. "Composers who lived unusual lives or flouted norms, writing works their contemporaries found incomprehensible, even unplayable, have a long history in American music," writes Michael Broyles in *Mavericks and Other Traditions in American Music*. "Americans have revelled in the idea of the maverick."[1] Never one to play safe, Russell was always searching for new sound combinations, and insisted that others be equally bold. "I have known only one other artist to rival Don Van Vliet (a.k.a. Captain Beefheart) for both sheer musical genius and sheer bloody-minded contrariness, and that is the late, great Arthur Russell," wrote Gary Lucas in 1994. "Arthur could musically deliver the kind of quirky goods that simultaneously melted your heart and forced you to listen to music in a new way — and do it all with a sense of high-spirited panache and good humor."[2]

Because his openness was so developed, however, Russell lacked the singularity and ambition of some of his maverick contemporaries, and he paid for this with his diminished profile. "What Philip Glass and Steve Reich, in particular, and La Monte Young in his own way also did, was bring a sense of musical 'branding' into the equation," comments Peter Gordon. "There was no way to not identify the Glass or Reich sound, and it has remained that way. Their own musical growth has remained totally within the context of the parameters which they set for themselves early on." Jon Gibson adds that Glass and Reich developed a "real rigidity to what they were doing" in order to establish their reputations. "Terry Riley's the same way, and La Monte Young is the ultimate possessive, having established his turf around drones and tuning," he adds. "They're all very, very territorial." In contrast, Russell showed so little interest in doing the same thing twice he was left to question his rigorously diverse approach toward the end of his life. "I ran into him on the street and he told me, 'Well, I didn't get as far as I wanted to, or make the impact I wanted to,'" remembers Gibson. "'I didn't make the right moves at the right time. I blew it.'" But Gibson wonders how success might be meaningfully measured, as does Donald Murk. "Arthur was always looking to refresh things, and as a result he didn't have the commercial success he might have had if he was more focused," comments Murk. "Then again, everything he touched became imbued with this broad outlook."

Suffused with the Buddhist-hippie ethos of San Francisco and the butt-shaking codes of downtown disco, Russell also lacked the rugged sensibility and authoritarian self-confidence that the most forthright mavericks tend to possess in abundance. Nor was he individualistic, for although he could be unbending and self-absorbed, he was also committed to the creation of collective music, and prioritized this above his own individuality. In contrast to the maverick tradition, Russell tended to remain friendly with his peers, because although he could drive people crazy, he wasn't invested in declaring sole authorship over an idea. "Arthur stands up to investigation," comments Ned Sublette. "You can look at the most embarrassing parts of his life, cross-check what everybody remembers about him, and he comes through it very well. He could be exasperating, but he was never cruel to anybody. He never deliberately fucked anybody over. And despite misunderstandings, paranoia, and the rest, there aren't any villains in his story because he worked with good people." Sublette adds: "If Arthur could have had five more productive years, your book might have been twice as long. Who knows what he might have accomplished if he had been allowed to reach that next phase of life, where you start to put it together."

Russell's form of musicianship was rooted in history. He enrolled at the San Francisco Conservatory of Music and the Ali Akbar College of Music in 1970, the same year Miles Davis released *Bitches Brew*. Fashioned by artists ranging from Bob Ashley to the Beatles to Manu Dibango to Sly and the Family Stone to Frank Zappa, the international movement toward fusion encouraged younger musicians to work beyond genre. A few years later, by the time Russell had relocated to New York, the flux and flow became an increasingly striking element of the downtown milieu. "There was, as rumoured, a nice rubbing together between disciplines during the later part of that time—borders were definitely fuzzy, which was inspiring," comments David Byrne, while Laurie Anderson maintains there "weren't any boundaries or categories."[3] Venturing into the mist of intergeneric sound, Russell went as far as, if not further than, any of his downtown peers. "Peter

[Gordon], Laurie [Anderson], Jill [Kroesen], and I focused our efforts within the context of one scene, however merged our music might have been," notes Rhys Chatham. "Arthur didn't and simultaneously wore many hats."

At the same time Russell also struggled to pursue an unconscious sonic because downtown could obstruct as well as facilitate. As Carlo McCormick writes, the "dichotomy between external disillusion and insider membership is a relationship Downtown struck not only against the mainstream but also consistently upon itself," and the critic adds that almost every "congregation that mattered was invented on its own conditions and fabricated its own turf." In the final instance, he argues, "each [scene] was relatively self-contained."[4] Chatham and Glenn Branca experienced these territorial tensions when they were branded "art fags" by the CBGB's no-wavers (no wave being the name given to the experimental rock bands that aimed to break with new wave).[5] And as downtown charged into its partly fictitious peak of free-flowing collaboration it was beginning to appear as though dance was experiencing a form of erasure when the New York Rocker surveyed an impressive cross-section of venues only to exclude the likes of the Loft, the Paradise Garage, and the Saint.[6] With the exception of Gordon, who explored dance with LOLO as well as with the visual artist Colette, and to a lesser extent James Chance, Russell remained the only downtown musician to explicitly embrace disco.[7]

Perhaps downtowners from the postpunk/new-music crossover scene still didn't know how to assimilate the nonmasculine culture of dance. As Lydia Lunch writes of the downtown era: "Anger. Isolation. Poverty. Soul murder. The connective tissue where the cultural division of art, film, music, and literature was cauterized, creating a vast insane asylum, part Theater of Cruelty, part Grand Guignol. All Dada, all the time."[8] Russell wouldn't have identified with Lunch's description of downtown—which she also portrays as the "blood-soaked bones of New York's underbelly" that was akin to "a filthy specter who refuses a final exorcism"—and he wouldn't have sided with what McCormick maintains was "a politics not of engagement but of estrangement."[9] Open to everything except the nihilistic and the aggressive, Russell had warmed to Sublette's queer cowboy song "Cowboys Are Frequently Secretly (Fond of Each Other)," yet he also objected to another song Sublette worked on at the same time with the poet and performance artist John Giorno that included the lines "I don't recommend to anyone to be alive / And I can't imagine anyone wanting to be alive / Except if they're completely deluded." "Arthur thought that was terrible," recalls Sublette, "not because of the music, but because he disagreed with the sentiment."

Russell was concerned with the creation of a tolerant, integrated, non-individualistic community. Although he didn't become involved in any form of activist politics, his interest in affective music scenes — scenes that were organized around sound and sensation — paralleled some of the most compelling philosophical interventions of the 1970s. There is no reason to believe that Russell read the writings of contemporary cultural theorists such as Michel Foucault, but his concern with building a community through the experience of music, in which musicians and dancers were encouraged to give up their individuality in favor of a collective experience, marked a parallel trajectory. While a number of musicians from the new-music and new-wave scenes came to appreciate downtown disco's heightened quest to experience a form of transcendence through sonic mutation and social ritual, none of them could be found on the dance floors of the Gallery, the Loft, and the Paradise Garage week in, week out, and none of them could come up with lines that captured the thrust of this adventure in a few simple words. "I wanna see all my friends at once," ran the timeless line from "#5 (Go Bang!)" "I'd do anything to get the chance to go bang. / I wanna go bang / I wanna go bang."

Whenever he could, Russell worked along the nonhierarchical, interconnected, tangential lines of the rhizome — the horizontal root structure evoked by Gilles Deleuze and Félix Guattari — and in so doing established the framework for an egalitarian, cooperative practice. He created music within a range of collaborative networks, and emphasized the group over his own individual presence when it came to releasing music, as evidenced by his use of pseudonyms. He democratized the music-making process by encouraging his co-musicians and vocalists to improvise. He immersed himself in editing, establishing a discontinuous universe of takes, tracks, and effects. He recorded several versions of the same song in order to dismantle the idea of the definitive version. He prioritized the open process of live performance above the closed circuit of the commodified recording. He made music that was aesthetically decentered, loosely structured, nonhierarchical, and nonteleological. He explored orchestral/compositional music, folk/pop/rock music, and disco/dance music, often working on these sounds simultaneously. He favored cultures that were socially inclusive rather than exclusive, and prioritized the strains of orchestral music, pop, dance, and hip-hop that were associated with the feminine, the black, and the gay (or the non-dominant). Finally, he made connections between sounds and scenes that were to varying degrees segmented. Russell's rhizomatic practice, in short, amounted to a polyvalent form of *roots music*.[10]

Twenty years later, this project risks looking inadequate. "The next generation of gay boys was more overtly political because after the onslaught of AIDS two things happened," notes Hall. "The focus shifted from the bacchanal, crazy, nonstop sex-drug parties, and the burgeoning gay culture represented by mentors like Allen Ginsberg and Andy Warhol was decimated. Political engagement bypassed our generation and was taken up by the next generation with groups such as ACT-UP." There is no knowing if Russell would have become explicitly critical of the deepening inequality, neocolonial war, religious evangelism, insidious censorship, and looming environmental catastrophe that marked the neoliberal opening of the twenty-first century. But considered in the context of the neoliberal philosophy of individualism, competition, materialism, and inequality, Russell's mode of musicianship suggested and continues to suggest an alternative to a framework that did so much to disrupt downtown's creative community during the second half of the 1980s. At the very least, the tiny steps taken by Russell and his downtown peers — their focus on getting a good sound and forming relationships that are collaborative and nonexploitative — provide a guide to ethical-creative living.

Arthur Russell's music has had to be durable in order to be heard, because his life ended in near silence — perhaps the most terrifying way a musician can die. Apart from a couple of twelve-inch dance singles, which could only be tracked down in specialist stores, the traces of his music were barely discernible at that time. Most of it lay in reel-to-reel format, stacked high on one of the walls of his old East Village apartment, where its latent potential weighed heavily. Preferring to create a whirlpool of recordings as he clung to the commissions of Philip Glass and Geoff Travis, Russell hadn't released a record since "Let's Go Swimming" came out in 1987, and a listener could only guess if any of the tapes were finished to his satisfaction. Those who knew him might have calculated that the answer was likely to be negative. Yet far from becoming a tragic epitaph to indecision, those tapes acquired the mystique of a complex and valuable archive just as the ageing process threatened to destroy their fragile magnetic form. "The fact is, wherever Arthur and organization coincided they clashed, and yet the artifacts we have were the result of those coincidences," says Donald Murk. "They are, meager as they may be, our only chance to be able to reconstruct the feelings, the teachings, of the maestro."

The first to make a move toward excavation, Glass approached Tom Lee about putting out a record right after Russell died, after which he enlisted the composer Mikel Rouse to catalogue his old friend's digital audio tapes, cassettes, reels, and masters. Having listened to a selection of the most promising material, Glass calculated "there were at least three good records if not more that could be made out of the stuff that we found," and he released *Another Thought* on his new label, Point Music, in 1994. The album showcased fresh voice-cello recordings, as well as the unreleased "In the Light of the Miracle" and a couple of songs from Russell's Rough Trade project. "Russell sang about kisses, miracles and eternity in a supple, dreamy voice, similar to John Martyn's, while his cello, plucked and bowed, provided propulsion and countermelody," wrote Jon Pareles in the *New York Times*, while *Rolling Stone* commented on the "confessional force and spatial beauty of his songs" before noting "potent echoes of Nick Drake and the chamber-art songs of John Cale and Laurie Anderson."[11] Those closer to Russell expressed reservations: Peter Gordon regarded the album as "a portrait of a tamed Arthur," while Peter Zummo found the collection to be "somewhat dissatisfying" and regretted the absence of his friend's surreal editing technique, as did Lee. Although a number of the recordings were drawn from the period before Russell knew he was sick, the specter of AIDS hung over the album, which ended with the song "A Sudden Chill."

Russell's early recordings with Ginsberg also became available when Rhino Records released *Holy Soul Jelly Roll* in 1994. "Immortality comes later," Ginsberg noted of his neighbor's contribution to the forthcoming album at Russell's Experimental Intermedia Foundation memorial event—but interest was already shifting to Russell's dance material. Twelve-inch singles such as "Is It All Over My Face?" and "Go Bang! #5" were played at the commemorative birthday parties staged for Larry Levan (who died in 1992) along with other nostalgic "classics" nights. Then, in 2000, Russell's dance influence was formally recognized when the London-based Strut

Records released *Disco Not Disco*, a collection of "leftfield dance classics from the New York underground" that featured Loose Joints' "Tell You (Today)," Dinosaur's "Kiss Me Again," and Indian Ocean's "School Bell / Treehouse," as well as "Let's Go Swimming" on the follow-up album, *Disco Not Disco 2* (2001). Taken together, the compilations suggested that Russell was the most prolific artist-producer of the least-recognized era in dance (and did so without including "Go Bang! #5" and "Is It All Over My Face?"). Lee was glad of this attention, yet wondered about the recordings that were barely known. "The dance music did not present a full picture of what Arthur was about, and it was a little frustrating to think that that was all people knew," he explains. "Arthur put his heart into his songs with equal vigor. The passion was equal, but it seemed like the public picked up on just the one side of him."

As Rough Trade stalled on its option of releasing an album of Russell's electronic pop recordings, his songs circulated in only the most private settings. "Joyce [Bowden] took me to meet Joey Ramone in his East Village luxury apartment a couple of years before he died," remembers Steven Hall. "At some point Joyce prompted me to sing, so I played guitar and sang a slow version of the first song that Arthur ever sang to me — 'Don't Forget about Me.' Joey listened with his eyes closed and kept them closed for a minute after I finished. Then he said, 'That song is a prayer.'" But how was anyone else supposed to listen in? "Steven and I were left with these unfinished projects with Arthur and the incredible weight of Arthur's talent," recalls Ernie Brooks. "He produced works of genius with ease and we both labored under his influence and his legacy, wondering how we were supposed to further it. Somewhere inside, both of us wanted to be in a band where we could play Arthur's music for the rest of our lives."

Russell's fragmented legacy continued to drift toward a fade-out until two posthumous compilation albums were released in quick succession at the beginning of 2004. David Hill, a London-based DJ and record collector who had started to negotiate the quagmire of Russell's musical archive in 1994, produced the first of these releases, having been turned on to Russell in the early 1990s. "I was introduced to the left-of-center disco, and then I got to hear his wonderful, stripped down avant-garde music that appeared on *World of Echo* and *Another Thought*," he explains. "The acoustic music grew to outshine the dance tracks." When he calculated the cost of treating the time-worn tapes, however, Hill began to question the viability of releasing Russell's music and became convinced that the songs would only sell if they were accompanied by Russell's better-known dance releases. "Even though I believed in and loved the music," comments Hill, "it didn't make commercial sense." He realized his vision as the executive producer of *The World of Arthur Russell*, which was released on Soul Jazz and interspersed Russell's most influential dance recordings with a couple of acoustic tracks. "We thought that the album would work well on its own, but would also warm up the market for Arthur's leftfield releases," he notes.

Compiled by Steve Knutson and Tom Lee, *Calling out of Context* appeared a couple of months later as the debut album on Knutson's new label, Audika. Knutson had been introduced to Russell's music while he was working for Tommy Boy Records, during which time he would speak regularly with Walter Gibbons, who was working behind the counter at Rock and Soul. "Walter played me 'School Bell / Treehouse' and I loved it," recalls Knutson. "I will forever be thankful to Walter for the introduction." Having parted company with Tommy Boy in April 2002, Knutson met Lee in September and remembers being "blown away" by the amount of unreleased material that lay in the archive. When Lee put on *Corn*, Knutson declared he "wanted to hear everything else from that period." Given that previous requests had come to little, Lee had every reason to be wary, but he warmed to Knutson, who "was one of the first people who didn't seem to think that the release of Arthur's music had to begin with the music people already knew." Knutson proceeded to set up Audika and compile an album that drew on *Corn* as well as the recordings Arthur made for Geoff Travis. "To me, the music remains fresh, new, and groundbreaking, even though it was written and recorded as long as twenty years ago," he says. "Arthur was on a path and who knows where that path would have led? The songs he wrote before he died were simple but very moving, very beautiful. As a musician and writer he got better as he got older."

Knutson had already been working on *Calling out of Context* for a year when news of Hill's *The World of Arthur Russell* album reached him. "It was serendipitous," says the Audika boss. "The timing could not have been better. So we agreed to release the projects around the same time and help each other." Knutson proceeded to contact David Toop (whom he knew from his time at Tommy Boy) and informed the musician and writer that a Russell story was taking shape; following a ten-year silence, two posthumous compilations were about to be released back-to-back. Published in the *Wire* in January 2004, Toop's ensuing feature caused a stir, and both the *New York Times* and the *New Yorker* followed with pieces on a musician who had been out of the news—with an archive of recordings hovering on the cusp of oxidization—since 1994. "Arthur's family and I were quite amazed," recalls Lee. "One article after another started appearing, and for the most part they were all very affirming and flattering. We were thrilled! Having Steve at the helm and so passionate about Arthur's music was critical to his exposure."

Since then the record releases have continued to flow. Audika has been the most prolific by far, reissuing *World of Echo* (along with Phill Niblock's previously unpublished films of Russell playing two songs); a compilation of Russell's orchestral compositions (*First Thought Best Thought*); further material from Russell's 1980s electronic pop repertoire (*Springfield*); and an album of folk and pop songs (*Love Is Overtaking Me*). Meanwhile Glass re-issued *Another Thought* on Orange Mountain Music, the Kitchen included a live performance of Russell performing *World of Echo* material on its "From the Kitchen Archives" series, and the Traffic Entertainment Group re-issued 24 —> 24 *Music* (and included three additional remixes). As Knutson works his way through the reels and reels of unreleased twenty-four-track tape bequeathed to Lee, and as the estate of Arthur Russell acquires the rights to previously published material, more releases will follow. "The most amazing thing of all is that a huge iceberg of still-unreleased music lurks under the receding, placid waters of Russell's anonymity," commented Jess Harvell in his review of *First Thought Best Thought* for *Pitchfork*. "Give Steve Knutson a knighthood or something already."[12]

A number of Russell's most influential collaborators have also worked to keep his legacy alive. Comprising Mustafa Ahmed, Ernie Brooks, Steven Hall, Elodie Lauten, and Peter Zummo, as well as guests such as Joyce Bowden, Bill Ruyle, and John Scherman, Arthur's Landing made its debut performance at the beginning of 2006 and promised (in the words of Hall) to "celebrate our fresh memories of the groovy genius of Arthur Russell and delight in performing his miracles (songs) throughout improvised states of Amerika resulting in world peace and joy." Other tribute projects, too numerous to detail here, have been outnumbered by precious recollections. "Sometimes I think of standing in front of a microphone in full absorption with Arthur's music, and I think of him encouraging me to dive in head first, as into a deep, dark pond, to trust the depth of the ripples all around me, and to then emerge back up the way I went down," says Bowden. "I did this knowing not where I'd been, but knowing that I had experienced a kind of reversal of my normal self. He insisted that I should never lose my sense of wonder at the unformulated question, the one to which there is no answer."

Contributing to Russell's increasing profile, DFA, Mimi Goese, Gary Lucas, the Memory Band, Polmo Polpo, and Tracey Thorn have covered his music, while Vera November, Jens Lekman, Taken By Trees, and Joel Gibb released *Four Songs by Arthur Russell* (2007), which included covers of "Our Last Night Together," "A Little Lost," "Make 1, 2," and "That's Us / Wild Combination." These and other musicians have been joined by a growing band of listeners who enjoy Russell's funky, unorthodox music, and want to be taken somewhere unexpected—because the task of piecing together the dispersed clues of his life has been enthralling, and because the recordings that have been released from those dusty tape archives still sound remarkably vibrant. "I often felt he overworked his music," says Eric Liljestrand. "But when I put on *Calling out of Context*, it didn't sound overworked or labored. It sounded very fresh and improvised. I only felt it was overworked because I knew how much work we had done."

Arthur Russell's resilience and modishness cannot mask the way in which it has become horribly difficult for performers to try and establish a foothold in downtown New York. As rising property prices drove out poorer artists, SoHo's ex-industrial infrastructure was converted into a chichi shopping oasis, and in a parallel movement, public spending cuts curtailed the activities of experimental music and art spaces, many of which started to introduce more conservative (and financially lucrative) programs in order to cover escalating costs. By 1987 Glass felt compelled to wonder in public about the potential for artists to live and work in New York, and his concerns might have deepened when Mayor Rudolph Giuliani's 1993 and 1997 administrations launched a sequence of punitive clean-up measures that gentrified the city at the expense of the under-regulated fissures where artists could flourish.[13] As the AIDS virus conducted its own sweep through downtown's gay male population and its drug-injecting peers, many record companies became more interested in reviving established artists and recycling familiar sounds than searching for new unorthodox talent. Though downtown may remain a favorite haunt for creative workers, further increases in the cost of living there mean that opportunities have become more restricted than at any point since manufacturers began to move out during the 1960s.

Considered in this context, it would be reasonable to assume that the recent surge of interest in Russell is guided by nostalgia. Many of his newer followers didn't live in lower Manhattan during the 1970s and early 1980s, but they can experience the period vicariously by listening to his music. The publication of a number of books that chart the twists and turns of downtowners and their sounds cannot help but bolster the impression that the creative flux of the so-called downtown era will never be repeated. In a parallel development, the broad shift in music culture from the material to the immaterial—whereby the tactile format of vinyl has been displaced by the progressively sterile alternatives of the CD and the MP3—might encourage listeners to dream of the visceral, communal prerogatives of the 1970s and early 1980s as they listen to the latest digitized reissue from the period. The advent of digitization also means that the music is easier to obtain—and dream about—than at any point since its original release.

At the same time, Russell's newer fans might understand that their hero didn't find acceptance during his lifetime, or at least nothing like the kind of acceptance that makes him such a relevant figure more than twenty years after his death. And although the recent chronicling of downtown disco has enabled a more developed appreciation of Russell's work, it's easy to work out that a return to the past is neither possible nor straightforwardly desirable.[14] "*It's senile.* And it wasn't all *that*," the downtown graffiti and conceptual artist Jeff Harrington wrote in a recent message-board thread on the history of downtown. "I think today's more chaotic, less holy, more eclectic and poorer scene is a lot more interesting."[15] Because Russell explored folk, pop, and disco idioms as well as the self-consciously serious forms of new music and new wave, his work, like Harrington's present, sounds more chaotic, less holy, and more eclectic than the sounds that have come to characterize the downtown era. And because Russell's recordings don't display the taut aggression and palpable anxiety that have become synonymous with downtown, they're less trapped in time. For these reasons, the act of listening to Russell indicates not an act of nostalgia but a commitment to an atemporal music culture that confounds chronology.

The spread of digital recording equipment, which accelerated during the 1990s, prepared the way for Russell's revival. Embarking on click-of-a-button tourist trips of musical genres that explored the lowest common denominator of sound, artists and producers used digital technology to release multigenre remixes that could help them renew jaded careers or reach out to a widening range of niche markets, and the results were often slick, predictable, and soulless. Yet as the crossover strategy became commonplace, it became easier to identify with Russell's priorities, even if the music industry had moved in this direction for profit-oriented motives. "In Arthur's case, his experiments in mixed music were decidedly not made for marketplace strategies; they represent an entirely spontaneous reaction to the music of his time," Glass wrote in LIFEbeat in 1994. "As a result, there is always a 'sureness' to his music and a total sense of authenticity. And it's important to remember that these were ventures into the unknown at that time."[16]

By the beginning of the new millennium, listeners had become more willing to travel beyond generic affiliations, and spurred on by the spread of burning, downloading, and file-sharing, they took to describing their taste in music as being "eclectic"—which meant they were ready for Russell. While the flat, impersonal, and precise quality of digital technology's os and 1s cannot be reconciled easily with Russell's idiosyncratic warmth, it remains the case that digital music culture has contributed to the possibility of his newfound popularity. The physical limitations of the traditional shop floor required retailers to sell from a limited catalogue of heavily marketed recordings, but online stores can maintain a much wider stock, and this has enabled consumers to spread their purchases across a long tail of formerly unavailable artists, including those previously consigned to the vaults of recording history. Relaunched within a markedly more pluralistic milieu that has encouraged new forms of musical fusion to proliferate, Russell's cross-generic and intergeneric archive sounds uncannily modern.

But if the shift to a pluralistic music culture lies close to the heart of Russell's revitalized profile, does it follow that his work has come to signal "a form of tolerance that does not threaten the status quo," as Hal Foster wrote in his trenchant critique of pluralism in 1985?[17] Analyzing the art world, Foster notes that "no style or even mode of art is dominant and no critical position is orthodox," and he maintains that this pluralist condition renders art impotent, allowing for "minor deviation" simply "in order to resist radical change." That is because the pluralist condition grants "a kind of equivalence" in which "art of many sorts is made to seem more or less equal—equally (un)important." He continues, "Posed as a freedom to choose, the pluralist position plays right into the ideology of the 'free market.'" Because pluralism lacks its own values, old values such as "the unique, the visionary, the genius, the masterpiece" are revived in their place, while "the critical is often evacuated by the merely risqué." As a result, pluralism leads "not to a sharpened awareness of difference (social, sexual, artistic, etc.) but to a stagnant condition of indiscrimination."[18]

Foster's analysis resonates with the present, in which listeners often jam their iPods with more music than they could ever hope to listen to, and import the material at a low-quality bit-rate that suggests that manic accumulation is more highly valued than careful listening, but it doesn't follow that Russell amounts to a "minor deviation" just because he has flourished in the same milieu. If Russell had lived long enough to swap his Walkman for an iPod, he would have surely used the technology to continue to listen both widely *and* deeply, and while Foster's "pluralist bazaar" resonates with Russell's dislike of hierarchy and penchant for hybridity, Russell was a mercilessly discriminating musician, even if he recognized that no single musical style could account for the populations of downtown New York in the post-countercultural moment.[19] Nor was there anything fleeting or careless about Russell's engagements; developing a progressive aesthetic that cut across the dominant articulations of race, sexuality, gender, and class, he encouraged a range of musical communities to forge sonic and social links with each other. And although he always kept an eye on the popular market, he also refused to submit his creative and collaborative impulses to its prerogatives. A walking headache for record-label bosses who wanted to rein in his resolutely rhizomatic outlook, Russell was no minor deviation.

Given the opportunity to survey his newfound popularity, Russell might have rallied against the way in which the easiest part of his ethos—the ethos of pluralistic openness—has been embraced. The digital is admittedly young, but for now it appears to be the case that consumers have yet to recognize the distinction between, on the one hand, a seductive pluralism that celebrates breadth for its own sake, and on the other, a historically grounded form of listening that interacts critically with the relationship between musical practice and the social. In other words, iPod culture appears to be contributing to a form of the ahistorical, decontextualized consumption described by Foster, in which listeners do not use music to reflect on their place in the world, yet are all too ready to celebrate artists as unique and visionary geniuses. Russell rarely doubted his own ability, but had absolutely no time for such talk. Seeking little more than the opportunity to surround himself in sound, he also brought the affective experience of music to bear on his everyday relations with friends, collaborators, communities, and record companies. He was ready for "radical change."

Temporal forces are nevertheless converging in unexpected ways. Russell's music might satisfy contemporary audiences because his analog struggle counters the disposable ease of the digital age, yet the complexity of the present has also helped prepare listeners for his fragmented sensibility. Once apparently impossible to translate beyond the limited confines of downtown New York during the 1970s and 1980s, Russell's music is becoming easier to comprehend in the contemporary era of not just pluralism but also mutation, hybridity, and uncertainty. If the soothing simplicity and implied spirituality of Norah Jones's *Come Away with Me* became a timely soundtrack for many U.S. citizens in the aftermath of 9/11, *Another Thought, Calling out of Context, First Thought Best Thought, Love Is Overtaking Me, Springfield, 24 —> 24 Music, The World of Arthur Russell,* and *World of Echo* offer all of those qualities along with restlessness, difficulty, and edginess. Russell won't have appealed to listeners who wanted to stick with the reassuring sound of musical chloroform, or those who rejected Jones in favor of a pumped-up sound that put them in the mood for a xenophobic war. But for those who hoped—and continue to hope—to come to terms with the intricacy and precariousness of the present, Russell's catalogue resembles a prescient time capsule from a bygone era. "Arthur was objective and pretty much right," says Zummo. "He was a visionary and if you followed his plan you would have been further into the future than you were by just doing your work. I just wonder what would have happened if he was still around while the rest of us matured more."

Although it has been gentrified beyond recognition, downtown continues to offer the promise of creativity, community, and dissent, with pioneering outposts such as the Experimental Intermedia Foundation, the Kitchen, and the Loft (to name three venues that Russell visited regularly) still committed to forging an alternative aesthetic and social milieu. Furthermore, an examination of the scope of downtown should not be restricted to New York, because downtowns are emerging all over the world. By the end of 2007 one in two of the world's population was living in a city, and it would require an act of extreme Westernism to assume that

New York, London, and the promising terrain of Berlin are the only urban centers that matter.[20] While the economic and social circumstances that resulted in the downtown era cannot be re-established in New York or copied step for step in other parts of the world, downtown communities will continue to develop as locations where artists converge, exchange ideas, and perform, if only because the global economy is so reliant on creative ideas and cultural production. As the Internet continues to generate a decentralized economy in which entertainment corporations hemorrhage money, it's possible to imagine the music sector reverting to an artisan-style milieu in which performers survive by playing live and selling their work across a range of interconnected local networks.

In this scenario, the star system that has dominated the strategic thinking of the music industry for so long will be difficult to sustain, and the original ethos of downtown — the creative, nonmaterialistic, communitarian ethos forged by Arthur Russell, his friends, and the friends of those friends — can thrive on an international scale. If the recent surge of interest in lower Manhattan's cultural ferment of the 1970s and 1980s is anything to go by, the downtown era might already be sustaining and inspiring new groups of artists. Their work is likely to benefit if they engage with the downtown era not as a fixed moment trapped in time but rather as a model of creative engagement that prioritizes collaboration and interdisciplinarity. Along the way, some might ponder the relevance of an awkward, acne-scarred cellist who hailed from Oskaloosa. That reflection would be welcome, because this book's focus on Arthur Russell is not supposed to describe a past life, but rather offer a present understanding of a past life that continues to cut across time.

While it is tempting to imagine Russell being satisfied with his belated acceptance — with the way his life is cutting across time with increasing vitality — he is likely to have wondered about the substance of the applause. "When it came to music, if you liked something he would change it because it was too easy," noted Kent Goshorn at the Experimental Intermedia memorial event. "If you didn't like it he would harass you on the phone for days trying to find out exactly what you didn't like."[21] Yet although he rarely relaxed his critical guard, Russell did want his music to have an effect, and having barely existed at the margins of U.S. culture, he can now be seen reverberating at its center — the awkward kid from the Corn Belt who crossed the country to become a low-key, high-energy figure in one of the most prolific periods in New York's music history. That means he hadn't done "it all wrong," as he feared at the end of his life, but had in fact done quite a bit right, as he dreamed for so long. "Arthur was convinced that he would reach a wider audience eventually," says Steven Hall. "He used to joke that everything he did would be recognized a decade later." Give or take a year or two, that forecast has turned out to be accurate.

Notes

Preface

1 Frank Owen, "Sleeping Around," *Melody Maker*, 27 September 1986, 11, and "Echo Beach," *Melody Maker*, 11 April 1987, 36–37; David Toop, "The Weird One," *Face*, January 1987, 27; Peter Zummo, "Eclectic Bubble Gum," *SoHo Weekly News*, 17 March 1977, 39; Gary Lucas, "Arthur Russell: An Appreciation," *Alternative Press*, November 1994, 16; Ned Sublette, "Arthur Russell 1951–92," *Reflex*, no. 26, April 1992; and Toop, "Past Futurist," *Wire*, April 1995, 20.

2 DeLanda, *A New Philosophy of Society*, 4–5.

Introduction

1 David Toop et al., "The State of Song," *Wire*, May 2004.

2 Quoted in Frank Owen, "Sleeping Around," *Melody Maker*, 27 September 1986, 11.

3 Sasha Frere-Jones, "Let's Go Swimming," *New Yorker*, 8 March 2004, 80–81.

4 Quoted in Thomas R. O'Donnell, "Death Can't Muffle Musician," *Des Moines Register*, 9 April 1995.

5 Baker, ed., *New York Noise*.

6 Arthur Russell isn't referenced in the original UK edition of *Rip It Up and Start Again*, in which Simon Reynolds develops the mutant disco chapter as an oral history. Reynolds rewrote the chapter for the much shorter U.S. edition, and Russell is included in that version.

7 Kyle Gann, "Square Rhythms," *Village Voice*, 28 April 1992, 94.

8 Gendron, *Between Montmartre and the Mudd Club*, 291–92. Gendron also contributed the chapter on music, "The Downtown Music Scene," to Taylor, ed., *The Downtown Book*.

9 Ben Ratliff, "The Many Faces, and Grooves, of Arthur Russell," *New York Times*, 29 February 2004.

10 McCormick, "A Crack In Time," 67.

1 **Formations** (1951–1973)

1 Chafe, *The Unfinished Journey*, 111.

2 Broyles, *Mavericks and Other Traditions in American Music*, 3, 6.

3 Quoted in Thomas R. O'Donnell, "Death Can't Muffle Musician," *Des Moines Register*, 9 April 1995.

4 From Kent Goshorn's speech at the private memorial event held for Arthur Russell at the Experimental Intermedia Foundation on 12 April 1992.

5 Lavezzoli, *The Dawn of Indian Music in the West*, 6–8. Alternatively, the explosion of interest in Indian music could be dated to 1965, when the Beatles released *Rubber Soul*, which included sitar instrumentation on the track "Norwegian Wood."

6 Ibid., 66.

7 Quoted in Whittier, *Good Is Never Lost*, 287.

8 Russell quoted in Toop, *Ocean of Sound*, 119–20.

9 Adorno, *Philosophy of New Music*, 101–2.

10 Potter, *Four Musical Minimalists*, 17.

11 Quoted in Schwarz, *Minimalists*, 114.

12 Jones, foreword to Glass, *Opera on the Beach*, xiii.

13 Potter, *Four Musical Minimalists*, 43.

14 At that time, notes William Duckworth, "no one could remember the last experimental composer who had used a key signature, much less written anything in C major." Duckworth, *Talking Music*, 268.

15 Nyman, *Experimental Music*, 139–71. Nyman wrote *Experimental Music* between 1970 and 1972, and the book was published in 1974.

16 Mertens, *American Minimal Music*, 121.

17 Ibid., 122, 124.

18 Allen Ginsberg, *Howl and Other Poems* (Fantasy Records, 1959); *Allen Ginsberg Reads Kaddish: A Twentieth-century American Ecstatic Narrative Poem* (Atlantic, 1966); and *William Blake's Songs of Innocence and Experience* (Verve/Forecast, 1970).

19 Allen Ginsberg, comments made at the private memorial event for Arthur Russell staged at the Experimental Intermedia Foundation, 12 April 1992.

20 Quoted in the sleeve notes to Allen Ginsberg, *Holy Soul Jelly Roll: Poems and Songs 1949–1993* (Rhino, 1994).

21 In the sleeve notes to Ginsberg's *Holy Soul Jelly Roll*, Ajari Warwick and the Kailas Shugendo Mantric Sun Band are referred to as Reverend Adjari and Buddhist Chorus.

22 Ibid.

23 Quoted in Jake Austen, "Sylvester," *Roctober*, summer 1997, http://www.roctober .com/roctober/greatness/sylvester.html. Retrieved on 9 August 2004.

24 A flyer from Arthur Russell's concert at the Kitchen on 19 March 1984 states that he started to play amplified cello in 1972. A copy of this flyer is in the author's personal collection.

25 The darbukka is an Egyptian tabla and is also known as a *doumbek*.

26 KPFA broadcast recording, 16–17 March 1973, accessed through Audika.

27 Hobsbawm, *Age of Extremes*, 323–43, 403–16.

2 **Explorations** (1973–1975)

1 Cannato, *The Ungovernable City*, 447.

2 Ibid., 447, 549; Schulman, *The Seventies*, 106.

3 Quoted in Taylor, "Playing the Field," 19.

4 Quoted in Mahler, *Ladies and Gentlemen, the Bronx Is Burning*, 8.

5 Cannato, *The Ungovernable City*, xi.

6 Quoted in William Zimmer, "Still Funky but Oh So Chic SoHo," *Art News*, November 1980, 90.

7 Dorothy Seiberling, "The Most Exciting Place to Live in the City," *New York*, 20 May 1974, 52.

8 Richard Kostelanetz uses this phrase in the subtitle of his book, *SoHo: The Rise and Fall of an Artists' Colony*.

9 Taylor, "Playing the Field," 31.

10 McCormick, "A Crack In Time," 69.

11 Gann, *Music Downtown*, 4; Kostelanetz, *SoHo*, 56.

12 Tom Johnson, "Phill Niblock on Fourth Street," *Village Voice*, 8 March 1973; re-printed in *The Voice of New Music*, n.p.

13 Peter Gordon, comment posted on the Sequenza 21/ Web site, www.sequenza21 .com, 17 February 2006. Retrieved from http://www.haloscan.com/comments/ jbowles/113950581534970678/ on 7 August 2006.

14 Taylor, "Playing the Field," 31.

15 Vincent Canby, "New York's Woes Are Good Box Office," *New York Times*, 10 November 1974; quoted in Shapiro, *Turn the Beat Around*, x.

16 Quoted in Frank Owen, "Echo Beach," *Melody Maker*, 11 April 1987, 36–37.

17 Inviting several other musicians to join him in the studio, including John Bergamo on the tablas, Arthur Russell recorded a version of "Goodbye Old Paint" in May 1973. The recording appears on the album *Love Is Overtaking Me* (2008) and is almost certainly the version Russell handed to David Van Tieghem.

18 Postcard, Allen Ginsberg to Arthur Russell, 15 September 1973. The postcard is held by Tom Lee in his private archive. A photocopy is on file with the author.

19 Rhys Chatham, "Composer's Notebook: 1990 Toward a Musical Agenda for the Nineties," published as the sleeve notes to his album *Angel Moves too Fast to See: Selected Works, 1971–89* (Table of Elements, 2003).

20 Tom Johnson, "Rhys Chatham: One-Note Music," *Village Voice*, 17 August 1972; reprinted in *The Voice of New Music*, n.p.

21 Details of the incident can be found in Murray Schumach, "Broadway Central Hotel Collapses," *New York Times*, 4 August 1973.

22 For a report of the concert, see Tom Johnson, "Christian Wolff: Exercises and Songs," *Village Voice*, 6 June 1974; reprinted in *The Voice of New Music*, n.p.

23 For a report of the concert, see Tom Johnson, "Richard Landry," *Village Voice*, 14 November 1974; reprinted in *The Voice of New Music*, n.p.

24 Information on the event comes from Stearns, ed., *The Kitchen, 1974–1975*, 17.

25 A video of the performance appears in Matt Wolf's documentary film *Wild Combination* (Plexi, 2008). Recorded shortly before the "Soup and Tart" performance, a studio version of the song appears on *Love Is Overtaking Me*.

26 Peter Zummo, "Eclectic Bubble Gum," *SoHo Weekly News*, 17 March 1977, 39.

27 McCandlish Phillips, "Mercer Stages Are a Supermarket," *New York Times*, 2 November 1971.

28 Arthur Russell's linguistics class is noted in Owen, "Echo Beach."

29 "I Forget and I Can't Tell" appears on *Love Is Overtaking Me*. The sleeve notes for the album cite John Hammond as having produced the song at CBS in 1975, but the presence of Jerry Harrison on the track suggests that Paul Nelson was the producer, because Harrison didn't appear in the Hammond session. The other songs have not been released.

30 Peter Gordon, "Public Music," *Ear*, 1 April 1975, n.p.

31 Broyles, *Mavericks and Other Traditions*, 232, 235.

32 The references to Soft Machine through to Eno are drawn from Potter, *Four Musical Minimalists*, 91, 149, 249, 340.

33 Gendron, "The Downtown Music Scene," 47.

34 Jerry Leichtling, "Modern Lovers: Did You Come?," *Village Voice*, 31 March 1975. Leichtling mentioned the Kitchen setting only in passing.

35 Gordon, "Public Music," n.p.

36 Muriel Fujii remembers Arthur Russell talking about John Hammond while they were living on the West Coast.

37 While the sleeve notes to *Love Is Overtaking Me* cite 22 October 1974 as the recording date of Russell's recording session with John Hammond, Russell described the session in a letter to Muriel Fujii that is postmarked 8 August 1974. *Love Is Overtaking Me* contains three songs from the Hammond session: "Close My Eyes," "Maybe She," and "Eli."

38 Dunstan Prial's biography of John Hammond, *The Producer*, contains very little information on the A&R executive's post-Springsteen career at Columbia. Arthur Russell isn't cited in the book.

39 Two songs from the March 1975 recording session—"Nobody Wants a Lonely Heart" and "I Couldn't Say It to Your Face"—appear on *Love Is Overtaking Me*.

40 Peter Frank, "Performances and/or Publications," *SoHo Weekly News*, 30 January 1975, 14, 32.

41 Arthur Russell, untitled and undated notes on *Instrumentals*. A photocopy is on file with the author.

42 Jon Gibson and Garrett List made these comments in a set of notes that were probably compiled by Russell in preparation for a grant application. They are held by Tom Lee in his private archive. A photocopy is on file with the author.

43 Ernie Brooks tells the story of this struggle in his contribution to the sleeve notes for Arthur Russell, *First Thought Best Thought* (2006). Several extracts from the performance can be heard on *First Thought Best Thought*.

44 David Toop, "Past Futurist," *Wire*, April 1995, 20.

45 McCormick, "A Crack In Time," 70.

46 Quoted in "La Monte Young and Marian Zazeela at the Dream House," transcribed by Frank J. Oteri, Randy Nordschow, Amanda MacBlane, and Rob Wilkerson, *New Music Box*, 1 October 2003, http://www.newmusicbox.org, retrieved 24 January 2007.

47 Hiller, introduction to Reich, *Writings on Music, 1965–2000*, 4.

48 "Minimalism was a historic reaction to a sort of music which had a stranglehold on American musical institutions, and which none of us really liked," the composer David Lang told Keith Potter. "What most people really hated was the way that this other world had theorised that it was the only music possible. I look at minimalism . . . as being just the battleground that was necessary to remove those forces from power." Potter, *Four Musical Minimalists*, 20.

49 Piekut, "Taking Henry Flynt Seriously."

50 *Love Is Overtaking Me* includes three songs — "Hey! How Does Everybody Know," "This Time Dad You're Wrong," and "Time Away" — that were recorded by Ernie Brooks and Arthur Russell (along with, variously, Andy Paley, Jonathan Paley, David Van Tieghem, Steve Warren, and Darrius Thabit) at the Kitchen, in all likelihood on the Teac tape recorder, in 1974 and 1975.

3 **Alternatives** (1975–1977)

1 Christopher Mele describes the urban disinvestment that besieged the East Side from the early 1970s onwards. Mele, *Selling the Lower East Side*, 188–200. Also see Freeman, *Working-Class New York*, 107.

2 The Nuyorican Poets Café opened in the East Village apartment of the poet Miguel Algarín around 1973, with the New Rican Village, which was situated on Avenue A between Sixth and Seventh Streets, following in 1976. The New Rican Village music program provided an alternative outlet for Puerto Rican performers such as Mario Rivera and the Salsa Refugees, Brenda Feliciano, and Conjunto Libre. For more on the New Rican Village, see Roseman, "The New Rican Village." Roseman notes that Conjunto Libre "could not get work in the mainstream commercial network of Latin music in New York City" (140).

3 David Toop, "The Flying Heart," *Wire*, January 2004, 34.

4 Gilles Deleuze and Félix Guattari develop the rhizome as a materialist metaphor in *A Thousand Plateaus*.

5 Quoted in Potter, *Four Musical Minimalists*, 261–62.

6 Suggesting a philosophy and practice composed of tangential alliances, Deleuze and Guattari note, "the fabric of the rhizome is the conjunction 'and . . . and . . . and . . .'" Deleuze and Guattari, *A Thousand Plateaus*, 25.

7 Toop, "The Flying Heart," 34.

8 Peter Gordon references his performance of "Atonal Variations" in a comment posted on the Sequenza 21/ Web site, www.sequenza21.com, 17 February 2006. Retrieved from http://www.haloscan.com/comments/jbowles/113950581534970678/ on 7 August 2006.

9 Frank Owen, "Echo Beach," *Melody Maker*, 11 April 1987, 36.

10 Allen Ginsberg told the story to several people, including Jim Merlis, a DGC/ Geffen publicist who was friendly with Arthur Russell, and also to Thomas R. O'Donnell, a journalist for the *Des Moines Register*, who responded by saying it amounted to "way more information" than he wanted to know. O'Donnell, "Death Can't Muffle Musician," *Des Moines Register*, 9 April 1995. Russell confirmed Ginsberg's version of events with a close acquaintance (who wishes to remain anonymous).

11 Quoted in Erik Davis, "DeLanda Destratified," *Mondo 2000*, winter 1992. Retrieved from http://www.techgnosis.com/delandad.html on 21 June 2007.

12 Garrett List, "The Development of the New Eclecticism in Music," unpublished version of List, "Twenty Years Is a Long Time," c. 1991. A photocopy is on file with the author.

13 Stanley Crouch, "Jazz Lofts: A Walk through the Wild Sounds," *New York Times*, 17 April 1977.

14 Ibid.

15 Gary Giddins, "Weather Bird: Goings On about Town," *Village Voice*, 29 August 1977, 76.

16 Lewis, *A Power Stronger than Itself*, 351.

17 Ibid.

18 List, "Twenty Years Is a Long Time," 24.

19 The Experimental Intermedia Foundation concerts took place on 7 and 19 May 1975. The first performance, which featured Beth Anderson (another graduate from Mills College) and Dan Salmon, appears on *First Thought Best Thought* (2006). At the second concert, the piece was retitled "Music with Two Fender Rhodes Electric Pianos."

20 See, for example, Erika Munk, "Falling, But into the Month of May," *Village Voice*, 19 April 1976, 113, 115.

21 Taylor, "Playing the Field," 31.

22 Rockwell, *All American Music*, 237–38.

23 Frith and Horne, *Art into Pop*, 113, 112–13.

24 A photo of the Fast Food Band taken by Bob Bielecki appears in Goldberg, *Laurie Anderson*, 18.

25 Quotes are taken from Kurt B. Reighley's interview with Laurie Anderson, original transcript, February 2002. A digital copy is on file with the author.

26 Quoted in Stearns, ed., *The Kitchen, 1975–1976*, 40.

27 Quoted in Hagger, *Art after Midnight*, 13.

28 Quoted in Owen, "Echo Beach," 36–37.

29 Quoted in Sylvie Simmons, "Ten Questions for David Byrne," *Mojo*, May 2004, 42.

30 The version containing Russell's cello was eventually released on the reissue of the album in 2006.

31 Quoted in Simmons, "Ten Questions for David Byrne," 42.

32 Quoted in Miles, "Flying Hearts," *New Musical Express*, 2 April 1977, 48.

33 Ibid, 48.

34 Gendron, *Between Montmartre and the Mudd Club*, 272.

35 "Anthems of the Blank Generation," *Time*, 11 July 1977, 48–49.

36 The recording of "What It's Like" appears on the album *Love Is Overtaking Me* (2008).

37 *Chromatic* is the musical term for the half-steps, or accidentals, that come into play when a musician goes outside the key of tune.

38 Peter Zummo, "Eclectic Bubble Gum," *SoHo Weekly News*, 17 March 1977, 39.

39 Ibid.

40 Robert Palmer, "Pop Music: Modern Meets Rock," *New York Times*, 6 May 1977.

41 Ibid.

42 A section of the concert can be heard on track eleven of *First Thought Best Thought*.

43 From Bill Ruyle's speech at the private memorial event held for Arthur Russell at the Experimental Intermedia Foundation on 12 April 1992.

44 Rhys Chatham, "Composer's Notebook: 1990 Toward a Musical Agenda for the Nineties," published as the sleeve notes to his album *Angel Moves too Fast to See: Selected Works, 1971–89* (Table of Elements, 2003).

45 Ibid.

46 Ibid.

47 The name "Fernanda" and not "Fernando" appears on an undated handwritten transcription of the song, but both Ernie Brooks and Steven Hall remember being taught to sing "Fernando" and assumed at the time that "Fernando" was an Italian man Russell had met in Italy. It's possible that Russell taught two different versions of the song, or that the sex of Fernanda/Fernando changed over time. Tony Pagliuca wonders if "Fernando" was a substitute for Le Orme. "Oh Fernando, *perche*?" he says. "Why didn't it work out?" The catalogue of Russell's tapes compiled by Point Music in July 1992 uses "Fernando."

4 **Intensities** (1977–1980)

1 The first English-language account of disco's French roots can be found in Albert Goldman's *Disco*. My own book *Love Saves the Day* provides a detailed historical analysis of the development of U.S. dance culture in the 1970s. Peter Shapiro's *Turn the Beat Around* examines pre-1960s discotheque culture in France and Germany and develops an overview of the disco culture across the 1970s and 1980s.

2 Mertens, *American Minimal Music*, 124. Writing before Mertens, Tom Johnson described the emerging sound of orchestral minimalism as "hypnotic music" when he noticed that Philip Glass, Steve Reich, Terry Riley, and La Monte Young were generating short, repeated phrases that would mutate slowly over the course of a piece. Tom Johnson, "Steve Reich's 'Drumming,'" *Village Voice*, 9 December 1971; reprinted in *The Voice of New Music*, n.p. "The music never entertains or stimulates in an overt way," Johnson later added. "It simply lulls, hypnotizes, and draws him [the listener] into its world." Johnson, "La Monte Young, Steve Reich, Terry Riley, Philip Glass," *Village Voice*, 7 September 1972; reprinted in *The Voice of New Music*, n.p. The shifting planes of intensity in the DJ-dancer interaction suggested the title of Gilles Deleuze and Félix Guattari's *A Thousand Plateaus*. Like Mertens, Deleuze and Guattari published their book in 1980.

3 David Toop, "The Weird One," *Face*, January 1987, 27.

4 Vince Aletti, "Disco File," *Record World*, 2 December 1978, 44.

5 Larry Levan's selections are listed in Vince Aletti, "Disco File," *Record World*, 9 December 1978, 16.

6 Following an exchange of emails I had with Killian, he wrote an essay about his encounters with Arthur Russell, as well as with Allen Ginsberg, from which these and other quotes are drawn. Kevin Killian, "Arthur Russell."

7 Sweet, *Music Universe, Music Mind*, 85–86.

8 In addition to Arthur Russell's and Steven Hall's vocals, the Japanese version contains a grinding organ and a more obviously misaligned bass. Looser and funkier than the final Sire release, it matches Donald Murk's suggestive description of the original acetate pressing.

9 John Holmstrom, editorial, *Punk*, January 1976; reprinted in Holmstrom, ed., *Punk*, 8.

10 Lester Bangs, "White Noise Supremacists," *Village Voice*, 30 April 1979; reprinted in Bangs, *Psychotic Reactions and Carburetor Dung*, 272–82.

11 Ibid.

12 Quoted in Frank Owen, "Echo Beach," *Melody Maker*, 11 April 1987, 36.

13 Russell mentioned his possible influence on "I Zimbra" during his interview with Frank Owen. Ibid.

14 Steve D'Acquisto referenced the *White Album* in an interview with Chris Menist. "Arthur Russell," *Faith*, winter 2001, 29–31.

15 The list of compositions is drawn from Mary Jane Leach, "In Search of Julius East-

man," *New Music Box*, 8 November 2005, http://www.newmusicbox.org, retrieved 25 August 2006. Leach, a "pursuer of impossible dreams," is the producer of *Unjust Malaise*, the first commercial CD of Julius Eastman's music, which was released by New World Records in 2005.

16 *First Thought Best Thought* (2006) contains several sections from this performance.

17 Owen, "Echo Beach," 37.

18 Rhys Chatham's sleeve notes for *Guitar Trio*, reprinted in the sleeve notes for *Amplified: New Music Meets Rock, 1981–1986*, the third release in the "From the Kitchen Archives" series (Orange Mountain Music, 2006).

19 These recordings were eventually released on 24 → 24 *Music* (1981), and the album jacket documents that the album was recorded on 9 June 1979. However, Bob Blank notes that the material was laid down over a number of months and that 9 June was the day of the mix. Although John Bradley was credited as the sole engineer, Bradley only worked with Russell when Blank wasn't available. Blank suggests that his name didn't appear on the credits because of an argument he had with Will Socolov.

20 Quoted in Owen, "Echo Beach," 37.

21 David Toop, "The Flying Heart," *Wire*, January 2004, 36.

22 The original, twelve-minute version appears on the first volume of *David Mancuso Presents The Loft* (Nuphonic, 1999). In this version, Russell's cello is introduced at an early point in the mix, and the horn section is deployed more liberally. The mix also includes the lines, "It's many friends catch the wave, catch the love wave. Feel it up, catch the wave, catch the love wave."

23 Corbett and Kapsalis, "Aural Sex," 99.

24 Quoted in Andy Thomas, "Arthur Russell: Twisted Disco Visionary," *Seven*, November 2000, 26.

25 This argument is developed in more detail in Lawrence, "'I Want to See All My Friends at Once.'"

26 "Reviews," *Dance Music Report*, 29 March 1980, 5.

27 Brian Chin, "Disco File," *Record World*, 12 April 1980; Barry Lederer, "Disco Mix," *Billboard*, 26 January 1980, 35.

28 Chin, "Disco File."

29 Rockwell, *All American Music*, 243.

30 In 1981 the New York–based ZE records released an album titled *Mutant Disco*, which consisted of tracks that blended disco and new-wave aesthetics. The London-based Strut Records helped revive interest in the sound with its *Disco Not Disco* albums, released in 2000 and 2001, which featured a number of Arthur Russell recordings.

31 Walter Hughes analyzes the relationship between the gay dancer and the female diva in "In the Empire of the Beat."

5 **Variations** (1980–1984)

1 Rockwell, *All American Music*, 118.

2 Performances of works by David Behrman, Barbara Benary, Joel Chadabe, Tony Conrad, Jon Gibson, Philip Glass, Tom Johnson, George Lewis, Garrett List, Meredith Monk, Charlie Morrow, Gordon Mumma, Phill Niblock, Michael Nyman, Pauline Oliveros, Charlemagne Palestine, and Steve Reich that took place during the "New Music New York" festival can be heard on *From the Kitchen Archives: New Music New York 1979* (Orange Mountain Music, 2004).

3 Smith Brindle, *The New Music*; Peter Gordon, "Public Music," *Ear*, April 1975, n.p.

4 Tom Johnson, "New Music New York New Institution," *Village Voice*, 2 July 1979; reprinted in *The Voice of New Music*, n.p.

5 John Rockwell, "Music: 53 Composers In 9-Day Festival," *New York Times*, 18 June 1979.

6 Johnson, "New Music New York New Institution," n.p.

7 Ibid.

8 Rockwell, "Music: 53 Composers In 9-Day Festival."

9 Lewis, *A Power Stronger than Itself*, 384.

10 Dessen, "Decolonizing American Art Music."

11 Tom Johnson, "John Zorn and Other Improvisers," *Village Voice*, 24 September 1980; reprinted in *The Voice of New Music*, n.p.

12 George Lewis provides a list of performers and artists booked during his tenure in *A Power Stronger than Itself*, 588.

13 Ibid., 385.

14 John Rockwell, "Avant-Gardists in Midtown for Benefit," *New York Times*, 13 June 1981.

15 George Lewis is referring to Hal Foster's essay "Against Pluralism," which appears in Foster, *Recordings*, 13–32.

16 Revised by Mary Jane Leach for *Hold On to Your Dreams*, this comment was originally posted on the Sequenza 21/ Web site, www.sequenza21.com on 11 February 2006. Retrieved from http://www.haloscan.com/comments/jbowles/1139505815 34970678 on 7 August 2006.

17 Martin Carnoy notes the African American working-class conditions of the time in *Faded Dreams*, 13–14.

18 Hobsbawm, *Age of Extremes*, 249.

19 Vince Aletti, "SoHo vs. Disco," *Village Voice*, 16 June 1975, 125.

20 Richard Kostelanetz notes that real-estate prices started to rise in SoHo in 1979 (*SoHo*, 223).

21 Tim Carr et al., "That Downtown Sound . . . From A to Z," *New York Rocker*, June 1982, 27.

22 Ibid.

23 Foster, *Recordings*, 13.

24 Bogue, *Deleuze on Music, Painting, and the Arts*, 34.

25 Steven Hall described Tom Lee's and Arthur Russell's interaction in an interview with Daniel Wang that took place on 7 October 2004 (original transcript). An edited version of this interview was published in *Keep On*, no. 4 (2005), 16–17.

26 Gavin Bryars, "Medea," posted at Bryars's official Web site, n.d., http://www .gavinbryars.com/Pages/medea_first_note.html, retrieved 4 September 2006.

27 Russell, letter to Chuck and Emily Russell, 20 February 1980. A photocopy is on file with the author.

28 David Byrne's comment is drawn from the promotional video for *Another Thought* (Point Music, 1994).

29 Don Howland, "The Necessaries," *New York Rocker*, October 1982, 40.

30 The information on *Instrumentals Volume 1* is drawn from Steve Knutson's essay in the sleeve notes to Arthur Russell, *First Thought Best Thought*.

31 The Les Disques du Crépuscule release gives the title of the track as *Sketch for "Face of Helen."* The longer recording, released on *First Thought Best Thought*, transcribes the composition's title as *Sketch for the Face of Helen*.

32 In occasional CVs and press releases, Russell notes he also played electronics in John Cage's composition *Empty Words*, but no further details are provided.

33 "RTZ" by Bill's Friends is included on *Amplified: New Music Meets Rock, 1981–1986*, the third release in the "From the Kitchen Archives" series (Orange Mountain Music, 2006).

34 From Bill Ruyle's speech at the private memorial event held for Arthur Russell at the Experimental Intermedia Foundation on 12 April 1992.

35 *Instruments* was later released on Side A of *Zummo with an X* (Loris Records, 1985).

36 *Billboard*, "Format Frontiers," Spotlight: Disco Dance Music, 19 June 1982, DD–9; Adrian Thrills, "It's Nasty," *New Musical Express*, 5 June 1982, 12; *Dance Music Report*, "Reviews," 1 May 1982; Steven Harvey, "Dinosaur L," *New York Rocker*, July/August 1982, 22.

37 Elodie Lauten comments, "I don't know if there ever was a final version," while Don Christensen, who produced *Another Thought* (1994), is uncertain about the status of the six-minute version of "In the Light of the Miracle" that is included on that album. "Whether Arthur thought it was the 'final' mix would be pretty hard to say," he comments. "Arthur often made many mixes and versions of the same tune. I probably chose that one because I liked it the best." Lauten was disappointed with the selection. "I didn't feel that the correct tracks were used, but none of the original participants were consulted," she says. Running at twice the length, the version that appears on *The World of Arthur Russell* (2004) was remixed by Steve D'Acquisto, Steven Hall, and Tony Morgan under the auspices of Point Music.

38 The Larry Levan remix of "Cornbelt" was included on the compilation *Sleeping Bag's Greatest Remixers II* (1987).

39 Tom Lee notes the goal-driven basis of their club outings in his article "Point Music Honors Arthur Russell with 'Another Thought,'" LIFE*beat*, October 1994, 4.

40 Johnson, "New Music New York New Institution," n.p.

41 Arthur Russell asked Alan Abrams to film the recording session with Joyce Bowden in order to create a music video for "My Tiger, My Timing." Abrams also shot Russell and Bowden performing the song with Mustafa Ahmed, Ernie Brooks, Steven Hall, and David Van Tieghem at La MaMa. The video remains unfinished, as does footage shot for another Russell song, "I Kissed the Girl from Outer Space," which Russell worked on in the early 1980s. Abrams completed three experimental films for Russell that remain unreleased. "Street Seen #2" is set to music from the album 24 $\rightarrow$ 24 Music; "Reach" is set to the composition *Reach One (With Two Fender Rhodes)*; and "Tugboat Pilot" uses music from the *Medea* recording.

42 "Keeping Up," "Losing My Taste for the Nightlife," "Lucky Cloud," and "See through Love" appear on *Another Thought* (1994). "Hop on Down" and "Wild Combination" appear on *Calling out of Context* (2004). "The Letter" appears on *Love Is Overtaking Me* (2008). The other recordings were never released.

43 All of these songs appear on Arthur Russell, *Another Thought*.

44 "The Kitchen, Monday Series IV / Arthur Russell, David Linton," undated press release. The original is held by Tom Lee in his private archive. A photocopy is on file with the author.

45 Jon Pareles, "Music: Linton and Russell," *New York Times*, 22 March 1984.

46 A full list of contributors to the album is not available; no information on the players was included on the album's striking, conceptual sleeve art, which was designed by Kathleen Cooney (a former girlfriend of Alan Abrams) and silk-screened by Tom Lee.

47 J. Stacey Bishop, *Sound Choice*, January/February 1985; J. D. Considine, "Music from the Glass Menagerie," *Washington Post*, 20 September 1985.

48 Quoted in Mertens, *American Minimal Music*, 122.

6 **Reverberations** (1984–1987)

1 Taylor, ed., in *The Downtown Book*, 188. For more on the New York State (NYS) Multiple Dwelling Law (MDL), see http://www.soho-lofts.com/loftlaw/mdl/index.html.

2 Musto, *Downtown*, 4, 5.

3 Quoted in David Toop, "The Flying Heart," *Wire*, January 2004, 34.

4 Peter Gordon, comment posted on the Sequenza 21/ Web site, www.sequenza21 .com on 17 February 2006. Retrieved from http://www.haloscan.com/comments/jbowles/113950581534970678/ on 7 August 2006.

5 Musto, *Downtown*, 2.

6 Bill T. Jones, untitled essay, in Baker, ed., *New York Noise*, 204.

7 Gann, *Music Downtown*, 7.

8 "Planted a Thought" and "Love Is Overtaking Me" appear on *Love Is Overtaking Me* (2008).

9   The *Corn* versions of "Calling out of Context," "The Deer in the Forest Part One," and "The Platform on the Ocean" appear on *Calling out of Context* (2004); "Corn," "Hiding Your Present from You," "See My Brother, He's Jumping Out (Let's Go Swimming #1)," and "You Have Did the Right Thing When You Put That Skylight In" on *Springfield* (2006); and "They and Their Friends" on the *Let's Go Swimming* EP (2005). A later mix of "Keeping Up" can be found on *Another Thought* (1994).

10 Quoted from "Music for Modern Ears," WUSB Stony Brook interview with Arthur Russell, April 1987.

11 Stuart Cosgrove, "Funk to the Future!," *NME*, 15 March 1986, 20–21.

12 Gary Lucas, "Arthur Russell: An Appreciation," *Alternative Press*, November 1994, 16.

13 Ibid.

14 For a more detailed account of this episode, as well as the influence of Walter Gibbons on DJ and remix culture, see Lawrence, "Disco Madness."

15 Arthur Russell told David Toop that he met Walter Gibbons at West End in an interview conducted on 7 October 1986 in preparation for Toop's article "The Weird One," *Face*, January 1987, 27. The original transcript is held by David Toop. A photocopy is on file with the author.

16 David Toop, "Past Futurist," *Wire*, April 1995, 20.

17 Toop, "The Flying Heart," 37.

18 Frank Owen, "Echo Beach," *Melody Maker*, 11 April 1987, 36.

19 Edwin J. Bernard, "Arthur Russell, 'Let's Go Swimming' (Rough Trade)," *Record Mirror*, 27 September 1986.

20 Barney Hoskins, "Arthur Russell: Let's Go Swimming," *New Musical Express*, 4 October 1986, 54.

21 James Hamilton, "BPM," *Record Mirror*, 4 October 1986, 56–60.

22 Simon Reynolds, "Arthur Russell: Let's Go Swimming," *Melody Maker*, 11 October 1986, 26.

23 Frank Owen, "Sleeping Around," *Melody Maker*, 27 September 1986, 11.

24 Jay Strongman, "Bomb Culture," *New Musical Express*, 27 September 1986, 6.

25 John Leland, "Arthur Russell: 'Let's Go Swimming' / Indian Ocean featuring Arthur Russell: 'School Bell/Tree House,'" *Spin*, December 1986.

26 In occasional CVs and press releases, Russell notes he played a concert at Cunningham Dance. The date of the performance is unknown.

27 *Turbo Sporty* was staged in several venues, including the St. Mark's Poetry Project and the Living Art Museum in Reykjavik. Arthur Russell participated live in all the U.S. performances and contributed a cassette recording of cello drones for the Reykjavik installation.

28 Govinda, *The Way of the White Clouds*, 7.

29 A form of polyester resin called Mylar, which could be bought cheaply on Canal Street, was used to create the lighting effects for *Turbo Sporty* and the *World of Echo*

video. "We developed a technique of hanging up the Mylar and shining colored lights onto it so that it would move in the heat, or else be movable by hand," notes Steven Hall. "The effect was of shimmering water, and sometimes we showed the Mylar itself as if it were water. The dreamy, psychedelic, undulating colors were just what Arthur was looking for."

30 Phill Niblock's videos were stashed away until Audika released them—as *Some Imaginary Far Away Type Things / Lost in the Meshes* and *Terrace of Unintelligibility*—on DVD in tandem with its reissue of the *World of Echo* album.

31 *Arthur Russell and Group*, concert program, Institute of Contemporary Art, Boston, 13 May 1988. The original is held by Tom Lee in his private archive. A photocopy is on file with the author.

32 Owen, "Sleeping Around," 11.

33 John Hull, quoted in Rodaway, *Sensuous Geographies*, 102.

34 Another thirty-nine songs were recorded in Phill Niblock's loft and catalogued as *Sketches for World of Echo*, but Russell decided to hold them back from the LP. Four of these takes—"The Name of the Next Song," "Happy Ending," "Canvas Home," and "Our Last Night Together"—are included on Audika's re-release of *World of Echo* (2004). In addition, live recordings of "All-Boy All-Girl" and "Hiding Your Present from You" appear on the Kitchen compilation *Amplified: New Music Meets Rock, 1981–1986*, the third release in the "From the Kitchen Archives" series (Orange Mountain Music, 2006). At the time of the Orange Mountain release it appeared the recordings of "All-Boy All-Girl" and "Hiding Your Present from You" might have been recorded at the Kitchen, but it has since been confirmed they were recorded at the Experimental Intermedia Foundation.

35 Jonathan Romney, "Arthur Russell: World Of Echo," *New Musical Express*, 4 April, 1987, 32.

36 "Arthur Russell: World Of Echo," *Billboard*, 10 May 1987; Owen, "Echo Beach," 36.

37 David Stubbs, "Arthur Russell: World Of Echo," *Melody Maker*, 11 April 1987, 33.

38 Tom Petersen, "Osky Native Makes Unusual Music with Electric Cello," *Oskaloosa Herald*, 24 December 1986.

39 Quoted in Owen, "Echo Beach," 37.

40 Quoted in Chang, *Can't Stop, Won't Stop*, 174. It could be argued that the Funhouse, the Loft, the Paradise Garage, and other downtown dance clubs had already generated a "legitimately mixed scene."

41 Owen, "Sleeping Around," 11.

42 David Toop, "The Weird One," *Face*, January 1987, 27.

43 Toop "Past Futurist," 20. Interviewed by JW [Jonh Wilde] in May 1987 for *Blitz*, Russell would comment: "Why have I made a record with just vocals and cello? Well, it's like you want to go to outer space but you're not allowed to take your drums with you. It's like some huge soundtrack to some pornographic science-fiction movie, absolutely drenched in irony, of course."

44 Toop, "The Weird One," 27.

45 Thomas R. O'Donnell, "Death Can't Muffle Musician," *Des Moines Register*, 9 April 1995.

46 "A Sudden Chill" appears on *Another Thought*.

47 "Music for Modern Ears," WUSB Stony Brook interview.

48 Jonh Wilde, "Arthur Russell: The Kitchen, New York," *Melody Maker*, 9 May 1987, 17.

49 Robert Palmer, "Concert: Russell and Marti," *New York Times*, 26 April 1987.

50 Kyle Gann, "Revolution Now," *Village Voice*, 28 April 1987, 78.

51 JW [Jonh Wilde], "Untitled," *Blitz*, May 1987.

7 **Tangents** (1987–1992)

1 The quotation comes from "La MaMa to Present Second Annual New Music Festival," an undated press release for the festival. The original is held by Tom Lee in his private archive. A photocopy is on file with the author.

2 Kyle Gann, "Don't Speak Up," *Village Voice*, 14 June 1988, 90.

3 Peter Watrous, "Music: Elodie Lauten," *New York Times*, 16 February 1988.

4 Kyle Gann, "The Rising Yin," *Village Voice*, 8 March 1988, 90.

5 Sleeve notes to Peter Zummo, *Experimenting with Household Chemicals* (Experimental Intermedia Foundation, 1995).

6 Bill Ruyle's essay in the sleeve notes to *Experimenting with Household Chemicals*.

7 This version of "Don't Forget about Me" appears on *Love Is Overtaking Me*. It features Arthur Russell on lead vocals and Joyce Bowden on background vocals.

8 Jill Pearlman, "The Devil Made Him Do It," *New York City Paper*, November 1987.

9 Barry Walters discusses Sylvester and AIDS in "Stayin' Alive," *Village Voice*, 8 November 1988, reprinted in Kureishi and Savage, eds., *The Faber Book of Pop*, 645. Joshua Gameson describes the development of Sylvester's sickness in detail in *Sylvester*, 246–60.

10 These recordings appear on *Another Thought*.

11 These recordings appear on *Calling out of Context*.

12 The quotation comes from "La MaMa to Present Second Annual New Music Festival," an undated press release for the festival.

13 Quoted in Shilts, *And the Band Played On*, 149.

14 "Music for Modern Ears," WUSB Stony Brook interview with Arthur Russell, April 1987; JW [Jonh Wilde], "Untitled," *Blitz*, May 1987.

15 Guy Wingate, "Todd the God," *Mixmag*, November 1988, 48–49.

16 Sheryl Garratt, "Can U Feel It?," *Face*, October 1988, 70.

17 Jess Harvell, "Arthur Russell: First Thought, Best Thought," *Pitchfork*, 18 April 2006, http://www.pitchforkmedia.com, retrieved 10 January 2007. The *Springfield* EP includes two of Russell's original takes (recorded in 1988), a remix by DFA

(James Murphy and Tim Goldsworthy), and four previously unreleased tracks from *Corn*.

18 Jennifer Dunning, "The Dance: New Works By 6 Choreographers," *New York Times*, 19 January 1988.

19 Deborah Jowitt, "Minutes Like Hours / Hours Like Minutes," *Village Voice*, 2 February 1988, 89.

20 Quoted in Wilma Salisbury, "Clumsy, Funky and Anti-dance," *Cleveland Plain Dealer*, 8 February 1988.

21 Tom Lee, "Point Music Honors Arthur Russell with 'Another Thought,'" LIFEbeat, October 1994, 4.

22 Russell is credited with cowriting "Facing the Fire" and "The Doctors Lie," two of the LP's better-received songs. Bowden remembers Russell providing her with precise instructions on how to deliver the melody for "The Doctors Lie" over the phone while she recorded with Brooks and Harrison in Milwaukee, and adds that he later complained that some of the intervals weren't exact. Part of the album was mixed in New York. It was then that Brooks asked after Russell's health.

23 The reflection on sound is made by John Hull in Rodaway, *Sensuous Geographies*, 103.

24 Kyle Gann, "Choices: Arthur Russell," *Village Voice*, 19 March 1991, 88.

25 Allan Kozinn, "Music in Review: Music at the Anchorage," *New York Times*, 10 September 1991.

26 Tom Johnson, "Christian Wolff: Exercises and Songs," *Village Voice*, 6 June 1974; reprinted in *The Voice of New Music*, n.p.

27 "Love Comes Back" appears on *Love Is Overtaking Me*.

28 From Allen Ginsberg's speech at the private memorial event held for Arthur Russell at the Experimental Intermedia Foundation on 12 April 1992.

29 The Allen Ginsberg quote comes from an essay he wrote while at the Kerouac School of Disembodied Poetics, Naropa Institute, Boulder, Colorado, 30 June 1975, and appears in the sleeve notes to *First Blues: Rags, Ballads and Harmonium Songs* (Folkways, 1981). The album was reissued as *Allen Ginsberg New York Blues: Rags, Ballads and Harmonium Songs* by Locust Music in 2002. Somewhat confusingly, Ginsberg also released an entirely different album titled *First Blues* on John Hammond's label, Water, in 1983, and it was this second album that included contributions from Arthur Russell.

30 From Allen Ginsberg's speech at the private memorial event held for Arthur Russell at the Experimental Intermedia Foundation on 12 April 1992.

31 "Charles Arthur Russell Jr., 40, Cellist, Dies," *New York Times*, 14 April 1992, B8.

32 "Lifelines: Deaths," *Billboard*, 18 April 1992, 56.

33 Kyle Gann, "Square Rhythms," *Village Voice*, 28 April 1992, 94.

Epilogue

1 Broyles, *Mavericks and Other Traditions in American Music*, 2.

2 Gary Lucas, "Arthur Russell: An Appreciation," *Alternative Press*, November 1994, 16.

3 Quoted in Baker, ed., *New York Noise*, 1, 49.

4 McCormick, "A Crack In Time," 78, 79.

5 Quoted in Foege, *Confusion Is Next*, 30.

6 The *New York Rocker* listed ABC No Rio, Art on the Beach, Brooklyn Academy of Music, CBGB's, Danceteria, Dance Theater Workshop, Ear Inn, Inroads, the Kitchen, the Mudd Club, New Pilgrim Theater, P.S. 1, Public Theater, Roulette, and White Columns in its survey of venues. The only dance venue to make the cut, Danceteria, had its dance element stripped from its description. "Promoter Jim Fouratt always booked new music," ran the entry. "So far: Branca, Rhys Chatham, Phillip [*sic*] Glass, Red Decade, and T-Venus, with more to come." Merle Ginsberg, "Venues," in Tim Carr et al., "That Downtown Sound . . . From A to Z," *New York Rocker*, June 1982, 36.

7 Peter Gordon's and Colette's artist name was Justine and the Victorian Punks. Arranged by Gordon, "Beautiful Dreamer" was performed by LOLO with additional vocals by Gordon. The record was released as a limited edition twelve-inch single, with "Still You (Ancora Tu)" on the B-side, on Colette Is Dead Records in 1980.

8 Lunch, untitled essay, in Taylor, ed., *The Downtown Book*, 95.

9 Ibid., 95; McCormick, "A Crack In Time," 78.

10 While critics such as Ronald Bogue, Jeremy Gilbert, Drew Hemment, Tim Jordan, and Simon Reynolds have applied Gilles Deleuze's and Félix Guattari's critical framework to music in their examination of composers who work within a single genre, or genres that feature rhizomatic aesthetics, the question of how a musician might work according to these principles has yet to be addressed. Russell's career suggests how a musician might operate rhizomatically, not just in terms of the final structure of the music, but also in terms of how that music is created. This argument is developed in more detail in Lawrence, "Connecting with the Cosmic." For earlier writings on the relevance of Deleuze and Guattari to music, see Bogue, "Violence in Three Shades of Metal"; Gilbert, "Becoming-Music"; Hemment, "Affect and Individuation in Popular Electronic Music"; Jordan, "Collective Bodies"; and Reynolds, *Energy Flash*.

11 Jon Pareles, "A Gentle Soul's Songs, Accompanied by His Cello," *New York Times*, 26 November 1994; David Fricke, "On the Edge," *Rolling Stone*, 20 April 1995, 72.

12 Jess Harvell, "Arthur Russell: First Thought, Best Thought," *Pitchfork*, 18 April 2006, http://www.pitchforkmedia.com, retrieved 10 January 2007.

13 Speaking at a press conference at the Kitchen in 1987, Philip Glass commented: "The thing that I worry about, not just about the Kitchen but about New York, is its remaining a community of artists who work together, artists who see each other's work, artists who are influenced by each others' work, and artists who can

create a community of other artists who, together, create the kind of art that we've identified with New York and with the United States." Quoted in Kostelanetz, *SoHo*, vii.

14 The main books that chronicle disco are my own *Love Saves the Day* and Peter Shapiro's *Turn the Beat Around*. Marvin J. Taylor's edited collection, *The Downtown Book*, and Simon Reynolds's detailed analysis of postpunk, *Rip It Up and Start Again*, have contributed to the broader historicization of downtown.

15 Jeff Harrington, comment posted on the Sequenza 21/ Web site, www.sequenza21 .com, 17 February 2006. Retrieved from http:// www.haloscan.com/comments/ jbowles/113950581534970678 on 7 August 2006.

16 Philip Glass, "Point Music Honors Arthur Russell with 'Another Thought,'" LIFE-*beat*, October 1994, 1.

17 Foster, *Recordings*, 17.

18 Ibid., 13, 15, 17, 23, 31.

19 Ibid., 24.

20 The figure is drawn from the "Global Cities" exhibition at the Tate Modern, London, 20 June to 27 August 2007. For more information, visit: http://www.tate.org .uk/modern.

21 From Kent Goshorn's speech at the private memorial event held for Arthur Russell at the Experimental Intermedia Foundation on 12 April 1992.

Discography

This is the first full discography of the published recordings on which Arthur Russell appeared as an original artist or as a member of a band or studio outfit, as well as releases where he made an appearance as an instrumentalist, mixer, or guest songwriter. Promotional copies and bootlegs are listed only when the record didn't receive a commercial release, while Russell's twelve-inch dance reissues and compilation appearances are too numerous to list here in their entirety.

Producers and remixers are referenced when their names were included on the original release, but details of musicians and engineers and song lengths have been omitted for consistency and brevity. In cases of multiple issues across format and country, CD numbering systems are used instead of vinyl numbering systems, while original publishing agreements are listed instead of licensing parties. The use of "Side 1" and "Side A" follows original usage.

This discography is provisional, in part because so many of Russell's recordings exist only on tape, and in part because the ongoing excavation of the archives means that old recordings will continue to be released after the publication of this book. Other anomalies exist: for example, three different versions of the twelve-inch single "Tell You (Today)" are in circulation, but inconsistent labeling makes them difficult to distinguish from one another. Because of the fluctuating nature of the market, no attempt has been made to indicate the availability of any recording. Finally, I have corrected apparently unintentional mistakes, such as the misspelling of names.

1978
Dinosaur, "Kiss Me Again"
  Seven-inch promotional single, Sire, 1978 (SRE-1034)
  Side 1. "Kiss Me Again"

Side 2. "Kiss Me Again"
Produced by Arthur Russell and Nicky Siano; remixed by Jimmy Simpson

Dinosaur, "Kiss Me Again"
Twelve-inch single, Sire, 1978 (SRD-1035)
Side 1. "Kiss Me Again." Remixed by Jimmy Simpson
Side 2. "Kiss Me Again (Version)"
Produced by Arthur Russell and Nicky Siano
Note: This record was also released as a red vinyl promotional twelve-inch single (PRO-A-0771)

1979
Dinosaur, "Kiss Me Again"
Twelve-inch promotional single, Sire, 1979 (PRO-A-0785)
Side 1. "Kiss Me Again (Edit)." Remixed by Dinosaur
Side 2. "Kiss Me Again." Remixed by Jimmy Simpson
Produced by Arthur Russell and Nicky Siano

Loose Joints, "Pop Your Funk"
Seven-inch promotional single, West End, 1980 (WES-1228)
Side 1. "Pop Your Funk (Vocal)"
Side 2. "Pop Your Funk (Instrumental)"

1980
Loose Joints, "Is It All Over My Face?" / "Pop Your Funk"
Twelve-inch single, West End, 1980 (WES-22128)
Side A. "Is It All Over My Face?"
Side B. "Pop Your Funk"
Produced by Arthur Russell and Steve D'Acquisto

Loose Joints, "Is It All Over My Face? (Female Vocal)" /
"Is It All Over My Face? (Male Vocal)"
Twelve-inch single, West End, 1980 (WES-22129)
Side A. "Is It All Over My Face? (Female Vocal)." Remixed by Larry Levan
Side B. "Is It All Over My Face? (Male Vocal)"
Produced by Arthur Russell and Steve D'Acquisto

1981
Dinosaur L, *24* → *24 Music*
Album, Sleeping Bag Records, 1981 (TLX-0)
Side 1. "#1 (You're Gonna Be Clean on Your Bean)" / "#5 (Go Bang!)" /
"#2 (No, Thank You)" / "#7"
Side 2. "#3 (In the Corn Belt)" / "#6 (Get Set)"

Produced by Arthur Russell, except track #1 produced by Arthur Russell and Peter Gordon

Necessaries, *Big Sky*
Album, Sire, 1981 (SRK-3573)
Side A. "Back to You" / "Driving and Talking at the Same Time" / "Born Yesterday" / "My Baby's Explosive" / "Sahara"
Side B. "Europe" / "Algebra" / "Detroit Tonight" / "State-of-the-Art" / "On the Run" / "Cuba Mortis"
Produced by Bob Blank

Various, *The Fruit of the Original Sin*
Compilation album, Les Disques du Crépuscule, 1981 (TWI-035)
Side D, track 4. Arthur Russell, "Sketch for 'Face of Helen'"

1982

Dinosaur L, "Go Bang! #5" / "Clean on Your Bean #1"
Twelve-inch single, Sleeping Bag Records, 1982 (SLX-0 / SLX-000)
Side A. "Go Bang! #5." Produced by Arthur Russell and Will Socolov
Side B. "Clean on Your Bean #1." Produced by Arthur Russell and Peter Gordon. Rap by Andre and Abel
Mixed by François K

Necessaries, *Event Horizon*
Album, Sire, 1982 (SRK-3574)
Side 1. "Rage" / "More Real" / "Like No Other" / "Driving and Talking at the Same Time" / "AEIOU" / "Sahara"
Side 2. "Europe" / "State-of-the-Art" / "The Finish Line" / "Detroit Tonight" / "On the Run" / "Paceways"
Produced by Bob Blank

1983

Loose Joints, "Tell You (Today)"
Twelve-inch single, 4th and Broadway, 1983 (BWAY401)
Side A. "Tell You (Today)." Mixed by Larry Levan, Eddie Garcia, and Robert Moraty
Side B. "Tell You (Today) (New Shoes) Part I" / "Tell You (Today) (New Shoes) Part II." Mixed by In the Cornbelt
Produced by Killer Whale [Arthur Russell] and Steve D'Acquisto

Arthur Russell, *Tower of Meaning*
Album, Chatham Square, 1983 (CLS-145)
Conducted by Julius Eastman

1984

Arthur Russell, *Instrumentals (1974—Vol. 2)*
  Album, Another Side, 1984 (SIDE-8401)

1986

Indian Ocean, "School Bell / Treehouse"
  Twelve-inch single, Sleeping Bag Records, 1986 (SLX-023)
  Side A. "Treehouse / School Bell"
  Side B. "School Bell / Treehouse"
  Produced by Arthur Russell and Peter Zummo; mixed ("with love")
    by Walter Gibbons

Arthur Russell, "Let's Go Swimming"
  Twelve-inch single, Logarhythm, 1986 (LR-1002–1)
  Side A. "Let's Go Swimming (Gulf Stream Dub)" / "Let's Go Swimming
    (Puppy Surf Dub)"
  Side B. "Let's Go Swimming (Coastal Dub)." Mixed ("with love")
    by Walter Gibbons
  Produced by Arthur Russell and Mark Freedman; edited by Killer Whale
    [Arthur Russell]

Arthur Russell, *World of Echo*
  Album, Upside Records, 1986 (UP-60009)
  Side A. "Tone Bone Kone" / "Soon-to-Be Innocent Fun / Let's See" / "Answers
    Me" / "Being It" / "Place I Know / Kid Like You" / "She's the Star / I Take
    This Time"
  Side B. "Tree House" / "See-Through" / "Hiding Your Present from You" / "Wax
    the Van" / "All-Boy All-Girl" / "Lucky Cloud" / "Tower of Meaning / Rabbit's
    Ear / Home away from Home" / "Let's Go Swimming"
  Produced by Arthur Russell

1987

Various, *Sleeping Bag's Greatest Mixers II*
  Compilation album, Sleeping Bag Records, 1987 (TLX-42012)
  Side X, track 5. Dinosaur L, "Cornbelt." Mixed by Larry Levan

1994

Arthur Russell, *Another Thought*
  Album, Point, 1994 (438–891–2)
  1. "Another Thought" (1985) / 2. "A Little Lost" (1982) / 3. "Home away from
    Home" (1986) / 4. "Lucky Cloud" (1984) / 5. "This Is How We Walk on the
    Moon" (1984) / 6. "Hollow Tree" (1985) / 7. "See through Love" (1986) /
    8. "Keeping Up" (1988) / 9. "In the Light of the Miracle" (1982) / 10. "Just a

Blip" (1986) / 11. "Me for Real" (1990) / 12. "Losing My Taste for the Night
Life" (1987) / 13. "My Tiger, My Timing" (1988) / 14. "A Sudden Chill" (1986)
All words and music by Arthur Russell, except "In the Light of the Miracle,"
words by Arthur Russell, music by Elodie Lauten and Arthur Russell
Produced by Don Christensen

1999

Various, *David Mancuso Presents the Loft*
Compilation album, Nuphonic, 1999 (NUX-136)
Disc 1, track 2. Loose Joints, "Is It All Over My Face? (Unreleased Original Full-
Length Version)"
Compiled by David Mancuso.

2000

Various, *Disco Not Disco*
Compilation album, Strut, 2000 (STRUTCD-008)
Track 3. Loose Joints, "Tell You (Today)"
Track 7. Dinosaur, "Kiss Me Again (Original Edit)"
Track 10. Indian Ocean, "School Bell / Tree House [*sic*] (Part 1)"
Compiled by Dave Lee and Sean P.

2001

Various, *Disco Not Disco 2*
Compilation album, Strut, 2001 (STRUTCD-020)
Track 8. Arthur Russell, "Let's Go Swimming"
Compiled by Sean P. and Dave Lee

2004

Dinosaur L, "Go Bang (Walter Gibbons Unreleased Mix)"
Twelve-inch single, bootleg, 2004 (Slebb-05)
Remixed by Walter Gibbons

Arthur Russell, *Calling out of Context*
Album, Audika, 2004 (AU-1001–2)
1. "The Deer in the Forest Part One" / 2. "The Platform on the Ocean" /
3. "You and Me Both" / 4. "Calling out of Context" / 5. "Arm around You" /
6. "That's Us / Wild Combination" / 7. "Make 1, 2" / 8. "Hop on Down" /
9. "Get Around to It" / 10. "I Like You" / 11. "You Can Make Me Feel Bad" /
12. "Calling All Kids"
All words and music by Arthur Russell
Tracks 1, 2, 4 produced and mixed by Killer Whale [Arthur Russell] and Arthur
Russell, 1984–85; tracks 3, 5–12 produced and mixed by Arthur Russell, 1986–

90; track 12 produced by Arthur Russell and remixed ("with love")
by Walter Gibbons

Compiled by Steve Knutson, Tom Lee, and Melissa Jones

Arthur Russell, *Terrace of Unintelligibility*

DVD (limited edition) issued with *World of Echo*, Audika, 2004 (AU-1002–3)

Track 1. "Terrace of Unintelligibility"

Track 2. "Some Imaginary Far Away Type Things, a.k.a, Lost in the Meshes"

Filmed at the Experimental Intermedia Foundation on 22 September and
27 October, 1985

Video by Phill Niblock, music by Arthur Russell

Arthur Russell, *The World of Arthur Russell*

Compilation album, Soul Jazz Records, 2004 (SLR-LP83)

1. Dinosaur L, "Go Bang" / 2. Lola, "Wax the Van" / 3. Loose Joints, "Is It All
Over My Face (Female Vocal)" / 4. Arthur Russell, "Keeping Up" / 5. Arthur
Russell, "In the Light of the Miracle" / 6. Arthur Russell, "A Little Lost" /
7. Loose Joints, "Pop Your Funk" / 8. Arthur Russell, "Let's Go Swimming" /
9. Dinosaur L, "In the Corn Belt" (Larry Levan mix) / 10. Arthur Russell,
"Treehouse" / 11. Indian Ocean, "School Bell / Treehouse" (Walter Gibbons
mix)

Compiled by David Hill

Arthur Russell, *World of Echo*

Album reissue with additional tracks, Audika, 2004 (AU-1002–2)

1. "Tone Bone Kone" / 2. "Soon-to-Be Innocent Fun" / 3. "Answers Me" /
4. "Being It" / 5. "Place I Know / Kid Like You" / 6. "She's the Star / I Take
This Time" / 7. "Tree House" / 8. "See-Through" / 9. "Hiding Your Present
from You" / 10. "Wax the Van" / 11. "All-Boy All-Girl" / 12. "Lucky Cloud" /
13. "Tower of Meaning / Rabbit's Ear / Home away from Home" / 14. "Let's
Go Swimming" / 15. "The Name of the Next Song" / 16. "Happy Ending" /
17. "Canvas Home" / 18. "Our Last Night Together"

Tracks 15–18 from *Sketches for World of Echo*, produced by Arthur Russell, 1986
(previously unreleased)

2005

Arthur Russell, *Let's Go Swimming*

MP3 EP, Audika, 2005 (AU-1003–2)

1. "Let's Go Swimming (Gulf Stream Dub)" / 2. "You Have Did the Right Thing
When You Put That Skylight In" / 3. "Hiding Your Present From You" /
4. "They and Their Friends"

Produced by Steve Knutson

2006

Arthur Russell, *Another Thought*

> Album reissue, Orange Mountain Music, 2006 (OMM-0027)

Arthur Russell, *First Thought Best Thought*

> Album, Audika, 2006 (AU-1005-2)
>
> Disc 1. 1–10. "Instrumentals — 1974: Volume 1" (previously unreleased), recorded 27 April 1975 at the Kitchen / 11. "Instrumentals — 1974: Volume 2, Part 1," recorded 23 June 1977 at the Franklin Street Art Center / 12–15. "Instrumentals — 1974: Volume 2, Part 2," recorded 10 May 1978 at the Kitchen / 16. "Reach One (With Two Fender Rhodes)" (1973), recorded 7 May 1975 at the Experimental Intermedia Foundation
>
> Disc 2. 1–7. "Tower of Meaning," recorded February 1981. Julius Eastman, conductor / 8. "Sketch for the Face of Helen," recorded sometime in the early 1980s
>
> Compilation produced by Steve Knutson and Ernie Brooks

Arthur Russell, *Springfield*

> Album, Audika, 2006 (AU-1007-2)
>
> 1. "Springfield" / 2. "Springfield (DFA remix)" / 3. "Springfield (Detail)" / 4. "See My Brother, He's Jumping Out (Let's Go Swimming #1)" / 5. "Corn #3" / 6. "Hiding Your Present from You" / 7. "You Have Did the Right Thing When You Put That Skylight In"
>
> Arthur Russell: vocals, cello, keyboards, and all drum programming; Peter Zummo: trombone. Additional keyboard and drum programming by the DFA on track 2.
>
> All tracks written and produced by Arthur Russell, except for track 4, produced by Arthur Russell and Mark Freedman. All tracks previously unreleased. Tracks 1–3 recorded in New York City in 1988, and tracks 4–7 from *Corn*, recorded 1985.

Various, *Amplified: New Music Meets Rock, 1981–1986 ("From the Kitchen Archives" series, Vol. 3)*

> Compilation album, Orange Mountain Music, 2006 (OMM-0024)
>
> Track 6. Arthur Russell, "Hiding Your Present From You." Music and words by Arthur Russell; cello, voice, and electronics by Arthur Russell. From an unlabeled, eight-track test pressing, recorded at the Experimental Intermedia Foundation, New York, 1986.
>
> Track 7. Arthur Russell, "All-Boy All-Girl." Music and words by Arthur Russell; cello, voice, and electronics by Arthur Russell. From an unlabeled, eight-track test pressing, recorded at the Experimental Intermedia Foundation, New York, 1986.

2007

Dinosaur L, *24 → 24 Music*
> Album, Traffic Entertainment Group, 2007 (TEG-76530-2)
> 1. "#1 (You're Gonna Be Clean on Your Bean)" / 2. "#5 (Go Bang!)" /
> 3. "#2 (No, Thank You)" / 4. "#7" / 5. "#3 (In the Corn Belt)" /
> 6. "#6 (Get Set)" / 7. "Clean on Your Bean #1" / 8. "#5 (Go Bang!)
> (François K Mix)" / 9. "Go Bang! (Thank You Arthur Edit)" /
> 10. "In the Corn Belt (Larry Levan Mix)"
> Produced by Arthur Russell, except track #1 produced by Arthur Russell and
> Peter Gordon

2008

Arthur Russell, *Love Is Overtaking Me*
> Album, Audika, 2008 (AU-1010-2)
> 1. "Close My Eyes" / 2. "Goodbye Old Paint" / 3. "Maybe She" / 4. Turbo Sporty,
> "Oh Fernanda Why" / 5. "Time Away" / 6. "Nobody Wants a Lonely Heart" /
> 7. "I Couldn't Say It to Your Face" / 8. "This Time Dad You're Wrong"
> 9. Flying Hearts, "What It's Like" / 10. "Eli" / 11. "Hey! How Does Everybody
> Know" / 12. "I Forget and I Can't Tell" / 13. "Habit of You" / 14. "Janine"
> 15. "Big Moon" / 16. "Your Motion Says" / 17. "The Letter" / 18. "Don't Forget
> about Me" / 19. Bright and Early, "Love Is Overtaking Me" / 20. Bright and
> Early, "Planted a Thought" / 21. "Love Comes Back"
> Compilation produced by Ernie Brooks, Steve Knutson, and Tom Lee

Appearances

Jill Kroesen, "I Really Want to Bomb You" / "Jesus Song"
> Seven-inch single, Lust/Unlust Music, 1980 (JMB-747)
> Arthur Russell: cello

Various, *The Fruit of the Original Sin*
> Compilation album, Les Disques du Crépuscule, 1981 (TWI-035)
> Side D, track 2. Thick Pigeon, "Sudan." Arthur Russell: cello

Jill Kroesen, *Stop Vicious Cycles*
> Album, Lovely Music, 1982 (VR-1501)
> Side B, track 2. "Fay Shism Blues." Arthur Russell: cello

Allen Ginsberg, *First Blues*
> Album, John Hammond Records, 1983 (W2X-37673)
> Disc 1, track 5. "CIA Dope Calypso." Arthur Russell: cello, tambourine
> Disc 2, track 2. "Gospel Noble Truths." Arthur Russell: cello, tambourine
> Disc 2, track 6. "Father Death Blues." Arthur Russell: cello

Powerman, "Lost Tribe"
Twelve-inch single, Battery Sound, 1983 (BS-1013)
A2. "Lost Tribe." Arthur Russell: cello

Sounds of JHS 126 Brooklyn, "Chill Pill"
Twelve-inch single, Sleeping Bag Records, 1983 (SLX-004)
Side B, track 2. "Chill Pill (Under Water Mix)"
Mixed by Killer Whale [Arthur Russell]

Jah Wobble, The Edge, and Holger Czukay, Snake Charmer
Mini-album, Island Records, 1983 (90151-1-B)
Side A, track 2. "Hold On to Your Dreams." Arthur Russell: lyrics

Bonzo Goes to Washington, "5 Minutes"
Twelve-inch single, Sleeping Bag Records, 1984 (SLX-013, SLX-666–13)
Side A. "5 Minutes (R-R-R Radio Mix)" / "5 Minutes (B-B-B Bombing Mix)"
Edited by Arthur Russell

Clandestine featuring Ned Sublette,
"Radio Rhythm (S-I-G-N-A-L-S-M-A-R-T)"
Twelve-inch single, Sleeping Bag Records, 1984 (SLX-011)
Side A, track 2. "Radio Rhythm (S-I-G-N-A-L-S-M-A-R-T) (Extra Cheese Mix)"
Side B, track 1. "Radio Rhythm (S-I-G-N-A-L-S-M-A-R-T) (Dub Mix)"
Both tracks remixed by Killer Whale [Arthur Russell] and NS [Ned Sublette]

Felix, "Tiger Stripes"/"You Can't Hold Me Down"
Promotional twelve-inch single, Sleeping Bag, 1984 (SLX-008)
Lyrics by Killer Whale [Arthur Russell]; side B mixed by Killer Whale

Nicky Siano "Tiger Stripes"/"Move"
Twelve-inch single, Splash, 1984 (31855)
Lyrics by Killer Whale [Arthur Russell]

Elodie Lauten, The Death of Don Juan
Album, Cat Collectors, 1985 (CC-713)
Arthur Russell: cello, tenor vocals

Lola, "Wax the Van"
Twelve-inch single, Jump Street, 1985 (JS-1007)
Side A. "Wax the Van (Kenny's Club Version)" / "Wax the Van (Cherry's Club)"
Side B. "Wax the Van (Radio Edit)" / "Wax the Van (Jon's Dub)"
Written by Lola Blank, Arthur Russell; produced by Bob Blank and Lola Blank
Keyboards: Arthur Russell, Kenny Blank

Peter Zummo, Zummo With an X
Album, Loris Records, 1985 (LR-001)
Side 1. "Instrumentals" (1980) / "Half Steps" / "Sixths" / "Whole Steps" /

"Sevenths" / "Chromatic Fourths" / "Unisons" / "Four Notes, Large
Intervals"
Side 2. "Song IV," from the suite *Six Songs*
Arthur Russell: cello

Peter Gordon, *Innocent*
Album, CBS, 1986 (BFM-42098)
A4. "That Hat." Arthur Russell: vocals

Jerry Harrison, *Casual Gods*
Album, Sire, 1987 (9-25663-2)
Track 6. "A Perfect Lie." Written by Arthur Russell and Ernie Brooks

Lola, "I Need More"
Twelve-inch single, Vinylmania, 1988 (VMR-015)
Side A. "I Need More (Club Mix)" / "I Need More (Radio Edit)"
Side B. "I Need More (Kenny's Club Mix)" / "I Need More (Attic Mix)"
Keyboards: Arthur Russell, Fred Zarr

Jerry Harrison, *Walk On Water*
Album, Fly/Sire, 1990 (25943)
Track 12. "Facing the Fire." Cowritten by Arthur Russell
Track 13. "The Doctors Lie." Cowritten by Arthur Russell

Allen Ginsberg, *Holy Soul Jelly Roll: Poems and Songs, 1949–1993*
Album, Rhino, 1994 (R2-71693)
Disc 3: 11. "A Cradle Song" (Arthur Russell: cello) / 12. "Infant Joy" (Arthur
Russell: cello) / 13. "The Fly" (Arthur Russell: cello) / 14. "Voice of the
Bard" (Arthur Russell: cello) / 15. "School Boy" (Arthur Russell: cello) /
16. "A Dream" (Arthur Russell: cello) / 19. "Pacific High Studio Mantras
(Om Ah Hum Vajra Guru Padma Siddhi Hum)" (Arthur Russell: cello)
All tracks recorded in 1971 and previously unreleased

Peter Zummo, *Experimenting with Household Chemicals*
Album, Experimental Intermedia, 1995 (XI-116)
1. "Fresh Batteries" / 2. "Includes Free Information" / 3. "Sung, Played,
Heard" / 4. "Rocket Scientist" / 5. "In Three Movements" / 6. "Peaceful
Transportation"
Arthur Russell: cello

Jon Gibson, *Two Solo Pieces*
Album, New Tone, 1996 (NT-6756-2)
Track 5. "Song 1." Arthur Russell: cello

Talking Heads, *Talking Heads: 77*
Album reissue, Sire Records, 2006 (8122-73297-2)
Track 14. "Psycho Killer (Acoustic)." Cello: Arthur Russell

Bibliography

This bibliography contains references to books and journal articles. Newspapers, magazines, and other ephemera are cited in the notes.

Adorno, Theodor W. *Philosophy of New Music*. Translated, edited, and with an introduction by Robert Hullot-Kentor. Minneapolis: University of Minnesota Press, 2006.

Attali, Jacques. *Noise: The Political Economy of Music*. 1977. Translated by Brian Massumi. Minneapolis: University of Minnesota Press, 1989.

Baker, Stuart, ed. *New York Noise: Art and Music from the New York Underground, 1978–88*. London: Soul Jazz Records Publishing, 2007.

Bangs, Lester. *Psychotic Reactions and Carburetor Dung*. Edited and with an introduction by Greil Marcus. New York: Knopf, 1988.

Bogue, Ronald. *Deleuze on Music, Painting, and the Arts*. New York: Routledge, 2003.

———. "Violence in Three Shades of Metal: Death, Doom and Black." In Buchanan and Swiboda, *Deleuze and Music*, 95–117.

Broyles, Michael. *Mavericks and Other Traditions in American Music*. New Haven: Yale University Press, 2004.

Buchanan, Ian, and Marcel Swiboda, eds. *Deleuze and Music*. Edinburgh: Edinburgh University Press, 2004.

Cannato, Vincent. *The Ungovernable City: John Lindsay and His Struggle to Save New York*. New York: Basic, 2001.

Carnoy, Martin. *Faded Dreams: The Politics and Economics of Race in America*. Cambridge: Cambridge University Press, 1994.

Chafe, William H. *The Unfinished Journey: America Since World War II*. New York: Oxford University Press, 1999.

Chang, Jeff. *Can't Stop, Won't Stop: A History of the Hip-Hop Generation.* London: Ebury, 2005.

Cheren, Mel. *My Life and the Paradise Garage: Keep On Dancin'.* New York: 24 Hours for Life, 2000.

Corbett, John, and Terri Kapsalis. "Aural Sex: The Female Orgasm in Popular Sound." In *Experimental Sound and Radio,* edited by Allen S. Weiss, 97–106. Cambridge, Mass.: MIT Press, 2001.

Crawford, Richard. *America's Musical Life.* New York: W. W. Norton, 2001.

DeLanda, Manuel. *A New Philosophy of Society: Assemblage Theory and Social Complexity.* New York: Continuum, 2006.

Deleuze, Gilles, and Félix Guattari. *A Thousand Plateaus: Capitalism and Schizophrenia.* 1980. Translated and with a foreword by Brian Massumi. Minneapolis: University of Minnesota Press, 1987.

Dessen, Michael. "Decolonizing American Art Music." PhD diss., University of California, San Diego, 1983.

Duckworth, William. *Talking Music.* New York: Schirmer, 1995.

Dyer, Richard. "In Defence of Disco." In Kureishi and Savage, *The Faber Book of Pop,* 518–27.

Foege, Alec. *Confusion Is Next: The Sonic Youth Story.* New York: St. Martin's, 1994.

Foster, Hal. *Recordings: Art, Spectacle, Cultural Politics.* Port Townsend, Wash.: Bay Press, 1985.

Freeman, Joshua. *Working-Class New York: Life and Labor Since World War II.* New York: New Press, 2000.

Frith, Simon, and Howard Horne. *Art into Pop.* London: Methuen, 1987.

Gameson, Joshua. *Sylvester: The Legend, the Music, the Seventies in San Francisco.* New York: Henry Holt, 2005.

Gann, Kyle. *Music Downtown: Writings from the Village Voice.* Berkeley: University of California Press, 2006.

Gendron, Bernard. *Between Montmartre and the Mudd Club: Popular Music and the Avant-Garde.* Chicago: University of Chicago Press, 2002.

———. "The Downtown Music Scene." In Taylor, *The Downtown Book,* 41–65.

Gilbert, Jeremy. "Becoming-Music: The Rhizomatic Moment of Improvisation." In Buchanan and Swiboda, *Deleuze and Music,* 118–39.

Glass, Philip. *Opera on the Beach: Philip Glass on His New World of Music Theatre.* Edited and with supplementary material by Robert T. Jones. London: Faber, 1988.

Goldberg, RoseLee. *Laurie Anderson.* London: Thames and Hudson, 2000.

Goldman, Albert. *Disco.* New York: Hawthorn, 1978.

Govinda, Lama Anagarika. *The Way of the White Clouds.* 1966. London: Rider, 1998.

Haden-Guest, Anthony. *The Last Party: Studio 54, Disco, and the Culture of the Night.* New York: William Morrow, 1997.

Hagger, Steve. *Art after Midnight: The East Village Scene.* New York: St. Martin's, 1986.

Hemment, Drew. "Affect and Individuation in Popular Electronic Music." In Buchanan and Swiboda, *Deleuze and Music*, 76–94.

Hobsbawm, Eric. *Age of Extremes: The Short Twentieth Century, 1914–1991*. London: Abacus, 1995.

Holmstrom, John, ed. *Punk: The Original*. New York: Trans-High, 1996.

Hughes, Walter. "In the Empire of the Beat: Discipline and Disco." In *Microphone Fiends: Youth Music and Youth Culture*. Edited by Andrew Ross and Tricia Rose, 147–57. New York: Routledge, 1994.

Johnson, Tom. *The Voice of New Music: New York City, 1972–1982; A Collection of Articles Originally Published by the Village Voice*. Eindhoven, Netherlands: Het Apollohuis, 1989; reprinted as a digital book in 2002 (available at http://www.kalvos.org/pdf/johnsonvoice.doc).

Jordan, Tim. "Collective Bodies: Raving and the Politics of Gilles Deleuze and Félix Guattari." *Body & Society* 1, no. 1 (1995): 125–46.

Kaiser, Charles. *The Gay Metropolis, 1940–1996*. 1997. London: Weidenfeld and Nicolson, 1998.

Killian, Kevin. "Arthur Russell." In *Screen Tests*. Forthcoming from Fanzine Press, 2010.

Kostelanetz, Richard. *SoHo: The Rise and Fall of an Artists' Colony*. New York: Routledge, 2003.

Kureishi, Hanif, and Jon Savage, eds. *The Faber Book of Pop*. London: Faber and Faber, 1995.

Lavezzoli, Peter. *The Dawn of Indian Music in the West: Bhairavi*. New York: Continuum, 2006.

Lawrence, Tim. "Connecting with the Cosmic: Arthur Russell, Rhizomatic Musicianship, and the Downtown Music Scene, 1973-92." *Liminalities* 3, no. 3 (2007): 1–84.

———. "Disco Madness: Walter Gibbons and the Legacy of Turntablism and Remixology." *Journal of Popular Music Studies* 20, no. 3 (2008): 276–329.

———. "'I Want to See All My Friends at Once': Arthur Russell and the Queering of Gay Disco." *Journal of Popular Music Studies* 18, no. 2 (2006): 144–66.

———. *Love Saves the Day: A History of American Dance Music Culture, 1970–1979*. Durham, N.C.: Duke University Press, 2003.

Leach, Mary Jane. "In Search of Julius Eastman." *New Music Box*, 8 November 2005, http://www.newmusicbox.org. Accessed 25 August 2006.

Lewis, George. *A Power Stronger than Itself: The AACM and American Experimental Music*. Chicago: University of Chicago Press, 2008.

List, Garrett. "Twenty Years Is a Long Time." In Morrissey, *The Kitchen Turns Twenty*, 23–27.

Lunch, Lydia. Untitled essay in Taylor, *The Downtown Book*, 95.

Mahler, Jonathan. *Ladies and Gentlemen, the Bronx Is Burning*. New York: Farrar, Straus, and Giroux, 2005.

Masters, Marc. *No Wave*. London: Black Dog, 2007.

McCormick, Carlo. "A Crack In Time." In Taylor, *The Downtown Book*, 67–94.

Mele, Christopher. *Selling the Lower East Side: Culture, Real Estate, and Resistance in New York City*. Minneapolis: University of Minnesota Press, 2000.

Mertens, Wim. *American Minimal Music: La Monte Young, Terry Riley, Steve Reich, Philip Glass*. 1980. Translated by J. Hautekiet, with a preface by Michael Nyman. London: Kahn and Averill, 1988.

Morrissey, Lee, ed. *The Kitchen Turns Twenty: A Retrospective Anthology*. New York: Kitchen Center for Video, Music, Dance, Performance, Film and Literature, 1992.

Musto, Michael. *Downtown*. New York: Vintage, 1986.

Nyman, Michael. *Experimental Music: Cage and Beyond*. 1974. Rev. ed. with a foreword by Brian Eno. Cambridge: Cambridge University Press, 1999.

Piekut, Benjamin. "Taking Henry Flynt Seriously." *Institute for Studies in American Music Newsletter* 34, no. 2 (2005): 6–7, 14.

Potter, Keith. *Four Musical Minimalists: La Monte Young, Terry Riley, Steve Reich, Philip Glass*. Cambridge: Cambridge University Press, 2000.

Prial, Dunstan. *The Producer: John Hammond and the Soul of American Music*. New York: Farrar, Straus, and Giroux, 2006.

Reich, Steve. *Writings on Music, 1965–2000*. Edited and with an introduction by Paul Hillier. Oxford: Oxford University Press, 2002.

Reynolds, Simon. *Energy Flash: A Journey through Rave Music and Dance Culture*. London: Picador, 1998.

———. *Rip It Up and Start Again: Post-Punk 1978–1984*. London: Faber, 2005; New York: Penguin, 2006.

Rockwell, John. *All American Music: Composition in the Late Twentieth Century*. New York: Alfred A. Knopf, 1983.

Rodaway, Paul. *Sensuous Geographies: Body, Sense and Place*. London: Routledge, 1994.

Roseman, Marina. "The New Rican Village: Artists in Control of the Image-Making Machinery." *Latin American Music Review / Revista de Música Latinoamericana* 4, no. 1 (1983): 132–67.

Schulman, Bruce J. *The Seventies: The Great Shift in American Culture, Society, and Politics*. New York: Free Press, 2001.

Schwarz, K. Robert. *Minimalists*. London: Phaidon, 1996.

Shapiro, Peter. *Turn the Beat Around: The Secret History of Disco*. London: Faber and Faber, 2005.

Shilts, Randy. *And the Band Played On: Politics, People, and the AIDS Epidemic*. New York: St. Martin's Press, 1987.

Smith Brindle, Reginald. *The New Music: The Avant-Garde Since 1945*. 2nd edition. Oxford University Press, 1987.

Stearns, Robert, ed. *The Kitchen, 1974–1975*. New York: Haleakala, 1975.

———, ed. *The Kitchen, 1975–1976*. New York: Haleakala, 1976.

Sweet, Robert E. *Music Universe, Music Mind: Revisiting the Creative Music Studio, Woodstock, New York.* Ann Arbor, Mich.: Arborville, 1996.

Taylor, Marvin J., ed. *The Downtown Book: The New York Art Scene 1974–1984.* Princeton: Princeton University Press, 2006.

————. "Playing the Field: The Downtown Scene and Cultural Production, an Introduction." In Taylor, *The Downtown Book,* 17–39.

Toop, David. *Haunted Weather: Music, Silence and Memory.* London: Serpent's Tail, 2004.

————. *Ocean of Sound: Aether Talk, Ambient Sound and Imaginary Worlds.* 1995. London: Serpent's Tail, 1996.

Toynbee, Jason. *Making Popular Music: Musicians, Creativity and Institutions.* London: Arnold, 2000.

Walters, Barry. "Stayin' Alive." In Kureishi and Savage, *The Faber Book of Pop,* 644–53.

Whittier, Jeff. *Good Is Never Lost.* Palo Alto, Calif.: Eastern Gate, 2006.

Williams, William Carlos. *William Carlos Williams: Selected Poems.* 1949. Rev. ed. with an introduction by Randall Jarrell. New York: New Directions, 1969.

Internet References

This list of Web addresses was updated on 31 July 2008. All were functional at that time.

Mustafa Ahmed: http://www.myspace.com/drumsongcollaborations

Stuart Aitken: http://www.fleeeg.blogspot.com/2007/06/arthur-russell-wax-poetics-june-2007_04.html

Arthur-O-Rama: http://www.myspace.com/arthurorama

Arthur's Landing: http://www.myspace.com/arthurslanding

Artists with AIDS: http://www.artistswithaids.org/artforms/music/catalogue/Russell.html

Audika: http://www.audikarecords.com

Bob Blank: http://www.blankproductions.com

Joyce Bowden: http://profile.myspace.com/index.cfm?fuseaction=user.viewprofile&friendid=162126456

Rhys Chatham: http://www.rhyschatham.net

DFA Records: http://www.dfarecords.com

Arnold Dreyblatt: http://www.dreyblatt.net

Julius Eastman: http://www.en.wikipedia.org/wiki/Julius_Eastman; http://www.mjleach.com/eastman.htm

Experimental Intermedia Foundation: http://www.experimentalintermedia.org

Sasha Frere-Jones: http://www.newyorker.com/archive/2004/03/08/040308crmu_music

Jon Gibson: http://www.jongibson.net

Allen Ginsberg: http://www.allenginsberg.org

Steven Hall: http://www.myspace.com/buddhistarmymusic

Jess Harvell: http://www.freakytrigger.co.uk/old-ft/essays/2001/09/russell

Kevin Killian: http://www.epc.buffalo.edu/authors/killian/

The Kitchen: http://www.thekitchen.org

Joan La Barbara: http://www.joanlabarbara.com

Elodie Lauten: http://www.elodielauten.net

Tim Lawrence: http://liminalities.net/3-3/russell.htm; http://www.timlawrence
.info/articles/2006/ArthurRussellqueering.php; http://www.timlawrence.info

Mary Jane Leach: http://www.mjleach.com

George Lewis: http://www.music.columbia.edu/people/bios/lewis-george

Eric Liljestrand: http://www.oldnordicfolksongs.com

Garrett List: http://www.garrettlist.com

The Loft: http://www.theloftnyc.com

Gary Lucas: http://www.garylucas.com

Walter Allaudin Mathieu: http://www.coldmountainmusic.com

Rome Neal: http://www.myspace.com/romeneal

Vera November: http://profile.myspace.com/index.cfm?fuseaction=user.view
profile&friendid=69494994

Ben Ratliff: http://www.nytimes.com/2004/02/29/arts/music-the-many-faces-
and-grooves-of-arthur-russell.html

Rough Trade: http://www.roughtrade.com

Arthur Russell http://profile.myspace.com/index.cfm?fuseaction=user.viewprofile
&friendid=87863158

Soul Jazz Records: http://www.souljazzrecords.co.uk

Taken By Trees: http://profile.myspace.com/index.cfm?fuseaction=user.viewprofile
&friendid=101175133

Tracey Thorn: http://profile.myspace.com/index.cfm?fuseaction=user.viewprofile&
friendid=102188224

David Toop: http://www.davidtoop.com

David Van Tieghem: http://www.vantieghem.com

Wikipedia: http://www.en.wikipedia.org/wiki/Arthur_Russell_(cellist)

Wild Combination: A Portrait of Arthur Russell: http://www.arthurrussellmovie.com

Matt Wolff: http://profile.myspace.com/index.cfm?fuseaction=user.viewprofile&
friendid=39730040

Ellen Ziegler: http://www.ellenziegler.com

Robert Ziegler: http://www.myspace.com/robertziegler360

Peter Zummo: http://www.kalvos.org/zummope.html

Index

Songs, albums, and other works are by Arthur Russell unless otherwise indicated.

Arthur's Landing, 350–51

Ashley, Robert, 29, 67–68, 73–74, 180, 183, 188

Association for the Advancement of Creative Musicians (AACM), 98, 182

astrology, 90, 270

atonality, 27–29, 53

Audika, 349, 350, 372n30, 372n34

"Avant-Garde Festival" of 1973, 55

Babbitt, Bob, 130–31

Babbitt, Milton, 27–28, 51

Balinese gamelan, 140–41

"Ballad of the Lights, The," 106, 109, 334

Bambaataa, Afrika, 224, 281–82

bands: Blue Green, 250; Bright and Early, 250–51, 256, 316; Dinosaur, 137, 146, 195, 214; Dinosaur L, 214–23, 348; Fast Food Band, 103; Flying Hearts, 105–9, 111–23, 134, 189, 195–99, 298–301, 338; Kailas Shugendo Mantric Sun Band, 23, 37–38, 360n21; Le Orme, 120–22, 365n42; Loose Joints, 172–73, 175, 188–89, 193; Love of Life Orchestra (LOLO), 113–16, 134, 184, 258; Necessaries, 2, 6, 189, 199–204, 209, 246; Normal Music Band, 110; Palo, 250; Sailboats, 193–94, 250, 266; Singing Tractors, 213–14, 294, 338

Bangs, Lester, 143–45

Bartel, Jonni Sue, 42–43, 45, 75

Bascomb, Wilbur, 130–31, 160–64

Basquiat, Jean-Michel, 247

Battery Sound, 239–41, 256

Beastie Boys, 249

Beatles, 24, 143, 360n5

Beckett, Samuel, 28, 102–3

Behrman, David, 62, 80, 114, 180

Bergamo, John, 39–40

Berger, Karl, 69, 98

Bernd, John, xix, 242, 270–71, 288, 314

Between Montmartre and the Mudd Club (Gendron), xviii, 8, 69

"Big Blue Bus," 338

Big Game (Woodard), 209, 312

"Big Moon," 333

Big Sky (Necessaries), 202–3, 209

Bill's Friends, 208–9, 369n33

"Birthday," 320

Blank, Bob, 2, 203; Connecticut studio of, 295, 305, 320, 328; Lola promoted by, 255, 320; Necessaries viewed by, 199–200; negotiating of, 239, 305–6; Russell's orchestral disco viewed by, 149–54, 161, 165, 172, 238–40, 366n19; Sleeping Bag Records viewed by, 227, 256–57

Blank, Lola, 215–16, 219, 221–22, 255, 305–6, 310, 320

Blondie, 8, 108, 143, 144

"Bobby," 106, 109, 199, 338

Bohannon, Hamilton, 140, 157

Bonzo Goes to Washington, 255

Boulez, Pierre, 27–28, 53, 181

Bowden, Joyce, 193; in Flying Hearts, 195–98, 298–301; goodbyes to Russell by, 331, 334, 337–38; Milwaukee visited by, 298–301; Russell's AIDS viewed by, 313–14, 326; Russell's Buddhism viewed by, 225–26; Russell's legacy viewed by, 348; on Russell's songs, 227–28, 233–35, 297, 309, 370n41, 373n7; tributes to Russell by, 350–51

Branca, Glenn, xix, 8, 158, 179–80, 183–84, 188, 344

Braxton, Anthony, 69, 98, 183

Bright and Early, 250–51, 256, 316

Brooklyn Academy of Music, 258–59

Brooks, Ernie: in Arthur's Landing, 350–51; Blank viewed by, 306; compositions by, 118; in Flying Hearts, 105–9, 120, 195–99, 298–301; goodbyes to Russell by, 331, 334, 336, 337–38; on *Instrumentals*, 75–76, 115; "Kiss Me Again" recording, 129–32, 195;

Coltrane, Alice, 39
Columbia Records, 2, 70–73, 75
Community Health Project, 294
compositional music, 2, 4, 8–9, 205–14, 232; equal temperament tuning in, 212–13; Flying Hearts performances of, 112–15; funding of, 111, 129; generation gap in, 232; generative aesthetic of, 5–6, 55, 59, 163; minimalism in, 27–32, 69–70, 79–80, 360n14, 363n48, 366n2; mixed media explorations in, 67–68; for modern dance, 270–72; neotonal music in, 159; new music in, 180–87; postminimalist response in, 79–80; recordings of, 238–46; rock collaborations in, 67–70, 116–18; scoring and the studio in, 163; serialism in, xviii, 27–29, 50–51, 360n14; West Coast style of, 28–29
Contortions, 144
Cooper, Paula, 49
Corn, 252–54, 266, 371n9; reworking of, 301–8; unreleased tracks from, 373n17
"Corn," 252, 371n9
counterculture, 95–96
"Cowboys are Frequently Secretly (Fond of Each Other)" (Sublette), 207–8, 344–45
Crocker, Frankie, 174, 222, 226
"C-Thru," 270
Cunningham, Merce, 87, 270–71

D'Acquisto, Steve, xv–xvi, xix, 148–54, 160; gay sexuality and, 169–70; mutant disco mixes of, 165–66, 178; Russell's collaboration with, 215, 228
Dahl, Steve, 143, 145
dance music, xv–xvi, 2, 341; backlash against, 142–48; commissions for, 270–73; Gibbons's collaborations on, 261–70; histories of, 352, 376n14; HIV/AIDS impact on, 308–9; improvisation and reinvention in, 161–64,

190; Kevorkian's collaborations on, xxi, 3, 220–23, 266; "Kiss Me Again," 129–37; "Let's Go Swimming," 261–67, 270, 272, 283–84, 291; Levan's collaborations on, 3, 147–48, 171–74, 223, 226–30, 261, 266, 369n38; by Love of Life Orchestra (LOLO), 113–16, 160; other composers on, 146, 154, 157–60, 164, 179, 344; repetitive variation in, 128–30, 164, 366n2; re-releases of, 347–48; at rock clubs, 179–80; Russell's legacy in, 3; sales of, 164–65; "School Bell / Treehouse," 267–68, 270, 272–73, 291; Siano's collaborations on, 127–28; 24 → 24 Music, 215–23, 279. See also disco; mutant disco; twelve-inch singles
dance party scene, 125, 343–45, 375n6; compositional scene vs., 128–29; drug use in, 127, 346; gay scene in, 126, 130, 138, 141–42, 336; rock clubs, 179–80; trance-like states in, 129. See also modern dance
dance productions, xv, 1–2, 6; modern dance, 41–45, 270–72, 312–13, 371n26; by Zummo and Woodard, 110, 271–72
Danceteria, 2, 179, 200–201, 209, 375n6
Davis, Miles, 39, 71, 343
Death of Don Juan, The (Lauten), 295
"Deer in the Forest, The," 252, 371n9
Defunkt, 144, 183
DeLanda, Manuel, xviii, 96
Deleuze, Gilles, 29, 345, 364n6, 366n2, 375n10
Delgado, Vince, 39–40, 146
DePino, David, 171, 174
Desperately Seeking Susan, 249
"Detroit Tonight" (Brooks and Russell), 202
DFA, 351, 373n17
digital technology, 352–55
Dinosaur: "Dumbo Dumbo," 146; "Kiss

Gordon, Peter (*cont.*)

74, 179, 336; dance music explored by, 344, 375n7; on demo for Hammond, 71–72, 75; downtown viewed by, 51–52, 247; in Fast Food Band, 103; in Flying Hearts, 107–8; *Innocent*, 260; on *Instrumentals*, 75–76, 157; "Kiss Me Again" recording, 131; Kitchen performances of, 97; Love of Life Orchestra (LOLO) and, 113–16, 134, 160, 180, 184, 258, 344; at memorial events for Russell, 333–34, 337–38; Modern Lovers viewed by, 66; at "New Music New York" festival, 180, 181; new wave viewed by, 108, 143; Normal Music Band and, 110; Russell's collaboration with, 87, 160–64, 166, 174, 208, 232, 258–60, 347; Russell's lack of recognition viewed by, 342; *Secret Pastures*, 258–59; at Sobossek's, 89–90; success and influence of, 112–13, 155, 257–60, 273; *Symphony in Four Movements*, 100–101, 103; "Trust in Rock" concert, 112; on 24 $\rightarrow$ 24 *Music*, 217, 223

Goshorn, Kent, 16–17, 19, 93, 153, 315–16; goodbyes to Russell by, 330, 334, 337–38, 355; Russell's orchestral disco recordings viewed by, 160–64, 217–18

gospel, 140–41

Govinda, Anagarika, 22, 25, 273

Grandmaster Flash and the Furious Five, 281

Green, Al, 144, 167, 173

Green, Robert, 152–53

Guattari, Félix, 345, 364n6, 366n2, 375n10

Guitar Trio (Chatham), 116–17, 158

Hall, Steven, 91–96, 294; *Active Driveway*, 322; in Arthur's Landing, 350–51; Blank viewed by, 149, 306; in Bright and Early, 250–51, 316; D'Acquisto viewed by, 151; experimental music

of, 213–14; friendship with Russell of, 133, 139–41; gay sexuality viewed by, 169–70, 219; Ginsberg's collaborations with, 193; goodbyes to Russell by, 330–31, 337–38; Freedman viewed by, 239–40; Lee viewed by, 178; Russell's AIDS viewed by, 316–17, 327; Russell's cello work viewed by, 276; Russell's collaborations with, 152–53, 157, 159, 166, 167, 172, 193–94, 227–28, 235–36; Russell's legacy viewed by, 348; Russell viewed by, 145–46, 190, 257, 322, 336, 357; Sleeping Bag Records viewed by, 257; *Turbo Sporty*, 270–71, 371n27; Winslow viewed by, 270

Hammond, John, xvi, xix, 2, 87; Ginsberg's recordings by, 95; Russell's demos for, xxv, 70–73, 75, 119–20, 130, 134, 362n29, 362nn36–38

"Happy Ending," 372n34

Haring, Keith, 247, 258–59, 314

Harrison, Jerry: Reagan lampooned by, 255; Russell's work with, 65, 362n29; solo recordings of, 298–301, 316, 374n22; in Talking Heads, 103, 105

Harvell, Jess, 311–12, 350

Harvey, Steven, 223, 341

Hell, Richard, 8, 143

"Hey! How Does Everybody Know," 363n50

"Hiding Your Present from You," 252–53, 371n9, 372n34

Hill, David, 348–50

hip-hop, xvii–xviii, 2, 3, 189, 249, 254, 281–85; at "Aluminum Nights" festival, 184; as black scene, 211–12; in mixed downtown scene, 281–82, 372n40

HIV/AIDS, 186, 336, 351; AIDS Memorial Quilt, 339; Bernd's performance of, 271; Community Health Project clinic, 294; Kaposi's sarcoma, 313–

Johnson, Tom, 7, 51, 59, 97, 181–82, 325, 366n2

Jolly Monk, 102

Jones, Bill T., 258–59

Jones, Robert T., 28

"Just a Blip," 302

Kailas Shugendo commune, 22–26, 32–36

Kailas Shugendo Mantric Sun Band, 23, 37, 38, 360n21

"Keeping Up," 118, 233, 234, 252, 313, 370n42, 371n9

Kerouac, Jack, 22, 95

Kerouac School of Disembodied Poetics, 56, 374n29

Kevorkian, François, xvi, 2, 171, 236–37; remixes by, xxi, 3, 220–23, 266; sample sets of, 320

Khan, Ali Akbar, 24–25, 27, 43

Killer Whale, 228, 229, 266

Killian, Kevin, 138–39, 366n6

"Kiss Me Again," 145, 232, 266; Japanese version of, 140, 366n8; original of, 129–32, 195; Sire's remix of, 3, 135–37, 223

Kitchen Center for Video and Music, xix, 58, 355; art-rock conversation at, 63–70; Chatham as music director of, 59–60, 154–55; composer rule of, 154; experimental composition at, 2, 59–70, 80–81, 204–6; "Five Generations of Composers at the Kitchen" retrospective at, 325; "From the Kitchen Archives" series at, 350, 372n34; funding of, 185–86, 247; Gordon's *Symphony in Four Movements* at, 100–101; influence of, 100; jazz at, 97–98; Lewis as music director of, 182–85; List as music director of, 97, 154, 182; media reviews of, 69; minimalist rock at, 158; "Music: It's the Ocean" series at, 288–89; "New Music New York"

festival at, 180–82, 368n2; Russell as music director of, xix, 62–70, 80–82; Russell's *Instrumentals* at, 75–79, 85, 154–57; Russell's orchestral disco at, 157–64, 211, 243; "Soup and Tart" event, 63, 103; Talking Heads at, 104–5; tenth anniversary celebration of, 182–85, 325; video program at, 60, 64; *World of Echo* project at, 237, 274

Knitting Factory, xix, 296, 324

Knutson, Steve, xvii, 244, 305, 349–50

Konk, 144, 188, 254, 256

Kroesen, Jill, 69, 73, 81, 188; disco viewed by, 159; downtown viewed by, 247; Kitchen performances by, 100; in Love of Life Orchestra (LOLO), 113–16, 184; at "New Music New York" festival, 180; Normal Music Band, 110; recordings by, 208; Russell's collaborations with, 160–64, 217; Russell viewed by, 103

Kukai: Major Work, 33

La Barbara, Joan, 97, 183, 276–77

La Mama, 110, 294–96

Landry, Richard, 62–63, 68

"Last Look at Love," 109

Lateral Pass (Brown), 271–72

Lauten, Elodie, 56, 294, 297, 331; in Arthur's Landing, 350–51; *The Death of Don Juan*, 295; media reviews of, 296; at memorial events for Russell, 334–36; the Pass Concert Series, 237–38; *Remembrance of Things Past* installation, 295; Russell's collaborations with, 209, 212–14, 224–27, 240–41, 243, 324, 369n37

"Laying by Your Lover," 301

Leach, Mary Jane, 185–86, 366n15

Leary, Timothy, 18, 36

Lee, Tom, xvii, 9, 139; Bowden viewed by, 234; memorial events for Russell

Love of Life Orchestra (LOLO) (*cont.*)
work for, 134; performances by, 134,
180, 184, 258; recordings by, 258
Love Saves the Day (Lawrence), 366n1,
376n14
Lower Manhattan Ocean Club, 2, 107–8,
194
LSD, 18, 21, 36, 48, 127
Lucas, Gary, xvii; cover of Russell's
music by, 351; at memorial events for
Russell, 336, 337–38; Russell's collabo-
rations with, 259–61, 280–83; Russell
viewed by, 6–7, 319, 342; Upside
Records, 260–61
Lucier, Alvin, 55, 109, 180
"Lucky Cloud," 233, 236, 370n42
Lunch, Lydia, 8, 344
"Luv Dancin'" (Sanchez), 310–11

Mabou Mines, 102–3
Mac Low, Jackson, 55, 57–58, 80, 183,
306–7
Madden, Diane, 312
Madonna, 203, 249
Maine, 53, 65, 264, 285, 314–15, 329–30,
339
"Make 1, 2," 302, 351
Mancuso, David, xvi–xvii, 6, 125–26,
148–49, 230; response to "Go Bang!"
of, 220, 221; Russell viewed by, 170;
SoHo viewed by, 186–87
Manhattan School of Music (MSM),
52–58
Mantronix, 254, 256
marijuana, 17–18, 21, 139–40, 239, 305
Masters, Marc, xix
Mathieu, William Allaudin, 29–32, 34–
35, 43, 93, 241, 317
*Mavericks and Other Traditions in Ameri-
can Music* (Broyles), 342
Max's Kansas City, 194
McCormick, Carlo, 9, 50, 79, 344
McElroy, Leon, 152–53, 166, 167, 173

McIntosh, Daniel, 312
Medea, 190–93, 211, 242, 270, 370n41
media coverage, 4, 53; of Anchorage
performance, 325; in *Face*, 284,
372n43; interviews, xix, 109, 111–12,
290–91, 301, 309; of "Is It All Over My
Face?," 170; of Kitchen Center, 69;
of "Let's Go Swimming," 266–67; of
modern dance songs, 312; of "Music:
It's the Ocean" performance, 289;
obituaries, 336–37; of performances
with Lauten, 296; posthumous feature
articles, xvii, 6, 349–50; of posthumous releases, 347, 349–50; of *Tower
of Meaning*, 244–46; of Wolff retrospective, 289–90; of *World of Echo*,
280–81
"Me for Real / Home away from
Home / Lucky Cloud," 338
Mercedes, Denise, 84, 94, 160–64, 176
Mercer Arts Center, 59–60, 64, 103, 108
Mertens, Wim, 29, 129, 366n2
microtonal music, 189, 212–13
Middle Eastern music, 140–41
Midwest, 138; Oskaloosa, Iowa, 11–18, 53,
57, 170, 330; in Russell's music, 264–
66; Singing Tractors, 213–14; University High, 19–21
Mills, Lorna, 22–23
Mills, Terry, 22–23
Mindset (McIntosh), 312
minimalism, 27–32, 70, 363n48; Buddhist aspects of, 69; on *Corn*, 252–53;
in disco, 128–29; hypnotic states in,
129; in jazz, 98; in pop, 252–53; post-
minimalist response to, 79–80; repetition in, 164, 366n2; in rock, 68–69,
108, 116, 158, 180
modern dance, 41–45, 110, 270–72, 312–
13, 371n26
Modern Lovers, 63–70
Monk, Meredith, 180, 336

Moog synthesizer, 59, 73

Moorman, Charlotte, 55

Moran, John, 307–8, 329

"More Real," 202–3, 333

Moroder, Giorgio, 163, 168

Moulton, Tom, 163, 261

"Mr. Problems," 234

Mudd Club, 179, 180, 224

multiculturalism, 182–85

Murk, Donald, 5, 336; Anderson viewed by, 104; managerial role of, 134, 147–48, 154–55, 165–66, 173, 175–76; Russell's AIDS viewed by, 319–20; Russell's lack of recognition viewed by, 343, 347; Russell's relationship with, 133–37, 139, 169, 175, 225; Russell viewed by, 152, 159

Murray, Sydney, 85–86, 88, 102–4, 141, 146, 151

"Music: It's the Ocean" series, 288–89

Music for 18 Musicians (Reich), 79–81

Music for the Trine (Lauten), 295

Music in Twelve Parts (Glass), 79–80

Music with Changing Parts (Glass), 67

Musique, 140, 149, 171

musique concrète, 206

Musto, Michael, 7, 247–48

mutant disco (disco-not-disco, post-disco), 3, 164–75, 270, 341, 359n6; "Is It All Over My Face?," 166–67, 171–72; "Kiss Me Again," 130–32, 137; "Pop Your Funk," 166; 24 → 24 *Music*, 161–64, 216–19, 223, 270

Mutant Disco (various), 367n29

"My Tiger, My Timing," 118, 233, 234, 302, 313, 316, 370n41

Naked (Talking Heads), 321

"Name of the Next Song, The," 372n34

Naropa Institute, 56, 91, 95, 374n29

Nath, Pandit Pran, 28, 29, 30

nature themes, 214, 264–66

Neal, Rome, 152, 157, 160–64, 211, 217–18

Necessaries, 2, 6, 160, 189, 199–204, 209, 246

Nelson, Paul, 65, 71

"New and Newer Music" series, 181

new music, xviii, 2, 27–29, 157, 180–83, 187, 344–45; diversity valorized in, 184–85; funding of, 185–86

New Music, The (Smith Brindle), 181

"New Music America" festivals, 185–86

New Music Festival, 294, 295

"New Music New York" festival, 180–82, 368n2

Newport Jazz Festival, 98

New Rican Village, 84, 363n2

new wave, xvii–xviii, 1–2, 52, 108, 344, 352; dance in, 144–45, 170, 172, 345, 367n30; the Necessaries, 199–204, 246; racial aspects of, 143–45

New York City, 47–52, 62, 138. *See also* downtown music scene

New York Dolls, 8, 65

New York Noise (Baker), 7

Niblock, Phill, 63, 102, 336; goodbyes to Russell by, 331; at "New Music New York" festival, 180–81; "World of Echo" project, 273–81, 372n30

"Nobody Wants a Lonely Heart," 362n39

"No Hearts Free," 149, 152, 193

NoHo, 49

non-intentional composition, 55

Nonomura, Yuko, 317; Buddhist practice of, xix, 33, 35–36, 95, 225; slides for *Instrumentals* by, 75–76, 78, 112, 333

Normal Music Band, 110

"No, Thank You," 217

November, Vera, 351

no wave, xvii–xviii, xix, 344

No Wave (Masters), xix

"#5 (Go Bang"!), xvi, 3, 212, 217–23, 226–27, 269–70, 310–11, 333, 347–48

"#7," 217

numerology, 270

Nuyorican Poets Café, 84, 363n2
Nyman, Michael, 29

"Oh Fernando Why?," 121–22, 232, 328, 338, 365n42
1-800-Dinosaur, 294–95, 301–8, 322
"Only Usefulness, The," 109, 152, 193
Ono, Yoko, 50–51
"On the Run" (Tomney and Russell), 202
orchestral disco, 157–59, 189, 211; improv work in, 161–64; 24 → 24 Music recordings, 160–64, 279
Orlovsky, Peter, 38, 93, 137, 151
Oskaloosa, Iowa, 11–18, 53, 57, 170, 330
Other End, 106
"Our Last Night Together," 351, 372n34
"Out by the Porch," 335–36, 338
"Over the Line," 234
Owen, Frank, xvii, 104–5, 130–31, 264–65, 278, 280–82

Pagliuca, Toni, 120–22, 365n42
Paik, Nam June, 328
Palestine, Charlemagne, 63, 97
Paley, Andy, 65, 71–72, 76, 108
Palmer, Robert, 112, 289
Palo, 250
Paradise Garage, 2, 138, 171, 174, 229–30, 308, 344, 372n40
Pareles, Jon, 237, 347
Paris Is Burning, 320
Partch, Harry, 11, 342
Pass Concert Series, 237–38
Paula Cooper Gallery, 49, 60
Peck, Richard, 97, 99
"Perfect Lie, A" (Russell and Brooks), 298
performance art, 103, 179–80, 270–71, 371n27
Perron, Wendy, 110
Perry, Lee, 163
Peter Zummo Orchestra, 271–72

Petronio, Stephen, 271–72, 295
Pettet, Simon, 84
Philosophy of New Music (Adorno), 27
photos: of Acker, 117; of Ahmed, 303; of Albani, 162; of Allaudin, 31; of Aquilone, 127; of Behrman, 114; of Blank, 150; of Bowden, 197, 300; of Brooks, 67, 106, 117, 299, 300; of Chatham, 116, 117; of Dreyblatt, 205; of Eastman, 156; of East Twelfth Street, 85, 140, 329; of Experimental Intermedia Foundation, 275; of Freedman, 240; of Friedman, 116; of Fujii, 41; of Gibbons, 262; of Gibson, 58; of Ginsberg, 85, 94, 140; of Gordon, 114, 116, 117; of Hall, 92, 94, 194, 251, 307, 317; of Haring, 259; of Johnson, 116; of Jones, 259; of Kitchen, 61, 238; of Kroesen, 116; of Lauten, 296; of Lee, 177, 194, 286, 326; of LOLO, 114, 116, 117; of Lucas, 282; of Maine, 315; of Mercedes, 94; of Murray, 86; of the Necessaries, 201; of Nonomura's slides for Instrumentals, 78; of the Poet's Building, 85, 140; of the Russells, 20, 24; of Ruyle, 162, 210; of Siano, 127, 131; of Sublette, 207; of Tyranny, 114; of Woodard, 210; of Zane, 259; of Zummo, 117, 162, 210
Pizarro, Gladys, 310–11
"Planted a Thought," 250
"Platform on the Ocean, The," 252–53, 266, 371n9
pluralism, 184–85, 189, 353–55
poetry, 2, 80, 84, 290; by Hall, 139, 316; Russell's work with Ginsberg, 37, 56, 328, 334; Trungpa on, 95
Poetry Project at St. Mark's, 74
Poet's Building, East Twelfth St., 84–89, 134–35, 137–38, 140, 177, 337
Point Music, 321, 347

Russell, Arthur (*cont.*)

—appearance of, 1, 4, 15, 214

—birth and childhood of, 11–16, 19, 151, 194

—cello music of, xvii, 2–4, 6, 84; at Ali Akbar College of Music, 25–32, 34; with amplifiers and special effects, 39, 77, 87, 173, 275–76, 361n24; Anderson's approach to, 104; on dance-music recordings, 131, 151–52, 166–67, 366n22; education in, 14, 23; with Ginsberg, 37–38, 138, 328; on Glass's *Cascando*, 102; in *Instrumentals* project, 75, 77; at Kailas Shugendo commune, 23–24; playing style of, 57–58, 151–52, 173, 276, 328; at San Francisco Conservatory, 39; with Talking Heads, 105, 321; on 24 → 24 *Music*, 217. *See also* voice-cello songs

—day jobs of, 175–76

—death and tributes for, 6, 332–39, 369n34

—drug use by, 17–18, 23, 139–40, 257

—eccentricity of, 36, 56–57, 81–82, 102, 204

—emotional disposition of, 16, 32, 257–58, 262–63

—financial challenges facing, 174–78, 320

—health challenges facing, xxi, 6, 287–88, 293–94, 301, 309, 313–33

—horoscope of, 90, 270

—interest in affective music scenes of, 344–46, 355, 375n10

—lack of recognition of, 5–7, 188–89, 325, 336–37, 342–43, 359n6

—musical aesthetic of, 1–9, 13, 51, 204; affective music scenes of, 344–46, 355, 375n10; amateur performance in, 4–5, 312; animal, water, and nature themes of, 214, 264–66; black and gay aesthetic in, 8–9, 159–60, 272; Buddhist goals of, 69, 75, 94–95, 224–25, 257, 262, 279–80; collaborative outlook of, xviii–xix; disco's repetitive variation in, 128–30, 164; drum machines in, 5, 302; drumming in, 77, 106, 108–9, 115, 120, 151, 195, 221; electronic pop in, 109–12, 117–18, 254–55; fusion, 291; genre-crossing focus of, 39–41, 63–73, 76–81, 140–41, 188–89, 244–46, 252, 341–46, 354–55; Indian classical influence on, 24–32; intentional slackness in, 289–91; music without drums, 4, 278–79, 284, 309, 372n43; non-narrative structure in, 53–54; of orchestral disco productions, 154–64; postminimalistm in, 79–80; post-party sensibility in, 309; reinvention and indeterminacy in, 5–6, 133, 146, 189–93, 252, 272, 322–23; rhizomatic musicianship in, 345–46; rhythmic groove of, 251; singing in, 276–78, 304–5; in solo cello work, 275–76; unconscious sonic in, 245–46, 344; vernacular communication in, 65; water themes in, 264–65. *See also* Russell, Arthur: cello music of

—musical education of, 33, 276; at Ali Akbar College of Music, 24–32, 34; in cello, 14, 23; at Manhattan School of Music, 52–58; at San Francisco Conservatory of Music, 27–32, 38–39, 62

—musical legacy of, 1–9, 341–57

—names and nicknames of, xx, 12, 19, 23, 25

—parents of, xvii, 11–13, 57; Arthur's correspondence with, 33–34, 36, 89, 109, 115, 174–77; Arthur's later relationship with, 285–87, 330–31; Arthur supported financially by, 174–78, 320; Charles Arthur Musical Enterprise (C.A.M.E.), 176; family vacations of, 19–20, 34–35, 194, 264–65, 285, 314,

329–30; gay sexuality viewed by, 287–88; goodbyes to Arthur by, 331, 333, 339; Lee's relationship with, 314–15; musical interests of, 13–14; New York visited by, 314; social and political success of, 15–17

—performances by, 101–2, 128–29, 193–204, 208–14, 294–97; at Avant-Garde Festival of 1973, 55; of Beckett's *Cascando*, 102–3; at CBGB's, 214; at Experimental Intermedia Foundation, 102, 112, 237–38, 273–74, 324; with Flying Hearts, 107–8, 114–15, 119; with Gibson in Washington Square, 57–58; with Ginsberg, 93–96, 138, 139, 194, 224, 328; in Gordon's *Symphony in Four Movements*, 100–101; with Hall, 270–71, 316, 371n27, 371n29; during illness, 323–26; at Kitchen, 62–63, 100–101, 154–59, 325, 361n24; with Lauten, 209, 212–14, 237–38, 295, 324; with Love of Life Orchestra, 113, 184; at Lower Manhattan Ocean Club, 107; at "Music: It's the Ocean" series, 288–89; of mutant disco, 173; with Necessaries, 199–201; at Pass Concert Series, 237–38; with Sailboats, 193–94; at 1750 Arch Street, 39–41; with Singing Tractors, 213–14, 224; at Sobossek's, 89–90, 110; with Wolff, 57–58, 289–90; with Zummo, 271–72, 323–24. *See also* bands

—recording work of, xv–xvi, xxi, 6–7, 9, 281, 346; amateurs in, 152–53; with Blank, 238–39, 255, 320; of Bright and Early project, 250–51, 256, 316; with Brooks, 65–66, 81, 363n50; of *Corn*, 252–54, 266; of dance music, xvi, 2–3, 129–37, 146–54, 223–31, 255–56, 262–65, 267–68; discography of, 377–86; with Dylan, 38; with Flying Hearts, 108–9, 196–99, 240, 301, 373n7; with

Freedman, 239–41; with Ginsberg, 37–38, 94–96, 328, 347–48, 360n21, 374n29; of "Go Bang! #5," xvi, 3, 222–23, 226–27, 333; for Hammond, 70–73, 75, 109, 119–20, 362nn36–38; of hip-hop, 282–85; home studio of, 306, 320–21; with Indian Ocean, 250–54; of *Instrumentals*, 206–7, 242–45, 265–66, 279; of "Kiss Me Again," 129–37, 140; at Kitchen, 81, 363n50; for Les Disques du Crépuscule, 207, 243–44, 369n31; of "Let's Go Swimming," 261–67, 270, 272, 291, 333, 347; of *Medea*, 191–93, 242, 270; with Necessaries, 199–204, 209; for Nelson, 65, 362n29; of orchestral disco, 160–77; posthumous compilations, xvii, 3–4, 6, 243–44, 311–12, 341, 347–51, 369n31, 369n37, 370n42, 371n9, 372n30; for Rough Trade, 283–84, 288, 294–95, 301–5, 322; sampling of, 309–12, 373n17; of "School Bell / Treehouse," 267–68, 270, 272–73, 291; with Singing Tractors, 224–38; for Sire Records, 108–9, 203–4; of *Sketch*, 206; of *Sketches for World of Echo*, 372n34; with Talking Heads, 105; of "That Hat," 258–60; of "That's Us / Wild Combination," 302–4, 313, 333; of *Tower of Meaning*, 242–46, 265–66, 336, 370n46; of 24 $\rightarrow$ 24 *Music*, 214–23, 279, 370n41; unfinished nature of, 5–6, 146, 252, 272, 322–23; of voice-cello songs, xvii, 2, 4, 189; with Warnes, 118–20, 234, 302; for West End Records, 149, 160–66; of *World of Echo*, 273–81, 284, 291, 293, 302, 309, 372n30. *See also* Sleeping Bag Records

—relocations of, xviii–xix, 13, 19–21, 43–45, 141–42

—shyness of, 7, 14–16

Russell, Julie, 11, 15, 285–86, 329–31

project of, 250–51, 256, 316; *Corn*, 252–54; Fresh Records subsidiary of, 255–56, 310; Indian Ocean, 250–54, 267–68; "In the Light of the Miracle," 224–27, 369n37; koala bear logo of, 214–15, 222; Russell's departure from, 256–57; "School Bell / Treehouse," 267–68, 270, 272–73; Socolov's role in, 226–27, 229–30, 254–57; "Tell You (Today)," 227–28; "Tiger Stripes," 229; 24 → 24 *Music*, 214–23, 239, 370n41; "Weekend" (Class Action), 226–27; "You Can't Hold Me Down," 229

Smith, Patti, 8, 60, 108

Smith, Willi, 258–59

Smith Brindle, Reginald, 181

Snake Charmer (Kevorkian), 236–37

Sobossek's, 2, 89–90, 110

Socolov, Will, xvi, 214–15; Blank viewed by, 306; Gibbons viewed by, 269; goodbyes to Russell by, 330; marketing practices of, 226–28; role in Sleeping Bag of, 229–30, 239, 254–57, 321; Russell viewed by, 252

SoHo, 47, 49–50, 83, 103; gentrification of, 186–88, 247–48, 351–52, 368n20; jazz scene in, 97–98. *See also* downtown music scene

SoHo Weekly News, 109, 111–12

Some Imaginary Far Away Type Things / Lost in the Meshes, 372n30

Song IV (Zummo), 271–72

songs, 232, 237–38, 246, 328, 338, 370n42; with Blank (Lola), 320; with Bowden, 233–35, 309, 313, 370n41, 373n7; electronic pop, 294–95, 301–8; with Hall, 235–36; "Love Comes Back," 326, 327; posthumous releases of, 347; synthesizers and keyboards in, 233; with Warnes, 118–20, 234. *See also* bands; voice-cello songs

Sonic Youth, 8, 188

"Soon-to-Be-Innocent-Fun," 338

Spector, Phil, 111, 163

Springfield, 6, 350, 355, 371n9, 373n17

Springsteen, Bruce, 72

Stearns, Robert: as Kitchen's manager, 60–63, 66, 80–81, 97; multicultural programming viewed by, 99; Russell supported by, 71

Stein, Seymour, 108, 135, 147–48, 195, 200, 203

Stockhausen, Karlheinz, 27–28, 163, 181

Stop Vicious Cycles (Kroesen), 208

"Street Seen #2" (Abrams), 370n41

Strictly Rhythm, 310–11

Stubbs, David, 281

Studio 54, 138, 142

Studio Rivbea, xix, 98

Studio We, 98

Sublette, Constance, 330

Sublette, Ned, xvi, xvii, 6, 155, 207–8, 213–14, 344–45; downtown music scene viewed by, 100, 247; goodbyes to Russell by, 330, 332–34, 336–38; on *Instrumentals*, 156–57; Kitchen performances of, 183; in Love of Life Orchestra (LOLO), 184; Modern Lovers viewed by, 68; at "New Music New York" festival, 181; orchestral disco viewed by, 160; rock clubs viewed by, 179–80; Russell's dance music viewed by, 166, 174, 229; Russell viewed by, 202, 246, 343; stagflation of 1970s viewed by, 48; studio innovation viewed by, 163

Subotnick, Morton, 42, 59

"Sudden Chill, A," 288, 347

Sugarhill Gang, 281

Suicide, 8, 64

Summer, Donna, 114, 168

"Sunshine Lover," 234

Swans, 8

Tim Lawrence leads the Music Culture: Theory and Production degree program at the University of East London. He is the author of *Love Saves the Day: A History of American Dance Music Culture, 1970–1979*, also published by Duke University Press.

Library of Congress Cataloging-in-Publication Data

Lawrence, Tim, 1967–
Hold on to your dreams : Arthur Russell and the downtown
music scene, 1973–1992 / Tim Lawrence.
p. cm.
Includes bibliographical references and index.
ISBN 978-0-8223-4466-7 (cloth : alk. paper)
ISBN 978-0-8223-4485-8 (pbk. : alk. paper)
1. Russell, Arthur.
2. Composers — United States — Biography.
3. Avant-garde (Music) — New York (State) — New York
   — History and criticism.
4. Manhattan (New York, N.Y.) — Intellectual life — 20th century.
I. Title.
ML410.R9523L39 2009
780.92 — dc22 [B]
2009029298